The Frankenfood Myth

The Frankenfood Myth
How Protest and Politics Threaten the Biotech Revolution

BY HENRY I. MILLER AND GREGORY CONKO

FOREWORD BY NORMAN E. BORLAUG
PROLOGUE BY JOHN H. MOORE

Westport, Connecticut
London

Library of Congress Cataloging-in-Publication Data

Miller, Henry I.
    The Frankenfood myth : how protest and politics threaten the biotech revolution / Henry
I. Miller, Gregory Conko ; foreword by Norman E. Borlaug ; prologue by John H. Moore.
        p. cm.
    Includes bibliographical references and index.
    ISBN 0–275–97879–6 (alk. paper)
        1. Biotechnology—Social aspects.   2. Biotechnology—Political aspects.
    3. Biotechnology—Government policy.   I. Conko, Gregory P.   II. Title.
    TP248.23.M556   2004
    303.48′3—dc22   2004048059

British Library Cataloguing in Publication Data is available.

Library of Congress Catalog Card Number: 2004048059
ISBN: 0–275–97879–6

First published in 2004

Praeger Publishers, 88 Post Road West, Westport, CT 06881
An imprint of Greenwood Publishing Group, Inc.
www.praeger.com

Printed in the United States of America

The paper used in this book complies with the
Permanent Paper Standard issued by the National
Information Standards Organization (Z39.48–1984).

10 9 8 7 6 5 4 3 2 1

To Sherri and Carrie,
for tolerating and supporting us
as we worked on this volume

Contents

Foreword

Henry I. Miller and Gregory Conko have written a brilliant account of how self-interest, bad science, and excessive government regulation have profoundly compromised the potential of the new biotechnology. This book is a call to action to resist a pernicious political process that is currently denying enormous potential benefits to consumers throughout the world.

All of life involves weighing risks against benefits. Through our own experience, and by observing that of others, we assess the risks of familiar activities and, sometimes almost subconsciously, we adapt to them. A child soon learns—sometimes painfully—about the high risk of touching a hot stove. Usually without a great deal of thought, we run the hazard of shark attacks at the beach. Academics and insurance company experts have been able to quantify the risks of, say, smoking a pack of cigarettes a day, commuting to work by car, or undergoing cardiac surgery.

Risk is more problematic when we are confronted with unfamiliar activities or products. In the absence of sufficient experience (what scientists would call "data") to make a confident assessment of risk, we tend to become anxious and to compensate for our lack of knowledge by overestimating the risk.

The authors use an apposite contemporary example to illustrate public policy run amok—the regulation in the United States and abroad of the new biotechnology, or gene-splicing, which has great potential to improve plants and microorganisms for agriculture and food production. Henry I. Miller and Gregory Conko make a persuasive case not only that the benefits of the technology far exceed its risk but also that there has been an abject failure in the formulation of public policy. The result has been, they argue correctly, gross overregulation of the technology and its products, disincentives to research and development, and fewer choices and inflated prices for consumers.

As a plant pathologist and breeder, I have seen how the skeptics and critics of the new biotechnology wish to postpone the release of improved crop varieties in the hope that another year's, or another decade's, worth of testing will offer more data, more familiarity, more comfort. But more than a half-century in the agricultural sciences has convinced me that we should use the best that is at hand, while recognizing its imperfections and limitations. Far more often than not, this philosophy has worked, in spite of constant pessimism and scaremongering by critics.

I am reminded of our using the technology at hand to defeat the specter of famine in India and Pakistan in the 1950s and early 1960s. Most "experts" thought that mass starvation was inevitable, and environmentalists like Stanford's Paul Ehrlich predicted that hundreds of millions would die in Africa and Asia within just a few years "in spite of any crash programs embarked upon."[1] The funders of our work were cautioned against wasting resources on a problem that was insoluble.

Nevertheless, in 1963, the Rockefeller Foundation and the Mexican government formed the International Maize and Wheat Improvement Center (known by its Spanish acronym CIMMYT) and sent my team to South Asia to teach local farmers how to cultivate high-yield wheat varieties. As a result, Pakistan became self-sufficient in wheat production by 1968 and India a few years later.

As we created what became known as the "Green Revolution," we confronted bureaucratic chaos, resistance from local seed breeders, and centuries of farmers' customs, habits, and superstitions. We surmounted these difficult obstacles because something new *had* to be done. Who knows how many would have starved if we had delayed commercializing the new high-yielding cereal varieties and improved crop management practices until we could perform tests to rule out every hypothetical problem, and test for vulnerability to every conceivable type of disease and pest? How much land, for nature and wildlife habitat, and how much topsoil would have been lost if the more traditional, low-yield practices had not been supplanted?

At the time, Forrest Frank Hill, a Ford Foundation vice president, told me, "Enjoy this now, because nothing like it will ever happen to you again. Eventually the naysayers and the bureaucrats will choke you to death, and you won't be able to get permission for more of these efforts."[2] Hill was right. His prediction anticipated the gene-splicing era that would arrive decades later. As Henry I. Miller and Gregory Conko describe in this volume, the naysayers and bureaucrats have now come into their own. If our new varieties had been subjected to the kinds of regulatory strictures and requirements that are being inflicted upon the new biotechnology, they would *never* have become available.

From 1950 to 1992, the world's grain output rose from 692 million tons produced on 1.70 billion acres of cropland to 1.9 billion tons on 1.73 billion acres of cropland—an increase in yield of more than 150 percent. Without high-yield agriculture, either millions would have starved or increases in food output would have been realized only through drastic expansion of acres under cultivation—with losses of pristine wilderness a hundred times greater than all the losses to urban and suburban expansion.

Today, we confront a similar problem: feeding the anticipated global population of more than eight billion people in the coming quarter of a century. The world has or will soon have the agricultural technology available to meet this challenge. The new biotechnology can help us to do things that we could not do before, and to do it in a more precise, predictable, and efficient way. The crucial question today is whether farmers and ranchers will be permitted to use that technology. Extremists in the environmental movement are doing everything they can to stop scientific progress in its tracks, and their allies in the regulatory agencies are more than eager to help.

We owe a debt of gratitude to the environmental movement for raising global awareness of the importance of air and water quality and of wildlife and wilderness preservation. It is ironic, therefore, that if the platform of anti-biotechnology extremists were to be adopted, it would have grievous consequences for both the environment and humanity. If the naysayers do manage to stop agricultural biotechnology, they might actually precipitate the famines and the crisis of global biodiversity they have been predicting for nearly forty years.

For a decade, the United States has produced ever-larger quantities of gene-spliced, insect-resistant corn that yields as much as or more than the best traditional hybrids but with far less need for chemical pesticides. No negative health or environmental effects have been observed. Yet there is an immensely strong, rabid anti-biotech lobby, especially in Europe, where activists have convinced many governments to thwart new approvals and have opposed the use of gene-spliced corn and soybeans as food aid in famine-stricken parts of Africa and Asia. Recently, in the southern African countries of Zambia, Zimbabwe, and Angola, where many people are dying of starvation, this anti-biotech movement has helped to persuade government authorities to refuse food aid from the United States because it contains gene-spliced corn. But the risk-benefit characteristics of gene-splicing in general, and of this insect-resistant corn in particular, are extraordinarily favorable; this rejection is an obscene exaggeration of risk.

Tragically, this is not an isolated case. There are many other examples of overreaction and resistance to technology. The American Council on Science and Health has documented a series of twenty cases—including pesticides on cranberries in 1959, the supposed hazards of cyclamates in 1969, "agent orange" in 1979, and Alar® on Pacific coast apples in 1989—in which scare stories trumpeted by the media became widely known and accepted but later were shown to be of little or no consequence. The resistance to gene splicing is yet another sordid episode in this larger anti-technology, junk-science movement.

In spite of the many powerful and precise new tools and the greater health and well-being that science and technology have offered us, our society has become overly risk averse. We obsess over impurities that are detectable at levels of one part per billion, for example, while not so many years ago we would have declared a product pure if adulterants were present at less than one part per five hundred thousand. Not infrequently, regulators worry about levels of contamination not because they are worrisome but because they are detectable. They regulate not because they should but because they can. This is both foolish and destructive. Sometimes greater analytical sensitivity requires greater intellectual perspicacity.

Regulators are not alone in their demands for ever-increasing margins of safety. It seems we are born with an instinct to resist change and to regard what is new with suspicion, while forgetting the faults and risks that were readily tolerated in the past and that were eliminated or ameliorated by new technologies; chlorination of water, pasteurization, and vaccination readily come to mind. Our very wealth and well-being, made possible by technology, now seem to offer the luxury of forgoing additional advances. But we are hard put to equal the immortal observation of the head of the U.S. patent office at the dawning of the twentieth century who suggested that the office be closed because surely everything possible had already been invented.

We must be more rational about our approach to risks. We need to think in broader terms, recognizing, for example, that the world cannot feed all its 6.3 billion people from organic farms or power all its cities and industries by wind and solar energy.

Although we must be prudent in assessing new technologies, these assessments must not be based on overly conservative—or overtly inaccurate—assumptions or be swayed by the anti-business, anti-establishment, anti-globalization agendas of a few activists, or by the self-interest of bureaucrats. They must be based on good science and good sense. It is easy to forget that science offers more than a body of knowledge and a process for adding new knowledge. It tells us not only what we know but what we don't know. It identifies areas of uncertainty and offers an estimate of how great and how critical that uncertainty may be.

The authors of this book address the problems of the new biotechnology that have arisen not from limits of the technology itself or from the science underlying it but from the machinations and peregrinations of policy makers. We must begin to solve *those* problems before it is too late.

Norman E. Borlaug
Distinguished Professor of International Agriculture
Texas A&M University
Nobel Peace Laureate, 1970

Prologue

W<small>E LIVE IN</small> an age of government regulation that expands literally by the day. Federal departments and agencies annually issue literally thousands of regulations, guidelines, advisories, and the like, filling countless volumes of the government's journal of record, the *Federal Register*. These directives from on high range from the listings of endangered species to the conditions under which over-the-counter preparations for ingrown toenail relief are recognized as safe and effective.[1] State and local governments likewise issue innumerable lists of regulations that cover everything from taxes and zoning to the licensing of dogs and tattoo parlors. Nor are we Americans alone in our regulatory zeal. The European Union, for example, has its own immense body of regulations, which seems to grow exponentially.

These regulations affect a vast spectrum of citizens' activities: their movement across national borders, how they can and cannot express themselves, the payments they may receive for work, the amounts they pay for goods and services, how they are educated, the characteristics of the buildings in which they work and live, the modes of transportation they use, the products they can buy, and the quality of the very air they breathe. Indeed, it is hard to think of any aspect of human life in the twenty-first century that is not in some way subject to government regulation. Even our religious institutions are granted certain tax advantages in return for agreeing to various constraints.

IRRATIONAL CONSTRAINTS ON FREEDOM

Government regulation is so pervasive, so intrusive upon our freedoms, that it should be carefully measured and based on rational considerations. After all, more than two centuries after the Enlightenment—when we are supposed to have shed our earlier mystical and irrational ways—twenty-first-century humans take pride in their rationality. We also highly prize our individual autonomy. Taking these modern tendencies together, one might think that any some sacrifice of our freedom should require both a compelling interest of the state and justification based on objective facts. Anything other than a rational basis for such wide-ranging interference and intrusion into our lives should be unthinkable.

Nothing could be further from reality. The regulatory process (like the lawmaking that precedes it) is rife with manipulation for political, economic, and social advantage. All too often, self-interest and special interests overrule the best available information and knowledge about the matters that the laws and regulations are meant to address.

Examples abound. In 1897, at the behest of a crank mathematician, the Indiana House of Representatives unanimously passed a bill defining the value of *pi*, the ratio of the circumference of a circle to its diameter, as 9.2376 rather than the true value of 3.14159. Science eventually prevailed, and the Indiana House corrected its error and rejoined our galaxy, but later examples have had worse outcomes. Although economic theory and empirical evidence argue compellingly that the minimum wage increases unemployment and diminishes economic well-being among the very people it is intended to help, legislatures persist not only in keeping the minimum wage on the books but regularly *increasing* it, thereby exacerbating the problem.[2]

Wrong-headed public policy can have widespread effects. One egregious example of the unintended consequences of ill-considered regulation is the Corporate Average Fuel Economy (CAFE) regulations, which were intended to conserve energy by reducing the overall consumption of gasoline by automobiles. Instead, it has had the effect of shifting American consumers' preferences for larger vehicles toward gas-guzzling light trucks, including sport utility vehicles, or SUVs. This, in turn, has stimulated greater production and use of these vehicles, which has *increased* energy consumption.

The culprit is, in part, the legislation that imposed the fuel economy restrictions on automobiles. Because the efficiency of internal combustion engines has changed little in the past few decades, the response by vehicle manufacturers was to make smaller, lighter automobiles. Auto purchasers still preferred larger vehicles, however, which increased the demand for light trucks, a category not covered by the fuel efficiency mandate. (This is reminiscent of the more recent electric power regulations adopted by the state of California, which capped retail but not wholesale prices of electricity and thereby helped to precipitate the energy crisis that swept the state in the summer of 2001.)

The CAFE regulations not only generated a proliferation of large, low gas-mileage vehicles, but may have contributed to more highway fatalities by downsizing a large portion of the U.S. auto fleet.[3] The effect of making ordinary passenger cars smaller and lighter was to reduce their crashworthiness. As anyone who drives on freeways knows, there can be frightening discrepancies in vehicle weights between small, fuel-efficient cars and the SUV and truck behemoths. But this accounts for only part of the problem. The likelihood of passenger injuries is also greater in accidents involving two small cars than in accidents involving two large cars, so the net effect of the CAFE legislation was to make auto travel less safe without having a significant impact on energy use.

The most profoundly important scientific public policy issue of our day is the development of civilian nuclear power, eclipsing even the use of the new biotechnology, or gene-splicing, the subject of this volume. The very steep legal and political obstacles to expanding nuclear energy production are extraordinarily costly to society. Given the serious concerns about the stability and availability of fossil fuel supplies, as well as speculation (justified or not) that carbon-based fuels cause global climate change, nuclear power seems to offer the most viable solution to our long-term energy needs. It produces no greenhouse gases. Unlike wind farms, it does not require vast spaces on land or sea. Unlike solar power, it can be produced economically and efficiently with existing technology. It does produce hazardous wastes, but reasonable, safe means of storing those wastes exist.[4]

Nuclear power becomes even more attractive when one considers the inevitable dangers and huge expense of the exploration and recovery of fossil fuels—the periodic coal mine disasters (to say nothing of miners' occupational hazard of lung disease, and the environmental damage from the mines), oil spills, and refinery accidents. Yet exaggerated concerns about safety have resulted in stupendously complex and costly regulation that, along with endless objections from activists, has priced nuclear power out of the American market. Interestingly, several other nations, notably France, rely heavily on it.

In a way, nuclear power serves as a good leitmotif for all the regulation that involves or affects modern science and technology. Because so many people consider nuclear power, and science and technology in general, to be arcane, these subjects produce awe and sometimes fear. People somehow overlook the spectacular advances that have occurred in science and technology during the last century and have brought stunning improvements in the length and quality of human life. People almost everywhere live longer, are better nourished, and enjoy better health than ever before. They move more freely about the world, learning of other peoples and cultures. The telecommunications revolution allows access to the great cultural events of the time and permits people to maintain instantaneous contact with friends and family in the most remote locations.

At the same time, modern technology has been put to objectionable and even evil uses. Employing the results of scientific knowledge, people have created and used weapons of mass destructive capability. It bears mentioning, however, that some of the most horrendous slaughters of recent times have been carried out with weapons no more sophisticated than those in common use hundreds of years ago. Consider the 1994 slaughter of nearly one million people of the Tutsi ethnic group by members of the Rwandan armed forces and Hutu militia, committed with little more than knives and machetes.

Also, just as with many other kinds of human actions, applications of technology for noble purposes have sometimes had unintended and even disastrous consequences—the Thalidomide™ tragedy, the *Exxon Valdez* oil spill, and the explosion at a pesticide plant in Bhopal, India, being prominent examples. The very power and mystery of modern science only add to the fear of its potential misuse or unexpected consequences.

It is human nature for people to perceive risks differently, depending on the nature of the risk and their individual experiences. Researchers from various fields, including psychology, social psychology, and decision analysis, have identified several characteristics related to products or activities that influence risk perceptions. People are affected by how much choice and control they have, who will bear the risks, and how widespread, familiar, and dreaded are the effects. Perceptions also are influenced by the benefits derived from accepting the risks, and by considerations of fairness, equity, and the distribution of risks and benefits.

People seem to be affected more profoundly by the negative consequences of decisions and activities than by positive ones. Studies have shown, for example, that people respond more emotionally to losses in the stock market than to gains of the same or even greater magnitude. Similarly, we seem often to take the enormous benefits of science and technology for granted, while we allow the fear of their power to dominate public policy. It is in this phenomenon—which is often exploited by self-interested activists and others—that irrationality is founded.

THE FEAR OF THE NEW BIOTECHNOLOGY

With the exception of nuclear power, there is perhaps no better example of the power of irrational fear of new technology to overcome the potential benefits than foods produced with the new biotechnology, or gene-splicing techniques. The history of agriculture is a story of genetic modification. For thousands of years, farmers and agriculturalists have selected and crossbred plants with desirable characteristics in order to increase yields, improve resistance to pests and disease, and add or enhance other useful traits. Traditional techniques involved cross-pollination of plants, which results in the more or less random mixing of vast numbers of genes, sometimes entire genomes. Along with the desired traits may come other, unwanted traits, however, such as weediness or susceptibility to disease, not present in either of the original parental specimens. Even so, the overall result of thousands of years of use of such gradual, incremental improvement has been an epochal improvement in agriculture, which has led to cheaper, more nutritious, and more varied foods.

Thirty years ago came the advent of modern biotechnology, with its promise of vastly more precise means to improve plant characteristics. Instead of mixing entire genomes in a trial-and-error process—which at times gives rise to unpredictable outcomes in the characteristics of the offspring—the newer techniques move or add small numbers of known genes to the plants. These modifications are far less likely to cause unintentional, unwanted changes. The results have been impressive; both field trials and the experience with commercialized varieties show such benefits as higher yields, lower pesticide use, improved disease resistance, and reduced need for artificial fertilizer.[5] The potential for improved nutrition, especially in poor countries, is enormous, as is the potential for reducing the negative ecological and occupational impacts of agriculture.[6]

Yet there is fierce resistance, especially in Europe, to the planting of gene-spliced seeds and to the consumption of gene-spliced foods. This resistance, coupled with European tendencies toward protectionism, has translated into European Union policies that have effectively stopped not only new regulatory approvals in the EU but also the importation of gene-spliced products—as either commercial seeds and food or food aid—into most of Africa. On the entire continent, no government except South Africa's has given approval to cultivate gene-spliced crops commercially. The usual explanations for these refusals—lack of scientific capabilities to perform adequate risk analysis, problems with intellectual property rights, and fears about food safety—do not provide an adequate explanation. The most powerful factor appears to be the fear of losing export sales to Europe and Asia. In 1998, the EU began to refuse bulk imports of corn from the United States because they might contain unapproved gene-spliced varieties. In 1997, the EU began to require labeling of all imported gene-spliced foods—labeling that requires paperwork, testing and guarantees that poor nations cannot offer.[7]

The situation in Zambia affords a recent illustration of the problems posed by these policies. This desperately poor country, plagued by widespread malnutrition and starvation, has refused to distribute corn donated by the United States to its hungry people. Why? Not for reasons related to safety, but because the American corn might contain superior, pest-resistant, gene-spliced seed that Zambian farmers could subsequently plant—causing the Europeans to reject the import of any food suspected to have been grown from gene-spliced seed.[8] Testing to guarantee that the crops contained no gene-spliced material, as required by EU labeling regulations, would be prohibitively expensive.

There is a unifying, intellectual principle behind such pointless and costly regulation. The opponents of gene-spliced foods—and of genetic modification in general—often rely on the so-called precautionary principle. This volume includes a chapter devoted to the abuses of this sophistic concept, which also has been extensively discussed elsewhere.[9] In its purest manifestation, the principle demands that no action or product be permitted until there is proof that it will have no ill effects. This places an exceedingly high burden of proof on anyone who wishes to introduce a new product, technique, or even a new service. It is a recipe for stagnation; it is anathema to innovation.

The late William Nierenberg, former director of the Scripps Institute of Oceanography and a member of the National Academy of Engineering, coined a corresponding principle—the Law of Constant Concern. According to his formulation, no matter how much reassuring evidence is produced, another concern always arises. Nierenberg coined his "law" in the context of global climate change, but it is equally applicable to much of the argument over the new biotechnology—and also to science and technology more generally. Nierenberg's Law captures the idea that many radical activists are ideologues searching for justification—justification that shifts along with circumstances and perceived opportunities to proselytize.

The Western world enjoyed an unprecedented period of growth during the nineteenth and twentieth centuries. The explanations for this growth are complex and involve many factors, including investment, population growth, education, culture, institutions, the accumulation of private property, and the rule of law. But prominent among these are scientific research and discovery and the technological advances that they spawned. Estimates of technology's contribution to economic growth put it in the range of 30 percent to 50 percent of the total.[10] Widespread adoption of the philistinism represented by the precautionary principle and similar policy approaches would surely diminish greatly the rate of adoption and the diffusion of new technologies—especially biotechnology—and all of the promise they represent. Economic misfortune is not democratic; although we will all pay a price, the poor peoples of the world will be most harmed.

OVERCOMING IRRATIONAL REGULATION

This volume analyzes the foibles, errors, and inconsistencies of current regulatory policy and of regulatory overreach in the context of biotechnology. The spectacular applications of biology—in medicine, animal science, and agriculture—surely rank among the most dramatic examples in the last century of the use of scientific advance for practical purposes. The new biotechnology has enormous potential for good—for example, to prevent and treat disease, enhance agricultural yields, conserve water, and protect the environment. But, like many scientific advances, it also has the potential for harm, both intentional and inadvertent. Because it deals with the basic materials of life itself, its use raises special fears and even deep philosophical and moral qualms. Furthermore, the fears that it raises are often fed by sensational reports in the popular media and by the alarmism of self-interested activists.

The new biotechnology often has been singled out for extreme regulatory scrutiny, although that course is inconsistent with good science and good sense. The precautionary principle has been applied, often in its most uncompromising form, giving rise to regulation that is wholly at odds with the scientific consensus. Inconsistencies in regulatory treatment abound. Risks that are minimal and that for centuries have been routine and accepted in traditional practice have been deemed unacceptable with the new technology. Scientific knowledge has been trumped by political and bureaucratic maneuvering. Advances that represent great benefits for humankind have been delayed and possibly lost altogether. As a result, both our public and individual lives are diminished. Perhaps this volume will serve as a wake-up call to the deficiencies of current public policy and will chart a course to better prospects for the future.

John H. Moore
President, Grove City College (1996–2003)
Deputy Director, National Science Foundation (1985–1990)

Acknowledgments

THE AUTHORS WISH to express their gratitude to the Hoover Institution and Competitive Enterprise Institute for providing not only material support and encouragement but also nurturing and stimulating intellectual environments.

We thank the Rathmann Family Foundation, William J. Rutter, the Bruce and Giovanna Ames Foundation, the Koshland Foundation, and the D&D Foundation for generous support.

We also thank Drew Kershen for his collaboration, Norman Borlaug and John Moore for their insightful contributions to this volume, and Robert Paarlberg for graciously sharing his research with us.

We wish to express our gratitude to Alan Rinzler, David Longtin, Sam Kazman, and Paula Duggan King for their extraordinary efforts on our behalf.

Finally, we express our appreciation to all of our colleagues upon whose work ours has built.

CHAPTER 1

A Brave *New* World
of Biotechnology?
More Like a Brave *Old* World!

IMAGINE A SITUATION in which an impoverished developing country suffering severe food shortages in the midst of a years-long drought receives food aid shipments of grain from industrialized nations to help fill the void. Instead of saving the day, though, the food aid sits untouched in warehouses. Grain that could help prevent malnutrition in millions of people is locked away from starving villagers by government edict because it contains kernels of the same gene-spliced, genetically improved corn varieties consumed daily by scores of millions of Americans and others around the world but that allegedly have not been "proven" to be safe. Eventually, starving citizens storm the warehouses to "liberate" the grain.

If it weren't real, this scenario would be almost too implausible to believe, especially in the twenty-first century. Yet this was precisely the situation in the southern African countries Zambia and Zimbabwe during fall and winter 2002–2003.

With some 2.5 million of his countrymen at risk of starvation, Zambian President Levy Mwanawasa told a UN gathering in South Africa, "We would rather starve than get something toxic."[1]

Tony Hall, the U.S. ambassador to the UN food agencies, responded quickly, lashing out at Zambian and Zimbabwean leaders who refused food aid because of baseless fears of new biotechnology products. "People that deny food to their people, that are in fact starving people to death, should be held responsible . . . for the highest crimes against humanity, in the highest courts in the world."[2]

This is where the new biotechnology—variously known as recombinant DNA technology, gene-splicing, or genetic modification (GM)—applied to agriculture finds itself after twenty years of stunning scientific and commercial achievements. We have had two decades of widespread precommercial and commercial cultivation of environment-friendly, enhanced-productivity crops—including more than a hundred million acres annually for most of the last decade—and yet the new biotechnology remains widely misrepresented and beleaguered by anti-technology and anti-globalization activists, poorly defended by its own practitioners, and discriminated against in public policy.

Although the new biotechnology may be the closest thing to a free lunch in the technological firmament, its future remains uncertain. Two things *are* certain, however. First, distorted, unscientific public policy will prevent the breadth and impact of applications that many predicted during the technology's early days in the 1970s and 1980s. Second, if those failures are not corrected, the new biotechnology could go the way of nuclear power and become a magnificent anachronism.

In this volume, we dissect various aspects of public policy toward the new biotechnology: its roots, which are buried in the self-interest of bureaucrats, agribusiness companies, and activists; its nurturing by media eager for stories about "the tomato that ate Toledo"; and its complex relationship with culture and agriculture. Finally, we map out reforms that could salvage some of the new biotechnology's potential to contribute to agriculture and the production of food and pharmaceuticals. We hope, but do not assume, that the logic and import of rational, science-based arguments will overcome the demonization, obstruction, and overregulation of this proven, superior technology.

THE ORIGINS OF "BIOTECHNOLOGY"

Thirty years ago headlines in scientific journals and popular media announced the arrival of a "biological revolution" and the resulting transformation of research, industries, and consumer products in ways never thought possible. "Biotechnology" would convert bacteria into miniature factories to make drugs and fine chemicals, and "genetically engineered" plants and animals would be used for food products with characteristics unachievable through traditional breeding. Companies were founded by the hundreds, private investment soared, and stock markets couldn't get enough of their newfound darlings.

Early Applications

With the advantage of hindsight, would we now characterize this biotechnological new era as revolution, or merely evolution? Certainly, the latter. But in order to understand why, some background is necessary.

The term "biotechnology" means very different things to different people. The Hungarian agricultural engineer Karl Ereky first used the word in 1917 to describe his use of an improved pig feed supplemented with sugar beets to carry out more intensive animal husbandry. More generally, it has been used by scientists to describe the use of living organisms to create consumer or industrial products.[3] This broad definition clearly encompasses a spectrum of old and new processes and products as different as fish farming, the production of enzymes for laundry detergents, and the genetic modification of bacteria to enable them to clean up oil spills or synthesize human insulin.

Since the invention in the early 1970s of recombinant DNA technology, biotechnology has come to connote the use of these techniques for genetic improvement at the molecular level. Today, "biotechnology" is often used interchangeably with other terms, such as "genetic engineering," "genetic modification," and "bioengineering"—each of which may at times mean something very different to scientists, consumers, lawyers, government regulators, and others.

To scientists, "genetic modification" simply means any intentional alteration to the genomes of living organisms, whether it is done with selection pressures over repeated generations, by hybridizing two different but related organisms, by intentionally mutating an organism's DNA with radiation, or by splicing new genes into the organism's genome. Even the term "genetic engineering" dates back to the early 1940s, some three decades before the advent of recombinant DNA technology.[4] The most precise terms to describe the newest type of biotechnology are "recombinant DNA" and "gene-splicing," which we will use interchangeably throughout this volume.

The ancients practiced early biotechnology by using yeasts to produce alcoholic beverages and by selecting and hybridizing plants with desirable traits in order to retain and exaggerate them. As early as 6000 BC, the Sumerians and Babylonians used yeast to brew beer.[5] An Egyptian cave painting shows people preparing and fermenting grain and storing the brew. In these poorly understood but still quite useful applications, early biologists and agriculturists worked empirically. They sought changes in phenotypes (the observed characteristics of the cell or organism), while accompanying changes in the genotypes (the information encoded in the DNA of the chromosomes) occurred invisibly.

In modern times, this conventional genetic modification—often by crude, "brute force" techniques—has produced many valuable variants of yeast and bacteria. For example, the capacity of the mold *Penicillium chrysogenum* to produce penicillin has been increased more than a hundredfold during the past several decades.[6] Other microorganisms have been selected and genetically enhanced in their ability to produce foods, beverages, industrial detergents, antibiotics, organic solvents, vitamins, amino acids, polysaccharides, steroids, and vaccines. By the mid-1980s, these pre-recombinant-DNA biotechnology products had a value in excess of $100 billion annually[7]—a figure that does not include the even greater worth of agricultural products from genetically improved plants.

Many people are surprised to learn that one of the ubiquitous uses of pre-recombinant-DNA genetically improved organisms is the vaccination of human and animal populations with live, weakened viruses. Live viruses modified by various techniques in order to reduce or limit their disease-causing capabilities have been used for over a century. In the nineteenth century, Louis Pasteur and his collaborator Emile Roux discovered that they could weaken, or attenuate, the virulence of rabies virus by drying nerve tissue from rabid rabbits and treating it with chemicals. Such vaccines now are used to prevent mumps, measles, rubella, smallpox, poliomyelitis, and yellow fever. Inoculation of a live viral vaccine entails the controlled "infection" of the recipient in an effort to stimulate the immune system to confer protection against subsequent uncontrolled, "natural" infections.

The practical applications of pre-recombinant-DNA genetic modification extend far beyond vaccines. In agriculture, they include not only virtually every plant that is cultivated commercially but also a wide spectrum of organisms used in pest control—including many organisms often considered to be pests themselves in other settings.[8] Insect release was used successfully to control troublesome weeds in Hawaii in the early twentieth century and St. John's wort ("Klamath weed") in California in the 1940s and 1950s. More recently, an introduced plant pathogen has been used to control rush skeletonweed in Australia. Hundreds of successful planned introductions of natural predators, such as the Australian Vedalia beetle in California in 1988, have made research into biological control of weeds, nematodes, insects, and diseases a priority at the U.S. Department of Agriculture and Department of the Interior. Currently, dozens of microbial biocontrol agents, including bacteria, viruses, and fungi—in hundreds of formulations—have been approved and registered with the Environmental Protection Agency (EPA). They control a broad spectrum of important plant pests and provide effective alternatives to chemical pesticides, which have fallen into disfavor among regulators and environmentalists.

Biological agents are also used as critical growth promoters for plants. Preparations of the bacterium *Rhizobium*, which have been sold in the United States since the late nineteenth century, stimulate the development of plant root structures that, in turn, enable the bacteria to convert nitrogen into compounds needed by the plant. The bacteria "fix" atmospheric nitrogen, converting it into nitrogen-containing ions that are essential plant nutrients, and thereby enhance the growth of leguminous plants such as soybeans, alfalfa, and beans. The use of nitrogen-fixing microorganisms decreases the need for chemical fertilizers.

The crowning glory of improved genetic varieties used in agriculture is surely the collection of plants that created the "Green Revolution," which has dramatically increased human longevity and improved the quality of life in developing countries. The Green Revolution might be viewed as the culmination of a long quest begun by the ancient agriculturists who first cultivated and domesticated wild plants. With the rediscovery in 1900 of Gregor Mendel's concepts of inheritance, plant breeders ushered in the era of scientific application of genetic principles to crop improvement. Long before the advent of recombinant DNA methods, twentieth-century plant breeders sought ways to take advantage of useful genes and gradually found a progressively wider range of plant species and genera on which to draw.

Beyond Simple Hybridization

Early plant improvement relied on using selection pressures to choose plants with the best characteristics for the following year's seed stock. Next came the intentional mating of two plants of the same species or variety. Most nonexperts still believe that selection and hybridization between closely related varieties remained the only options for plant improvement until the advent of gene-splicing techniques in the 1970s, but nothing could be further from the truth. Breeders first achieved interspecies hybridization in the early twentieth century, transferring "alien" genes between different but related species. Next came ways to perform even wider crosses, between members of different genera (organizational groupings within families of organisms, comprising many species). These "wide crosses," which by definition break the "species barrier" much revered by biotechnology's opponents, routinely introduce thousands or tens of thousands of entirely new genes into crop plants.

Critics of the new biotechnology often disparage it as "unnatural." But as we will point out repeatedly throughout this volume, context is critical. Wide crosses, whose fruits we enjoy every day, are at least as "unnatural" as gene-splicing—if by that term one means a process that does not occur in nature. The offspring of such crosses normally are not viable, because the resulting embryo has an abnormal endosperm and will die shortly after fertilization. But with the development of tissue culture techniques in the early twentieth century, the wide-cross hybrid embryos could be "rescued" and cultured in a laboratory environment to provide conditions similar to those supplied in early development by the normal endosperm and maternal tissues. Even when such rescued embryos do grow to maturation, however, they typically produce sterile offspring, which can occasionally be made fertile again by using still other techniques to add additional sets of chromosomes.[9]

The plant triticale, an artificial hybrid of wheat and rye, is one such example of a wide-cross hybrid made possible solely by the availability of embryo-rescue and chromosome-doubling techniques.[10] This entirely new species generally produces superior protein content and higher yields than wheat, tends to be hardier than wheat, and is grown as food or animal feed in numerous countries; however, it is unnatural, in that it is not found in nature and sophisticated laboratory equipment was necessary to create it—yet gene-splicing played no role at all in its development.

Many such "unnatural" combinations are grown commercially in the United States and abroad, and are often used in breeding programs to produce additional new varieties. Other wide-cross hybrids include familiar and widely used varieties of tomato, potato, oat, sugar beet, bread and durum wheat, rice, and squash. Many, if not most, of the bread wheat and durum pasta wheat varieties grown by farmers in the United States are the products of wide-cross breeding programs in which different species of plants (some even from an entirely different genus), such as ryegrass, or weed species such as goatgrass or couchgrass, were artificially crossed with wheat.[11]

Another pre-recombinant-DNA breeding technique is mutation breeding, in which breeders expose seeds or young plants to chemicals or ionizing radiation—such as X-rays or gamma rays—to induce random genetic mutations. These treatments most often kill the plants or seeds, or cause deleterious genetic changes. On rare occasions, though, the result is a desirable mutation—for example, one producing a new trait in the plant that is agronomically useful, such as altered height, more seeds, or larger fruit. But because of the random and severe damage inflicted on the DNA, breeders have no real knowledge of the exact nature of the genetic mutation that produced the useful trait or of what other mutations might have occurred in the plant.[12]

Nevertheless, more than 2,250 mutation-bred varieties of corn, wheat, rice, squash, beans, and dozens of other crop species have been introduced over the last half-century, and thousands more have been bred from these first-generation plants. These crops and their offspring have been grown in more than fifty countries around the world, including the United States.[13] Many are still being cultivated, and most have been used at one time or another as parental lines for other commercial varieties that are now planted all around the world. Wheat, which itself resulted from the natural combination of three different grass species from two different genera, has been among the most commonly mutated species. According to the International Atomic Energy Agency, nearly two hundred different varieties of bread wheat (*Triticum*) have been produced with mutation breeding, as well as some twenty-five varieties of durum pasta wheat.[14]

These are just some of the methods categorized as "conventional" plant breeding that are neither opposed by critics of biotechnology nor scrutinized case-by-case by regulators. How widely are these consumed? Unless one's diet is limited to wild berries, wild mushrooms, wild-caught fish and shellfish, and wild game, it is virtually impossible to avoid these genetically improved organisms. That is the irony of those who oppose or have reservations about "genetically modified" organisms. By enabling plant breeders and biologists to identify and transfer *single* genes encoding specific traits of interest, recombinant DNA techniques have greatly refined the less precise, brute-force methods of "conventional" genetic modification.

Breeders can now readily transfer selected and well-characterized genetic material from virtually any source in nature, exploiting nature's ingenuity, and greatly increasing the diversity of useful genes and germplasm available for crop improvement. In addition, the safety assessment of plants and food is enhanced by the greater sensitivity and precision of recombinant DNA techniques. If a new plant variety differs from its antecedent by only the introduction of a single gene, it is far easier to assess its agronomic traits, and to perform pharmacological, toxicological, and ecological testing, than if thousands of new genes were introduced or modified.

The Birth of the New Biotechnology

The seminal recombinant DNA experiment was described in a 1973 paper, "Construction of Biologically Functional Bacterial Plasmids in Vitro," by Stanley Cohen, Herbert Boyer, and their collaborators. Cohen and Boyer first isolated a ringlet of DNA called a "plasmid" from the cytoplasm of bacteria. They then used certain natural enzymes to splice a gene from another bacterium into the plasmid, and then introduced the resulting *recombinant*, or chimeric, plasmid DNA back into the original species of bacterium. When these modified bacteria were cultivated, the plasmids containing the segment of "foreign" DNA had become stably incorporated into the bacterial cytoplasm, the new gene functioned in its new environment, and "recombinant DNA technology" and the "new biotechnology" were born.[15]

This experiment was a landmark, because it provided the all-important "proof of concept," not unlike the demonstration that heavier-than-air machines can fly or that nuclear fission can release huge amounts of energy. The idea for this experiment came not as a sudden epiphany but as the logical extension of earlier work in several discrete scientific areas. It emerged from the synergy of several lines of biological and chemical research extending over several decades. Prodigious research in enzymology had led to the discovery of naturally occurring "restriction" enzymes that cut DNA molecules at defined sequences, and of enzymes called "DNA ligases" that rejoin DNA fragments to form linked recombinant DNA molecules.

Another essential contribution was the array of advances in fractionation procedures that permitted the rapid detection, identification, and separation of nucleic acids and proteins. These techniques made it possible to sort through, identify, and purify the fragments of genetic material to be manipulated and moved. This, in turn, eventually led to the ability to find and move virtually any snippet of DNA from one genome to another.

The final essential element was the accumulated knowledge of microbial physiology and genetics that made possible the introduction of recombinant plasmids into bacterial cells (a process called "transformation") and the appropriate expression of introduced genes. Later discoveries would identify tools for introducing recombinant DNA into plant and animal cells. These "foreign" genes could then be made to function at high levels in their new intracellular environments.

This new process of creating and obtaining expression (that is, function) of genes with recombinant DNA opened up the tantalizing commercial reality of converting certain well-domesticated microorganisms into miniature factories for producing important pharmaceuticals. For example, inserting into baker's yeast the gene that codes for the surface antigen of the virus that causes hepatitis B induces the yeast to synthesize large amounts of the virus-specific molecule, which can then be purified and used as a vaccine. Vaccines produced in this way have reduced the incidence of hepatitis B in the United States by more than 75 percent.

By reprogramming certain harmless bacteria with the introduction of the single gene that codes for human insulin, they can be directed to produce large amounts of that medically critical protein. Even though it is produced by bacteria, the recombinant DNA–derived insulin protein is identical to that produced by the human body. It thus provides a safer and more effective medical therapy than the more traditional alternatives—insulins purified from the pancreas of cows or pigs. Today, tens of millions of diabetics daily inject themselves with this superior human insulin, which was first marketed in 1982.

The first food product made with the new biotechnology became available in 1990, with the introduction of a gene-spliced enzyme, chymosin, used to produce cheese. Chymosin is synthesized in microorganisms reprogrammed with a calf gene and serves as a substitute for the "natural" clotting agent rennet, an enzyme scraped from the stomach lining of calves. Because it is produced in a laboratory environment, chymosin is generally considered to be a safer product and of higher quality than natural rennet, and today it is used to produce more than 80 percent of the hard cheese in the United States.[16]

The first commercial gene-spliced plant, the Calgene corporation's FlavrSavr™ slow-ripening tomato, was introduced in 1994. Since that time, more than sixty new gene-spliced plant varieties have been approved by the U.S. Department of Agriculture for commercial cultivation in the United States. Approved varieties include canola, corn, cotton, papaya, potato, tomato, soybean, squash, and several others; they express a range of improved traits, such as heightened resistance to certain insects and diseases, tolerance to herbicides, and longer shelf life. Although farmers have not readily adopted some varieties, 46 percent of all corn, 86 percent of all soybeans, and 76 percent of all upland cotton grown in the United States in 2004 were gene-spliced varieties.[17]

Genetic Modification Is a Continuum

As we have seen, the process of genetic modification and improvement is a continuum, and recombinant DNA technology offers far more precise, better understood, and more predictable ways to modify genetic material than was possible with conventional biotechnology. The desired "product" of recombinant DNA modification may be the engineered organism itself—for example, bacteria modified to clean up oil spills, a weakened virus used as a vaccine, or a pest-resistant crop plant. Or the modified organism can be used as the source of a useful end product—such as the insulin, chymosin, and hepatitis vaccine described above or cooking oils pressed from engineered corn kernels or canola seeds.

The technical successes of recombinant DNA technology have offered not only myriad commercial applications but extraordinary tools for studying the genetics, biochemistry, and physiology that underlie fundamental biological processes in normal and disease states—how genes duplicate, the mechanism(s) of natural genetic recombination, the details of macromolecular synthesis, and the nature of control over cellular growth and senescence.

PRODUCT VERSUS PROCESS

Used in the vernacular, "biotech" has become a catchword for an emerging entrepreneurial business sector and a wide spectrum of medical and agricultural products. By 2003, the approximately 1,400 biopharmaceutical companies in the United States boasted a market capitalization over $200 billion and were spending more than $15 billion annually on research and development. The hundred-plus recombinant DNA–derived drugs and vaccines on the market have benefited some 250 million patients worldwide.

These medicines include life-saving therapies for anemia, cystic fibrosis, hemophilia, hepatitis, organ-transplant rejection, and leukemia and other cancers. Millions of American diabetics inject themselves daily with recombinant DNA–derived human insulin, and hundreds of thousands of heart attack survivors owe their lives to the clot-dissolving drug known as tissue plasminogen activator (tPA). More than three-quarters of processed foods in our supermarkets contain ingredients from recombinant DNA–modified plants—mostly products refined from corn and soybeans. High school students perform basic DNA purification and gene-splicing experiments in classrooms across the nation.

These are some of the bright spots in a complex picture marked both by remarkable promise and sometimes vitriolic, often divisive controversy. The fate of new spin-off industries has turned on governmental decisions about the regulation of biotechnology research and products. The Food and Drug Administration's early decision to treat the products of the new biotechnology in the same way as other drugs and devices catalyzed intense investment activity in biopharmaceutical firms and rapid progress on a host of innovative new medicines.

Commercialization of agricultural and environmental products, by contrast, has fared less well—in large part arguably because federal regulators decided to discriminate against the use of recombinant DNA technology by creating new regulatory requirements and procedures for the new bio-technology, and also because of activists' intransigent opposition.

Why such different outcomes? Early on, the new biotechnology was viewed as something approaching science fiction. For an American public known to have a love-hate relationship with high technology, biotech stirred both excitement and deeply rooted suspicion of the "new" and of "tamper-ing with nature." By the mid-1980s, even as advances in biotechnology were becoming synonymous with the cutting edge of medical progress, gene-splicing techniques and its products were proving to be fodder for myth makers and apocalyptics.

The mythology quickly took root in agricultural and environmental ap-plications of biotechnology. Demands were made for governmental protec-tion against unseen, unlikely, and often largely imaginary risks. The products of the new biotechnology often were regarded as though they were myste-rious and alien substances transported here from another galaxy, instead of the result of precise and well-understood scientific processes. The reality is that the new biotechnology yielded products not so different from the old biotechnology—which gave us products like the mutant peach we call a "nectarine," the tangerine-grapefruit hybrid we know as a "tangelo," and the wheat varieties from wide crosses discussed above.

First Federal Guidelines

It wasn't long before the new biotechnology encountered the world of federal policy makers. In 1975, scientists convened a historic conference at the Asilomar Conference Center in Pacific Grove, California, at which par-ticipants called on the National Institutes of Health (NIH)—the federal agency that promotes and funds much biological and medical research—to oversee the use of the new research methods.[18]

The conclave focused on the potential risks of recombinant DNA tech-nology, many of them highly speculative. The discussions of risk assessment and management were as much influenced by the brouhaha the meeting provoked in the national media as by a legitimate scientific debate about the likelihood of biosafety problems. There was rampant speculation about laboratory creations run amok; talk of Frankenstein's monster and *Androm-eda Strain* scenarios enlivened the news (*Jurassic Park* had not yet been written). Some of those assembled believed that the risks were negligible but that the public needed reassurance in the form of stringent regulation, a recurring theme that persists to this day. Many of the scientists at the meeting, usually relegated to windowless laboratories, appeared to be in-toxicated with their unaccustomed celebrity.

According to James Watson, co-discoverer of the double helix structure of DNA and a co-convener of the Asilomar conference, many scientists left the meeting fearing that their colleagues "had compromised their better judgment as scientists just to be seen by the assembled press as 'good guys' (and not as potential Dr. Frankensteins)." The press, in turn, exaggerated even those already inflated fears, arguing, "if scientists themselves saw cause for concern, then the public at large should *really* be alarmed."[19]

In the end, the Asilomar participants called on the NIH to develop a formal "biosafety" system to provide guidance to researchers about the safety precautions needed for various kinds of research (including the prohibition of certain classes of experiments) and to ensure that laboratories employing the new techniques were properly equipped to prevent inadvertent release of organisms modified by recombinant DNA techniques.

In response, the NIH established the Recombinant DNA Advisory Committee (RAC) and in the mid-1970s implemented the first version of the *Guidelines for Research with Recombinant DNA Modified Organisms.* This move sent a powerful message that the scientific community and the federal government were taking the speculative risk scenarios seriously, a message that has affected—and afflicted—biotechnology regulation worldwide ever since.

Partly in order to reassure the public that sufficient oversight was in place, and partly because no one thought to seek the viewpoints of some critical scientific and medical specialties (such as infectious diseases, immunology, toxicology, oncology, and endocrinology), the guidelines ended up being overly risk averse. They used what has proved to be an idiosyncratic and largely invalid set of assumptions that exaggerated the potential risks associated with the process of gene transfer and with recombinant DNA–modified organisms.

The assumptions incorporated into the *Guidelines for Research* would likely have been more valid if a broader range of experts had been present at Asilomar for their creation. For example, concerns that recombinant bacteria producing human hormones could colonize the human gastrointestinal tract and expose people to toxic doses of the substances proved to be grossly overblown and extraordinarily unlikely—but without gastroenterologists and endocrinologists to offer opinions, the exaggerated concerns dictated policy. These erroneous assumptions and overly conservative guidelines have left a quarter-century's legacy of false assumptions, excessive risk-aversion, and unscientific public policy.

Within a year after the Asilomar meeting, many of the scientists who had been there recognized that the restrictions they proposed made little sense, and they eventually led an unsuccessful effort to retract them. In a 1977 article for *The New Republic,* James Watson expressed regret for supporting the meeting. In retrospect, Watson called it "an exercise in the theater of the absurd," arguing that the scientific community's initial trepidation about recombinant DNA technology was "a massive miscalculation in which we cried wolf without having seen or even heard one."[20] But the damage had already been done. The world had already heard from many leading scientists that the fears were legitimate, and no amount of remorse or retraction could unring the bell.

The Acceleration of Public Debate

Because it affects so many aspects of public policy toward the new biotechnology, the seminal policy question was, and remains: Should regulation focus on the characteristics of a given *product*, or on the use of a certain *process*, or technique, of genetic modification? Other important corollary questions include: Is the use of recombinant DNA techniques, per se, risky? Does the use of these techniques affect product safety in a systematic way that warrants a special oversight regime for all products made with them? In other words, with respect to safety issues, are recombinant DNA–derived products a meaningful "category"?

Inevitably, these questions give rise to other, bureaucratic concerns. In order to protect public health and environmental safety, should government regulate recombinant DNA research, or the end product, or both? Should the federal government have a regulatory agency that oversees all biotechnology activities, the equivalent of the airline industry's Federal Aviation Administration? Or should products made with recombinant DNA technology be treated like other similar products made with other technologies, where the intended use of the end product determines the oversight—that is, drugs from recombinant organisms regulated by the Food and Drug Administration (FDA), recombinant organisms used as pest control agents regulated by the Environmental Protection Agency (EPA), and so forth?

Scientists and policy makers have debated all of these questions at considerable length. But while the scientific debate generally was sober and dispassionate, the public debate very often was driven by the outlandish claims of anti-technology campaigners—that field-tested plants would be "unrecallable" and become "superweeds," that small-scale field tests of microorganisms would alter the climate and disrupt air-traffic control, and so on and on. Regulations were proposed and draft legislation introduced into Congress; none of them were enacted into law, fortunately. All of this occurred with little input from the broader scientific community. The American Society of Microbiology expressed concern about "the apparent intemperate rush to establish legislation to regulate recombinant research without first consulting with the appropriately qualified scientific experts" and spoke of the "need to understand that early allegations concerning recombinant DNA research were characterized by uncontrolled imagination."[21]

Fortunately, cooler heads prevailed. In 1977, Senator Adlai Stevenson Jr. wrote in a letter to the president's science advisor that the pending legislation was poorly conceived and probably incapable of protecting the public without impeding research.[22] By the end of that decade, the drive among politicians for new legislation specific for the new biotechnology had begun to wane, and efforts were refocused on identifying ways to regulate recombinant DNA technology within the boundaries of existing laws.

A Landmark FDA Approval

Fast-forward to the next decade, when Henry I. Miller, a coauthor of this book, was the FDA's primary reviewer for the first therapeutic drug produced by recombinant DNA techniques to come to the agency for market approval. The drug was human insulin, marketed by Eli Lilly as Humulin®, and the year was 1982. When the dossier for marketing approval of Humulin® was submitted, the FDA reviewed it on what has proved to be historic terms; based on the considered judgment of numerous scientific bodies, recombinant DNA techniques were determined to be no more than an extension, or refinement, of long-used and familiar methods for the genetic improvement of organisms for various products and purposes. Regulators were aware that these powerful new techniques enabled scientists to move genes between organisms at will and that they provided the means to craft genetic changes more precisely and predictably. It was a time of great anticipation.

Based on a thorough review of data submitted by the manufacturer, gained from years of preclinical testing in animals and clinical trials in diabetic patients, the FDA rapidly granted marketing approval for Humulin®. The review required only five months, at a time when the agency's average for new drugs was 30.5 months. This sent a message that was trumpeted on the *New York Times*' front page to biotechnology firms and the world. Miller, who headed the FDA team that conducted the review, observed that the speedy approval affirmed the "scientific and commercial viability" of a stunning new technology.[23] Developers were reassured that, at least for pharmaceuticals, products made with the new biotechnology would compete on a level playing field.

Since 1982, thousands of biotech drugs and vaccines have been tested, and more than one hundred have been approved for marketing, in addition to thousands of diagnostics tests, many of which, such as screening tests for infectious agents in blood products, have been public health milestones. Hardly a week passes without press coverage of a significant biotechnology development in medicine or agriculture—or even criminology. The identification of genes involved in obesity, cystic fibrosis, cancer, cellular senescence, fruit ripening, biological pest control, and drought resistance has wrought advances in many fields. DNA sequencing and analysis have even become a mainstay of law enforcement, useful for acquiring evidence of both guilt and innocence.

The Not-So-Well-Coordinated Coordinated Framework

In 1986, the Reagan White House's Office of Science and Technology Policy published a "Coordinated Framework for Regulation of Biotechnology," to clarify the regulations and procedures the major federal agencies had in place or were proposing for oversight of the new biotechnology.[24] Following the advice of the scientific community, the Coordinated Framework apportioned regulatory jurisdiction for the products of gene-splicing not to a special biotechnology regulator but to the various agencies that already oversaw product regulation. The FDA would regulate gene-spliced pharmaceuticals and foods, just as it regulated conventional pharmaceuticals and foods. The U.S. Department of Agriculture (USDA) was given jurisdiction over new plant varieties with the potential to disrupt agriculture, and the EPA would have jurisdiction over pesticides and microorganisms used for pest control, bioremediation, and other (nonmedical) purposes.

This milestone policy statement, however, soon revealed a schism among the federal agencies. Unlike the FDA, the EPA and USDA identified supposed "gaps" in their existing policies and procedures that allegedly could leave the new biotechnology inadequately regulated. The EPA and USDA crafted new definitions of the scope of what would require case-by-case review—on the assumption that the use of recombinant DNA techniques, per se, creates new or incremental risk in products.

Six years earlier, the FDA had judged that the vast majority of new biotechnology products would be fundamentally similar to familiar and well-accepted products made with older, less sophisticated techniques. The FDA had based this landmark decision partly on a consideration of first principles and also on extensive experience with microorganisms that had been genetically modified (using older, far less precise techniques) for the production of various regulated products, including therapeutic proteins, antibiotics, and vaccines.

The EPA and USDA, in contrast, rejected centuries of experience with genetically modified plants used in crop breeding and decades of experience with genetically improved microorganisms used in biological pest control, mining, nitrogen fixation, and bioremediation (the cleanup of toxic wastes). The agencies' actions implied that the new techniques and products were unfamiliar, uniquely risky, and worthy of special governmental control.

Coming a decade after the issuance of the NIH guidelines, the decisions by the EPA and USDA added new fuel to the product-versus-process debate. That led us back to the seminal question: Are the molecular techniques of recombinant DNA a straightforward extension of older genetic methods, or are they sufficiently different that they are likely to create novel and unfamiliar risks? If the former is true, then the EPA and USDA should simply have extended existing regulatory regimes to products of the new biotechnology. After all, both had ample experience with the oversight of various plants, animals, and microorganisms modified with conventional genetic techniques. If the latter were true, an entirely new risk analysis paradigm and new regulatory systems might be justified.

In the late 1980s, the U.S. National Academy of Sciences (NAS) and its research arm, the National Research Council (NRC), published a white paper[25] and a special report,[26] respectively, that addressed the potential risks of recombinant DNA–modified plants and microorganisms. Both documents, prepared by blue-ribbon panels of scientific experts, concluded that effective risk management for products made with recombinant DNA techniques can be achieved in basically the same way as for similar products of older techniques, and that recombinant DNA–modified plants and microorganisms typically present both a high degree of "familiarity" and a greater degree of certainty about genetic changes.

The NAS and NRC findings resonated with the FDA's earlier judgments and were also consistent with empirical observations. As expected, recombinant human insulin (purified from a harmless strain of modified *E. coli* bacteria into which the human gene that codes for insulin had been incorporated) was found to be therapeutically similar to insulin extracted from cows or pigs, with the notable exceptions that it was more pure and less likely to elicit allergic reactions. Even just the *deletion* of a gene from an organism was found to have useful applications. The "silencing" of a gene in tomatoes and carnations that plays a role in ripening can slow the post-harvest aging of the fruits and flowers, lengthening their shelf life. Aside from lasting longer, these plants are otherwise indistinguishable from their conventional counterparts.

Nonetheless, the EPA and USDA proceeded with plans for a vastly increased scope of regulation and more stringent case-by-case governmental review than for products crafted with the less precise, pre-recombinant-DNA genetic techniques.

Those regulations and proposals, the creation of which required bureaucrats to distort the original intent of federal statutes, were a capitulation to radical environmentalists and consumer activists (and also, paradoxically, to big agribusiness, as discussed in chapter 3). They exacted a high cost. These regulatory strictures have required companies and academic researchers to perform thousands of unnecessary field experiments at great expense, supposedly in order to measure or take into account the alleged "unique" risks of recombinant DNA-modified plants and microorganisms. Directly and indirectly, regulatory compliance has hugely inflated the costs of performing routine field validation experiments. For the emerging commercial biotechnology sector, these policies have spawned a whole spectrum of undesirable side effects. Specifically:

1. By raising the cost of biotechnology research and development, the new regulations drain capital resources and slow the pace of research, which can delay or block altogether the entry of new products into the marketplace. Viewed from a competitive business perspective, bureaucratic disfavor may redirect corporate strategic planners away from a superior technology, process, or product toward less efficient, less precise, less predictable, and more hazardous alternatives.

2. The financial community considers that the higher operating costs, regulatory uncertainty, extended development times, and legal liability associated with using recombinant DNA techniques raise investment risk and doubts about the long-term viability of agricultural biotech companies. The resistance of potential customers to products that are disfavored by regulators magnifies this problem. These financial risks lead to depressed valuations of start-up firms and of subsequent financial offerings. Less capital and higher "burn rates," due to the inflated expense of performing research and development, conspire to jeopardize smaller firms' ability to achieve research and development milestones. As a result, agricultural and environmental biotechnology companies, as well as academic and nonprofit research centers, have found their capital streams diminishing or drying up completely, in contrast to their more equitably regulated counterparts in the biopharmaceutical sector. Ultimately, a reduction in resources means that fewer worthwhile research projects can be initiated and completed, and fewer beneficial products ever make it to market. Those that do make it to market will necessarily have to be highly profitable and able to command artificially inflated prices.

3. The new regulations disproportionately affect the academic research community, an important source of fundamental scientific knowledge, improved germplasm, and a highly skilled workforce—all of which are essential to the long-term health of agricultural biotech. The paperwork involved in obtaining government permits is at the very least an unwelcome distraction, and often has been debilitating. The significant costs of performing and reporting on required environmental assessments divert funds from meager research budgets. Many academic scientists choose, therefore, not to pursue early field research with recombinant DNA-modified plants and microorganisms because their resources are spent more cost-effectively on less onerously regulated laboratory research, or on field experiments with organisms modified by other (less efficient and less precise) techniques. They may forego field validation research that is essential to develop recombinant DNA-modified plants and microorganisms for use in agriculture or environmental bioremediation. Without this needed proof of concept, many biotechnology innovations remain on the bench, are not transferred to the commercial research and development pipeline, and never become available to end-users and consumers.

4. Viewed from the perspective of vulnerability to legal delays, disruptions and challenges, the EPA's and USDA's regulations provide legal avenues by which an individual or group ideologically opposed to biotechnology generally or to a particular application can easily and repeatedly interrupt the process of research and development. Unnecessary regulation exposes scientists and companies to extraordinary jeopardy because agencies are typically required to publish their decisions to authorize field trials or grant marketing approval, and to seek public comment. Making matters worse, members of the public can challenge agency decisions in court, delaying the process almost indefinitely. Product by product and experiment by experiment, researchers, manufacturers, and regulatory agencies then become vulnerable to petitions, lawsuits, demonstrations, and boycotts.

Tilting the Playing Field

The endorsement by regulators of the myth that using recombinant DNA technology for gene transfer conveys incremental or unique risks and therefore requires more burdensome oversight has created a kind of ripple to effect—producing a wave that has become a tsunami. The myth has helped erect a variety of obstacles to research and development. For example, once the agencies settled on recombinant DNA–modified organisms as the target for discriminatory, enhanced oversight regimes, they introduced various regulatory subregimes. These include vastly excessive data requirements and complex, arbitrary, and often flawed algorithms to measure such things as transmission of pollen and potential allergenicity. They also include inappropriate, one-size-fits-all requirements for the physical and procedural design of all field trials—fences, disposal of plants (and dirt) following the trials, prohibition of mixing gene-spliced and conventional plants in transit, and so forth.

Regulators are nothing if not creative. Performing an arguably unnecessary review of a perfectly innocuous corn variety that contains a bacterial protein that confers resistance to certain insects, the EPA granted a "split," or partial, approval, that permitted the product to be consumed only by animals. That inappropriate decision (discussed further in chapters 5 and 6) precipitated a cascade of wrong-headed, unscientific decisions that caused no end of mischief. Other ill-conceived policies include the agencies' practice of publishing the location of field trial sites, which has made possible vandalism of experiments and harassment of farmers.

Taken together, the EPA's and USDA's approach to biotech oversight has tilted the playing field against researchers and companies that use the techniques of the new biotechnology. In doing so, regulators have defied the primary goal of the U.S. government's own Coordinated Framework, which was intended to limit potential product risks *while encouraging innovation and economic development.*

EPA and USDA officials have defended their policies as bolstering public confidence in products of the new biotechnology. Charles Hess, USDA Assistant Secretary for Science and Education from 1989 to 1991, said that if the public *believes* a risk is real, the government has a responsibility to regulate it. Hess's rationalization is unconvincing. As the president of the consumer-advocacy group Consumer Alert testified to a federal investigative panel a decade ago, "For obvious reasons, the consumer views the technologies that are *most* regulated to be the *least* safe ones. Heavy involvement by government, no matter how well intended, inevitably sends the wrong signals. Rather than ensuring confidence, it raises suspicion and doubt."[27]

Public policy that panders to public misapprehensions only serves to enhance anti-biotechnology (and more general anti-technology) mythology, but it is not surprising. Princeton physicist and writer Freeman Dyson has observed that resisting a new technology is generally safer for regulators than embracing it, although this course often has larger costs for society, a dynamic we discuss further in chapter 4.[28] Society would surely benefit if government officials were to choose progressive, rational public policy that defies the myths, and then vigorously educate the public as to its appropriateness.

CHAPTER 2

Myths, Mistakes, Misconceptions . . . and Mendacity

THERE IS A place in society for myths. Like Parson Weems's parable about George Washington chopping down the cherry tree ("I cannot tell a lie . . ."), they illustrate simple moral lessons. Learning from fables about the apocryphal actions of heroes can be empowering, but when misinformation is cloaked in a pretense of reality, myths can mislead, misinform, and undermine social goals.

The new biotechnology has been plagued by several insidious misconceptions:

1. That it is a fundamentally new, discrete technology
2. That it is unsafe, untested, and unpredictable
3. That it is likely to give rise to dangerous pathogens, "superweeds," and other nasty outcomes.

These misapprehensions derive from concerns about technology and from a limited understanding of science in general, and of genetics and biology in particular.

NEW? UNSAFE? UNTESTED? UNPREDICTABLE?

Biotechnology is neither a discrete new technology nor a "category" of products. It refers to a continuum of useful, widely applicable enabling technologies, new and old. At the most recent, and most sophisticated, end of this continuum are recombinant DNA techniques, which permit precise modifications at the molecular level.

The new biotechnology already has enjoyed wide application in research, development, manufacturing, and commerce. Its universe is so diverse as to defy meaningful generalizations. Over the past several decades, the techniques of the new biotechnology have become so integrated into the work of plant breeders, medical scientists, and life scientists of all sorts, and so commingled with conventional techniques, that distinctions between old and new have become blurred.

How does society ensure the quality and safety of the products of conventional biotechnology? Regulators and the public over time have embraced a principle called "proportionality"—the idea that the degree of oversight of an activity or product should be commensurate with its estimated risk. Thus, a new variety of tomato or pluot, a plum-apricot hybrid, poses far less risk than a new drug or vaccine and should not be regulated as stringently. Clinical trials are quite appropriate for new pharmaceuticals, but for new varieties of fruits, vegetables, and grains, professional standards adopted voluntarily by plant breeders routinely and effectively suffice. In addition, federal regulators oversee the rare uses of genuinely risky plants, such as those known to be, or suspected of being, "noxious weeds" and the like.

Not only do plant breeders carefully test yield, flavor, toxicity, and such properties as resistance to insects, mold, and viruses, in order to protect breeding programs (as well as farmers and consumers) from unsafe or otherwise unacceptable plants, there exists as well another formal level of quality assurance—the certification of plant seeds sold to agricultural producers or growers, in order to prevent any compromise of seed quality or consistency. In California, for example, oversight is performed by the nonprofit California Crop Improvement Association (CCIA), which provides a voluntary quality assurance program for the maintenance and increase of crop seed.[1] Each variety that enters this program is evaluated for its unique characteristics such as pest resistance, adaptability, uniformity, quality, and yield. Seed production is closely monitored by CCIA to prevent outcrossing, weed contamination, or other crop or disease contamination that may negatively affect seed quality. Seed movement is monitored from field harvest through the conditioning plant and into the bag. Samples can be rejected if "off-type" seeds are found at a percentage greater than standards permit, as is occasionally the case with beans, cereals, and sunflowers. The CCIA is just one of many different private-sector authorities for the international seed certification scheme administered by the Paris-based Organization for Economic Cooperation and Development in forty countries.

Plant breeding has achieved an impressive record of safety based on well-established professional, rather than government-imposed, standards of practice. The products of conventional plant breeding are subject to formal government oversight prior to marketing only in those rare cases in which an actual health or ecological risk is identified. The extraordinary safety of the food supply demonstrates the ability of plant breeders and government regulators to work together to identify high-risk products.

Since the 1970s recombinant DNA techniques have provided an important new set of tools for scientists in disciplines ranging from medicine and biology to anthropology and criminology. They enable researchers to precisely identify, characterize, enhance, and transfer individual genes involved in the biosynthesis of target products, in the expression of desirable traits, or as biological markers. They also enable biopharmaceutical companies to use microorganisms, plants, and animals as biological factories for synthesizing therapeutic substances like human insulin, human growth hormone, and erythropoietin—a process called "biopharming." They make possible revolutionary breakthroughs in the safety, nutrition, yield, and overall versatility of plants. The long search for useful organisms begun by the ancients is now driven by a continuum of biotechnologies that has culminated in the myriad manifestations of recombinant DNA techniques.

It should be emphasized that the new techniques only supplement traditional processes of developing new varieties but do not wholly replace them. By virtue of their greater power and precision, gene-splicing and other new methods merely accelerate the earliest phases of research and development. After transformed plants or seeds are developed, they undergo a process that is virtually indistinguishable from the traditional pathway—progressively less contained testing in growth chambers, greenhouses, and under field conditions; only then do they become candidates for seed certification. Only when an identifiable high-risk trait is involved should formal government oversight be required. Fortunately, recombinant DNA techniques actually make it easier to identify and eliminate such risky traits.

Unfamiliar and Likely to Spawn Dangerous Organisms?

Does the introduction of one, two, or several genes, judged against the background of tens or hundreds of thousands of the host organism's own genes, create a "novel" organism?

How novel is a corn plant, for example, that harbors a newly inserted gene for a bacterial protein toxic to certain insect larvae when they feed on the plant, when one considers that every crop plant already has hundreds or thousands of its own natural pest-resistance genes? How novel is a gene-spliced canola plant enhanced to withstand a particular herbicide, given that conventional herbicide-tolerant canola plants have been produced and used commercially for more than two decades?

The issue of "novelty" is important when considering whether the introduction of a single gene from a known pathogen could convert an otherwise benign organism into a pathogen or weed. For example, does a tomato plant become pathogenic or weedy after the insertion of a small amount of well-characterized and noninfective DNA from the common soil bacterium *Agrobacterium tumefaciens*, a known plant pathogen? Should such a construction trouble us? Should it elicit greater regulatory scrutiny? These questions have been widely debated by scientists, and the answers are reassuring.

Consider, first, whether genetic recombination itself—which links two or more DNAs that may originate from different sources—should be of concern. We have already noted that people engaged in the purposeful domestication of microorganisms, plants, and animals have for millennia purposefully "promoted" the mixing and recombination of genes. But the potential impact and importance even of these genetic changes must be viewed against the background of what occurs continuously in nature. Innumerable recombinations among related and unrelated organisms occur constantly, through several mechanisms.[2]

Sexual reproduction randomly combines genes in the offspring of two parents, which then pass along a unique set of genes to the next generation. In the gut, infected wounds, decomposing bodies, and decaying plant material, bacteria take up naked mammalian DNA (albeit inefficiently) when they encounter disintegrating cells. Over the past million years and longer, mammalian-bacterial, plant-bacterial, and other genetic hybrids have appeared, been tested by competition within bacterial populations and by environmental stresses, and have been conserved or discarded by natural selection. This sort of genetic recombination also has been widespread among fungi and viruses. Think of the rampant genetic recombination that occurs continuously among the organisms, living and dead, on the underside of a dead log in the forest, or in an organic gardener's compost heap. When critics argue that the swapping of genes between various unrelated organisms makes recombinant DNA uniquely worrisome, they can only do so by ignoring the biological facts of life.

Similar to the wide crosses in plants described in the previous chapter, certain kinds of gene transfers thought until recently to be impossible in nature because of phylogenetic distances are now known to occur. Researchers at the Pasteur Institute in Paris, France, have demonstrated that a gene (or genes) for resistance to the antibiotic erythromycin could be transferred through natural interaction between two entirely different classes of bacteria—from *Campylobacter*, known as gram-positive due to specific characteristics of its thick cell walls, to an unrelated gram-negative *Escherichia coli BM2570* bacteria.[3] In other laboratory experiments, it was demonstrated that gene transfer can occur between *E. coli* and streptomyces,[4] or yeast,[5] and that crown gall disease in plants results from a natural transfer of DNA from the bacterium *Agrobacterium tumafaciens* to plant cells.[6]

In fact, detailed knowledge of the mechanism by which *Agrobacterium* transfers its own genes into the cells of plants led to the development of an effective recombinant DNA tool for modifying plants. This natural soil bacterium causes crown gall disease by infecting wounds in the plant tissue and injecting a plasmid containing pathogenic genes into the plant cells. Working independently, three different teams of scientists (two in the United States and one in Belgium) discovered how to hijack *Agrobacterium*'s natural infection pathway to introduce beneficial genes instead of pathogenic ones.[7]

Evolutionary studies are an additional source of data relevant to the "novelty" of molecular chimeras created by gene-splicing—whether, for example, the transfer of a jellyfish gene into a zebrafish (which has given rise to an eye-catching fish that glows fluourescently) somehow affects its "fishness" or transfers "jellyfishness" to the zebrafish. The sequencing of various genomes during the past quarter-century reveals that nature has been remarkably conservative about using and maintaining efficient molecules as they evolved. Nearly identical DNA sequences and biochemical pathways are found in different species, across genera, and even across phylogenetic kingdoms (the division between plants, animals, and microorganisms). Scanning the DNA sequence of the *E. coli* genome to search for similar structures, for example, reveals gene sequences that are virtually identical to those in a variety of organisms, including other bacteria, plants, insects, amphibians, birds, and humans.[8]

Humans share more than 50 percent of their genes with those in a simple plant, *Arabidopsis thaliana*, known as thale cress or mustard weed.[9] In a background of tens of thousands of genes in common, surely the addition of one or two genes from a human into that plant would not make it less of a plant or more of a person. With such broad conservation and "sharing" of genes in nature, debates about the proprietary nature of "human," "plant," and "bacterial" genes—or, for example about the essential "novelty" of a squash plant that contains a viral gene—become moot. Taken together, the evidence on genetic recombination and evolutionary conservation of genes makes distinctions drawn between "natural" and "unnatural," or "familiar" (a favorite concept among certain regulators) and "novel," seem neither clear nor relevant.

New Pathogens?

The issue of conversion of a nonpathogen into a pathogen, or a nonweed into a weed, as the result of limited genetic recombination, is best considered within the context of the natural phenomena that underlie pathogenicity, a process that is both complex and multifactorial. Pathogenicity is not a *trait* produced by a single gene. Rather, it is the coordinated activity of a set of genes that determines essential properties.

A pathogen must possess three general characteristics, each of which involves multiple genes. First, it must survive and multiply in or on host tissues. The oxygen tension and pH must be favorable, the temperature (and for plant pathogens, the tissue water potential) must be suitable, and the nutritional milieu must be adequate. The pathogen must be able to adhere to specific surfaces on or in the host and to thrive on nutrients available in the host environment. Second, the pathogen must be able to resist or avoid the host's defense mechanisms for the period of time necessary to produce sufficient numbers of offspring to cause disease. For human and animal pathogens, this includes resistance to enzymes, antibodies, and phagocytic (bacteria- and virus-killing) cells in the host. Third, the pathogen must be able to survive outside of the host, and it must somehow be disseminated to new, susceptible host organisms.

The organism must be meticulously adapted to this complex pathogenic lifestyle. A single gene, even one encoding a potent toxin, will not convert a harmless bacterium into a pathogen capable of causing epidemics or even localized disease. On the other hand, a mutation that interferes with a gene essential to one of the three characteristics of a pathogen can *eliminate* pathogenicity. It is worth noting that just as naturally occurring pandemics of influenza lethal to hundreds of millions are far more rare than the usual modest outbreaks, *severe* pathogenicity is even more dependent upon favorable conditions and is, therefore, much rarer in nature than mild pathogenicity. Thus, in the unlikely event that a nonpathogen did exhibit some characteristics of pathogenicity, we would expect those characteristics to be mild rather than pronounced.

New Weeds?

A similar situation pertains to weediness in plants, which is not a simple trait that is mediated by a single gene or two. Analogous to the multifactorial nature of pathogenicity, weed biologists have discovered thirteen characteristics that contribute to weediness. Most serious weeds have eleven or twelve of these, which include rapid seedling establishment, high growth rates, prolific root systems, large leaf areas, and the ability to alter growth and development in order to optimize reproductive output. Crop plants, in contrast, typically have, at most, only five or six of these thirteen characteristics.[10] Because one or perhaps multiple genes code for each of the characteristics, it is unlikely that a crop plant could suddenly acquire the genetic information necessary to transform it into a weed. A corollary is that the introduction into a crop plant of a small number of genes unrelated to weediness is unlikely to confer weediness.

This theoretical conclusion has been validated by empirical research. A ten-year study by British scientists of four crops (rapeseed, potato, corn, and sugar beet) grown in twelve different habitats and monitored over a period of ten years found that neither gene-spliced nor conventional crop plants survive well in the wild and that biotech varieties are no more likely than their conventional counterparts to invade wild ecosystems.[11]

A more realistic scenario is the transfer of genes from crop varieties to wild plants through cross-pollination—but only in regions where wild species related closely enough for ordinary sexual reproduction grow near cultivated fields. Even then, this "outcrossing" could constitute a significant problem only if the genes in question could enhance the fitness of the recipient weed—by, for example, enabling it to survive predation by a significant pest, better withstand frost or drought, or produce and scatter seeds that survive better in the wild.

But cross-pollination of crop plants and wild plants is not new; gene flow between crops and wild plants has been happening for millennia. It is by no means unique to biotechnology, new or old, and it has rarely been a problem, because most genes that are introduced into crop plants, conventional or gene-spliced, have little survival value in the wild. In fact, while some traits added with either gene-splicing or conventional breeding methods *could* provide an ecological advantage, most newly introduced crop traits make plants *less* likely to survive the rigors of nature.

Biotech's critics and skeptics fret about the possibility that genes conferring herbicide tolerance could flow from gene-spliced plants to weeds and create so-called "super-weeds." But herbicide-tolerant canola, soybean, and wheat plants have been produced with conventional breeding for more than twenty years, and no unmanageable weed problems have been reported as a result of their use.[12] Thus, although the transfer of a gene for herbicide tolerance into a wild relative could create a (temporary) nuisance for farmers, it is unlikely to have any impact on wild biodiversity, because the herbicide tolerance trait would not confer on wild plants any selective advantage relative to other weeds. In the event that herbicide tolerance genes were transferred to a weed species, farmers could control it with other herbicides to which it was not tolerant. Thus, just as the scientific consensus maintains, it is the new characteristic of the plant in question that matters, not the methods used in its development.

The probability of inadvertently creating an organism capable of producing a medical or ecological catastrophe, therefore, is vanishingly small. There is no support for the notion promoted by some biotechnology critics that genetic recombination of the sort achieved with recombinant DNA techniques will create pathogens from nonpathogenic organisms, or significant weeds from nonweedy organisms. There is likewise no foundation for the speculation that although the likelihood is small that a problem would be created through the use of recombinant DNA techniques, the outcome should one occur will be cataclysmic—the "low probability, high impact" fiction. Such cataclysmic effects would require the addition or alteration of one or a few genes of known function to induce severe pathogenicity in a nonpathogenic organism, which, as discussed above, is extraordinarily unlikely. Just as for other common technologies, such as kitchen knives, automobiles, microwave ovens, and prescription drugs, when mishaps occur they are usually of modest impact rather than catastrophic.

Finally, we should bear in mind that consideration of safety and risk does not exist in a vacuum, but is context specific. The new biotechnology is essentially a refinement, or extension, of the kinds of genetic experimentation and improvement that have long been performed by far less precise and predictable techniques. It builds and improves upon the extraordinary accomplishments of those techniques, and any consideration of its risks should be placed squarely in the context of the risks that are created by other breeding methods, the knowledge of how those other risks have been managed, and also the risks of *not* introducing the new technology. Without consideration of the proper context, one cannot draw valid conclusions about the ability of breeders and farmers to manage the risks of gene-spliced organisms.

The Record of Safety

The safety record of recombinant DNA techniques in many thousands of laboratories worldwide is illustrative, a point that we will revisit while discussing regulatory approaches that focus on and discriminate against the new biotechnology. For more than a quarter-century, scientific research on gene-spliced microorganisms has been conducted in tens of thousands of minimal-containment laboratories in the United States and Europe alone. In spite of "incidental releases" measuring on the order of one hundred million recombinant microorganisms per worker per day from standard, minimal-containment laboratories, not a single adverse reaction has been observed in humans, animals, or the environment.[13] It is worth noting that these "incidental" releases, which are virtually *unregulated*, have been ignored by regulators and activists alike (but more on this later). The reason for this admirable safety record is that the organisms handled in minimal-containment laboratories—whether genetically modified or not—are quite innocuous.

Researchers who work with pathogenic or otherwise hazardous organisms employ appropriate containment equipment and handling procedures. Although some biotechnology critics would place obviously innocuous domesticated plants, animals, and microorganisms that have been precisely and minimally modified with gene-splicing techniques within this context, both theory and practice militate against such an approach. Not only are gene-spliced organisms neither "exotic" nor likely to be newly pathogenic or invasive, but they are also, on average, far more predictable than new strains or varieties produced in other ways. Moreover, far from making them more competitive in the evolutionary lottery, many kinds of modification—useful as they may be for myriad purposes—appear to be a drain on the energy of the organism and to make it *less* fit outside the protective care of human beings.

RISK PERCEPTION VERSUS REALITY

No responsible person would contend that gene-spliced organisms pose no risk. The presence of undesirable characteristics—pathogenicity, toxigenicity, weediness, and so forth—in the parental organism and the nature of the trait transferred to the new organism are important predictors of the likely risk of the final construct.

Research with smallpox virus or foot-and-mouth disease virus—whether recombinant or not—must be done with extraordinary circumspection and care, unless the investigators (and regulators who might have jurisdiction) are convinced that the organism has been sufficiently and irreversibly attenuated (weakened). Similarly, before deciding to commercialize a food plant containing a gene that codes for a potent toxin—such as, say, a preservative or a pesticide harmful—to humans, one had better be very sure that the toxin will not be expressed in the edible parts of the plant, or that potential risk is managed in some other way. However, there is no evidence that modification of an organism with recombinant DNA techniques, per se, confers *inherent* or *incremental* risk, compared to the introduction of similar traits using conventional techniques. That is not the same as saying that there is no risk, or even that the risk is invariably negligible, but the risks are the same in kind as plant breeders and farmers have been successfully managing for decades—and in some cases for centuries.

The Fear of the Unknown

Human beings have been gripped by fear of the unknown as long as they have invented new technologies. There is a cartoon that depicts prehistoric cave dwellers gathered around a campfire, when a lookout peering into the distance shouts a warning: "Quick, put it out; here come the anti-fire activists!" In more recent times, skeptics predicted that Jenner's immunizations against smallpox would cause grotesque, homunculus-like growths at the injection site; that telephones would electrocute their users; and that if humans traveled in trains at speeds faster than a horse could run, their rib cages would collapse.

Today, the Cassandras warn that because "the unknowns far outweigh the knowns,"[14] the use of gene-spliced organisms will run amok and lead to Andromeda Strains and Jurassic Parks. However, what matters is not how much is unknown but whether what we know enables sufficiently accurate predictions of risk. Prior experience, science, and common sense applied to risk analysis provide a rational process through which one can make useful predictions about potential hazards.

There is much that remains unknown, for example, about the mutations induced in poliovirus that attenuate and make it useful as a vaccine: As a result of intense mutagenesis the live Sabin vaccine has dozens of uncharacterized mutations in addition to the critical ones that make the virus incapable of causing disease. Yet the existence of these numerous, poorly understood genetic changes has not prevented our using the vaccine with monumental success for half a century. Likewise, for thousands of commercially important new plant varieties and microorganisms modified with conventional techniques, it would be accurate to say that although there is much that we do not know, we have benefited greatly from their use. Indeed, the very nature of recombinant DNA techniques means that plant breeders will actually know considerably *more* about the genotype and phenotype of new gene-spliced plants than about wide-cross hybrids or mutant varieties. Nevertheless, practitioners of the new biotechnology have systematically developed and adopted standard practices that are far more stringent than necessary to ensure the safety of their research and testing and the quality of their products.

Unless they are employed in research or industry, members of the public have little reason to know about these safeguards. It is a popular belief that new technology is invariably dangerous. This view, which may be an expression of an atavistic fear of disturbing the natural order or of breaking primitive taboos, is probably little affected by scientists' statistics-based assurances about the risks of a new technology. Few people understand the subtle relationship between mathematical probability and risk. The media—not known for scientific literacy but always eager to report a story of technology-run-amok—are no help.

We find it surprising that technophobia thrives in the face of the skeptic's own direct experience with unequivocal successes like telephones, air travel, vaccination, microprocessors, and pasteurization, as well as genetically improved plants, animals, and microorganisms. It appears, however, that few people spontaneously make those connections or think in terms of the dependence of our modern lifestyle on the routine availability of safe, powerful, innovative, technological processes and products. The DuPont Company was probably wise to abandon its erstwhile well-known motto, "Better Things For Better Living, Through Chemistry."

Certain of the practices, processes, or products of both conventional modification and new biotechnology are potentially hazardous under specific conditions to be sure. Beekeepers are stung, workers purifying antibiotics experience allergic reactions, laboratory technicians inadvertently become infected by pathogenic bacteria, and vaccines occasionally elicit serious side effects. The infrequency of these occurrences can be attributed to the application of risk analysis that relies heavily upon both first principles and empirical evidence. So it is with gene-splicing techniques.

Faulty Research

The scientific method and the body of knowledge it generates are essential to our understanding of the risks posed by the world in which we exist. Science is subverted, however, when inaccurate assumptions are used and when experiments are poorly designed or performed, misrepresented, or inadequately peer-reviewed. As the old computer science adage has it, "garbage in, garbage out."

For biotechnology, at least, these kinds of subversions—amplified by the press, who are always alert for a "Frankenfood" story—are unquestionably part of the answer to why technophobia survives and thrives. A review of the news coverage of biotechnology found that between 1997 and 2000, the *New York Times* and the *Times* of London used fewer and fewer university-based scientists as sources and were more than twice as likely to quote representatives from such extremist groups as Greenpeace, the Environmental Defense Fund, and the Union of Concerned Scientists.[15] Indeed, gene-spliced crop plants were effectively unknown to most Europeans until 1998, when the British news media seized on the unvalidated results of a methodologically flawed laboratory experiment conducted by Scottish microbiologist Arpad Pusztai.

Pusztai claimed, during a televised interview, that his research showed a certain variety of gene-spliced potatoes had negative health effects in lab rats. He fed his rats either conventional potatoes or an experimental biotech potato variety he had altered by adding a gene from the snowdrop plant that codes for a protein known to be toxic to certain insects.[16] He claimed that his experiments showed that the gene-spliced variety damaged the immune system and stimulated abnormal cell division in the digestive tract of the lab rats. But many scientists have shown that Pusztai's research methodology was critically flawed and that no conclusions about the safety of biotech foods can be drawn from his data.[17]

Pusztai fed the rats only potatoes and made no attempt to provide nutritionally balanced diets. As a consequence, *all* the rats in the study experienced adverse health effects. Moreover, Pusztai used an experimental potato variety that lacked several key vitamins. Any effects that Pusztai might have observed were almost certainly due to these factors.[18] What he did was rather like designing a five-hundred-horsepower automobile without brakes and concluding that cars are unacceptably dangerous.

After an extensive review, the British Royal Society issued a statement explaining the ways in which the experiment was fatally flawed: "On the basis of this paper, it is wrong to conclude that there are human health concerns with the process of [gene-splicing] itself, or even with the particular genes inserted into these [gene-spliced] potatoes."[19]

The editors of the British journal *The Lancet*, in which Pusztai's research appeared, wrote that despite the article's flawed methodology, they published it to "make constructive progress in the debate between scientists, the media, and the general public" about what was clearly a very politically charged issue.[20] Unleashing such a sham has proved to be anything but constructive, because its appearance in *The Lancet* is frequently trotted out as presumptively validating its result—not unlike referring to pre-Galileo literature as proof that the sun revolves around the earth. The Pusztai study should never have been published in a reputable journal.

Although no scientist has replicated the results of Pusztai's study with gene-spliced potatoes, a team of Chinese scientists conducted its own studies of gene-spliced sweet peppers and tomatoes, and found no such biological changes.[21] A Japanese study likewise found no negative effects on the immune system of rats fed gene-spliced soybeans.[22] Nearly two dozen other scientific papers evaluating the effect of various biotech animal feeds on livestock have found no evidence of harm.[23] Nevertheless, Pusztai's flawed research has become one of several touchstones for anti-biotechnology activists, who persist in claiming that it highlights the "dangers" of gene-spliced food.

Although the European press made Arpad Pusztai a household name, the mainstream press in the United States largely ignored the story. American activists were provided with a homegrown biotech scare story in 1999, however, when the results of a laboratory test suggested that pollen from a type of gene-spliced corn could kill Monarch butterfly caterpillars.[24] This was hardly news to plant scientists, because the corn had been modified by the introduction of a gene from the soil bacterium *Bacillus thuringiensis* (Bt) specifically to kill the caterpillars that are the major insect predators of corn. Nevertheless, the paper's publication triggered a frenzy of anti-biotech stories in the media. When a second Monarch study,[25] which attempted to simulate field conditions of corn pollen dispersal, found that pollen distribution onto milkweed plants in and around cornfields could be high enough potentially to kill the Monarch caterpillars, it seemed as though biotechnology might never recover from this public relations disaster.

Many scientists pointed out, however, that neither study accurately simulated real-world conditions. Corn pollination and Monarch larval development occur at different times of the year, and the amount of pollen that is spread decreases rapidly beyond twenty to thirty feet from the edges of cornfields.[26] Moreover, both the critics and the media consistently ignored the real-world context of pesticide use. The alternative to the cultivation of gene-spliced, insect-resistant corn is not simply to permit the pests an all-they-can-eat buffet in the field; rather, it is the extensive spraying of synthetic chemical insecticides, which kill not only the pests and Monarchs, but other beneficial insects as well. In summary, most scientists concluded that a minuscule effect on Monarchs should not lead to widespread condemnations of gene-spliced corn.

Ultimately, even the modest effects on Monarchs predicted by the initial research seemed to be contradicted by several factors, such as the limited exposure of butterflies in the wild to corn pollen of any type, and the fact that Monarch butterfly populations actually *increased* following the 1996 introduction of biotech corn in the United States.[27]

Any substantive concerns about the effects of Bt-pollen on Monarch butterflies were put to rest in October 2001, with the publication of six peer-reviewed papers in the highly respected *Proceedings of the National Academy of Sciences*. The papers describe two full years of intensive field research by twenty-nine scientists (including three of the five authors of the two original reports), who found little or no effect of Bt-pollen on Monarchs.[28] Additional research shows little or no impact on other beneficial insects and soil organisms. Nevertheless, these robust scientific results have not stopped activists from dressing up as Monarch butterflies in their street-theater protests of biotechnology. The relentlessly anti-biotech Union of Concerned Scientists continues to use images of Monarch butterflies on its website and fund-raising envelopes as a way of perpetuating the politically useful myth that crop biotechnology causes environmental damage.[29]

As illustrated by the publication of the Pusztai experiments, we are concerned about prominent journals' apparent tendency to err on the side of publishing inaccurate or merely substandard work that exaggerates biotech risk and ignores or distorts risk-benefit analyses. This appears to represent a failure of both peer review and editorial judgment.

Another example is the publication in *Science* of an analysis of the literature ostensibly to evaluate the "ecological risks and benefits of genetically engineered plants."[30] The authors, L. L. Wolfenbarger and P. R. Phifer, ignored obvious incontrovertible theoretical and experimental evidence of the safety and utility of these products and concluded . . . that no conclusion is possible. Even if the authors had been more knowledgeable and conscientious about exploring and interpreting the literature, the value of their work would have been compromised by its focus on the noncategory of "transgenic" plants, defined unproductively as those that contain genes transferred across species lines by (and only by) recombinant DNA techniques. They also chose to ignore the fact that not a single risk identified in their research is unique to gene-splicing, a shortsighted approach to reviewing the safety of this technology. Thus, even if they had performed a careful analysis and considered all the available data on transgenic, or gene-spliced, plants, the study still would have foundered on the principle that, as microbiologist and Nobel laureate Salvador Luria used to say, something that isn't worth doing at all isn't worth doing well.

Millions of new genetic variants of plants produced through hybridization, mutation breeding, and other traditional methods of genetic improvement are field-tested each year, and dozens enter the marketplace without any governmental review. Many such products are from wide crosses, hybridizations in which genes have been moved from one species or one genus to another to create a plant variety that cannot exist but for man's intervention.

Why did Wolfenbarger and Phifer not consider in their analysis any of the thousands of such non-gene-spliced varieties that are planted, harvested, and consumed every day? Why would they limit their analysis to the risks and benefits of recombinant DNA–engineered plants without including what might be termed "non-gene-spliced transgenics"—that is, the products of wide crosses—as a comparison? As *Nature* editorialized, "amid all the fuss about [gene-spliced] crops, there's been little acknowledgment that similar questions about biodiversity and gene flow must be asked about conventionally bred varieties. . . . [S]cientists, regulators, and politicians must seize the initiative and widen the debate about the future of farming beyond an obsession with transgenics."[31]

After invoking the tired (and tiresome) ecologists' tautology that "the complexity of ecological systems presents considerable challenges for experiments to assess the risks and benefits and inevitable uncertainties of genetically engineered plants," it is hardly surprising that the authors concluded about recombinant DNA–modified transgenic plants that no conclusions can be drawn, and that "collectively, existing studies emphasize that [risks and benefits] can vary spatially, temporally, and according to the trait and cultivar modified." In other words, Wolfenbarger and Phifer concluded exactly what for a century scientists have known to be true about plants modified with *any* genetic technique.

Designer Genes for Designer Jeans

Also troubling is the fact that so few of the proven benefits of gene-spliced crop plants and microorganisms have been described in the peer-reviewed scientific literature. A good example of the kinds of ecological benefits of recombinant DNA technology that Wolfenbarger and Phifer should have considered can be summarized with the following case: the use of designer genes to make designer jeans. The two principal components of blue jeans are, of course, cotton fabric and the indigo die that confers the characteristic color, both of which can now be produced with ecologically friendly recombinant DNA techniques. Bt-cotton is used to control several major pests, the cotton and pink bollworm and the tobacco budworm, which account for a quarter of all losses due to pest infestations in the United States and cost farmers more than $150 million annually.

U.S. and foreign farmers who have adopted Bt-cotton are experiencing a significantly reduced need to treat fields with chemical pesticides. Insecticide applications were cut nearly in half in the United States, and by three-fourths in China.[32] Between 1996, when it was introduced, and 2000, Bt-cotton alone eliminated the need for more than two million pounds of chemical pesticides.[33]

The advantages of this significant reduction in the use of chemical pesticides are obvious. In purely economic terms, Bt-cotton produces benefits to farmers both by reducing the need to buy and apply chemical pesticides and by increasing the crop's yields. Bt-cotton provides the highest per-acre monetary benefits to farmers of all the Bt-containing commodity crops, which also include corn and potatoes. The aggregate advantage to cotton farmers in the United States—the net value of crops not lost to pests, savings in insecticides, and so on—is in the range of $100–$150 million per year. In China, the average Bt-cotton farmer has been able to reduce pesticide sprayings for the Asian bollworm from an average of 12 to just 3 or 4 per growing season, and to achieve a nearly four-fifths' reduction in quantity.[34] Mexican and South African farmers also increased their yields while reducing their costs.[35]

But these commercial returns pale beside the environmental advantages. According to environmental regulators, aquatic wildlife is threatened by three of the chemicals that must be used in much greater amounts on conventional, non-Bt-cotton: endosulfan, methyl parathion, and profenos. The smaller the amounts of pesticides that are applied, the less runoff into waterways, a significant problem in many of the nation's agricultural regions. The adoption of Bt-cotton and the resulting lessened need for chemical pesticides also reduces occupational exposures to the toxic chemicals by the workers who mix, load, and apply the pesticides, and who perform other activities that require their presence in the field. (*Homo sapiens* is also part of the environment.) The reduction in pesticide use with Bt-cotton was found to reduce the incidence of insecticide poisonings in China by roughly 75 percent.[36]

Cotton is only half the story when we're talking about blue jeans, however. The standard chemical process for producing the indigo dye is an ecological and occupational monstrosity. Synthetic indigo production involves eight discrete operations, and it uses and produces as by-products several highly toxic chemicals. The process requires special precautions and physical facilities to protect workers and the environment. By contrast, the process of making indigo with recombinant bacteria involves only three operations, uses water instead of toxic organic solvents, employs corn syrup (which is safe and cheap) as the primary substrate, and yields biomass and carbon dioxide as by-products instead of potentially hazardous chemical waste products.[37]

The cotton-indigo story is only one of many—and one of many missed by Wolfenbarger and Phifer—in the unfolding saga of recombinant DNA technology applied to agricultural and industrial uses. Given the absence of any demonstrable ecological damage from the prodigious cultivation of gene-spliced crops during the past decade, the conclusion that their benefits outweigh the risks seems incontrovertible. In a letter published in *Science*, Janet Carpenter, then of the National Center for Food and Agricultural Policy, made this point and offers a succinct but devastating critique of Wolfenbarger and Phifer:

> Their discussion of changes in pesticide use includes little of the evidence available on pesticide use trends, and thus they underestimate reductions in pesticide

use. In particular, the authors cite analyses of trends in corn and soybeans, but do not discuss cotton, the crop for which the most dramatic reductions in pesticide use have been observed. Further, the authors mischaracterize the need for additional studies on changes in pesticide use and the impact of these changes on the environment [and] by focusing solely on potential ecological benefits, the authors overlook the other reasons U.S. farmers have planted [gene-spliced] crops on millions of acres: decreased costs, increased yields, and ease of management.[38]

One must wonder how these fundamental points could have escaped *Science*'s editors and peer-reviewers.

Runaway Corn

Another example of science subverted is the claim by two University of California, Berkeley, researchers to have found that "transgenes" (genes moved across "natural breeding boundaries" with recombinant DNA techniques) were transferred from recombinant varieties into the genome of Mexican corn landraces (local varieties largely removed from and unaffected by scientific plant breeding) and that the transgenes had fragmented and acted in unpredictable ways.[39] This report was seized upon by the new biotechnology's professional critics, who, immediately charging "contamination" and "genetic pollution," demanded a global ban on the planting of corn that contains Bt proteins—all of this widely publicized by the media. It was only later revealed that the researchers, David Quist and Ignacio Chapela, had sent samples to a scientist in the Swiss Ministry of Health, where tests for transgenes were negative.[40]

Moreover, many in the plant research community were highly skeptical that the transgene had fragmented because the evidence offered was insufficient and the claim was contrary to the experimental literature.[41] Indeed, based upon evidence that *was* presented in the paper, some researchers suggested that Quist and Chapela did not find transgenes at all, but that they merely recorded a false positive result known to be common with the testing method they used.[42] Quist and Chapela refused to release the data that described their negative controls, and they denied requests by other researchers for samples of the material in which the "contaminants" were found.

Finally, after an intensive search for evidence of "contamination" by gene-spliced corn in Mexico, scientists at the prestigious International Center for the Improvement of Maize and Wheat concluded that there was no evidence of an intrusion.[43] It is possible that a Bt gene may have been introduced into Mexican landraces by farmers unknowingly breeding their crop with a gene-spliced corn variety, but Quist and Chapela provided no evidence of this. Nevertheless, similar to the earlier, highly publicized "pseudo-crisis" that followed the report that pollen from Bt-corn killed Monarch butterflies, once critics seized on this example, they easily captured media attention with their bogus scare stories. But even if there were movement of transgenes into native landraces or teosinte (the closest wild relative of corn), this would be neither unexpected nor a cause for concern.[44]

Correspondence calling into question the scientific validity of the Quist and Chapela article deluged *Nature*, which published two of these letters.[45] Quist and Chapela were given an opportunity to defend themselves with additional data,[46] but *Nature*'s editors were unconvinced and concluded, "In light of these discussions and the diverse advice received, *Nature* has concluded that the evidence available is not sufficient to justify the publication of the original paper."[47]

The abject failure of the initial peer review and the decision by *Nature* to publish the original Quist and Chapela paper are ironic, given the journal's predilection for self-righteous moralizing about the need for those who are involved in science in general, and biotechnology in particular, to conduct themselves in a way that is beyond reproach: "Risk [to scientists' reputations] comes from pushing, or appearing to push, controversial practices opposed by large segments of the population, such as genetic manipulation of foods or stem-cell research. This is more than a question of who's 'right.' Too many scientists dismiss opposition based on emotion or differences in world-view, arrogantly believing that if the public is simply told the facts, they will fall in line."[48]

The public is certainly not likely to fall in line if they are told false and alarmist "facts." Moreover, we disagree that scientists have a special responsibility to mold their research programs and findings to accommodate the public's fears, or that they should hold town hall meetings at which they explain the value of their work. We believe that scientists' primary responsibility *is* to be "right," in the sense that their research should follow recognized rules, be reproducible, and add to the sum total of our knowledge and understanding. Not every scientist should feel bound to join in the debates on public policy, because few have that special combination of skills required to communicate accurately but effectively with a congressional committee or newspaper editorial board. Although playing such a public role can be very useful—and we encourage those who *are* effective communicators to do so— many scientists are more comfortable in the lab and have far more value there. If they choose to act as public spokesmen, however, scientists should espouse what they know to be accurate and relevant, and avoid venturing beyond their expertise.

No More Myths

Critics frequently misrepresent by asserting that gene-spliced organisms are analogous to "exotic" species—organisms introduced to ecosystems in which they haven't coevolved—and that once "released," they can cause ecological disruption. It is undeniably true that introductions of non-coevolved species such as English sparrows, gypsy moths, and kudzu vines have had seriously detrimental ecological and economic consequences. In their new settings, these organisms were no longer constrained by controlling factors found in their native ecosystems; and able to compete effectively in their new environments, they won the evolutionary lottery, thrived, and dominated. This enhanced competitiveness does not depend upon one or a few genes, however, but rather on highly complex traits and ecological systems.

By contrast, domesticated organisms have been systematically and gradually modified to enhance commercially important traits that are commonly of little advantage in the native environment and often place the organism at a competitive *dis*advantage. Small, discrete, incremental genetic changes in domesticated species are unlikely to confer the sort of adaptive advantage presented by non-coevolved species, which are not, therefore, an appropriate model for judging the likely risks of introductions of recombinant DNA–modified domesticated organisms. In the latter, one or a few genes have been modified for a particular purpose, and the organisms are introduced into a familiar ecosystem. Regulatory oversight appropriate to non-coevolved species would be overly precautionary and unnecessarily burdensome, were it to be applied to domesticated organisms.

What, then, is the appropriate oversight paradigm for recombinant DNA–modified organisms? The scientific assumptions that should serve as the basis for oversight, as well as both existing and proposed models for risk-based approaches, are discussed in the following chapters.

CHAPTER 3

Science, Common Sense, and Public Policy

For MORE THAN a quarter century, international scientific organizations and professional groups have grappled with the fundamental question of which assumptions should be used as the basis for public policy toward the new biotechnology. Because it determines so many aspects of public policy, ranging from regulatory and trade policy to legal liability, the pivotal question is whether the use of the new techniques requires a new paradigm, a unique approach. The consensus among scientists has been a remarkably consistent "No." At least, that was their answer until several years ago, when the anti-biotechnology lobby began to stuff the ballot box with a few contrary votes. (More on this later.)

Without intending to belabor the point, it is necessary to describe in some detail the consensus that no new regulatory paradigm is required, because the "product versus process" issue—whether regulation should focus on the characteristics of a product or on the use of a certain process—has such sweeping ramifications.

THE SCIENTIFIC CONSENSUS ON REGULATING BIOTECH

In 1987, the U.S. National Academy of Sciences (NAS) published a white paper on the planned introduction of genetically modified organisms into the environment.[1] It noted that recombinant DNA techniques provide a powerful and safe means for modifying organisms, and it predicted that the technology would contribute substantially to improved health care, agricultural efficiency, and the amelioration of many pressing environmental problems. The paper had wide-ranging impacts in the United States and internationally. Its most significant conclusions and recommendations include:

- There is no evidence of the existence of unique hazards either in the use of re-combinant DNA techniques or in the movement of genes between unrelated organisms. The risks associated with the introduction of recombinant DNA–modified organisms are the same in kind as those associated with the introduction of unmodified organisms and organisms modified by other methods.
- Assessment of the risks of introducing recombinant DNA–modified organisms into the environment should be based on the nature of the organism and of the environment into which the organism is to be introduced, and independent of the method of engineering per se.

In a 1989 follow-up to this white paper, the National Research Council (NRC), the research arm of the NAS, concluded that "no conceptual distinction exists between genetic modification of plants and microorganisms by classical methods or by molecular techniques that modify DNA and transfer genes," whether in the laboratory, in the field, or in large-scale environmental introductions.[2] The NRC report supported this statement with extensive discussions of experience with plant breeding and the cultivation of these pre-recombinant-DNA genetically modified plants and microorganisms:

- "Crops modified by molecular and cellular methods should pose risks no different from those modified by classical genetic methods for similar traits. As the molecular methods are more specific, users of these methods will be more certain about the traits they introduce into the plants."[3]
- "Recombinant DNA methodology makes it possible to introduce pieces of DNA, consisting of either single or multiple genes, that can be defined in function and even in nucleotide sequence. With classical techniques of gene transfer, a variable number of genes can be transferred, the number depending on the mechanism of transfer; but predicting the precise number or the traits that have been transferred is difficult, and we cannot always predict the phenotypic expression that will result. With organisms modified by molecular methods, we are in a better, if not perfect, position to predict the phenotypic expression."[4]
- "Information about the process used to produce a genetically modified organism is important in understanding the characteristics of the product. However, the nature of the process is not a useful criterion for determining whether the product requires less or more oversight."[5]
- As a consequence, "the *product* of genetic modification and selection should be the primary focus for making decisions about the environmental introduction of a plant or microorganism and not the *process* by which the products were obtained."[6]

Thus, the NRC set a standard that has been reiterated subsequently by countless scientific bodies: The mere fact that an organism was modified by gene-splicing techniques should not determine how the organism should be regulated. The committee proposed that the evaluation of experimental field testing of any organism, whether gene-spliced, conventionally modified, or unmodified, be based on three considerations: familiarity, the sum total of knowledge about the traits of the organism and the test environment; the ability to confine or control the organism; and the likelihood of harmful effects if the organism should escape control or confinement.

The same principles were emphasized in the comprehensive report from the U.S. National Biotechnology Policy Board (on which one of us—Henry I. Miller—served as a charter member), which was established by Congress with representation from the public and private sectors. The report concluded: "The risks associated with biotechnology are not unique, and tend to be associated with particular products and their applications, not with the production process or the technology per se. In fact, biotechnology processes tend to reduce risks because they are more precise and predictable. The health and environmental risks of not pursuing biotechnology-based solutions to the nation's problems are likely to be greater than the risks of going forward."[7]

Various other national and international groups, including the American Medical Association, the United Kingdom's Royal Society, and the UN's Food and Agriculture Organization and World Health Organization, have repeatedly echoed or extended these conclusions. A joint statement from the International Council of Scientific Unions' (ICSU) Scientific Committee on Problems of the Environment (SCOPE) and the Committee on Genetic Experimentation (COGENE) concluded,

The properties of the introduced organisms and its target environment are the key features in the assessment of risk. Such factors as the demographic characterization of the introduced organisms; genetic stability, including the potential for horizontal transfer or outcrossing with weedy species; and the fit of the species to the physical and biological environment . . . apply equally to both modified or unmodified organisms; and, in the case of modified organisms, they apply independently of the techniques used to achieve modification. That is, it is the organism itself, and not how it was constructed, that is important.[8]

The report of a NATO Advanced Research Workshop concluded,

In principle, the outcomes associated with the introduction into the environment of organisms modified by recombinant DNA techniques are likely to be the same in kind as those associated with introduction of organisms modified by other methods. Therefore, identification and assessment of the risk of possible adverse outcomes should be based on the nature of the organism and of the environment into which it is introduced, and not on the method (if any) of genetic modification.[9]

Other analyses have focused specifically on the food safety aspects of gene-spliced organisms and their derivatives. For example, in a 1993 report the Paris-based Organization for Economic Cooperation and Development

(OECD) described several concepts related to food safety that are wholly consistent with the consensus discussed above:[10]

- "Modern biotechnology broadens the scope of the genetic changes that can be made in food organisms and broadens the scope of possible sources of foods. This does not inherently lead to foods that are less safe than those developed by conventional techniques."[11]
- "Evaluation of foods and food components obtained from organisms developed by the application of the newer techniques does not necessitate a fundamental change in established principles, nor does it require a different standard of safety."[12]

Finally, a comprehensive analysis of food safety published in 2000 by the Institute of Food Technologists addressed both the scientific and regulatory implications of recombinant DNA–modified foods and specifically took current regulatory policies to task. The report concluded that the evaluation of recombinant DNA–modified organisms and the food derived from them "does not require a fundamental change in established principles of food safety; nor does it require a different standard of safety, even though, in fact, more information and a higher standard of safety are being required." The report went on to state unequivocally that theoretical considerations and empirical data do "not support more stringent safety standards than those that apply to conventional foods."[13]

Again, we do not mean to belabor the point, but we include so many examples to demonstrate how completely and unreservedly the scientific community had embraced these principles.

SUBSTANTIAL EQUIVALENCE

Given this solid consensus of the scientific community regarding the safety of recombinant DNA techniques, how would plant breeders go about ensuring the safety of foods derived from newly modified varieties? As we discussed at the end of chapter 2, one cannot deny that some of the conceivable products of old and new biotechnology are potentially hazardous under specific conditions. For that reason, the OECD Group of National Experts on Safety in Biotechnology developed a simple approach for comparing the safety of new varieties with varieties already in the food supply known to be safe. This practical way to determine the safety of novel foods is "to consider whether they are *substantially equivalent* to analogous conventional food product(s), if such exist."[14]

The concept of substantial equivalence is important but often misunderstood. Because the scientific consensus holds that the products of either conventional modification or gene-splicing generally change just a few of the characteristics of the product, the concept of substantial equivalence focuses attention on the differences that are introduced, alerting regulators to the differences rather than the similarities. In that way, public resources can be spent on evaluating legitimate risks while leaving relatively low-risk research and development unencumbered.

Critics have often distorted and misrepresented the concept in an effort to frighten consumers into believing that regulatory authorities have deemed *all* products of gene-splicing to be, ipso facto, substantially equivalent to the products of conventional modification and therefore not to require testing or government oversight. This is not what substantial equivalence is about.

The concept of substantial equivalence was appropriated from the FDA, which uses it to define new medical devices that do not differ materially from their predecessors, and thus do not raise new regulatory concerns. In an analogous way, substantial equivalence as applied to foods made with the new biotechnology was intended to serve as a kind of benchmark for an acceptable level of safety. Products whose testing by their developers shows them to be without material differences from their closest conventional counterparts in nutritional value, metabolism, intended use, and other characteristics would be subject to minimal oversight. Those that could not be shown to be substantially equivalent would face higher regulatory scrutiny. But no one should be under the misapprehension that gene-spliced products found to be substantially equivalent to earlier conventional products undergo no testing. They would still be subject to at least the testing and government oversight required for conventional foods. After all, only through testing can a gene-spliced food be judged to be substantially equivalent.

ANTI-SCIENCE IS ANTI-SOCIAL

In spite of the broad consensus of the scientific bodies that have studied recombinant DNA techniques and gene-spliced foods, from the earliest days there has been a disconnect between science and policy.

At one point in the early 1980s, it seemed that this product-versus-process debate was on the verge of being put to rest in the councils of government, when Stanford biologist Allan Campbell and MIT virologist David Baltimore, eminent members of the NIH Recombinant DNA Advisory Committee (RAC), proposed that the NIH recombinant DNA guidelines be made voluntary. This would have been an historic development, because it would have acknowledged, at least implicitly, that the guidelines had been predicated on the incorrect assumption that recombinant DNA techniques, among all methods of genetic manipulation, were somehow uniquely worrisome with respect to risk.

Already, an impressive body of experimental data—as well as sober reflection by experts in many scientific disciplines—had made a persuasive case for reform. The majority of RAC members expressed support for the general arguments about the nature of recombinant DNA risks, and they agreed that recombinant DNA methods and products warranted no special precautions or oversight beyond that applied to standard microbiological practices. Paradoxically, they then proceeded to reject the proposal, many members of the committee members stating pointedly that the reforms would unacceptably diminish the RAC's role. They believed that RAC meetings served a valuable public relations purpose. The open meetings, they argued, provided a prestigious and democratic forum in which anyone could air concerns about the testing and use of new biotechnology methods and products. Although their ostensible goal was to gain public approval of scientific research, some members revealed an unmistakable element of self-congratulation and self-importance.

Vanity has its price. By sustaining the recombinant DNA guidelines—instead of relegating them to a museum of American history to join other relics—the RAC sent a signal that the NIH and the scientific community remained sufficiently concerned about the new genetic methods that they should be more stringently regulated than others. This decision reinforced the nagging perception that gene-spliced organisms are inherently dangerous and warrant extra governmental oversight. In the absence of concrete actions to correct that perception, the USDA and EPA followed the lead of the NIH and introduced scientifically indefensible regulatory schemes of their own—a process that has continued, as we discuss below and in chapter 5.

Some in both the public and private sectors abetted these errors of commission and omission. But whether their motivations were noble, crass, or naïve, the muted retort of these regressive policy decisions sounded through the decades of the 1980s and 1990s like a firecracker in slow motion. Federal bureaucrats eager to expand their regulatory domains, companies desperate to calm jittery investors or attempting to gain a short-term commercial advantage, and a few academic scientists eager for notoriety constituted the packets of gunpowder. The sensational claims of anti-biotechnology groups—promulgated by the media hungry for lurid scenarios—lit the fuse.

The Big Lie

Professional anti-biotechnology activists have promoted pseudo-controversy by raising a succession of phony issues that have included fanciful safety concerns, inaccurate economic forecasts, and trumped-up consumers' rights. They maintain that even the most modest, precise, and well-characterized genetic modification can have unpredictable and disastrous effects. For example, they claimed that using a recombinant version of the hormone bovine somatotropin (bST) to increase milk production in dairy cows would cause breast cancer in women who drink milk. They speculated that field trials of a gene-spliced bacterium (*Pseudomonas syringae*) intended to limit frost damage of crops could disrupt weather patterns and air traffic control. They also continue to argue that gene-spliced plants modified to tolerate certain herbicides will lead to the creation of *Attack of the Killer Tomatoes*–like "super weeds," even though exactly the same herbicide-tolerant trait can be bred into plants with conventional techniques.

Anti-biotechnology antics have ranged from the silly to the bizarre and pernicious. In the 1970s a group of activists disrupted a scientific conference chanting, "We shall not be cloned." Plants in field trials in at least half a dozen countries have been ripped from the ground—even when the purpose of the study was scientific risk assessment rather than precommercial testing. A few hard-core activists have campaigned relentlessly against *all* biotechnology applications, including even the production of pharmaceuticals that prevent or treat cancer, heart attacks, AIDS, hepatitis, and rabies. They continue to beleaguer and harass government agencies with petitions to restrict or altogether ban new biotechnology products and research. They terrify the populace with bizarre and bogus accusations and alarms, not unlike the "activists" who fomented the panics of the Middle Ages by spreading rumors that Jews or gypsies had poisoned the wells. They are not the first to use the technique of endlessly repeating The Big Lie.

Biotech's critics have capitalized not only on the public's scientific naiveté but also on others' concerns about the public's scientific naiveté. The critics have gambled successfully that, their own cupidity and self-interest aside, government regulators, industry executives, and university scientists would panic over the mere *possibility* that the public would be taken in by the anti-biotechnology controversies.

Unfortunately, little attention has been paid to public opinion polls that show that the public is not up in arms about biotechnology but that, on the contrary, American consumers by more than three to one consistently are enthusiastic about the current use of the new biotechnology to reduce farmers' use of chemical pesticides.[15] In an odd twist on George Orwell's observation about peoples' tendency to experience "vague fears and horrible imaginings," the activists have mined a vein of anti-capitalist puritanism laced with the desire for zero-risk lives.

Activists who are antagonistic toward globalization and science in general, as well as those opposed to biotechnology specifically, continue to work overtime to popularize their mythic visions of apocalypse. The unflagging efforts of professional agitators like the Union of Concerned Scientists' Margaret Mellon and Jane Rissler, Environmental Defense's Rebecca Goldburg, the Foundation on Economic Trends' Jeremy Rifkin, the Consumer Federation of America's Carol Tucker Foreman, Consumers International's Jean Halloran, and Consumers Union's Michael Hansen have been given considerable access and credibility in many quarters. These quarters include not only the media but also USDA, FDA and EPA officials, certain members of Congress and their staffs, and the Neville Chamberlain–

like naïfs in companies and universities who foolishly hope to appease the activists or to buy them off.

The anti-biotechnology activists discard like junk mail the considered findings of distinguished scientific organizations. They claim that there is no documentation, just opinions, on matters of recombinant DNA risk. Jeremy Rifkin has characterized biotechnology as threatening "a form of annihilation every bit as deadly as nuclear holocaust."[16] Greenpeace demands the "complete elimination [from] the food supply and the environment" of biotech products.[17] Greenpeace and similar groups advocate and have committed thefts and vandalism of field trials at universities and on private and corporate farms.

Although these groups portray themselves as idealistic Davids fighting the mighty, exploitative, corporate Goliaths, the magnitude of financial resources available to anti-biotech activists is staggering. Greenpeace alone is a $100 million a year operation. What may appear to be an inconsequential handful of vocal ideologues is actually a collection of well-financed professionals employed by organizations to pursue narrowly focused activism.

The same band has battled biotechnology for more than two decades, winning occasional successes. These self-appointed "representatives of the people" appear at public hearings claiming to represent the views of large numbers of concerned citizens—although not one of their organizations has demonstrated any evidence to support the claim. North Carolina State University survey researcher Thomas J. Hoban, who has long studied public attitudes about biotechnology, has said that protest groups "really only promote self-serving myths about what consumers know and think about these important developments. These groups try to shape public opinion for their own benefit, rather than reflect true consumer interests."[18]

Anti-biotech activists seem sometimes not even to represent the values of their own interest group. We wonder, for example, how the rank-and-file members of the National Wildlife Federation would have reacted had they known of the organization's intractable opposition to the development—or even the *testing*—of a rabies vaccine to protect wild animals from the horrible disease. What would Sierra Club members think of their organization's opposition to gene-spliced crops that can help conserve water and reduce agriculture's dependence on synthetic chemical pesticides?

Greenpeace and the Purloined Seeds

Greenpeace International personifies mendacious, the-end-justifies-the-means activism. The group may have attained the nadir of anti-biotechnology activism when, on April 6, 1995 the organization announced that it had "intercepted a package containing rice seed genetically manipulated to produce a toxic insecticide, as it was being exported . . . [and] swapped the genetically manipulated seed with normal rice."[19]

This incident is the apparent result of too little education and a poorly developed moral compass combined with exposure to too many *Mission Impossible* reruns. The rice seeds stolen by Greenpeace had been genetically improved for insect resistance and were en route from the Swiss Federal Institute of Technology in Zurich to the International Rice Research Institute in the Philippines, where the modified seeds were to be tested for the ability to produce high yields of rice using less chemical pesticide.

In the Philippines and elsewhere in Asia, where rice is a staple food, disease-resistant and insect-resistant varieties are desperately needed. Insect pests are a particular problem in the hot and humid tropical regions of Asia, Africa, and Latin America. Chemical pesticides, which are often hand-sprayed on crops by farmers wearing little or no protective gear, pose a significant occupational hazard. For example, the *New York Times* reported on the occupational hazards that exist for those who work around pesticides in Latin America: "The pesticides, fungicides and fumigants used to produce Ecuador's magnificent, baseball-sized flowers afflict untold numbers of greenhouse workers with maladies including headaches, nausea, fatigue and miscarriages."[20] An Ecuadorian doctor recalled workers spraying chemicals in street clothes with no protective equipment, pesticides stored in poorly sealed containers, and fumes wafting over the workers' dining halls.

New varieties of flowers and food crops with enhanced endogenous pesticidal activity are by no means a panacea for mistreated workers, but these kinds of innovations can reduce drastically the need for agricultural chemicals and thereby improve working conditions.

Greenpeace interfered with the research on insect-resistant rice only because the seeds had been improved using recombinant DNA techniques. Each year, thousands of other genetically modified seed samples are shipped to and from the International Rice Research Institute and other agricultural research centers around the world—without notice by or interference from Greenpeace. But Greenpeace targets only a single, superior technology:

> Transports of hazardous waste have to be approved by both export and import countries as well as by all transit countries along the way. In Switzerland, the Federal Office of the Environment (BUWAL) watches over the exports of toxic wastes. Unlike chemical substances, genetically engineered organisms have the potential to multiply, spread and simply get out of control. Obviously such organisms constitute a danger for people and for the environment. . . . It should be clear that the export of genetically manipulated organisms needs to be even more tightly regulated than the export of toxic wastes.[21]

This is an example of endless repetition of The Big Lie—in this case intentionally blurring the obvious distinctions between seeds and toxic wastes (which are, as the English would say, about as alike as chalk and cheese) and implying that "genetically manipulated" organisms are new and in need of the most stringent regulatory requirements possible. This is a conscious strategy. The activists are well aware that profit margins for fresh and processed foods are so narrow and competition so keen that unnecessary regulation can make a technology uncompetitive and ensure its demise.

If Greenpeace were to prevail, the exchange of plant germplasm and the enhancement of crops for indigenous farmers would be imperiled. Who would underwrite the costs of developing agricultural products that are, without justification of any kind, "more tightly regulated than the export of toxic wastes?" New technologies and products would become even more densely concentrated in industrialized countries, whose populations can bear the inflated costs of a small number of overregulated commodity crops and high-value-added consumer products. Fewer new tools for more environment-friendly and productive agriculture would become available overall. One must ask: What—and whose—interest is served by Greenpeace and other extremist groups?

Posing as Moderates

Not all anti-biotechnology activism comes from the bomb throwers like Greenpeace and Friends of the Earth, however. Other groups, such as the Center for Science in the Public Interest and the Pew Initiative on Food and Biotechnology, claim not to oppose biotech, only to want it "properly" regulated. They are subtler, and therefore arguably more insidious, than anti-biotech players who show their colors unambiguously.

Reports published by the Pew Initiative, for example, receive extensive media and government attention, largely because Pew touts itself as occupying the thoughtful, disinterested middle ground in the biotechnology debates. But the fact that Pew's PR machine says that doesn't make it so.

Contrary to their remonstrations that they are nonpartisan and agnostic about biotechnology, Pew's workshops, conferences, and publications show a pervasive pro-regulation bias. The key for Pew has been to hide behind a "stakeholder forum" composed of representatives of the food and biotechnology industry, farmer organizations, food retailers, and anti-biotechnology activists. The forum is portrayed as a "balanced" dialogue between biotech's supporters and opponents that included views across the entire spectrum. However, the reality is quite different: a kind of Potemkin Village town meeting.

Pew's notion of "balance" is to mix intractable, anti-technology radicals together with academics and industry representatives who have largely moderate, mainstream views. (And in order to mollify critics, even the middle-dwelling big agribusiness and biotech companies capitulated—unwisely, in our view—to the demands for greater, discriminatory regulation of gene-spliced organisms and products derived from them.) The anti-biotech faction includes such tenacious, mendacious opponents of agricultural biotechnology as Environmental Defense's Rebecca Goldburg, the Union of Concerned Scientists' Margaret Mellon, and U.S. Public Interest Research Group's Richard Caplan. The nineteen-person committee contains just three academic scientists—one of whom, Kathleen Merrigan, also has long been a biotechnology critic. It is transparently obvious in which direction the "consensus" was intended to go. It is also revealing that every member of Pew's stakeholder forum had to agree at the outset that the current, biased regulatory apparatus is still in some way *insufficiently* stringent.

In spite of the litmus test and the stacking of the committee, the stakeholder negotiations broke down when the most extreme anti-biotech ideologues overplayed their hand. They made demands that went beyond even the excessive restrictions that the food and biotechnology industry representatives were willing to concede. Although the industry representatives were prepared to endorse a wholly unwarranted new requirement for a formal premarket notification process for all new gene-spliced food crop varieties, the more radical faction insisted that FDA must reject its current scientific approach and require a formal premarket authorization of all gene-spliced food crops, regardless of the level of risk individual crops posed.

This agenda was pushed especially hard by one member of the stakeholder forum, Greg Jaffe, of the Center for Science in the Public Interest. Although his group poses as unbiased and moderate, it too has a hidden agenda. Jaffe is credited with drafting legislation introduced in Congress by Senator Richard Durbin (D-IL) to establish a mandatory approval process for gene-spliced foods. CSPI then orchestrated a campaign to garner support for the Durbin bill, all the while pretending to be nothing more than an uninvested bystander that favored the legislation on its merits.

By creating its stakeholder committee, Pew asserted a kind of moral equivalence between those who hold ideological, anti-biotechnology views and those who are committed to sound science as the basis for public policy—not unlike equating "creation theory" with "Darwinian theory." Nevertheless, the gullible media lap up the slick, expensively produced reports from the Pew Initiative as though they emanate from a disinterested, honest process.

The Pew Initiative and other groups also attempt to create a presumption of genuine controversy, where none exists, over the safety and usefulness of gene-splicing techniques. For example, Pew's 2003 report, "Public Sentiment about Genetically Modified Food," is a typically disingenuous pastiche of truisms, half-truths, and sleight-of-hand.[22] The survey found that "Americans' knowledge about [biotech] foods remains low," with 54 percent saying they have heard nothing or not much about them. Then, without enlightening the subjects or offering them any sort of context, the survey went on to pose leading questions about safety and regulation. Not surprisingly, 89 percent agreed with the statement, "Companies should be required to submit safety data to the FDA for review, and no genetically modified food product should be allowed on the market until the FDA determines that it is safe."

This polling technique is rather like the example of Idaho junior high school student Nathan Zohner, who found that 86 percent of survey respondents thought the substance dihydrogen monoxide should be banned when told that prolonged exposure to its solid form causes severe tissue damage, exposure to its gaseous form causes severe burns, and it has been found in excised tumors of terminal cancer patients. Only one in 50 of young Nathan's survey respondents correctly identified dihydrogen monoxide as *water*, or H_2O. As any pollster (as well as common sense) will tell you, it's not hard to design survey questions to elicit a desired response, and Pew has incorporated that trick into its repertoire.

What the almost nine-in-ten respondents in Pew's survey undoubtedly do not recognize is that: 1) with the exception of wild berries and mushrooms, game, and wild-caught fish and shellfish, virtually *all* the organisms—plants, animals, microorganisms—in our food supply have been modified by one genetic technique or another; 2) because the techniques of the new biotech are more precise and predictable than their predecessors, biotech foods are likely to be even *more* safe than other foods; 3) food producers are already legally responsible for assuring the safety of their products, and the FDA does not normally perform safety determinations, but primarily conducts surveillance of marketed foods and takes action if any are found to be adulterated or mislabeled; and (4) unwarranted, excessive regulation, including unnecessary labeling requirements, discourages innovation and imposes costs that are passed along to the consumer and are a disproportionate burden on the poor. The Pew survey purposefully exploits consumers' (understandable) lack of familiarity with the nuances of both the new biotech and the way that food is currently regulated.

With critics raising at every opportunity the possibility of one hypothetical risk or another of gene-splicing—and a compliant, sensation-seeking media printing every word—it's no wonder that many of those who *have* heard about biotechnology find it confusing and a little scary. But more generally, hoodwinking the public on scientific and technological subjects is not difficult. A study by the National Science Foundation found that fewer than one in four know what a molecule is, and only about half understand that the earth circles the sun once a year.[23]

Another example of the public's muddled view of biotechnology is reflected in the results of a survey of 1,200 Americans, released in October 2003 by the Food Policy Institute at Rutgers University. In an eleven-item true/false quiz that was part of the survey, more than half of the subjects received a failing grade (defined as less than 70 percent correct answers). Only 57 percent recognized that the statement, "ordinary tomatoes do not contain genes, while genetically modified tomatoes do," is false.[24] Perhaps most shocking of all, only two-thirds knew that eating genetically modified fruit would not alter their own genes! One wonders whether the one-third who got this question wrong think that if they eat rabbit stew, they will begin to hop?

When Science Becomes Politicized

Anti-biotechnology activists have attempted to deconstruct science in order to discredit it. As Ellen Haas, a biotechnology critic who became undersecretary of agriculture in the Clinton administration, put it, "You can have 'your' science or 'my' science or 'somebody else's' science. By nature, there is going to be a difference."[25] Leaving aside the fact that Haas herself became a policy maker, far too often government officials welcome anti-technology campaigners to their advisory committees, hearings, and conferences, in spite of the fact that among the public, anti-biotechnology groups enjoy the lowest credibility among all stakeholders.[26]

Biologist Donald Kennedy, a former FDA commissioner and former Stanford University president, has analyzed various aspects of governmental oversight of America's scientific enterprise. Bringing to this issue the experience of a scientist, educator, and regulator, Kennedy observes that bad public policies usually result when we respond politically to some popular movement, only to discover that we have mistaken its real motivation. "'We did what they wanted, but after we did it they turned out to want something else' is among the oldest of political complaints. It has all kinds of bad consequences. Not only is the wrong policy put in place, but those who have tried to be responsive experience alienation and disillusionment when they discover that they have not provided any satisfaction."[27]

Kennedy gently chides policy makers: "Frequently decision-makers give up the difficult task of finding out where the weight of scientific opinion lies, and instead attach equal value to each side in an effort to approximate fairness. In this way extraordinary opinions, even those like Mr. [Jeremy] Rifkin's, are promoted to a form of respectability that approaches equal status."

Kennedy is too kind. Often the policy makers *do* know where the weight of scientific opinion lies but use the blandishments and demands of activists as cover for their own overregulatory tendencies.

Reluctant to let the world know their real agendas, biotech's antagonists seldom tip their hand, but once in a while we get a revealing glimpse. The Pew Charitable Trusts, the parent of the Pew Initiative on Food and Biotechnology, has announced that it is changing its legal and tax status from the more restrictive "foundation" to a "public charity," in order to be able to undertake more overt and aggressive lobbying and advocacy—that is to say, what it was doing previously, but in a less surreptitious way.

There are more substantive, less legalistic examples. In 2000, a university research team based in Switzerland and Germany announced an extraordinary scientific tour de force that resulted in the addition of beta-carotene, or pro-vitamin A, to rice grains.[28] The creation of this "golden rice" (so called because of its yellow color) was widely hailed as an example of how gene-splicing can benefit society, especially the inhabitants of less developed countries. Vitamin A supplementation of the diet prevents blindness and can be lifesaving to the millions of children who are deficient in the vitamin.

Astonishingly, activists lost no time in attacking even this beneficent innovation. First, the critics claimed that the rice itself would be unhealthy, because too much Vitamin A can be toxic.[29] That claim was rapidly discredited by nutritionists, who explained that golden rice contains beta-carotene, the chemical *precursor* of Vitamin A, which is not toxic at any dose. Then, torturing the data and flip-flopping as they are wont to do, Greenpeace declared that golden rice had too *little* beta-carotene and that an adult "would have to eat around 9 kg [19.8 pounds] of cooked rice daily to satisfy his/her daily need of vitamin A."[30] Greenpeace's Benedikt Haerlin threatened direct action against test plants in the field.[31] Greenpeace's radical media allies, including the UK's *Guardian*, rushed to support them, and Michael Pollan of the *New York Times Magazine* dubbed golden rice "the great yellow hype."[32] All of them criticize golden rice's developers for working with for-profit companies to make seed available to the poor.

These reactions are the vilest sort of distortion and misrepresentation. Even small amounts of vitamin supplementation can have huge effects. Golden rice and other products like it can be life-enhancing, lifesaving adjuncts to persons with vitamin A deficiency—but only if their producers can overcome NGO opposition and regulatory hurdles, and get the new varieties to the farmers who wish to grow it.

Still, such blatant and rabid militancy might make those who "merely" demand stifling regulation appear temperate by comparison. But correspondence published in the journal *Science* in 2003 opened a window into the motivations of the so-called "moderate" wing of the anti-biotech lobby. Steven H. Strauss, a professor of Forest Science at Oregon State University, proposed in an article in that journal a very modest streamlining of the regulation of negligible-risk genetic constructions of gene-spliced plants.[33] The reform that he suggested would remedy, in a small way, the irreconcilable paradox in the current federal oversight of plant biotechnology: that the use of the most precise and predictable techniques is far more stringently regulated than techniques that are less precise and predictable. In other words, Strauss was lobbying for regulatory proportionality, a recognition of the basic principle that the degree of oversight should be commensurate with the degree of risk.

Jerry Cayford, of the Washington D.C.–based Resources for the Future, responded with a letter published in *Science*: "Steven H. Strauss makes a plea for less onerous field trial regulations for less radical genetic modifications . . . thereby helping smaller companies and public-sector investigators to be able to afford to try out crop variants. Unfortunately, his pleas ignore the politics of the genetically modified (GM) food debate. . . . Strauss' proposal, reasonable as it may be, asks critics to surrender a major bargaining chip—strict regulation of field trials—but offers them nothing in return."[34] In other words, although it would favor consumers, researchers, and the public interest, sensible regulatory policy is not a goal in itself but is merely a bargaining chip to be held or given up in a negotiation among radical groups, business interests, academic researchers, and government regulators!

Strauss's response to Cayford deplored this "hostage-taking" attitude, because "the costs to people and environment of effectively losing genetic engineering from most agricultural sectors as a result of excess regulation are too great for so simple-minded a political approach."[35] He added that there are few practices more "'democratizing' than protecting and promoting the ideas and work of society's innovators when applied to improve food quality, dependability, and affordability."

The *coup de grace* in Strauss's response serves as a worthy epilogue to the unworthy efforts and venal motivation of biotech's antagonists, whether they are blatantly belligerent or subtly shifty: "[W]ith the high level of regulation and stigma successfully implanted in places such as Europe, policies and attitudes may take a generation or more to change course. The opportunity costs in dollars, and costs to human health and environment, will be incalculable."

No one should mistake the anti-biotech NGOs' misdemeanors for naive exuberance or excessive zeal in a good cause. Their motives are self-serving and their tactics vicious, an ongoing example of the sentiments expressed by Linus van Pelt, a character in the *Peanuts* comic strip: "I love humanity; it's people I can't stand."

To well-meaning colleagues in academia, government, industry, and nonprofit organizations who would attempt to propitiate or carry on meaningful dialogue with the anti-science, anti-biotechnology activists, we would counsel that it is fruitless. Their agenda is to arrogate control over what research is performed, what tools are used, and what products are brought to market—and they are not persuaded by scientifically reasonable arguments or empirical evidence. There is little common ground. One cannot have a reasoned debate with a mugger.

The consequential lesson to be learned from all this is that although anti-biotechnology groups are entitled to their own views of science and technology, it is foolish—no, grotesque—to cede to them the responsibility for defining the public interest or to equate their deconstructionist, anti-establishment ravings with traditional science. The scientific community, which spans government, industry, and academia, should not gracefully or passively tolerate activist campaigns whose doctrines contradict empirical knowledge and defy scientific principles of risk analysis.

INDUSTRY'S ROLE IN OVERREGULATION

America learned long ago that what's good for General Motors isn't necessarily good for the country, an epiphany that applies equally well to the biotechnology industry, which suggests that we should be suspicious of its history of cultivating self-serving regulation. It might seem incredible that industry would wish to crank up the level of regulation on its own products. Indeed, if opponents of the technology were to be believed, the industry has vigorously sought permissive laissez-faire regulation and has bitterly opposed the gradual expansion of regulation over the last twenty years.

Yet at its best, the biotechnology industry has been only a tentative and hesitant opponent of unscientific and progressively greater regulation. Often it has embraced the policies and compromises that disadvantage many of its own members in the competitive marketplace.

Since the 1980s the larger agbiotech companies, packaged food companies, and their industry associations have actively and aggressively lobbied in favor of certain major regulatory and legislative initiatives that were more restrictive even than those sought by regulators themselves. Industry titans such as the Monsanto Company, Ciba-Geigy Corporation (first reorganized as Novartis, then spun off as Syngenta), and Pioneer Hi-Bred International (now a subsidiary of DuPont), as well as biotechnology and food industry trade associations, have all too often abandoned science and common sense as the basis for public policy.

Long before the first gene-spliced plants were ready for commercialization, a few agrochemical and biotechnology companies, led by Monsanto and Calgene, approached senior policy makers in the administration of President Ronald Reagan and requested that the EPA, USDA, and FDA create a regulatory framework specific to gene-spliced products. The policies recommended by the biotechnology industry were far more restrictive than could be justified on scientific grounds, and often were even more burdensome than those proposed by regulators. Ostensibly, the goal of these policies was to placate anti-biotech activists and provide reassurance to consumers that government regulators had evaluated and cleared gene-spliced products.

The overregulation sought by the big biotech companies also served to placate the packaged food industry. Food companies see great potential value in gene-spliced food crops, but cognizant of incipient anti-biotech consumer sentiment, they are willing to pay a high price to obtain what would amount to a federal government endorsement—although conventional products neither need nor receive any such stamp of approval. Because competition in the food industry is intense and profit margins are very small, individual companies and their trade associations fear the effects of anti-biotechnology activism and its resulting negative publicity. Also, while food companies benefit from less costly and higher quality inputs, a regulatory framework that burdens and disadvantages every firm in the industry equally could very well prove to be less costly than lost sales due to activists' scare campaigns and boycotts. In the end, they decided to request stultifying regulation in order to preempt activists' questions about the safety of foods that contain gene-spliced ingredients.

Be Careful What You Wish For . . .

Echoing the warnings of activists, it appears that the biotechnology industry *did* create a Frankensteinian monster—a regulatory one. While the technology was still in its infancy, the USDA and EPA promulgated new policies that focused specifically on and discriminated against plants and microorganisms crafted with gene-splicing techniques.

In 1987, USDA created rules that, through peculiar and circuitous logic, defined virtually all gene-spliced plants as posing an inherent risk of invasiveness or injury—treating the plants themselves as "pests." In 1994, the EPA published a proposed rule that treated gene-spliced plants with improved pest resistance as though they were analogous to chemical pesticides. It would be seven more years before the final rule was published, but during the interim period the agency reviewed new gene-spliced crop varieties under the terms of the 1994 proposal.

Although the EPA's approach and proposed rule were egregiously flawed, they enjoyed the enthusiastic support of big agribusiness/biotech companies and their trade associations. In 1995, when a congressional budget proposal put forward by Congressman James Walsh (R-N.Y.) would have denied EPA funding to regulate "whole agricultural plants" if they were "subject to regulation by another federal agency," the Biotechnology Industry Organization (BIO)—the industry's main trade association—lobbied feverishly to defeat it.

The Walsh amendment would have both limited the EPA's expanding influence and shifted the regulation of many of these products to the FDA, under that agency's risk-based 1992 policy on gene-spliced foods. Unblushingly, BIO reported that the organization and its member companies had "enjoyed a good working relationship with EPA" and described EPA officials as "flexible in their regulatory approach" as well as eager to minimize the impact of regulation on biotechnology.[36]

In their lobbying against the Walsh amendment, BIO and Monsanto worked closely to court key congressmen and to strong-arm supporters of the amendment. An official of the Institute of Food Technologists, a nationwide professional association that supported the amendment, described one encounter with industry lobbyists:

> I just had a meeting this morning with a delegation from BIO and Monsanto who trooped into town to educate me. All went well for the first hour and then, as time was nearing a close, they got down to the brass tacks of our [pro-

amendment] position on the Walsh amendment. Still in my "sweet" finding-common-ground way, I indicated that many [in our organization] supported our position and that we did not see any way to yield on that position. Bob Harness, VP for Registrations and Regulatory Services [at Ceragen, a Monsanto subsidiary], converted to Mr. Hyde when I indicated that we saw no reason to adjust our views. At that, he rose from the table, beet red, and declared that they would continue to fight us.[37]

The industry did continue to fight and eventually succeeded at ensuring that the scientifically challenged EPA retained significant, and often redundant, responsibility for regulating the field trials and commercialization of gene-spliced plants.

Although the FDA did not capitulate entirely to industry's demands for a separate, discriminatory, mandatory regulatory regime for foods derived from gene-spliced plants, in 1992 it did establish a "voluntary consultation procedure." Gene-spliced food crop varieties were not required to obtain a formal FDA approval prior to commercialization, but the agency made it clear that it "expected" producers to meet with FDA officials during the pre-commercialization process in order to resolve any consumer safety issues that might arise. This should have satisfied the biotech and food industries' desire for an FDA "stamp of approval," because in fact every gene-spliced plant variety commercialized so far has undergone premarketing review. Moreover, under the regulations that address food "adulteration" and "misbranding," the FDA also has the authority to take any food off the market if regulators believe it to be in any way unsafe.

Given the FDA's vast discretion, the consultation procedure is therefore voluntary in name only, and the agency still wields great control over the market for gene-spliced foods. Nevertheless, the word "voluntary" attached to the process has been a lightning rod for critics, who argue that FDA oversight is inadequate. Consequently, the industry has continued to lobby for stricter, compulsory FDA scrutiny.

Before Calgene marketed its FlavrSavr™ slow-ripening tomato in 1994, the first biotech whole food to hit the market, the company not only completed the voluntary consultation procedure but opted to undertake a much greater burden—a formal request that the FDA review one of the FlavrSavr's new genes and the protein produced by it as a food additive. After several years of deliberation, the FDA finally concluded what everyone already knew—the FlavrSavr™ was, indeed, a tomato, and safe to eat.

But neither the "compulsory voluntary" consultation procedure nor the food additive review option was sufficient for the biotech industry. In a 1994 letter to the FDA, the Biotechnology Industry Organization requested that the agency develop a special notification scheme for gene-spliced crop plants, even though there was no evidence that they posed any health risk, and foods derived from them were already subject to the FDA's routine, rigorous policing of the marketplace. In 2000, the agency announced that it planned to introduce such a requirement, and the proposal was published the following year. Much to the chagrin of the biotechnology industry, however, the FDA quietly dropped the rule from its official regulatory agenda in 2003.

The Ripple Effect of Overregulation

This strategy of the biotechnology and packaged food industries has backfired. It has produced unrealistic and unnecessary regulatory requirements, creating the foundation for various kinds of pseudo-crises that are precipitated whenever the inevitable but inconsequential transgressions of the overly stringent rules occur.

A prominent example is the recall of hundreds of products containing StarLink™ corn, further discussed in chapters 5 and 6. StarLink™ proved to be a public relations and legal nightmare, although not a single person was injured; in fact, the "contamination" was rather like finding a small amount of uniodized salt in a box of the iodized variety. However, the manufacturer was held legally liable for "adulteration" of food with a corn variety that had been approved only for consumption by animals. But that liability was created solely because of EPA's unwarranted treatment of gene-spliced plants as inherently dangerous. No consumers were ever put at risk by StarLink™ corn.

The food industry appears to be intent on striking another such Faustian bargain, with its opposition to the use of food crops in "biopharming"—the production of high-value-added pharmaceuticals and industrial products in plants. Food companies fear that gene transfer or "volunteer" biopharmed plants in the field could contaminate the food supply with vaccines, drugs, and other substances, triggering costly recalls and liability issues. Therefore, in comments filed with the FDA in early 2003, food producers called for unrealistically, unnecessarily stringent federal regulation—a quite literal example of the NIMBY (Not In My Back Yard) mindset. Some of the demands of the Grocery Manufacturers of America and other food trade associations are reasonable—but the packaged food industry's recommendations are predicated on the misapprehension that there is something inherently different and of greater concern about gene-spliced plants that produce industrially useful compounds than about conventional plants that produce similar products.

The North American Millers' Association (NAMA) has also weighed in on the issue:

> Plant-made pharmaceuticals and industrial products are not intended to be cultivated for food and feed use, and are not required to seek food and feed approvals. Therefore, their presence *at any level* is currently not allowed in products meant for consumption by humans or animals. A positive detection of

plant-made pharmaceuticals and industrial products in food or feed in any amount, therefore, would require the immediate recall and destruction of all products manufactured from that grain. Under current regulatory standards, this zero tolerance creates an intolerable risk for U.S. food processors.[38]

That is why NAMA has called for regulations requiring companies producing plant-made pharmaceuticals and industrial products to demonstrate mandatory liability insurance coverage or to indemnify all downstream traders, handlers, processors, and food manufacturers for the full cost of recall, destruction, and brand deregulation as a result of gene flow or other release of genetic material into the food or feed industries.

The millers' association position turns public policy on its head. Instead of eliminating the unwarranted requirement for zero tolerance, the millers wish, in effect, to get rid of a promising technology. Their statement puts parochial self-interest before the public interest. As the millers plead for special treatment, they conveniently disregard the broader context not only of agriculture and biotechnology but of the grain industry itself. The industry's (literally) dirty little secret is that its own products are in fact highly prone to contamination—by highly toxic fungi, rodent droppings, and insect parts, among other unpleasant substances (which are not intended for food and feed use, as the saying goes). If these substances were prohibited from grain *at any level*, and if regulators adopted zero tolerance instead of establishing reasonable tolerances for them, the industry would be out of business. However, farmers, millers, and government officials cooperatively have designed techniques for risk assessment and risk management, in order to handle, store, and process grain appropriately to ensure consumer safety (and also occupational safety—let us not forget the hazard of dust explosions in grain elevators).

What's grain for the goose should be grain for the gander. Instead of punishing biopharming to the point of oblivion, we need to reject the zero-tolerance mindset and approach safety scientifically and sensibly.

As discussed below, many nonfood compounds that can be produced in crops would be totally innocuous, even if they were to appear in the food chain in large amounts. Also, experience with conventionally modified specialty crops shows that when it is necessary for public health or commercial reasons, they can be effectively segregated. Consider the example of rapeseed and one of its variants, canola. Rapeseed, a plant in the *Brassicae* family, is grown in many countries to produce an industrial lubricant that is toxic when consumed by humans. Canola, a variety of the same species, now grown widely to produce an excellent and healthy cooking oil, was developed from rapeseed by plant breeders with conventional breeding methods by which they removed two genes that code for the production of the anti-nutrient glucosinolate and the toxic erucic acid. To avoid cross-contamination in the field and throughout processing, growers routinely segregate the two varieties. Canola could not be grown for cooking oil, however, if a reasonable tolerance for minute traces of industrial-grade rapeseed were not allowed.

The food industry was not alone in muddying this issue. In 2002 the Biotechnology Industry Organization and several member companies came out strongly for stringent regulatory oversight of biopharming and agreed to voluntary restrictions on biopharmed plants. BIO went so far as to suggest that companies refrain from growing biopharmed crops in entire regions of the country where the host crop in question is widely grown—for example, corn in the midwestern Corn Belt. This precipitated a political firestorm, particularly from powerful Iowa Senator Charles Grassley, and within a few months BIO had retreated from its position, issuing a wholly incomprehensible "clarification."[39]

The food and biotech industries have failed to heed important lessons from the introduction, almost twenty years ago, of the first gene-spliced veterinary product, bovine somatotropin (bST), also known as bovine growth hormone (bGH). The drug, a protein that stimulates milk production in cows, generated tremendous controversy, with some analysts predicting that its introduction would so frighten consumers that milk consumption could drop as much as 20 percent. Although the milk is in no way different or less wholesome from that obtained from untreated cows, some in industry (as well as many activists) advocated special regulations, including mandatory labeling of dairy products from recombinant bST–treated animals.

However, a decade after milk from rbST-treated cows began to be marketed, an analysis from the USDA's Economic Research Service concluded: "Scientific evidence about food safety will not prevent controversy. . . . Even intense controversy may have minimal or no effect on total demand [and] the absence of reports of harm from consumption contributes to continued consumption."[40] The bottom line: The mere presence of controversy should not cause industry—or government regulators for that matter—to overreact.

Overregulation Sends the Wrong Message

Does unnecessarily stringent premarket review of gene-spliced crops temper anti-technology activists' demands for ever greater regulatory oversight? Does it assuage consumers' ambivalence about these products?

Those who believe so argue that American consumers trust federal regulators implicitly and subscribe to the notion that more regulation is synonymous with more safety. Naturally, the thinking goes, consumers will be reassured by greater oversight. But regulatory requirements for gene-spliced plants and foods have been ratcheted up steadily for nearly twenty years, with no apparent positive impact on consumer attitudes, and certainly none on activists' demands.

Part of the problem undoubtedly has to do with a concept that economists and political scientists call "rational ignorance"—the fact that ordinary people choose to spend very little time thinking about government policies, because they believe (correctly) that as individuals they have very little control over the creation of statutes and regulations. The consequence of such rational ignorance for biotech regulation is that often the public will believe whatever a supposedly credible source tells them. Inasmuch as the regulatory agencies have not explained or defended rational science-based policy, it is easy for the public to be hoodwinked by anti-biotechnology activists who claim that regulation is too lax, or that there are "gaps" in oversight. However, while the rationally ignorant will certainly express opinions on questions of public policy when prompted for a response, these opinions typically are not deeply held. When making purchasing decisions, for example, most consumers are motivated considerably more by other qualities, such as price, taste, and convenience.

Consider that, in spite of seemingly widespread concern about "genetically modified" foods throughout Western Europe, some labeled gene-spliced food products can still be found on supermarket shelves. Where both gene-spliced and non-gene-spliced products are sold, there does not appear to be any price premium for non-gene-spliced foods. Indeed, most European consumers must actually have the "GM" label pointed out to them before they reject those products.[41]

This is not to suggest that European consumers cannot be frightened away from gene-spliced foods. They can. It does mean, however, that even the population least inclined to support the new biotechnology does not care enough to pay close attention. Thus, while the biotechnology and food industries may believe that incrementally greater regulation will placate an ambivalent public, it is likely to have minimal, if any, impact on public attitudes. The rationally ignorant public knows little about how stringently or inappropriately the new biotechnology is regulated already. Why should still more stringent regulation alter this situation? If anything, experience suggests that consumers view the products that are the most regulated to be the most dangerous.

Even if consumers *were* reassured by our excessive and hugely expensive precautionary regulatory regimes, surely the responsibility of government leaders is to *lead*—that is, to implement policies based on science and common sense, and then to widely and aggressively defend those policies. During the past twenty years, government regulators should have spent far less time regulating and more educating. Admittedly, this is difficult without the cooperation of industry, which has shown a myopic fixation on creating "transparency"—apparently subscribing to the theory that the guillotine blade hurts less if you see it coming—and on attempting to assuage activists' concerns by embracing unnecessary regulation.

Therefore, the business community has ignored the reality that environmental and consumer activists are not likely ever to support biotechnology, no matter how stringent and onerous the regulation, no matter how profound the concessions from industry and government, no matter how impressive the benefits and safety record. Recall Donald Kennedy's warning about trying to compromise with ideologues: "'We did what they wanted, but after we did it they turned out to want something else' is among the oldest of political complaints."[42]

The Financial Impact of Overregulation

What has been the result of this excessive and hugely expensive regulation? EPA and USDA regulatory policies place federal bureaucrats in the middle of virtually all field trials of gene-spliced plants, the direct and indirect effects of which have spelled disaster for small businesses and especially for academic institutions, whose scientists lack the resources to comply with burdensome, unnecessary regulation. The cost of field-testing gene-spliced plants is as much as twenty times higher than for virtually identical plants crafted with older, less precise genetic techniques.[43] For each cultivar, this can add millions of dollars, to development costs as well as divert limited research and development resources away from productive research to paperwork and gratuitous field-test requirements.[44] Added production costs are a particular disadvantage to products in this competitive, low-profit-margin market. Revenue streams from large-scale commodity crop varieties may be worth several million dollars each year, whereas many horticultural crop varieties and plant species grown primarily by subsistence farmers in developing countries are often worth less than half a million dollars during their entire marketable lives. Adding upwards of a half-million dollars or more in regulatory costs during the development phase prices gene-splicing technology out of reach for those crops.

Another casualty of excessive regulation is the long-term survivability of small, highly innovative start-ups spawned by the experimental research in university laboratories. The genesis of the new biotechnology was the confluence and synergy of virtually unregulated academic and industrial research on fundamental questions in biochemistry, genetics, microbiology, and analytical chemistry. Today, academic labs still are the source of most new ideas in these interrelated fields, but as excessive regulation has made many speculative research projects on low profitability organisms prohibitively expensive, the progression from early conceptual innovations to marketed products has become uncertain. For example, plant biologists at the University of California, Berkeley, have developed a gene-spliced, allergen-free wheat variety that could be of benefit to millions of consumers, but they have no plans to test it in the field because of the prohibitive costs of complying with federal regulation.[45]

As highly innovative small and mid-size companies and the nation's academic research enterprises find research and development blocked by excessive costs, American innovation, good old-fashioned competition, and free markets suffer. Virtually all of the independent agbiotech start-ups of the 1980s are gone. Many, including DeKalb, Agracetus, and Calgene, have been purchased by bigger competitors like Monsanto, Pioneer, and Ciba-Geigy, which themselves have been bought up.

This is a variation on the "bootleggers and Baptists" theory of regulation coined by Clemson University economist Bruce Yandle. He points out that in the American South, Sunday closing laws make it illegal to sell alcohol on Sunday, and that these laws are maintained by an inadvertent coalition of bootleggers and "Baptists." The Baptists (and other religious denominations) provide the public outcry against liquor on Sunday, while the bootleggers (who profit from selling liquor illegally on Sunday) quietly persuade legislatures and town councils to maintain the closing laws.[46] In other words, the Baptists claim the high moral ground, providing cover for legislators and regulators to do the bidding of the bootleggers.

A similar symbiosis is seen with many other public policies, including biotechnology regulation. The "Baptists" are the environmental groups and other activists. The bootleggers are the big agribusiness companies that see regulation as a useful market-entry barrier that can limit competition. Government regulators go along with a nod and a wink. The result is a coalition that conspires against the public interest while pretending to be public-spirited. Biotech's critics are correct in asserting that the biotechnology industry plays an influential role in the development of public policy— but that influence has almost invariably produced *more* regulation, not less.

This is not a new phenomenon. In the eighteenth century, the patron saint of capitalism, Adam Smith, was wary of the motives of some capitalists. Acutely aware of the potential conflict between self-interest and the public interest, he warned that any policy advocated by businessmen should be viewed with the greatest suspicion, and that, seeking unfair advantage, businesses often urge the government to interfere with free markets. Past examples include tariffs on steel and limits on imports of Japanese automobiles, lending support to Smith's observation, "People of the same trade seldom meet together, even for merriment and diversion, but the conversation ends in a conspiracy against the public, or in some contrivance to raise prices."[47]

When the late-stage development of new, gene-spliced crop varieties requires field trials, financial resources can be quickly consumed by paperwork burdens and superfluous tests and analyses. The biggest casualties have been research and development by small firms and university laboratories on products such as noncommodity crops, ornamental plants, trees, staple crops that are important only in less-developed countries, and microorganisms used for crop protection and bioremediation. To be sure, government research grants, donations from charitable foundations, and cooperative ventures with large biotech firms still allow some of this research to be conducted, but without the potential for profits, the resources available for these kinds of projects are minuscule.

Moreover, even when the technology is applied to the development of public goods, rather than to a profit-making endeavor, potential funders can be frightened off by both the high costs and unpredictability of excessive regulation. Consider the example of Harvest Plus, an alliance of primarily government-funded organizations devoted to producing and disseminating staple foods rich in micronutrients such as iron, zinc, and vitamin A. According to its director, the group has decided that although they will "investigate . . . the potential for biotechnology to raise the level of nutrients in target crops above what can be accomplished with conventional breeding . . . there is no plan for Harvest Plus to disseminate [gene-spliced] crops, because of the high and difficult-to-predict costs of meeting regulatory requirements in countries where laws are already in place, and because many countries as yet do not have regulatory structures."[48]

When the burdens of excess regulation are added to the trade-, liability, and public opinion-related obstacles to research and development discussed in chapters 6, 7, and 8, the disincentives to using a superior but "disfavored" technology are imposing indeed.

Today, the six remaining major agbiotech companies—BASF, Bayer, Dow, DuPont, Monsanto, and Syngenta—have achieved a virtual monopoly, but they are paying dearly for it. By early 2003, the time and cost to develop a major, gene-spliced commodity crop variety had soared to from six to twelve years and $50 million to $300 million.[49] Due to persistent scaremongering and burdensome regulation in the United States and abroad, even those six firms have generated meager returns from nearly two decades' and billions of dollars' worth of research.

The major beneficiaries from these unscientific policies are activist groups that have raked in hundreds of millions of dollars from gullible donors; the natural and organic food industry, which has exploited the surfeit of misinformation; and the regulators themselves. Spawning large new bureaucracies to regulate gene-spliced organisms, the EPA, USDA, and FDA have grown in size and power. All of us who foot the bill for government and who purchase consumer products—that is, society at large—are the real losers from public policy that affords no incremental protection from risks while it creates huge disincentives to the use of superior technologies.

USING BAD SCIENCE TO JUSTIFY OVERREGULATION

Serious scientists no longer debate whether recombinant DNA–modified organisms pose new or unique risks compared with conventionally modified ones. In spite of the institutional and public antagonism toward the new biotechnology in Europe (chapters 7 and 8), even the highly risk-averse European Commission concluded in 2001, on the basis of scores of risk assessment experiments and other data, that with respect to environmental safety and human consumption, gene-spliced crops are "probably. . . safer than conventional plants and foods."[50] Precisely because this consensus is so well established, advocates of increased regulation have had to resort to nonscientific and disingenuous stratagems in order to argue that gene-spliced organisms deserve more stringent oversight.

Disingenuous Reports

Unfortunately, a few within the scientific establishment have at times aided anti-technology activists in this endeavor. Two of the most insidious examples are a pair of disingenuous reports from committees working under the auspices of the National Research Council, the National Academy of Science's research arm. Plagued by bias and unable to conclude that heightened risk arises from the new biotechnology, they produced conflicting and problematical recommendations.

In 2000 and 2002 the academy conferred its imprimatur on these two questionable analyses of federal biotechnology regulatory policy toward field trials and commercialization of recombinant DNA–modified plants. The first report, *Genetically Modified Pest-Protected Plants: Science and Regulation*, examined oversight by the Environmental Protection Agency.[51] The second, *Environmental Effects of Transgenic Plants: The Scope and Adequacy of Regulation*, paid for by the USDA, evaluated that department's regulation.[52]

These studies have been widely quoted by anti-biotechnology activists and cited specifically as the basis for unscientific and excessively burdensome regulatory proposals.[53] Because these two NRC reports illustrate the lengths to which it is necessary to go—namely, tortuous logic and ignorance of proper context—in order to justify discriminatory regulation of the new biotechnology, it is worth exploring them in some detail.

A "PIP" of a Bad Regulation

The EPA, which regulates pesticides under the Federal Insecticide, Fungicide, and Rodenticide Act (FIFRA), has long regulated field testing—on areas greater than ten acres—and the commercial use of pesticides. In 1994, the EPA proposed a rule that brought under the jurisdiction of FIFRA all plants containing substances that mediate "host plant resistance" to pests, but *only if pest resistance traits were introduced with recombinant DNA techniques.*[54]

Essentially, the EPA decided to regulate all gene-spliced plants that had enhanced resistance to pests of all types—including insects, plant diseases, fungi, and others—as though they were chemical pesticides themselves. (Actually, because they did not receive the benefit of the ten-acre research exemption, gene-spliced plants were regulated *more* stringently than highly toxic chemical pesticides.)

In a final regulation published in 2001, seven years after the rule was first proposed, EPA coined the term "plant-incorporated protectants" (PIPs) in place of "pesticide" to describe what it would regulate.[55] These PIPs are defined in a way that places them within the FIFRA definition of a pesticide—a substance intended to prevent, repel, or mitigate any pest—but only if the plant was constructed by gene-splicing techniques. Plants modified with any of the less precise, less predictable techniques of "conventional breeding" are expressly exempted.

Under this rule, the EPA is required to conduct repeated case-by-case reviews of proposed field trials of gene-spliced plants that contain a plant-incorporated protectant—before the initial trial, when trials are scaled up to larger size or to additional sites, and again at commercial scale. If even minor changes are made in the genetic construct, those too are subject to additional case-by-case reviews, a requirement that discourages plant breeders from continually making minor refinements. And as we noted above, the EPA eliminated the ten-acre pesticide research exemption, but only for gene-spliced plants. This makes the likes of gene-spliced wheat, cotton, and marigolds more stringently regulated than toxic chemicals similar to paraquat or parathion, which would enjoy the exemption. Ultimately, these rules require the developer of new plant varieties to obtain permission repeatedly from regulators long renowned for their arbitrariness, unpredictability, and lack of scientific acumen.

The concept of "plant incorporated protectant" may be inventive, but it makes no sense, and it flies in the face of the disciplines of plant pathology and biology. Likewise, it fails to take into consideration the extraordinary overall safety record of genetic improvement in agricultural research throughout both the pre- and post-gene-splicing eras. Literally millions of genetically modified—but not gene-spliced—plants are field-tested each year without governmental oversight or strictures. The average plant breeder of corn, soybean, wheat, or potato, for example, may put into the field fifty thousand discrete, new genetic variants per year, many or all of which may be the products of wide-cross hybridization, in which genetic material has been transferred from weedy or poisonous plants across so-called natural breeding barriers. Pest- and disease-resistance are among the traits highly sought after by these plant breeders, and the enhancement of such characteristics often involves increases in the levels of natural toxins. Once again, we see the pitfalls of policy making in the absence of proper context.

Ignoring the Lessons of Conventional Breeding

University of California–Riverside plant pathologist George Bruening has written compellingly about the theoretical problems of conventional breeding of new varieties of tomato.[56] Wild tomatoes, which are in the same taxonomic family as the deadly nightshade plant (*Atropa belladonna*), contain naturally occurring toxins that make the plants poisonous to humans. But wild tomatoes and wild varieties of many other cultivated species typically have vastly superior resistance to pathogens, fungi, nematodes, and insects. Such hardiness may have been bred out either accidentally or intentionally when the plants were domesticated, but it can at times be reintroduced by mating cultivated tomatoes (*Lycopersicon esculentum*) with wild relatives (*Lycopersicon peruvianum*).

Backyard gardeners may be familiar with the designation "VFNT" on tomato seedling packages. The *N* indicates resistance for the root knot nematode, while *T* indicates resistance to the tobacco mosaic virus, both derived from *L. peruvianum*.

Using gene-splicing methods, one can precisely identify, then isolate, the N-coding gene from the wild tomato genome and transfer it to cultivated varieties. By contrast, when using hybridization techniques, the DNA segment transferred into the cultivated tomato is five hundred times larger than the N-coding gene. This almost certainly transfers several other genes from *L. peruvianum* into *L. esculentum*, any one of which could code for a potent toxin, or allergen, or some other substance that could make the fruits hazardous to eat. Nevertheless, neither anti-technology activists nor U.S. regulators have expressed any concern about these natural plant-incorporated protectants against pests—possibly because the history of plant breeding has shown that plant breeders can usually eliminate varieties likely to manifest problems.

Thus, we return to the NRC report. A *Nature* editorial, aptly titled "Missing the Big Picture," addressed the need to keep the new biotechnology in a proper context: "Amid all the fuss about [gene-spliced] crops, there's been little acknowledgment that similar questions about biodiversity and gene flow must be asked about conventionally bred varieties. . . . [S]cientists, regulators, and politicians must seize the initiative and widen the debate about the future of farming beyond an obsession with transgenics."[57]

Nevertheless, the National Research Council committee that produced the EPA report missed the big picture. In fact, its members made a conscious decision to do so by choosing to ignore crucial aspects of their charge—"to examine the existing and proposed regulations to qualitatively assess their consequences for research, development, and commercialization of [gene-spliced plants modified to enhance pest-resistance]" and to "provide recommendations to address the identified risk/benefits, and, if warranted, for the existing and proposed regulation of [gene-spliced plants modified to enhance pest-resistance]."[58] This point is essential because other analyses have found the EPA's regulation to be unscientific, illogical, and damaging to agricultural research.

Neglecting Fatal Flaws in the EPA Approach

A 1996 report by eleven scientific societies that represent eighty thousand biologists and food professionals had excoriated the EPA's approach and warned of a number of negative consequences for agriculture and consumers, were it to be implemented.

They predicted that it would discourage the development of new pest-resistant crops, thereby prolonging the use of synthetic chemical pesticides; increase the regulatory burden for the development of pest-resistant varieties of crops; expand federal and state bureaucracies; limit the use of biotechnology for the development of pest-resistant plants to a very few developers that can bear inflated regulatory costs; and handicap the United States in competition for international markets.[59] Events have proven them right on all counts.

In 1998 the Council on Agricultural Science and Technology (CAST), an international consortium of thirty-six scientific and professional groups, had reiterated the eleven societies' criticisms, characterizing the EPA's approach as "scientifically indefensible" and observing that treating gene-spliced plants as pesticides would "undermine public confidence in the food supply."[60]

It was extraordinary, therefore, to find in the 2000 report from the academy that "the committee has chosen to take EPA's proposed rule and the overarching [federal] coordinated framework as given." This critical decision enabled the committee to produce a report that accepted a repeatedly censured and discredited policy that:

1. Ignores the context of the long, distinguished history of breeding pest resistance into plants, and the resulting enormous improvements worldwide in food production and safety
2. Is devoid of either scientific or common sense
3. If applied to earlier, less precise technologies for genetic improvement would have thwarted the Green Revolution that has saved the lives of hundreds of millions of starving people in developing countries.

Ironically, the NRC analysis of the EPA's regulatory approach contains language that reflects and endorses the scientific consensus on the nature of risk: "The committee agrees that the *properties* of a genetically modified organism should be the focus of risk assessments, not the *process* by which it was produced."[61] That only emphasizes the logical inconsistency of choosing to overlook the flawed, central tenet of the EPA's approach to regulation—the use of gene-splicing techniques as the trigger for regulation.

Pathological Science

Perhaps one such scientifically indefensible report could be dismissed as an anomaly, but the National Research Council's following report on a parallel subject—the USDA's oversight of gene-spliced plants—contains similar flaws. USDA has the legislative authority (primarily under the Plant Pest Act) to regulate the importation and interstate movement of plants, plant products, and other organisms that may introduce plant diseases or pests. Though most nonexperts understand the word "pest" to mean predatory insects, agronomists and federal law also consider bacteria, viruses, and even weeds to be pests.

There has long been a permitting system for "plant pests," defined as any organism "which can directly or indirectly injure or cause disease or damage in or to any plants or parts thereof, or any processed, manufactured, or other products of plants."[62] The regulations were developed before the advent of recombinant DNA technology, but, intended as they are for the oversight of both modified and wild unmodified organisms, they are broadly applicable. It is important to note, however, that in this context the USDA only has authority to regulate plants that it believes to be "pests." Its approach is risk based, in that the only organisms required to undergo case-by-case governmental review are known to be pests and are therefore an enhanced-risk group.

Since 1987, however, the USDA has maintained a non-risk-based, parallel regime focused exclusively on recombinant DNA–modified plants. In order to establish this mechanism, in which what is regulated is essentially *independent* of risk, APHIS tortured the original concept of a plant pest as something known to be harmful and crafted a new category—a "regulated article," defined as "any organism or any product altered or produced through recombinant DNA technology, which is a plant pest, or for which there is reason to believe is a plant pest."[63] The vague phrase "for which there is reason to believe is a plant pest" was crafted by APHIS precisely because it can be broadly interpreted by the agency to capture virtually any organism modified with recombinant DNA techniques, as most gene-spliced plants incorporate small, noninfective snippets of DNA from organisms that are bona fide pests. Thus, every gene-spliced plant commercialized to date has been considered by APHIS to be a presumptive "plant pest" and consequently subject to a mandatory premarket approval process.

On the basis of the analysis above, the broad scientific consensus and the recognition by the NRC committee itself that government agencies are in the "difficult position of enforcing a higher environmental standard for transgenic plants than the standards currently used to regulate the impacts of other agricultural technologies and practices," one would logically have expected an endorsement and extension of the 1987 NAS white paper and 1989 NRC report, accompanied by a recommendation to rationalize the system and apply equivalent oversight of recombinant and conventional plants, except for those with newly introduced traits judged to confer higher risk. Instead, the NRC committee recommended maintaining or even *increas-*

ing the stringency of the current discriminatory, process-based regulatory system that focuses only on plants modified by recombinant DNA technology. It justifies this recommendation by invoking a succession of specious arguments.

First, the committee claims there is greater risk from gene-splicing than other techniques because "a much broader array of phenotypic traits can potentially be incorporated into plants than was possible two decades ago." But this is a second-order kind of concern that only increases risk if the new traits are themselves risky. Greater versatility is not the same as enhanced risk. Moreover, the committee did not take into consideration the far greater precision and predictability of gene-splicing techniques.

If this greater range of traits were a genuine concern, the committee could simply have recommended additional stringent oversight only for new traits that are known to be, or that could reasonably be expected to be, harmful—that is, traits that would make the new plant a pest.

Second, in spite of the weight of scientific consensus and empirical evidence, the NRC panel concluded that "the scientific justification for regulation of transgenic plants is not dependent on historically set precedents for not regulating conventionally modified plants. While there is a need to re-evaluate the potential environmental effects of conventionally improved crops, for practical reasons, the committee does not recommend immediate regulation of conventional crops."[64]

For practical reasons, indeed! Not a single conventional crop could meet the requirements being imposed by USDA on gene-spliced plants—nor should most conventional crops *have* to meet such requirements. Conventional plant breeding would grind to a halt if it were subjected to the regulatory regimes that the USDA and EPA apply to gene-spliced products. On the basis of such a scientifically unconvincing rationale, the NRC panel recommended not just continuing compulsory case-by-case USDA oversight of the field trials of all gene-spliced plants but requiring more stringent, comprehensive reviews.

Finally, the NRC committee acknowledged its real motivation—the specious belief that regardless of the relative safety of gene-spliced organisms, heightened regulatory scrutiny will promote consumer acceptance of the technology and that "given the public controversy," regulatory agencies need to maintain the discriminatory treatment of gene-spliced plants to maintain their own legitimacy. After reiterating the findings of the earlier NRC analyses and concurring that the use of recombinant DNA techniques does not itself confer risk, the 2002 report asserts that heightened scrutiny of gene-spliced plants plays a role in the "establishment and maintenance of regulatory legitimacy" and that taking public opinion into consideration is important even when it "lack[s] scientific rigor."[65] We believe that the opposite is true—that, to the extent consumers pay attention to the strictness of regulation, they take proportionality of oversight for granted, and that they interpret stringent regulation as being necessary to offer protection from potentially dangerous products.

The Politics of Stacked Committees

These two studies by the academy bring to mind the phrase "pathological science," which was coined by Nobel laureate Irving Langmuir and defined as "the science of things that aren't so."[66] An obvious question is how could the academy's science *twice* have been so pathological, *twice* have gone so far wrong in its assessment of the scientific basis for federal regulatory policy, *twice* have transgressed the basic principle that there should be proportionality between the stringency of oversight and the perceived degree of risk—and produced such contradictory and inaccurate reports?

It was easy. The game was "fixed" by stacking the committees with members known to support unscientific and excessive regulation. Unlike the academy's 1987 and 1989 committees, these latter-day panels were a virtual Who's Who of anti-biotechnology activists and former regulators with conflicts of interest. Moreover, unlike the earlier panels they contained few members of the academy. In 2002, the twelve-person committee contained only two academy members. The 2000 committee contained only one—the chairman. It was rather like selecting an all-star team filled with .150 hitters.

Three of the twelve committee members for the EPA report (Stanley Abramson, Fred Betz, and Morris Levin) are former EPA staff members who had helped to craft and defend a variety of process-based regulatory policies while at the agency. Another member (Rebecca Goldburg of Environmental Defense) had produced a succession of questionable anti-biotechnology tracts over the previous decade and a half. During the formal review process, the document was reviewed by another former senior EPA official (Lynn Goldman), who had been instrumental in crafting and defending the policy in question, and by an intractable anti-biotechnology activist from the radical Union of Concerned Scientists (Jane Rissler).

Three members of the USDA committee (its chairman, Fred Gould, and David Andow and Norman Ellstrand), though respected scientists, are long-time skeptics about the safety of recombinant plants and have consistently advocated process-based regulation. Another member (Ignacio Chapela) is the author of the discredited report of alleged contamination of indigenous varieties of gene-spliced corn in Mexico by recombinant varieties, discussed in chapter 2.[67] He was recently denied tenure at the University of California, Berkeley due to his shoddy research.

The 2000 report on EPA oversight caused the fallout sought by the committee. It offered sufficient cover for the EPA to issue a final rule, which emerged in 2001 after seven years of delays caused by the legitimate objections and opposition of the scientific community. Similarly, the prestige of the academy attached to the report on USDA's regulation virtually assures the permanence of stultifying, process-based regulation.

The academy's response[68] to these criticisms[69] is both noteworthy and risible. Authored by Fred Gould (who sat on both committees and served as chairman for the USDA report) and Jennifer Kuzma (an NRC staff member), the response is reminiscent of the story about the drunk searching for his lost keys under the streetlight. A friend who happens upon him asks if he's sure that he lost them there. The drunk answers, "No. In fact I'm sure they're *not* here, but the light is better."

Gould and Kuzma concede that the risk-related characteristics of a product, rather than the techniques used to make it, should determine the need for and extent of regulation—a conclusion found in the NRC report on which they collaborated. But from the scientific consensus on these points Gould and Kuzma make the insupportable leap to assuming that there are only "two options: regulate all plant varieties or regulate none," and that because both are unacceptable, an approach that applied scrutiny only to gene-spliced plants is the logical solution.

This is a false dichotomy, as illustrated by long-standing, risk-based, federal regulation of many other products and by models for regulating high-risk plants described in the scientific literature. In fact, like the drunk in the parable, the keys to this conundrum are not where Gould and Kuzma are looking. Contrary to their misrepresentations, the risk-based approach incorporated in the long-standing USDA policy for unmodified and conventionally modified plants, which circumscribes only known or suspected plant pests, could painlessly also have accommodated recombinant DNA–modified organisms. Other possible alternatives are discussed later in this volume.

Surrendering the High Moral Ground

In his analysis of misconduct in biomedical research, the late DeWitt "Hans" Stetten, revered biologist and scientific administrator, wrote, "Science cannot tolerate the man who takes lightly his moral obligation to report strictly what is true."[70] It appears, however, that on certain high-profile, politically charged subjects, the National Academy of Sciences lately has chosen to ignore that obligation. Not only does it tolerate people who dissemble for ideological and political reasons but also appoints them to "expert" committees and then confers the academy's imprimatur on their execrable work product.

The notions that new biotechnology products defy useful, accurate risk analysis or that they are too dangerous to introduce into the environment and commerce are obviously without merit. On the contrary, it is now clear that there are huge costs in unjustifiably risk-averse regulatory policies that slow or divert biotechnology innovation and research and development. For these reasons, the professional practitioners and regulators of the new bio-technology must strive to demystify it and provide an accurate perspective for the public. The stakes are high in terms of both economic and social benefits.

CHAPTER 4

. . . .

Caution, Precaution, and the Precautionary Principle

W̲ᴇ ʙᴇɢᴀɴ ᴛʜᴇ first chapter of this volume by describing several African countries' rejection of food aid shipments solely because they contained kernels of the very same gene-spliced, genetically improved corn varieties consumed daily by scores of millions of Americans and millions of others around the world. Food that could have helped prevent starvation or malnutrition in millions of people was actually locked away from starving villagers by the governments of Zambia and Zimbabwe because officials didn't believe the corn had been "proven" to be safe. Zambian president Levy Mwanawasa told a UN gathering in South Africa, "We would rather starve than get something toxic."[1]

Of course, the food was not toxic or harmful in any way. But the flawed decision making that followed from Mwanawasa's claim was the tragic but inevitable outcome of an increasingly popular tenet of public policy known as the "precautionary principle"—the idea that regulatory measures should be taken to prevent or restrict actions that raise even conjectural risks, even though scientific evidence of their existence, magnitude, or potential impacts is incomplete or inconclusive.

These developments in Africa illustrate one of the absurd problems created by groundless fears about technological change and the potentially dangerous overregulation to which they give rise. Consumers demand assurances of perfect safety from industries and governments, but such assurances can never be made. When we demand something approaching zero risk, the resulting attempts at caution are often done with a tunnel vision that blinds us to the potentially vast human costs of such an effort. Tragically, many precautionary cures are far worse than the maladies they are meant to prevent.

PRECAUTION WITHOUT PRINCIPLE

We live in a world that is replete with risks, including diseases, accidents, fires, harsh weather, and other forces of nature. The reason for adopting new technologies in the first place is that they often improve our well-being by protecting us from these age-old dangers—either directly, by insulating us from such risks, or indirectly, by providing the wealth and other resources that allow us to cope with or adapt to risks. Most of the new technologies and products that themselves pose risk—medicines, automobiles, electric power generation, new construction practices, pesticides, gene-spliced crops, and many others—are intended to reduce other, greater risks.[2] Consequently, delaying their introduction solely because they are new, and their risks allegedly not yet fully explored, can actually hurt the very people such precautions are intended to protect.

Many consumers, voters, and politicians view product safety and the regulation of risk in a way that lends itself to sound-bite oversimplifications. "New products and activities may be dangerous, so we need to regulate them." "The more regulation, the more protection." "When lives are at risk, we should spare no expense to save them." "We cannot put a price on human life."

Unfortunately, none of these clichés has much grounding in the real world. There is often no easy way to determine when something is "safe" and when something else is "dangerous." "Completely safe" is a never-realized ideal. Many products, technologies, and activities fall into a broad gray area of uncertainty where the questions that must be resolved include: How safe is safe enough? How dangerous must a product be before it is subject to restrictions? What kind of regulation is appropriate, and who will perform it? What kinds of tradeoffs will society tolerate?

Actually answering these questions in a way that translates into public policy is much more complex and nuanced than a simple choice between yes and no, safe or unsafe, permit or ban. We must acknowledge that there is a range of possible risk levels and that certain things may pose high risk in some circumstances and considerably less in others. Complicating matters further is the fact that even products that pose nontrivial risks can at times make us safer. For example, on one hand, chlorine is a highly toxic gas, and by-products of water chlorination are suspected of causing a small number of bladder cancers; on the other hand, chlorination prevents far more common—and more dangerous—water-borne illnesses, such as cholera and typhoid fever. Asbestos fibers can cause lung diseases and cancers when handled improperly, but in many more cases asbestos helps to prevent fires and improves transportation safety. Most medicines have some toxic side effects under certain circumstances, but they also prevent, treat, and cure diseases.

Comparative Risk Analysis

Many people naively believe that the failure to regulate stringently new products, processes, and activities invariably risks severe harm, and that over-regulation "only costs money."[3] But that assumption is both overly simplistic and insidious. Scientific and technological innovation always involves uncertainties and risk. It is appropriate—and also routine—to consider potential dangers before a new technology is adopted and to reject any that, on balance, are expected to do more harm than good. The outright rejection of hypothetically risky technologies does not necessarily make us safer, however. Thus, when we confront a situation in which the risks are uncertain but unlikely to be negligible, we should perform a task known as "comparative risk-analysis," which considers tradeoffs and the risks of various alternatives—including the risk of forgoing the new technology or activity.

Without realizing it, typical families conduct comparative risk analysis routinely in their everyday lives. Should we spend extra money to purchase a super-safe Volvo or Mercedes Benz, or should we economize on safety and save for a rainy day? If we applied the precautionary principle consistently, fuel-efficient compact cars would be banned, because they trade safety for monetary savings. But sometimes accepting certain heightened risks is actually the safer choice, because it frees up resources that are better spent by investing in other, more cost-effective safety or health improvements.

In practice, most precautionary regulation suffers from a kind of lopsided decision making. It is based on the false assumption that little real harm can come from delaying the introduction of new products (and technologies) into the marketplace. Thereby, it exaggerates the potential drawbacks of a new product and underestimates its benefits. In the end, our attempts to eliminate risks that are small or manageable distract us from bigger, pre-existing dangers, and they often reduce the resources available to us for addressing other, perhaps more pressing problems.[4]

Supreme Court Justice Steven Breyer cites the example of an EPA ban of asbestos pipe, shingles, coating, and paper, which the most optimistic estimates suggested would prevent seven or eight premature deaths over thirteen years—at a cost of approximately a quarter of a billion dollars.[5] Breyer notes that such a vast expenditure can be expected to cause more deaths simply by reducing the resources available for other public amenities than it would prevent from the asbestos exposure. Also, perversely, the very act of removing asbestos from existing structures poses greater risk to human health than simply leaving it where it is. During removal, long-dormant asbestos fibers are disturbed and spread into the ambient air, where they expose workers and bystanders to heightened risk.

At the time EPA banned asbestos, it was an old product, the risks and benefits of which were well understood. Nevertheless, political pressures from so-called safety activists still pushed EPA to make a risk-*increasing* decision.

When it comes to *new* products, public health and environmental regulators around the world are even more prone to this kind of tunnel vision in their attempts to control potential risks. Anything new is treated as though its very novelty must make it a source of great and unmanageable danger. Disproportionately little weight is given to the ability of new products and technologies to ameliorate the perils of everyday life—auto accidents, fire, hunger, electric shock, infectious diseases, and other illnesses. In many nations and in international agreements, precautionary thinking increasingly guides the regulation of consumer products, manufacturing processes, agricultural practices, and many other activities.

Why do we systematically and intentionally fail to consider both sides of the risk equation? Perhaps it is human nature to fear the novel and to find comfort in the status quo, especially if the basis of the new technology or practice is difficult for nonexperts to understand, or is perceived to be in some way "unnatural." Precautionary thinking exploits our recollection of Mother telling us that it is "better to be safe than sorry."

The tendency of people to fear some risks and tolerate others that are greater is a phenomenon that is common across cultures and has persisted through time.[6] Whatever the cause, societies often encourage their governments to restrict what is believed to be new or mysterious, a prejudice that most regulatory agencies are eager to indulge. Over the past few decades, this impulse has become ever more deeply ingrained in regulatory decision-making processes. Recently, it has taken on a more radicalized and malignant form, now commonly known as the precautionary principle.

The Precautionary Principle

The purpose of the precautionary principle is ostensibly "to impose early preventive measures to ward off even those risks for which we have little or no basis on which to predict the future probability of harm."[7] At face value, it seems that it simply codifies into law the old maxim "Look before you leap." Precautionary principle advocate Joel Tickner acknowledges that it "establishes a type of 'speed bump'" in the road of technological progress, and he claims it "creates bottlenecks in the development process but does not stop flows."[8]

Proceeding with due caution is appropriate, but the decision-making process dictated by the precautionary principle is intentionally weighted against new technologies even *after* they have been cautiously examined. It grants regulators the ability to disregard the findings of a lengthy risk analysis whenever there remains any question, however insignificant or even ridiculous, about the safety of a product or process. By eroding the value of science-based risk-management practices, the precautionary principle creates an anomalous situation where even net-beneficial products may fail to make it to the marketplace. Thus, it does much more than turn a commonsense rule of thumb into a formal rule of law. It is as though the principle were commanding risk analysts to look, and look, and look, but never leap—often heightening, not reducing, net risk.

In spite of these obvious flaws in the concept, policy makers and environmental activists have increasingly embraced the precautionary principle for a variety of political and ideological reasons. It has become pervasive in public and political debates about all manner of environmental and health regulation—from energy use and climate variability to sanitation and the use of certain lifesaving medical devices. The principle has been formally incorporated into the environmental laws of several countries, including Germany, Sweden, and France, as well as in the Maastricht Treaty on the European Union. It has been included as well in numerous multilateral environmental agreements, including the Convention on Biological Diversity (CBD) and the Cartagena Protocol on Biosafety (an offshoot of the CBD). In many countries, the precautionary principle already is being applied to regulatory decisions on a wide range of policy questions.

Few issues, however, have proven to be a more contentious battleground over the precautionary principle than the creation, testing, and use of gene-spliced plants. Literally dozens of scientific bodies have studied the issue and have concluded that neither the process of gene-splicing nor the movement of genes between organisms inherently creates new or unique risks (chapter 3). They have found no evidence that the techniques of gene-splicing pose any risks that did not already occur with conventional breeding methods.

Nevertheless, virtually all domestic and international environmental regulations treat gene-spliced plants and microorganisms in a discriminatory, overcautious fashion, based solely on the relative "newness" of their production methods. The European Union exemplifies this attitude most clearly.

Beginning in 1990, the European Commission (EC) implemented a set of biotechnology regulations for all EU member countries, imposing several layers of premarket evaluation.[9] In spite of these being arguably the most cautious laws in the world, several EU member states used the precautionary principle as a justification to force an EU-wide moratorium on all approvals of new gene-spliced plants from 1998 to 2004, and they have continued to resist approving new varieties since then.[10] The moratorium technically was lifted in the spring of 2004, after even stronger new rules for approving, labeling, and tracing gene-spliced products were implemented (chapter 8). As late as July 2004, however, many EU member governments were still trying to block EU-wide approvals while demanding still more regulatory hurdles.

In April 2004, Denmark, Greece, France, Luxembourg, Austria, and Portugal voted against approving Syngenta's Bt-11 sweet corn variety—which had been awaiting judgment since February 1999—even though the European Commission insisted it had been "subject to the most rigorous premarketing assessment in the world."[11] Only a feature of the new regulations that allows the European Commission to break a deadlocked vote made the approval possible. Even then, the variety was not authorized for commercial cultivation in the European Union; only the import of canned Bt-11 corn for consumption was permitted. That unwarranted moratorium and the continuing resistance of several EU members have inhibited the development of products that are environmentally friendly and beneficial to public health, and they divert legitimate regulatory attention away from higher-risk products. Moreover, as discussed in this volume, they have had a malign ripple effect on countries around the world that export, or wish to export, agricultural products to the EU.

Consider one example. Gene-spliced, herbicide-tolerant crop plants, such as soybeans and canola, have undergone extensive mandatory testing and premarket evaluation in nearly a dozen countries, to ensure the protection of the natural environment and human health. Nevertheless, invoking the precautionary principle, European governments still refuse to approve new varieties, even though conventionally bred varieties of soybeans and canola that express nearly identical herbicide-tolerance traits are subject to no mandatory safety testing or premarket approval requirements at all. Ironically, far less is known about the cellular and molecular bases of the herbicide tolerance trait in conventional varieties, or their potential impacts on human health or the environment.[12]

The bottom line is that if uncertainty about the risks of a product or process should elicit application of the precautionary principle, that criterion is far more easily met with conventional techniques of genetic improvement than with gene-splicing. Thus, if the proponents of precautionary regulation were genuinely interested in resolving uncertainty and reducing risk, surely greater precaution would be appropriate not to gene-splicing but to the cruder, less precise, less predictable conventional forms of genetic modification.

These sorts of inconsistencies are irreconcilable.

The formulation of regulatory policy will never be perfect—and few of us expect it to be—but seldom is it so completely out of phase as it is for the new biotechnology. A far more enlightened and scientific approach is necessary if public policy is truly to reduce overall risk. As discussed throughout this book, especially in chapter 9, such enlightenment is not at all difficult to attain.

Unjustifiable Regulation in Western Europe

Although many examples of scientifically unjustifiable regulation of the new biotechnology based on the precautionary principle can be found around the world, the countries of Western Europe are perhaps the most egregious and chronic offenders.

In 1998 the highest French court suspended commercialization of three gene-spliced corn varieties, although the French government had endorsed approval for those same varieties at the EU level just two years earlier.[13] In 1999, the British government imposed a moratorium on commercial planting of already-approved gene-spliced crops, pending the outcome of a three-year series of government-sponsored field trials. Yet because the precise location of each field was made public, crops were destroyed, equipment damaged, and farmers and their families threatened and hounded out of the program.[14] In the end, the British government decided to approve only one of the varieties being tested, an herbicide-tolerant corn variety that the trials found to be *less* effective in controlling weeds than its conventional comparator. Its producer, Bayer CropScience, ultimately decided not to sell that variety in the UK, because additional regulatory hurdles would delay commercialization for several more years.[15]

In February 2000, against the recommendation of the German Central Commission for Biological Safety, Germany rescinded the license for field-testing a gene-spliced corn variety, a single day before the agriculture ministry planned to approve the variety for commercial cultivation.[16] In August 2000, the Italian government suspended the commercialization of four gene-spliced corn varieties, allegedly over concerns about potential health risks, even after a report from the Italian National Institute of Health had found that "there is no reason to believe that a risk for human or animal health could ensue from the consumption of products derived from the [gene-spliced] plants in question."[17] The list could go on and on.

Even in the countries that lead in the cultivation of gene-spliced crops, such as the United States, Argentina, and Canada, overly strict, precautionary approaches to regulation have resulted in questionable and often redundant regulations that restrict new products, waste resources, and threaten overall public health. Incredibly, most precautionary principle advocates maintain that even this level of overregulation is insufficient!

In spite of the overregulation in these relatively pro-biotech countries, there has been a trickle of gene-spliced crops into the marketplace. They have increased farm productivity, reduced the use of chemical pesticides, and diminished the impact of farming on the environment. The regulatory practices in those countries are far from perfect (see, for example, chapter 5), and relatively few crop species have been commercialized, but the fact that gene-spliced crops can be field-tested and commercialized in these countries at all is an important difference between the European approach to precautionary regulation and that taken by the U.S., Argentina, and Canada.

In both the United States and Europe, public health and environmental regulations usually employ risk analysis to determine the extent of potential hazards, followed by judgments about how to regulate. The main difference between precautionary-style regulation in the United States and use of the precautionary principle per se in Europe revolves around procedural require-ments in U.S. law. A few environmental statutes and a series of executive orders from both Republican and Democratic presidents actually require regulatory agencies to consider the negative effects of new regulations be-fore agencies finalize the methodological procedures they will use to evalu-ate a product's risks.[18] Furthermore, U.S. administrative laws provide legal recourse for cases in which regulators do not follow those established pro-cedures, or in which they have ignored existing data or made arbitrary decisions that conflict with the available information.[19] Although these safe-guards are weak, they do rein in much of the overt political abuse that char-acterizes the application of the precautionary principle in many foreign countries.

THE INHERENT INTERCONNECTEDNESS OF RISK

No matter which system is used, however, a systematic flaw of all precau-tionary thinking is that it examines the risk of new products in a vacuum, ne-glecting the inherent interconnectedness of many seemingly different risks.[20]

For example, the vast majority of the toxins and carcinogens to which we are exposed occur *naturally* in our food, but these are seldom addressed by regulation (nor are they a problem). Synthetic chemicals in our foods, how-ever, are regulated strictly, even when they are present in considerably smaller, and less harmful, amounts. Indeed, we seem to focus on synthetic chemi-cals not because they are dangerous but because they are more amenable to regulation.[21] It is difficult to take Mother Nature to court.

The treatment of water offers a similar conundrum. If we fail to treat drinking water with low concentrations of disinfecting compounds like chlorine, it is likely to be contaminated with pathogens.[22] This intervention is unquestionably net positive, but regulations often focus much more sharply on the disinfectant than on the infectious agents that are eliminated. Some-times the risk-benefit balance is not so clear, of course, but the effort to determine the net risk profile of a technology or product is the essence of comparative risk analysis.

The determination of relative risks is often complex, but we cannot sim-ply assume, as precautionary principle advocates would have us do, that de-laying the introduction of a new technology—or restricting the use of an established one—will not itself be harmful. Consider, for example, the carnage that resulted from the environmental movement's crusade against chlorinated compounds, which has extended even to opposing the chlori-nation of drinking water.[23] On the basis of limited evidence from the U.S. Environmental Protection Agency that by-products of water chlorination could cause a low incidence of bladder cancer, environmental activists lob-bied governments around the world to discontinue adding chlorine to their drinking water.

In the midst of a severe budget crisis, Peruvian officials used this alleged risk to public health as an excuse to stop chlorinating part of their country's drinking water.[24] That decision, initially promoted by environmental activists as "better safe than sorry," contributed to the acceleration and spread of Latin America's 1991–1996 cholera epidemic, which afflicted more than 1.3 million people and killed at least eleven thousand.[25]

These are the results of a precautionary concern about an exceedingly small man-made health risk, which blinded activists and government officials to a far greater natural one. Putting it another way, discontinuing water chlorination was an abject failure to perform comparative risk analysis.

The Tradeoffs of Risk Taking

Whether or not we consciously recognize it, every decision about avoiding or taking on a given risk necessarily entails these kinds of tradeoffs. Virtually all of the plants cultivated for modern agriculture have been genetically improved in some way, and no one can deny that modern agriculture has affected the planet's ecology; genetic modification of crops, by either old or new techniques, may produce unintended effects in the plants or the foods derived from them.[26]

Whatever uncertainties there may be, many benefits of the already-commercialized gene-spliced plants are not in doubt. They include a reduction in pesticide use of tens of millions of pounds, reduced topsoil erosion, increased yields, and net savings to farmers of time and money[27]—with no known detrimental effects on the environment. Increasing the adoption and diffusion of gene-spliced crops can also improve human nutrition, reduce the amount of land and water needed to produce food, and help save ecosystems from fragmentation and development.[28]

As we have reaped the benefits of gene-spliced plants, what have we learned about their risks? As predicted by the experts two decades ago, none appears to be new or unique. Plant breeders, agronomists, and farmers all have vast experience in managing the risks that arise from changing the genetic structure of plants, including enhancement of pest-resistance or disease-resistance traits.[29] As discussed in chapter 3, this experience and knowledge are fully applicable to both gene-spliced and conventionally modified plants.

The history of mankind shows that, on the whole, technological progress tends to improve human and environmental health, not degrade it. Technological advances enhance productivity and create wealth. As the late University of California–Berkeley political scientist Aaron Wildavsky has pointed out, wealth is directly correlated with health. Although choosing or using any one technology may lead to an increase in risk along one axis, avoiding it may lead inexorably to an increase in risk along another. Where other alternatives are available, they too will bring their own constellation of risks and benefits.

The eternal dilemma for regulators, then, is how to maximize net benefits while minimizing net risks, but no policy maker who overemphasizes only one side of any risk-benefit or risk-risk tradeoff is likely to solve it. Yet this is exactly the approach taken by many advocates of the precautionary principle, who assert that the novel risks introduced by new technologies must always be presumed to be greater.

Perils of the Precautionary Principle

Aside from the loss of beneficial products, there are other indirect and subtle perils of the precautionary principle when it is used to justify government overregulation. University of Texas economics professor Frank Cross observes that the "unsupported presumption that an action aimed at public health protection cannot possibly have negative effects on public health" is the precautionary principle's "truly fatal flaw."[30] The expenditure of government and private sector resources to implement and comply with regulations—whether they are justified or not—reduces the resources available for other purposes.

For example, although it may be wise to expend government resources to review new plant varieties that have poorly understood or overtly negative traits, evaluating *all* new plant varieties—or, as is the case under current U.S. law, all new gene-spliced varieties regardless of the risk of their traits— needlessly wastes resources that could be spent more productively. Far better, surely, is to use finite public resources to address problems that are real than to try to prevent hazards that may well be purely hypothetical—especially if these hypothetical hazards are likely in any case to be minimal and manageable.

The direct and indirect expenses related to government programs—for purposes good, bad, or indifferent—also exert an "income effect," which reflects the correlation between wealth and health. The accumulation of wealth by societies is necessary to fund medical research, build schools, support infrastructure and sanitation, and even improve environmental amenities. It is no coincidence that richer societies have lower mortality rates and cleaner environments than poorer ones. Thus, to deprive communities, or individuals, of wealth is to increase their risks. Wealthier persons are able to purchase better health care, enjoy more nutritious diets, and lead generally less stressful lives. Conversely, the deprivation of income itself has adverse health effects, including an increased incidence of stress-related problems, including ulcers, hypertension, heart attacks, depression, and suicide.[31]

It is difficult to quantify the relationship between the deprivation of income and mortality, but academic studies suggest that every five to ten million dollars of regulatory costs will induce one additional fatality through this "income effect."[32] Sometimes, a given risk is so great that even costly regulation may prove to be well worth the price. However, the excess costs in the tens of billions of dollars required annually by precautionary regulation for various classes of consumer products can be expected to cause thousands of deaths per year—well in excess of any health benefit derived from the regulations themselves.

For example, a 2001 EPA rule requiring municipalities to reduce the amount of naturally occurring arsenic in drinking water from an already low level to an even lower one is expected to prevent approximately twenty-three to thirty-three cancer deaths each year. However, achieving such a reduction is tremendously expensive, and high natural arsenic levels occur most frequently in the largely poor, rural areas of the American southwest. A study by the American Enterprise Institute and Brookings Institution estimates that the regulation could actually lead to *more* deaths than it would save, because public health resources would have to be diverted from more cost-effective uses such as ambulance service and health care, and the higher price of public water would cause some consumers to opt for less expensive, but untreated, well water that poses considerable bacteriological health risks—and which still contains the higher natural level of arsenic.[33] Such consumers are made worse off by public policy based on the presumption that additional regulation must lead to additional safety. These are the real costs of "erring on the side of caution." "Regulatory overkill" is no exaggeration.

RISK AVERSION AND REGULATORS' SELF-INTEREST

Although advocates of the precautionary principle are correct that human health and the environment may be jeopardized when appropriate precautionary measures are not taken, it is also true that waiting for an assurance of safety can also be injurious. Consider again, for example, the situation in Zambia and Zimbabwe, where food aid shipments containing gene-spliced corn were rejected in the midst of a severe food shortage.

Zambian agriculture minister Mundia Sikatana explained that his government "decided to base its decision not to accept [gene-spliced] foods in Zambia on the precautionary principle," because their safety has not been proven.[34] With more than two million people at serious risk of starvation, this decision and the principle behind it were the height of absurdity, and worse. We agree with Ambassador Tony Hall's demand (noted in chapter 1) that those who commit such acts should be held accountable. In legal parlance, such behavior could variously be considered to be "depraved indifference to life," manslaughter, or crimes against humanity. Rather than promoting human health and well-being, the precautionary principle is doing just the opposite.

Another irony is that so much misery is being tolerated ostensibly to protect the "biodiversity" of Zambia's local landrace corn varieties from so-called "contamination" by gene-spliced varieties. In fact, corn is not native to Africa; it was imported from Central America and has displaced the native vegetation. One must ask: Which is more environmentally disruptive—mixing a couple of additional, agronomically useful genes into a nonnative food crop (which itself has been highly engineered over many centuries), or plowing under millions of acres of native plants? Surely the latter, but who would doubt that the original introduction of corn into Africa was more a blessing than a curse, as it has provided an important staple food for the inhabitants of central and southern Africa for hundreds of years? Why then should those people now be encouraged to reject a technology with the power to provide abundant and nutritious food for hundreds more?

The Impossibility of Zero Risk

These kinds of actions by government officials illustrate a fundamental flaw of the precautionary principle—science can never prove the complete absence of a risk. There is always the possibility that we just haven't yet gotten to the nth hypothetical risk or to the nth dose or nth year of exposure, when the risk will finally be demonstrated. It is logically impossible to prove a negative, and all activities pose some nonzero risk of adverse effects.[35]

Thus, precautionary rules that require innovators to demonstrate the absence of some hypothesized cause-and-effect relationship create a standard that is impossible to meet. The scientific method can only prove that things are dangerous, not that they are perfectly safe. Taken to its "logical" extreme, the precautionary principle would mean that no action could ever be taken, because no assurance of absolute safety can ever be given.

When pressed, advocates of the precautionary principle acknowledge that a zero-risk standard cannot be met, and they insist that they are not demanding one.[36] Nevertheless, giving government institutions the sole and unchallengeable authority to judge when this vague burden of proof is met creates a highly subjective standard of safety and allows biases and hidden agendas (such as political ambition and trade protectionism) to creep into the decision-making process. Due to the ambiguous nature of risk—especially in very low-risk situations—questions about the safety of new products are often difficult to resolve quantitatively.

Risk determinations become more problematical when they are made with arbitrary authority by regulators who are subject to influences such as public perception, lobbying, and political pressures. Governments are predisposed to overregulate new technologies, because in industrialized societies, exposure to products believed to be harmful is widely publicized and condemned, while the opportunity costs of excessive restrictions go largely unnoticed. This creates an asymmetrical incentive structure in which governments are compelled to ensure that no harm arises from new products, while being free to discount the hidden risk-reducing properties of unused or underused technologies.

To understand why, consider that there are two basic kinds of mistaken decisions that a regulator can make. First, a harmful product can be approved for marketing—called a "Type I error" in the parlance of risk assessment; or second, a useful product can be rejected or delayed, never achieve marketing approval, or be inappropriately withdrawn from the market—a "Type II error."

In other words, a regulator commits a Type I error by permitting something harmful to happen and a Type II error by preventing something beneficial from becoming available. Both situations have negative consequences for the public, but the outcomes for the regulator are very different.[37]

Type I and II Errors

Examples from U.S. and European public policy abound, but the Type I/ Type II error dichotomy perhaps is shown most clearly in the FDA's approval process for new drugs. A classic illustration is the FDA's approval in 1976 of the swine flu vaccine. That decision is generally perceived to have been a Type I error, because although the vaccine was effective at preventing influenza, it had a major side effect that was unknown at the time of approval— 532 cases of paralysis, including thirty-two deaths, from Guillain-Barré syndrome.[38]

The mistaken approval of such a product is highly visible and has immediate consequences. The media pounces, the public denounces, and Congress pronounces. Both the developers of the product and the regulators who allowed it to be marketed are excoriated and punished in such modern-day pillories as congressional hearings, television newsmagazines, and newspaper editorials. Because a regulatory official's career might be damaged irreparably by the good-faith but mistaken approval of a high-profile product, decisions are often made defensively—in other words, to avoid Type I errors at any cost.

Type II errors, in the form of excessive governmental requirements and unreasonable decisions, can delay commercialization of a new product, lessen competition to produce it, and inflate its ultimate price. The detrimental effects of FDA delays in approving certain new drugs that previously had been approved in other industrialized countries are well documented.[39] The more than three-year delay in the approval of misoprostol, a drug for the treatment of gastric bleeding, is estimated to have cost between eight thousand and fifteen thousand lives per year, and the delay of the approval of streptokinase for the treatment of blocked coronary arteries may have resulted in as many as eleven thousand lost per year.[40]

Although they can profoundly compromise public health, Type II errors caused by a regulator's bad judgment, timidity, or anxiety seldom gain public attention. It may be only the employees of the company that makes the product and a few stock market analysts and investors who are likely to be aware of them. Likewise, if a regulator's mistake precipitates a corporate decision to abandon a product, the cause and effect are seldom connected in the public mind. The companies themselves are loath to complain publicly about FDA misjudgments, because the agency wields so much discretionary control over their ability to test and market products. As a consequence, there may be little direct evidence or data to document the lost societal benefits or the culpability of regulatory officials.

Exceptions exist, of course. A few activists, such as the AIDS advocacy groups that closely monitor the FDA, scrutinize agency review of certain products and aggressively publicize Type II errors. But such examples are rare. Congressional oversight should provide a check on regulators' performance, but seldom does it focus on their Type II errors. Type I errors make for more exciting hearings, after all, with injured patients or their families paraded before the cameras. Even when Type II errors are exposed, regulators frequently defend them as erring on the side of caution—in effect, invoking the precautionary principle. Too often, legislators, the media, and the public accept this euphemism uncritically, making our system of pharmaceutical oversight progressively less accountable and less relevant to the public interest. Former FDA Commissioner Alexander Schmidt aptly summarized the regulator's conundrum:

> In all our FDA history, we are unable to find a single instance where a Congressional committee investigated the failure of FDA to approve a new drug. But, the times when hearings have been held to criticize our approval of a new drug have been so frequent that we have not been able to count them. The message to FDA staff could not be clearer. Whenever a controversy over a new drug is resolved by approval of the drug, the agency and the individuals involved likely will be investigated. Whenever such a drug is disapproved, no inquiry will be made. The Congressional pressure for *negative* action is, therefore, intense. And it seems to be ever increasing.[41]

Since the time Schmidt delivered this speech, a few hearings have been held to investigate Type II errors, but they remain rare exceptions—and certainly, they have never led to redress of the Type I/Type II asymmetry.

The FDA is not unique in this regard, of course. All regulatory agencies are subject to social and political tensions that cause them to be castigated for the dangerous products that make it to market (often even if those products produce net benefits) but to escape blame when they keep beneficial products out of the hands of consumers. This institutional tendency toward the commission of Type II errors is magnified by the precautionary principle's inherent bias against Type I errors; adding the precautionary principle into the public policy mix only exaggerates regulators' already pronounced propensities.

Is Regulation Too Permissive?

In spite of this systematic bias, could it still be possible, as claimed by precautionary principle advocates, that our regulatory policies are insufficiently risk averse? Could regulation actually be underestimating the novel risks of new technologies, as compared to more familiar risks we have lived with for years, decades, and even centuries?

Precautionary principle advocates Carolyn Raffensperger and Joel Tickner[42] believe that is the case, because, they say, the scientific method, or "laboratory standard of proof," is weighted against false positives and wary of weak associations. When searching for a cause-and-effect relationship, they argue, Type I errors (concluding incorrectly that there is no harm when one really exists) are far more likely than Type II errors (concluding incorrectly that there *is* a harm when none exists).

Although some harmful effects may indeed go undiscovered by standard testing protocols, risk analysts and regulators build safety margins into their methodology for precisely this reason. When estimating the "safe" level of exposure to a chemical, for example, toxicologists identify the maximum amount of the substance (per unit of weight) that will have no observable deleterious effect in laboratory animals. Regulators then add in a safety factor of ten to account for the difference between lab animals and humans, then add an *additional* safety factor of ten to account for variation among individuals in human populations, and often add yet *another* safety factor of ten to account for the difference between adults and children. Thus, no harmful effect should occur even if humans were exposed to regulated substances at a hundred or a thousand times the permissible exposure levels.[43] Given this extremely conservative approach to risk, the burden of proof should be on advocates of the precautionary principle to demonstrate that currently used risk-assessment methodologies are insufficient.

Furthermore, regulation is not society's only safeguard against potentially harmful products. As described in chapter 6, producers are increasingly fearful of *ex post* legal liability for harms (real or alleged) their products may cause. Nor are businesses eager to invest tens or hundreds of millions of dollars in the development and commercialization of products that, for whatever reason, cannot or will not be used.[44] Thus, in spite of fears that the use of the scientific method in regulatory decision making could lead to an excess of Type I errors, the evidence indicates that the opposite may well be the case. Aversion to novel risks will always be present in any regulatory system, whether or not the precautionary principle is formally adopted.

Just as novel harms may not appear until after a product has been approved, the full range of risk-reducing *benefits* is also impossible to predict at the time a regulatory decision is made—for example, the reduction in Bt corn of infestation by the toxic mold *Fusarium*, which results in lower concentrations of the potent *Fusarium*-produced toxin, fumonisin (discussed in

chapter 5).[45] Prior to the commercialization of Bt corn, few experts anticipated such a significant effect—although in hindsight the relationship seems
quite obvious. Such benefits are important, but because they cannot be fully
anticipated prior to commercialization, they are unlikely to be factored into
the calculus of precautionary decision making. Similar examples abound.

Even innovators themselves typically cannot predict all the productive uses
to which a new product may be put. It is well known that the inventors of
new technologies do not foresee many ultimately important applications;
rather, they are discovered or developed by others only after the products
reach the marketplace.[46] Hundreds of prescription and over-the-counter
pharmaceuticals are used in ways their inventors never imagined. New and
often more important therapeutic uses are discovered by accident or experiment only after the drugs are initially marketed. An estimated 60 to 70 percent of cancer medicines are administered for so-called "off label" uses, in
ways for which they were not approved.[47] The excimer laser, now used daily
in a range of eye surgery and other applications, was "dismissed as an invention looking for a job" when it was introduced in the 1960s.[48] In some
cases, the most significant benefits are unknown until the product has been
used for many years.

THE PRECAUTIONARY PRINCIPLE OPENS THE DOOR
TO POLITICAL MANIPULATION

The precautionary principle skews the regulatory system away from a scientific appraisal of risk and toward more government subjectivity and discretion—which, in turn, invites caprice and abuse. For example, the most
common formulation of the principle is the one incorporated in the Rio
Declaration from the 1992 United Nations "Earth Summit," held in Rio de
Janeiro: "Where there are threats of serious or irreversible damage, lack of
full scientific certainty shall not be used as a reason for postponing cost-
effective measures to prevent environmental degradation."[49] This means only
that uncertainty should neither be used as an excuse for government inaction
nor as a justification to prevent a regulatory response. Therefore, it grants
considerable discretion to regulators about when and how to enforce precautionary measures—discretion that has been used to justify trade protectionism and technophobia.[50]

Advocates of the precautionary principle, including representatives of the
European Commission, have denied vehemently that the precautionary principle
is prone to political abuse.[51] That is like denying that you get wet if you're caught
in a thunderstorm—real-world experience argues otherwise.

The Politics of Beef

In addition to the litany of precautionary principle-related abuses of the
new biotechnology documented in this volume, another salient example is

a dispute over restrictions on hormone-treated beef cattle that pits, on one side, the United States and Canada, and on the other, the European Commission.

In this case, the U.S. and Canadian governments challenged an EC policy that restricts imports of American and Canadian beef from cattle treated with certain naturally derived or synthetic growth hormones. Since 1989, the European Commission has argued that this policy is justified by the precautionary principle, but a scientific committee assembled by the World Trade Organization (WTO) found the EC's rationale invalid.[52] Even the scientific studies cited by the commission in its own defense failed to identify any safety problems, as long as the hormones in question are used in accordance with good animal husbandry practices.

Moreover, the reason supplemental hormones are used is merely to restore some of the natural hormones that are depleted after castration of the bulls, in order to make the animals fatten more quickly and make the meat more tender—a common practice among North American ranchers.

Significantly, EU health officials have expressed no concern about endogenous hormones that often occur at higher levels in the uncastrated animals more commonly found in Europe. (This may be another example of the "natural" versus "unnatural" mythology discussed in chapter 2.) Nor did the EU ban growth promoters in the pork industry, where many European livestock operations are internationally competitive.[53] Although representatives of the European Commission still remonstrate that the restriction on hormone-treated beef is not intended to be a trade barrier, it is difficult to see the EU's inconsistent application of the precautionary principle in this case as anything other than crass protectionism.

Gene-Spliced Food Labeling

Equally inconsistent and scientifically insupportable are the EU's policies on the labeling of gene-spliced foods. Beginning in 1997, European food producers were required to label any food or animal feed made from a gene-spliced crop plant if residues of the novel gene or protein could be detected in the final product.[54] In practice, that meant cooking oils from gene-spliced corn or canola were exempt because the heat and friction from the crushing process tend to break apart DNA chains and break down proteins, making it impossible to detect any differences between gene-spliced and conventional sources.

In April 2004, a new labeling law went into effect. It covers all food and animal feed produced from any gene-spliced organism, even if the items are completely indistinguishable from conventional foods. To ensure that gene-spliced products are accurately labeled, seed producers, farmers, shippers, processors, retailers, and others will be required to keep detailed records of all gene-spliced products so they can be traced all the way through the food chain.

An interesting wrinkle in the overall debate over labeling is the distinction made by the EU between foods or feeds that are produced *with* and produced *from* a gene-spliced organism.[55] This peculiarity is a legal nicety that favors European producers. While products such as whole fruits and vegetables or starches and cooking oils produced *from* gene-spliced grains and oilseeds must be labeled, products made *with* the aid of gene-spliced enzymes (such as chymosin for cheese production) and *with* gene-spliced yeasts to make beer and wine are exempted from both the previous and new labeling and traceability rules.

We find it curious that in both the cattle hormone and gene-spliced food labeling examples, European regulators find it necessary to protect consumers from foods developed with certain production methods, but only when the foods involved come primarily from outside the EU. Even if there were no other objections to real-world applications of the precautionary principle, this fact would give one pause. One must wonder at the validity of a "principle" that consistently militates against certain foods produced primarily in the United States, while exempting similar foods from industries in which European producers have a competitive advantage.

If the U.S.-EU squabbles over gene-spliced foods are a diplomatic game with high financial stakes, in developing countries they are a matter of life and death. Once again, we return to the tragedy in sub-Saharan Africa.

Until the onset of a debilitating drought in 2000, countries like Zambia and Zimbabwe were important exporters of corn, beef, and poultry to other countries in Africa and Europe.[56] The Zambian and Zimbabwean governments have acknowledged that the fear of losing important European export markets contributed to their decision to refuse food aid from the United States.[57]

Harvested corn kernels can be planted to grow new crops and, while uncommon, it is not unknown for small portions of food aid to be diverted to seed stock by forward-thinking recipients. Thus, once the drought ends, the presence of gene-spliced corn growing anywhere in those countries would all but disqualify them from exporting harvested corn to Western Europe.

Even though food exporters are relatively few in number in those countries, they are politically powerful, and African political leaders have decided that protecting tomorrow's export markets is more important than preventing widespread starvation in their countries today.

But they are not solely to blame. What is especially repugnant is that by erecting discriminatory regulatory barriers against gene-spliced foods (a class of products made with a *superior* technology, let us recall), political leaders in Europe have created the regulatory environment that has precipitated the grotesque decisions of African leaders. All the governments involved have hidden behind the precautionary principle to mask their true motives. This sordid situation, with its many nuances, illustrates the importance of the rule of law in international trade—specifically, the strictures against unscientific regulations, which WTO rules define as a prima facie nontariff trade barrier.

PRECAUTION AS AN ATTACK ON FREEDOM

We see the precautionary principle being embraced repeatedly by governments not to promote public health or environmental protection but to reward domestic interest groups, appease radical environmentalists, and feather the nests of regulators themselves.

As we noted in the previous chapter, this is a variant of the "bootleggers and Baptists" conspiracy, in which certain producers, seeking to use regulation as a market-entry barrier to limit competition, ally themselves with extremists who vilify the new biotechnology and demand excessive government regulation. Regulators, who also benefit from unnecessary mandates, play along. The result is a venal coalition that conspires against the public interest while pretending to be public-spirited.

The Real Motivation for the Activists' Agenda

No one should make the mistake of assuming that the protection of society from technological risk is part of the anti-technology activists' agenda. Most proponents of the precautionary principle are more anti-business, anti-technology, and anti-establishment than they are pro-safety. They are consummate opportunists. In their zeal to oppose business interests and disparage technologies they don't like or that they have decided we don't need, they seize on whatever opportunities appear. They are never silent, never still, and never satisfied.

In their quest to create barriers to the use of new technologies, advocates of the precautionary principle capitalize on the public's fear of change and on regulators' natural risk-aversion. The impossibility of proving absolute "safety" bolsters their arguments, which skillfully confuse *plausibility* with *provability*. The precautionary principle requires regulatory bodies to resolve unanswered questions about the safety of a new product before it is marketed (and often before it has even been tested!), and regulators are free to require arbitrarily any amount and kind of testing they wish.

There are no clear evidentiary standards that establish the basis for certifying "safety," and no procedural endpoints that require regulators to grant approval, no matter how much evidence has been mustered. Thus, in order to obstruct a regulatory approval indefinitely, opponents simply have to pose endless questions that must be addressed before the approval can be made. Inventors or producers must spend time and resources to answer these interminable queries, while the critics move on to yet another frightening possibility and still more questions.

The staunch environmentalist advocates of the precautionary principle insist that the proponents of any technology or behavior must bear the burden of demonstrating its safety.[58] All too frequently, these same environmentalists then reject the safety data generated by the producers of a technology as "tainted," the rationale being that because producers have a direct interest in seeing their products marketed, they cannot be trusted to provide an honest analysis. Thus, we are at a Catch-22—the producers of a technology must generate safety data, but when they do so, it cannot be accepted. Even when an otherwise independent third party (such as a university research laboratory or government agency) is commissioned to design and conduct the experiments, activists condemn the results as hopelessly biased by a financial conflict of interest.

In 2001, the EC Directorate-General for Research released a report that described some eighty-one different research projects on the safety of gene-spliced organisms, all funded by the European Union. This fifteen-year, $64 million investigation not only concluded that gene-spliced crops pose no new risks to human health or the environment but also that the more precise technology and the intensified regulatory scrutiny focused on them "probably make them safer than conventional plant breeding."[59] The editors of this scientific review have since charged that the EC has done a poor job of communicating the results to the European public and consequently has failed to alleviate their concerns.[60]

That such findings have not swayed the opponents of the new biotechnology should come as no surprise. After all, Lord Peter Melchett, the former head of Greenpeace in the United Kingdom, had testified a year earlier to a parliamentary committee that his organization's view of the new biotechnology is "permanent and definite and complete opposition based on a view that there will always be major uncertainties."[61]

Similarly, Greenpeace U.S., one of the foremost advocates of the precautionary principle, reported in its 1999 federal tax filings that the organization was committed not to sufficient testing and safe use of the new biotechnology but to the "complete elimination [from] the food supply and the environment" of gene-spliced organisms.[62] Many environmental activist groups, including Greenpeace, do not draw the line at proselytizing, lying, and demanding illogical and stultifying regulation or outright bans on product testing and commercialization. They advocate and carry out vandalism of the very experiments intended to resolve uncertainty. Activists from Greenpeace, Friends of the Earth, and other radical groups have destroyed crops undergoing field trials, vandalized laboratories and greenhouses, and even set fire to research offices at Michigan State University.[63]

Biotechnology and the Brown Shirts

Even if every question about health and safety could be answered, precautionary principle advocates would still want regulators to ask, "Do we need this activity in the first place?"[64] The goal of activists is to arrogate the power to make that decision, of course. Many are motivated by their own parochial vision of what constitutes a "good society" and how to achieve it. One prominent biotechnology critic at the Union of Concerned Scientists rationalizes her organization's opposition to gene-splicing by claiming, "Industrialized countries have few genuine needs for innovative food stuffs [*sic*], regardless of the method by which they are produced." In her opinion, therefore, society should not squander resources on developing them. (Persons who suffer life-threatening allergies from peanuts or wheat might disagree.) She concludes that, although "the malnourished homeless" are indeed a problem, the solution lies "in resolving income disparities, and educating ourselves to make better choices from among the abundant foods that are available."[65]

Even when the new products will spare animals the torture of rabies or save lives in less developed nations, the activists remain unmoved. At an Organization for Economic Cooperation and Development conference in March 2000, Greenpeace anti-biotechnology campaigner Benedikt Haerlin "dismissed the importance of saving African and Asian lives at the risk of spreading a new science that he considered untested."[66] Many environmental organizations have supported the Zambian and Zimbabwean governments' decision to forgo gene-spliced food aid from the United States.

Such arrogance and tortured logic illustrate that the current controversies over the expansion of the precautionary principle generally, and the testing and use of gene-spliced organisms in particular, stem from a social vision that is not just strongly anti-technology and antagonistic to genuine safety improvements but poses serious challenges to individual, academic, and corporate freedom.

The precautionary principle shifts decision-making power away from individual citizens and into the hands of government bureaucrats and environmental activists. It is precisely this aspect of the precautionary principle that makes it the darling of many activist groups.

Carolyn Raffensperger of the Science and Environmental Health Network asserts that the precautionary principle "is in the hands of the people," as illustrated, according to her, by violent demonstrations against economic globalization such as those in Seattle at the 1999 meeting of the World Trade Organization.[67] "This is [about] how they want to live their lives," says Raffensperger. We disagree. It is about how a small, vocal, and at times violent group of radicals want the rest of us to live *our* lives. There is no real health or environmental benefit to be gained from bans or discriminatory restrictions on the new biotechnology. The issue here is freedom and its infringement by ideologues who disapprove, on principle, of a certain technology, product, or activity.

The systematic and relentless vilification of the new biotechnology by a small cadre of radicals is uncomfortably reminiscent of the stigmatization of various aspects of culture and science in Germany during the 1930s. Manfred

Laubichler has noted that the close association between Nazism and eugenics and human experimentation should have led to a moral imperative in Europe that dictates, "Hands off from genetic engineering and biotechnology."[68]

Far from avoiding the barbarities of the past, however, the moral imperative in Europe toward the new biotechnology is now overtly fascistic. Field trials have been regularly vandalized (acts that have most often gone unpunished), scientists have been intimidated, and the press has been fed (and has eagerly published) wildly inaccurate propaganda. All of this recalls the Third Reich's persecution of the practitioners of what the regime called *entartete Kunst*, or "degenerate art," which was practiced by such "subversives" as Marc Chagall, Emil Nolde, Max Beckmann, Vincent van Gogh, Henri Matisse, Edvard Munch, and Pablo Picasso. Today, throughout Europe the new biotechnology has become a kind of *entartete Forschung*, or "degenerate research," thanks to environmentalists and government officials armed with the precautionary principle.

Paranoia and the Conspiracy against Biotechnology

The underlying theme of anti-technology activism is not new. It resonates well with historian Richard Hofstadter's classic analysis of religious and political movements in American public policy, "The Paranoid Style in American Politics."[69] Hofstadter described the religious and political activists' obsession as "paranoia": "The central image is that of a vast and sinister conspiracy, a gigantic and yet subtle machinery of influence set in motion to undermine and destroy a way of life." He goes on to note a characteristic "leap in imagination that is always made at some critical point in the recital of events." How ironic that these activists tend to imitate the very conspiracies that they imagine are threats to society.

Susanne Huttner, Associate Vice-Provost for Research of the University of California System, has placed the biotechnology critics squarely in Hofstadter's sights.[70] Viewing from Hofstadter's model of the paranoid style, she has observed that, for anti-biotechnology activists, the "conspiracy" here lies in large-scale agriculture performed with twenty-first-century technology, and that the "leap in imagination" lies in the assertion that the new biotechnology somehow is bad for agriculture, farmers, and less developed countries. Anti-biotechnology activists fear a world in which multinational corporations conspire to strip away individual choice from the world's farmers and consumers. Yet it is *they* who are stripping away the freedom of researchers to research, farmers to farm, and consumers to consume gene-spliced foods and other products.

The Impact of Regulatory Uncertainty

Even when precautionary regulation does permit a trickle of gene-spliced products into the marketplace, the uncertainty caused by overregulation itself poses a significant hurdle to business. Reliability, predictability, and impartiality of legal rules are essential for proper planning by businesses and individuals.[71] Without established, transparent rules for making objective evaluations, planning by innovators becomes a guessing game. When entrepreneurs and company executives are uncertain about regulatory boundaries and requirements, they are reluctant to take the financial risks necessary to develop new products.[72]

Regulatory uncertainty has already created market distortions by helping to create a situation in which only the largest, most financially secure firms can afford to develop products—and then, only those products that are likely to be hugely profitable. In an environment governed by the precautionary principle, academic, public sector, and charitable institutions will find it increasingly difficult to develop gene-spliced products that are targeted at less-developed countries. Even in major, relatively permissive markets such as the United States, research and development with gene-splicing technology has become so costly due to often-superfluous regulations that it must focus on large-volume commodity crops, while smaller-volume but high-value plants such as trees, vegetables, and fruits get short shrift.

We are deeply troubled by the fundamental unfairness of current public policy toward the new biotechnology. Established, publicly promulgated rules clearly defining what is and what is not unlawful behavior is an essential bulwark of the freedoms protected by constitutional democracies.[73] Yielding wide discretion to government regulators has led to dubious public policy outcomes that have unduly restricted legitimate research and commercial activities. The legal rights of researchers, producers, and consumers, as well as the legal obligations of regulators, must be clearly defined to prevent overly subjective governmental judgments from unnecessarily restricting freedom in the way that has plagued the new biotechnology.

SEARCHING FOR SAFETY

In spite of radical environmentalists' repeated warnings that the sky is falling and that the end of the world is nigh, people in much of the world are living longer, healthier lives. Every year, life expectancy in both industrialized and less developed nations increases.[74] If the environmentalists are right, and the degradation of public health and the environment is growing progressively worse, what accounts for our increasing longevity?

In fact, it is the introduction of a spectrum of new and improved technologies that makes us better able to accumulate the global resources—that is, wealth—necessary to improve health, clean up the environment, and enable more people to lead happier, more prosperous, and longer lives.[75] New technologies, products, and activities do sometimes bring with them unexpected problems, to be sure, but on balance these side effects are more than compensated by the enhancement of resilience and adaptability, and the resulting increase in resources. The net effect of prudent risk taking—or, to be more precise, the calculated risks inherent in technological progress—is to enhance, rather than to compromise, safety.

If Not "Safe," at Least Safer

Precautionary thinking fails to take into consideration that we live in a world replete with risks that can be mitigated and controlled. We cannot make the world *safe*, but we can make it *safer*. Enter the discipline of risk-management, whose function is to determine how to minimize, or at least control, risks once they are identified. Still, while caution is usually de rigueur, it is not in and of itself a prescriptive concept. Although we constantly run the risk of injury, we do not forgo traveling, working, or recreation. Nor should we.

Likewise, the possibility of food poisoning does not prevent us from eating. In fact, some cultures even place a premium on foods that may be dangerous. An example is the Japanese penchant for fugu, a fish that contains a poisonous sac containing the extremely potent tetrodotoxin, which must be dissected out before the flesh is consumed. In spite of the licensing of fugu chefs, dozens of Japanese die annually from fugu poisoning—a delicious irony in a country where many consumers are resistant to foods from gene-spliced plants!

Even new technologies and activities that pose nonnegligible risks can be used in ways that confer net benefits. That is, although they pose some potential for harm, their use reduces or replaces enough alternative sources of risk that the individual users or society as a whole are made healthier, safer, more productive, or in some other way better off. Many prescription drugs are in this category, as are chain saws, nuclear power generation, and open-heart surgery. We cannot escape risk or uncertainty, but we can strive to choose the options most likely to make our lives and our communities safer. Therein lies the challenge with which life confronts us and our government policy makers. Each new technology is likely to introduce both good and bad consequences, the net effect of which on cultures, livelihoods, and entire national economies is often difficult to predict a priori.[76]

Inevitably, inequities are rife. The introduction of the automobile has made our lives more efficient and enjoyable, but it devastated the manufacturers of buggy whips. More apposite to the new biotechnology is the recent obsolescence of rennin (a crude extract made from calf stomach) for cheese making, following the introduction of chymosin purified from a gene-spliced microorganism. Perhaps some day the inexpensive and reliable production of vanilla or cocoa in gene-spliced plants (possibly corn or tobacco) will adversely affect the economies of countries that export those commodities.

As Aaron Wildavsky observed, this inherent interconnectedness means that improvements in net safety and benefit must be "searched for" through a continuing process of trial and error. Attempting to anticipate and prevent all possible harms is a recipe for disaster, because it is impossible to do so without also sacrificing much (or even most) of the good. It is essential for governments to keep this in mind when formulating regulatory policies. As we will discuss in the next few chapters, however, most governments have failed to craft policies for regulating gene-spliced agricultural products that balance the risks of moving too quickly into the future against those risks of staying too long in the past.

The Vagaries of U.S. Regulation

T HE FEDERAL GOVERNMENT's involvement in regulating consumer products today is so pervasive that most Americans probably assume it is one of Washington's basic and historical functions, like national defense and collecting taxes. Virtually every consumer product sold in today's marketplace is subject to at least one, and in many instances several, federal regulatory statutes, plus a bewildering array of implementing regulations, guidelines, and policies. But these regulations are relatively recent phenomena. Prior to the twentieth century, there was no direct federal regulation of consumer products in the United States.

THE BIRTH AND GROWTH OF PREMARKET REGULATION

The Biologics Act of 1902 ushered in the Regulatory Century, and as is often the case with legislation, it was written in a crisis atmosphere. In 1901, a contaminated batch of smallpox vaccine caused an outbreak of tetanus in Camden, New Jersey, and a single lot of tetanus-contaminated diphtheria antitoxin resulted in the death of several children in St. Louis.

These events triggered historic legislation. The 1902 statute required that the federal government grant *pre*market approval of two complementary license applications for every biological drug (derivatives of living substances used for treatment or precaution, including vaccines, blood and blood products, natural substances used to treat allergies, and extracts of living cells). One application was a product license application for the product itself. The other was an establishment license application, certifying the production process and facility.

Never before had any European or American government required explicit government licensing or approval of a whole category of consumer products prior to marketing. Earlier lawmaking in Europe, the American colonies, and the United States had made the sale of adulterated or misbranded products illegal, but it had provided governmental authorities only with the power to police the marketplace—that is, regulators could review already-marketed products and bring legal action against any product found to violate the statutory requirements.

With the 1902 act, however, government was given the unprecedented administrative authority to prevent certain consumer products from being put on the market in the first place. It could prevent commercialization simply by turning down a marketing application or by taking no action at all on the matter. The same premarket authority was later enacted into law for animal biological drugs by the Virus, Serum and Toxin Act of 1913.

Congress did not grant this power promiscuously. In fact, the premarket approval requirements for human and animal biologics stood alone for more than fifty years. When Congress enacted the Federal Food and Drugs Act of 1906 to regulate the rest of the U.S. drug supply (that is, nonbiological medical drugs), it did not authorize any form of premarket testing or approval, or even the development of administrative regulatory standards. The Federal Meat Inspection Act of 1906 and the Insecticide Act of 1910 similarly relied entirely upon traditional police powers and imposed no regulatory review requirements prior to marketing.

As first drafted, even the Federal Food, Drug and Cosmetic Act of 1938—the principal enabling statute of today's FDA—included only policing authority. Before it became law, however, a hastily marketed drug containing an untested solvent (diethylene glycol, a potent poison) killed more than a hundred people within a few days. In response to this tragedy, Congress included in the 1938 act a new provision to require "sponsors" (companies) to submit a "New Drug Application" (NDA) to the FDA before introducing a new drug into interstate commerce. The NDA had to describe the proposed uses of the drug and the tests that demonstrated safety at the recommended dose.

Under the 1938 act, if a company submitted an NDA for a product and the FDA took no action within sixty days, the application was, in effect, approved and the drug could be marketed lawfully. In other words, Congress stopped short of requiring that new drugs obtain an *affirmative* premarket approval; the default position was permission for the drug sponsor to market the product. Moreover, only the safety of the drug was considered to be within the FDA's purview, not the effectiveness. Effectiveness was left for the marketplace to judge.

A decade later, following World War II, Congress replaced the Insecticide Act of 1910 with the Federal Insecticide, Fungicide, and Rodenticide Act (FIFRA) of 1947. For the first time, before any pesticide could be marketed lawfully, it had to be registered with the U.S. Department of Agriculture, which regulated pesticides at that time. The 1947 act contained no authority, however, for USDA to deny registration based upon an administrative determination that a product was adulterated, mislabeled, or unsafe.

The combined impact of these various federal regulatory statutes on commerce in legitimate products was negligible, and there were, in fact, public health benefits. The policing, or surveillance, of the marketplace—that is, *post*marketing regulation—by the FDA and USDA under these regulatory statutes was extremely successful in weeding out adulterated, misbranded, or otherwise unsafe products. By taking strong regulatory action, these two agencies removed thousands of hazardous and ineffective products from the market, benefiting both consumers and the legitimate industry. At the same time, neither the industry's ability to develop and market new products nor individual choice was compromised.

Because their scope was narrow, the premarket review requirements for human and animal biological products had little negative impact, and free choice in the marketplace was actually enhanced by the requirement for accurate labeling of regulated products. Beginning in the 1950s, however, the regulatory landscape changed dramatically. Congress enacted a series of statutes that required actual premarket *approval* of a large number of consumer products, including the following:

1. The Miller Pesticide Amendments of 1954, requiring premarket approval of pesticide residues in or on food
2. The Food Additives Amendment of 1958, requiring premarket approval of food additives
3. The Color Additive Amendments of 1960, requiring premarket approval of color additives
4. The Drug Amendments of 1962, which introduced mandatory premarket approval and required that marketed drugs be determined by the FDA to be both safe *and effective*
5. The Animal Drug Amendments of 1968, requiring premarket approval of new animal drugs and feed additives
6. The Federal Environmental Pesticide Control Act of 1972, requiring premarket approval of pesticides
7. The Medical Device Amendments of 1976, requiring premarket notification for all medical devices and premarket approval for Class III (high-risk) medical devices
8. The Toxic Substances Control Act of 1976, requiring premarket notification for chemical substances
9. The Infant Formula Act of 1980, requiring premarket notification for infant formulas
10. The Nutrition Labeling and Education Act of 1990, requiring premarket approval of nutrient descriptors and disease prevention claims for food.

Taken collectively, these laws have resulted in a revolution in product regulation. Since the 1950s federal responsibility has grown from simple policing after the product launch to almost universal premarket regulation—and often, even to pre*testing* regulation, with government permits or approval necessary before a product can even be evaluated in clinical trials or in the field.

Regulatory Creep

With its monopoly on product review and approval, the federal government has become the exclusive gatekeeper to the marketplace. Regulators in a veritable alphabet soup of agencies now have the final authority to determine whether and when countless products will reach consumers. No manufacturer of these products has the legal right to distribute them without premarket approval, and no member of the public has the right to obtain them, unless and until the relevant federal agency authorizes marketing. Statute by statute, regulation by regulation, and decision by decision, massive bureaucracies have arisen to rein in industry and control product flow, and often, as noted above, product testing.

By fiscal year 2002, administrative expenditures for federal regulation had reached an all-time high of $25.1 billion. What is worse is that for every dollar of direct budget outlay expended on regulatory activities, the private sector—companies and also individual consumers, investors, and workers—spends forty-five dollars for compliance. Ominously, the magnitude of this multiplier is increasing.[1]

An important reason for this continual expansion of government influence and its costs is that a regulatory statute (the actual law itself), even if it is not amended, is not static. When the statute is first enacted, its implementation is generally narrow and limited to the specific requirements of the law—and its impact, therefore, is often modest. As time goes on, however, each successive generation of administrators tends to redefine the scope of jurisdiction and add new requirements, sometimes without benefit of the formal rule-making process, which requires agencies to accept public input and provides for judicial review of the rule making. Seldom does the scope narrow; and almost never do requirements disappear. Regulation begins to take on a life of its own.

A prime example is the FDA's 1997 "pediatric rule," which obligated manufacturers of many new and already commercialized drugs to test them on pediatric populations even if the product was not intended for or marketed for children's use. In some cases, drug makers would be required to develop a pediatric formulation for breakthrough drugs that represented a significant therapeutic advance over existing treatments. This rule ignores the realities of drug testing and could actually be detrimental to children and delay the availability of new drugs, because FDA could withhold approval for adult uses while the required data from pediatric studies are being collected. It also exceeded the agency's authority, according to Judge Henry H. Kennedy, Jr., of the District of Columbia federal court, who overturned the rule, writing "The pediatric rule exceeds the Food and Drug Administration's statutory authority and is therefore invalid."[2] However, under great pressure from the FDA and activists, Congress and President George W. Bush legislatively restored the pediatric rule in 2003.

As regulators interpret statutes ever more broadly and comprehensively, they themselves become a special-interest group, intent upon expanding their responsibilities, functions, budgets, and bureaucratic empires. In the absence of conscientious, persistent, and effective congressional oversight, what develops is an increasingly burdensome, inefficient, and unresponsive regulatory system.

The Impact on the New Biotechnology

Nowhere can this be seen more clearly than in the evolution of pretesting and premarket regulatory mechanisms for products made with the new biotechnology. For this set of enabling technologies, which are applicable to many industrial sectors and myriad products, the current system of oversight necessarily encompasses several regulatory agencies. Unfortunately, it includes little public accountability.

This means, for example, that citizens who could benefit from various environmental, agricultural, and food applications of the new biotechnology—including hypoallergenic foods, microorganisms that can clean up toxic wastes, plants that grow with less water and fewer applications of agricultural chemicals, to name just a few—have little ability to participate in the process and no access to judicial review of whatever action is taken by the federal government. Thus, the requirement for prior governmental approval in order to market or even to test gene-spliced products—which seldom applies to products made with less precise and predictable techniques—severely limits individual freedom of choice. Personal autonomy is subordinated to government controls. Citizens are precluded from obtaining safe products they wish to purchase and have no recourse other than to await government approval.

By constraining individual choice and free markets, government regulation often creates unintended and unforeseen problems. When combined with other economic consequences, these kinds of constraints at the national and international level create an invisible crisis. For small businesses and academic research centers in particular, the investment required to jump through arbitrary, unscientifically constructed regulatory hoops can be prohibitive. The greater the investment required to bring products to market, the less competition there is to make them, the fewer products are pursued, and the higher the price to consumers for the products that ultimately gain approval. Especially for low-profit-margin sectors like agriculture and food production, inflated regulatory expense and uncertainty discourage potential users of a new technology that finds disfavor with regulators. When excessive and poorly conceived regulation also causes the kinds of negative ripple effects on trade and consumer acceptance that we have seen with the new biotechnology (discussed in detail in chapters 7 and 8), it can be a death knell.

A PRIMER ON BIOTECH REGULATION

In the United States, government regulation generally is organized not around technological processes but around products and their intended uses. As those uses vary, so do agency jurisdictions and evaluation procedures. The approach that an agency takes to what and how to regulate is driven by several factors, including enabling statutes, regulations that implement the statutes, case law, and their own discretion other precedents.

As discussed in chapter 1, the diversity of biotechnology products and their uses may trigger regulation by a variety of federal agencies the evaluation strategies and procedures of which vary widely in focus, nature, and rigor. Although there is additional detail below on these agencies' regulation of biotechnology products, comprehensive descriptions must be sought elsewhere (e.g., in work by J. L. Vanderveen,[3] and on the websites of the respective agencies).

In general terms, the regulation of gene-spliced products in the agricultural sector (as opposed to pharmaceuticals and strictly environmental applications) falls into three main categories. The first is the safety of cultivation of plants or of the use of microorganisms in the field. The primary concerns are plant pest issues, the creation of weeds, the spread of pathogens, and ecological disruption. Except for the organisms in the pesticide category described below, this area is the domain of the USDA, which traditionally regulates on the basis of the expected risk of the organism. Under the Federal Plant Pest Act (FPPA), the USDA regulates the testing, transport, or sale of what are called "plant pests," specified by an inclusive list of organisms; use of any of the organisms on the list requires permission from the USDA.[4] In 1987 the department decided that the presence of certain gene sequences used in virtually all gene-spliced plants would make a plant a possible pest (and in the process, coined the new term "regulated article"). The effect was to require repeated and redundant case-by-case reviews and approvals for the field testing of essentially all gene-spliced plants not already captured by the Environmental Protection Agency (see the section on the EPA below).

The second category concerns the use of "pesticides," a term that has been broadly defined by regulators to include not only substances that kill or repel pests but also plants that have been modified by recombinant DNA techniques in order to enhance their own pest or disease resistance. The EPA regulates pesticides under the Federal Insecticide, Fungicide, and Rodenticide Act (FIFRA), which encompasses pesticides and growth modulators.[5] The agency also enforces the catch-all Toxic Substances Control Act (TSCA), which provides oversight of "nonnatural" and "new" substances, and mixtures of substances, intended for use in commerce and that are not regulated elsewhere.

The third area focuses on the safety of foods for human or animal consumption. The FDA regulates food additives (such as artificial sweeteners and preservatives) via premarket review, but the vast majority of what we eat—fresh and processed foods—is not subject to premarket testing, review, or inspection. However, federal regulators do police the marketplace, and food products may be removed from commerce or seized by the FDA if they are found to be "misbranded" (i.e., mislabeled) or "adulterated" (that is, containing any additive "which may render [them] injurious to health")—both of these being forms of *post*marketing regulation.[6]

Defying the consensus of the scientific community, in 2001 the FDA proposed a flip-flop of its risk-based regulatory approach for foods from gene-spliced plants, in the form of a regulation that would have reversed the agency's scientific approach to biotechnology products by requiring gene-spliced foods to undergo a premarket review.[7] In spite of widespread support from the packaged food and biotechnology industries for the proposal (but in the face of criticism from the scientific community), the provision was quietly deleted from the FDA's formal regulatory agenda in 2003, without being issued as a final rule. The agency could easily resurrect this proposed change in the future, however, as many within the organization remain strong proponents.

Agencies Ignore A "Scope" That Makes Sense

The USDA and EPA seem to be troubled neither by internal inconsistencies nor by the disparity between their approaches and the official federal policy—developed with the formal agreement of both of these agencies and the FDA—which stipulates that regulation of biotechnology products should be "risk-based," "scientifically sound," and focused on "the characteristics of the biotechnology product and the environment into which it is being introduced, not the process by which the product is created."[8]

These strictures for federal agencies are contained in the Coordinated Framework for the Regulation of Biotechnology and the "scope announcement"—more formally, "Exercise of Federal Oversight within Scope of Statutory Authority: Planned Introductions of Biotechnology Products into the Environment," which clarified how the regulation of recombinant DNA–modified organisms should be managed. The documents call explicitly for "a risk-based" approach to the oversight of gene-spliced products, the latter asserting that "exercise of oversight in the scope of discretion afforded by statute should be based on the risk posed by the introduction and *should not turn on the fact that an organism has been modified by a particular process or technique.*"[9]

What we have is exactly the opposite: the use of gene-splicing techniques serves as the trigger for additional regulation regardless of the risk posed by individual organisms. But exploiting the old Washington, D.C., political tradition that once something has been said three times it becomes a fact, federal regulators continually remonstrate that their policies *are* scientifically defensible and risk based. What is remarkable is not that they are disingenuous (another old Washington tradition) but how consistently they get away with such obvious untruths. The harsh reality is that unscientific agency policies, combined with unwise decisions on individual products and the acquiescence of industry, have created a seemingly inescapable morass.

UNSCIENTIFIC POLICIES

The USDA has the legislative authority, primarily under the Federal Plant Pest Act and the Plant Quarantine Act, to protect the U.S. agricultural environment against pests and disease.[10] Under these statutes, the USDA's Animal and Plant Health Inspection Service (APHIS) regulates the importation and interstate movement of plants and plant products that may result in plant diseases or pests. The Plant Protection Act of 2000 offers additional authority to regulate plant pests and to prevent the dissemination of "noxious weeds."[11]

A plant pest is defined as any organism "which can directly or indirectly injure or cause disease or damage in or to any plants or parts thereof, or any processed, manufactured, or other products of plants."[12] The APHIS regulations incorporate an inclusive list of organisms that are or that harbor plant pests.

This approach is essentially binary. A plant that an investigator might wish to introduce into the field is either on the proscribed list of plants pests—and therefore requires a permit—or is exempt. This straightforward approach is risk based, in that the organisms that are required to undergo case-by-case governmental review are an enhanced-risk group—organisms that *can* injure or damage plants—compared to organisms not considered to be plant pests.

Tortured Logic, Unscientific Policy

USDA's regulatory authority over gene-spliced plants also arises from the Plant Pest, Plant Quarantine, and Plant Protection Acts. It would have been both simple and effective to regulate only gene-spliced plants with suspected or recognized high-risk traits using essentially the same rule book. For the past fifteen years, however, APHIS has maintained a parallel regime focused exclusively on plants altered or produced through recombinant DNA techniques. All gene-spliced plants are included, no matter how obviously innocuous individual varieties may be.

In order to establish this mechanism, in which the scope of what is regulated is essentially independent of risk, APHIS tortured the original concept of a plant pest as something *known* to be harmful to craft a new category—a "regulated article," defined as "any organism or any product altered or produced through recombinant DNA technology, which is a plant pest, or for which there is reason to believe is a plant pest."[13]

The phrase "for which there is reason to believe is a plant pest" has been broadly interpreted by APHIS to include any organism that includes any amount of DNA from a plant pest—even a snippet of DNA that is incapable of conferring pathogenicity. This definition captures virtually all gene-spliced plants for case-by-case review, because small sections of DNA from plant viruses or bacteria are almost always used in the gene-splicing process to aid in the transfer of DNA between organisms.

Two such DNA sequences that are commonly used are from the cauliflower mosaic virus (CaMV) and the bacterium *Agrobacterium tumefaciens*. The CaMV 35S promoter sequence is a segment used in conjunction with a transferred gene. It signals the host cell to "turn on," or activate, the gene, to produce the substance for which the gene codes. The promoter sequence has no other function and cannot possibly be considered a plant pest.

The second example, a modified version of the bacterium *Agrobacterium tumefaciens*, is used to transfer useful genes into plant cells. Naturally occurring *A. tumefaciens* is a soil bacterium that causes crown gall disease in plants—an infection that generates a bulbous growth of excess cells on the stems of plants just above soil level but usually does not cause serious damage to adult plants and is harmless to humans. When it infects a plant, *A. tumefaciens* transfers to the plant's cells some of its own genes, which are found on a circular piece of DNA called a "plasmid," and this causes the cell to synthesize excessive amounts of plant hormones that cause a tumorlike growth, or "gall," to form. The transferred genes become stably integrated into the chromosomes of a single plant cell and subsequently are inherited by all the progeny of this cell. By replacing disease-causing genes on the plasmid with genes that one wishes to transfer, genetic engineers have exploited this system, creating an infectious but nonpathogenic and harmless vector that can move genes of scientific or commercial interest into plant cells.

The gene sequences from the cauliflower mosaic virus and *A. tumefaciens* that are used in gene-splicing are perfectly innocuous, but because they are derived from plant pests, the USDA is able to categorize any organisms that include the sequences as "regulated articles" under the new regulations of the Plant Pest Act.

In order to field-test or introduce a regulated article, a researcher must apply to APHIS for a permit and submit comprehensive data that includes a description of the regulated article; identification of the donor organism from which genetic material was obtained or transferred; the intended date and location of importation, movement, or release; how the regulated article differs from the "unmodified" parental plant; the experimental protocol for the release; description of facilities to be used; measures to ensure confinement; and plans for disposition of the regulated article upon termination of the field trial. After a plant has undergone sufficient testing and evaluation, the sponsor can submit a petition to APHIS for a "determination of non-regulated status," which, if granted, permits a gene-spliced plant—at long last—to be treated by USDA like any other plant, with no limitations on experimentation, cultivation, or sale.

USDA's case-by-case permitting process and costly field-test design and other requirements have made recombinant DNA modified plants disproportionately expensive to develop and test. A field trial with a recombinant DNA–modified plant may be ten to twenty times more expensive than the same experiment performed with a plant that has an identical phenotype but that was modified with less precise genetic techniques.[14] This can add up to millions of dollars of excess development costs, a princely sum for all but the most profitable applications.

Will Regulators Let Us Reap What Biopharming Sows?

Among the newest USDA regulatory regimes is that for so-called "biopharm" plants. Biotech companies are using gene-splicing techniques to reprogram crops—mainly corn, initially—to produce significant concentrations of high-value pharmaceuticals or industrially useful proteins. The idea of "biopharming" is not new, however. Many common medicines, such as morphine, codeine, the laxative Metamucil™, and the anti-cancer drug Taxol™, are all purified from plants. But biopharming's great promise lies in using gene-splicing techniques to make old plants do radical new things.

There is also great potential for cost cutting in the process and making medicines much less expensive. The energy for product synthesis comes from the sun, and the primary raw materials are water and carbon dioxide. In addition, biopharming offers tremendous flexibility and economy when adjustments in production are necessary, and the quality of the final drug can meet the same standards as current biotech methods that use microorganisms or cultured cells to produce medically useful proteins.

But storm clouds are gathering on the horizon. The food industry fears that pollen flow, accidental post-harvest mixing, or "volunteer" plants (ones that sprout in a particular field after the crop in question has been harvested) could cause vaccines, drugs, and other products to contaminate the food supply, triggering costly recalls and presenting thorny liability issues—concerns that are not without some basis in reality.

In 2002, a Nebraska farmer allegedly planted soybeans in a field in which biopharmed corn produced by the Texas-based company ProdiGene had grown the previous season, but the farmer failed to provide adequate weed control to eliminate drug-containing corn volunteers from sprouting in the soybean crop. After the harvest, the soybeans with a very small amount of cornstalk residue were then pooled with other soybeans into a 500,000-bushel shipment before USDA finally ordered the entire batch destroyed. ProdiGene agreed to cover all the clean-up costs and compensate the farmers whose soybeans were lost. USDA also fined the company $250,000.[15]

Alarmed by this incident, the food industry filed comments with the Food and Drug Administration in early 2003 calling for excessively stringent federal regulation. Some of the demands of the food industry were reasonable, but not their recommendations to the FDA that food plants should be entirely off limits for biopharming "unless the company developing the drug product clearly demonstrates that it is not feasible to use non-food crops," and for "land, labor and equipment [to be] dedicated solely to growing" biopharmed products.[16] Although these restrictions would in certain cases offer minimal additional safety, there is no good reason to apply them broadly to all biopharmed products.

As with gene-spliced food crops, not all biopharmed varieties would produce harmful substances. Such restrictions would, however, severely stigmatize the technology and push the development costs of biopharmed products into the stratosphere, limiting development only to very high value-added substances, and inflating the ultimate costs to the consumer of the biopharmed drugs that reach the marketplace. It would be far more appropriate for regulations to differentiate between situations in which complete segregation from the food supply of biopharmed crops is necessary and those situations in which such measures are unnecessary.

Like the food industry, regulators, too, are risk averse, and in the wake of the ProdiGene case, they hurriedly proposed stringent new regulations. In March 2003, USDA's Animal and Plant Health Inspection Service announced onerous new restrictions on the cultivation of *all* biopharmed crops.[17] To a great extent, the new rules tracked the demands of the food industry, which, interestingly, were almost indistinguishable from those of the radical environmental lobby.

Predictably, most of USDA's new restrictions on the cultivation of the biopharmed plants are excessively burdensome. They impose highly prescriptive, one-size-fits-all, "design" standards, instead of more reasonable "performance standards" that specify an end point that must be achieved. Like the rest of APHIS's regulations for gene-spliced plants, they do not take into account the actual risks of a given situation. Among other things, the new requirements:

1. Require separate planting, storage, and harvesting equipment for biopharmed crops. (APHIS allows such equipment to be returned to general use, but only after it has been cleaned in accordance with extraordinary, expensive, government-approved procedures.) Many biopharmers have always used dedicated equipment to avoid quality-control problems that might arise in the development of their plant-based drugs,but this level of precaution—along with its attendant expense and inconvenience—is not appropriate for all biopharmers.

2. Substantially increase the buffer zones between biopharmed and food crops of the same species. In corn, buffers are doubled from a half-mile to a mile, whenever the drug-bearing crops are openly pollinated, and to at least a half-mile away from other cornfields when crops are detassled or bagged to prevent pollination. These new requirements may rule out many opportunities for highly valuable biopharmed varieties in the Midwestern Corn Belt, where large plots of land without corn growing on them are rare.

3. Require that farmers seek explicit USDA authorization before growing food or animal feed crops on any land that has been used to cultivate biopharmed corn within the previous year. This measure is supposed to guard against the possibility that after a field has been cultivated with biopharmed corn, drug-producing "volunteer" plants might sprout later and get mixed with a food crop grown in the same soil.

The new biopharmed crop regulations are an obvious reaction to the ProdiGene fiasco and the negative publicity it generated.

Challenging the Zero-Tolerance Mindset

Federal officials have tried to keep residues of biopharmed products out of the food chain, no matter how trivial the amount or the likely effects. They have declined to establish non–zero tolerance levels for these substances, perhaps out of concern that opponents of biopharming would take advantage of such a move to proselytize against this new technology. However, this overly risk-averse approach can be justified on neither scientific nor political grounds. It appeases neither anti-biotech activists nor the food industry, both of which have simply used USDA's zero-tolerance policy as an argument for imposing even greater regulation and other strictures on biopharming.

Instead of punishing biopharming to the point of oblivion, we must reject the zero-tolerance mindset and approach safety scientifically and sensibly: We need to establish realistic non-zero tolerances for biopharmed drugs, in the same way we do for the fungal toxins, rodent hair and droppings, and insect parts that commonly contaminate grains—for which regulators have set achievable, non-zero levels at which miniscule amounts of these substances would be harmless and legally tolerated.

Even if biopharmed crops were to be commingled with food crops, how likely is it that anyone would find harmful amounts of prescription drugs in his cornflakes, pasta, or tofu? A combination of factors all militate against such a possibility. In some cases, such as for drugs that are neither orally active nor likely to be allergenic, one might simply conclude that contamination at any level poses negligible risk (not unlike the level of concern about small amounts of pollen from a variety of yellow sweet corn pollinating white sweet corn in a nearby field). An example would be a gene-spliced corn variety altered to produce greater amounts of sugar to facilitate the production of ethanol. Since the purpose of the trait is to be used in the production of an industrial compound, the corn would legally be considered a biopharm product, but its accidental introduction into the food supply would be harmless.

For situations in which risk is uncertain or known not to be negligible, one would base tolerances on animal toxicology studies, as regulators do for pesticide residues. The EPA builds in a safety margin of several orders of magnitude to create a huge safety margin—excessively huge, according to many experts—when they determine the maximum safe dose for humans (as discussed in chapter 4). An analogous approach for biopharmed substances could work just as well, replacing USDA's current design standards with more realistic performance standards—that is, a non–zero tolerance level, below which trace amounts of individual substances would be considered safe.

Fortunately, we already have a prime example of how this can be done with a crop plant variety that produces an industrial substance: rapeseed. As we discussed in chapter 3, rapeseed is a conventional crop plant, and its oil is used not for cooking but as a lubricant. Because of high levels of a chemical called erucic acid that is naturally present in rapeseed, its oil can cause heart disease when ingested. Canadian plant breeders used a number of conventional techniques to develop rapeseed varieties with very low concentrations of erucic acid, and the new plants came to be known as canola (short for Canadian oil). In 1985, the FDA approved canola oil for food use, provided that it contained no more than 2 percent erucic acid—a *performance*, rather than a *design* standard. But since rapeseed oil is still used as a lubricant and plasticizer, farmers and processors must carefully segregate these distinct high- and low-erucic acid crops in the field and thereafter, a task they accomplish routinely, without difficulty, and with minimal government interference.

Although under this system, small quantities of rapeseed occasionally may get mixed into the canola, it is of no consequence as long as the finished product meets the federal safety standard. Although it might be politically unrealistic to expect that people will unquestioningly eat tiny quantities of biopharmed crops the way they regularly consume erucic acid, there is no scientific or medical objection to their doing so.

Even in a worst-case scenario, by the time a food contaminated with a biopharmed substance passes a consumer's lips, it is unlikely to exert a significant effect. Recall that in the ProdiGene case, some 500,000 bushels of ordinary soybeans allegedly came into contact with a very small amount of biopharmed corn stalks and leaves. All the data necessary for a detailed analysis of that situation are not publicly available, but we do know that for personal injury to occur, several highly improbable events would have to happen.

First, the active drug substance would have to be present in the final food product—say, tofu or salad dressing made with soybean oil—at sufficient levels to exert an adverse effect, the result of either direct toxicity or allergy. But there would have been a huge dilution effect, as the tiny amounts of biopharmed corn stalks and leaves were pooled into the massive soybean harvest. With very few exceptions (e.g., peanuts), even an allergic reaction requires more than a minuscule exposure. Second, the active agent would need to survive milling, other processing, and cooking. Third, it would need to be orally active; to take the example of ProdiGene's corn, the synthesized "drug" is not pharmacologically active, except in the sense that it elicits antibodies that are intended to confer immunity to *E. coli*.

The probability that *all* of these events would occur in succession is extremely low. Moreover, it is essential to consider the broader context of the kinds of chemicals that are commonly in our diet. We routinely consume hundreds of thousands of chemicals of all sorts—proteins, fats, carbohydrates, and minerals, among others. Bruce N. Ames and Lois S. Gold at the University of California–Berkeley have estimated that each day "on average, Americans ingest roughly 5,000 to 10,000 different natural pesticides and their breakdown products," as well as about 2,000 milligrams of "burnt material, which is produced in usual cooking practices," and which contains many carcinogens and mutagens.[18]

These observations emphasize the primary principle of toxicology—that the dose makes the poison. Unless we have the misfortune to eat something to which we are highly allergic, a poisonous mushroom, or a poorly dissected puffer fish, the chemicals present in food do not cause acute harm. The possible risks of adding one more chemical moiety to the diet, especially in a minuscule amount, must be considered in that context. Except for extraordinary circumstances (for example, the production via biopharming of a potent toxin), there is no scientific justification for the kind of burdensome oversight that USDA now imposes on biopharmers.

More Flaws Than Just Regulation

The discriminatory regulation by APHIS is the most far-reaching and costly biotech-related abuse by the USDA, but it is not the only one. Another is the National Biotechnology Impact Assessment Program (NBIAP), an expensive boondoggle that holds conferences, publishes newsletters, and makes grants for risk assessment, all focused on the meaningless pseudo-category of gene-spliced organisms. Similarly, there is a large set-aside within USDA's competitive grants program, the Biotechnology Risk Assessment Research Grants Program (BRARGP), for "biotechnology risk assessment."

The 2002 Farm Bill doubled its yearly funding to approximately three million dollars.[19]

These wasteful, superfluous programs exert a corrupting influence on scientific research and public opinion. The use of recombinant DNA techniques does not confer any new or incremental risk, compared to the use of conventional techniques; in fact, as discussed above, their precision makes them more predictable and controllable. Even so, our attention and risk-assessment resources seem driven by an irrational "obsession with transgenics." The existence of a special "pot" of money induces researchers to cast proposals of almost any sort (and often of little scientific merit) as "risk assessment," in order to be eligible for the set-aside. But by focusing assessments solely on gene-spliced organisms rather than on specific traits that may be particularly worrisome, or on a comparison of organisms modified by various methods, the inevitable response of activists and the press to new research findings is to highlight some "newly discovered" risk of gene-splicing.

EPA: NEITHER THE BEST NOR THE BRIGHTEST

Government actions may seem to have an uncertain relationship to everyday life, but occasionally events illuminate the real-world impacts of flawed public policies. In the realm of the EPA's regulation of the new biotechnology—where unwise and unscientific policies have inhibited or prevented the development of all manner of useful products—there is a surfeit of examples that demonstrate the consequences of flawed regulatory policies. They include the unpreparedness for killing frosts in South America that precipitously raised world coffee prices several years ago, and the lack of modern bioremediation techniques following the oil spills from the *Exxon Valdez* in Alaska and the *Prestige* off the coast of Spain—in spite of the potential of the new biotechnology to address such problems. These situations represent opportunities lost to the EPA's wrong-headed policies and flawed decisions.

The Ice-Minus Fiasco

The EPA's role in regulating agricultural biotechnology products began with a major fiasco in the 1980s, and it has gotten no better since then. During the early days of recombinant DNA research, scientists at the University of California and in industry took an ingenious approach to reducing frost damage to crops. (Of all the catastrophes that can befall farmers, frost damage to mature fruit is among the worst, because it destroys the end product after fertilizer, water, labor, gasoline, and other resources already have been invested.) They knew that a harmless bacterium called *Pseudomonas syringae* found on many plants contains an "ice nucleation" protein that actually promotes frost damage to the crop. This occurs in a mechanical way—the protein serves as the initiator of the growth of ice crystals that damage the fruit and leaves of plants, including fruits and vegetables.

In the presence of the bacterium's ice-nucleation protein, ice forms at higher temperatures than it would otherwise. Sometimes, though, the bacteria spontaneously, and naturally, mutate in a way that makes them unable to express the ice-nucleation protein; such bacteria are said to be "ice–minus." The scientists reasoned that intentionally spraying "ice–minus" mutants on plants might occupy all the available space and displace the common "ice-plus" variant, thereby lowering the temperature at which ice crystals would form, and reducing frost damage.

Initial experiments with spontaneous ice-minus variants, however, were plagued by the problem of the bacteria reverting to "wild type"—that is, resuming production of the protein—so gene-splicing techniques seemed an ideal solution. The entire gene that codes for the ice-nucleation protein could be irreversibly removed, rendering the bacterium permanently ice-minus. Some experimental success was achieved with this innovative approach; nonetheless, government regulations were to pose insurmountable barriers.

In one of its earliest decisions about how to regulate the new biotechnology, the EPA astonished the scientific and regulatory communities by classifying as a *pesticide* the obviously innocuous ice-minus variant of the bacterium, which was to be sprayed on small, enclosed test plots of potatoes and strawberries in order to assess its ability to prevent frost damage. The EPA reasoned that the natural ice-plus bacterium is a "pest" because its ice-nucleation protein serves as a point of origin for ice crystal formation, and that a mutant intended to displace it is therefore a pesticide—a convoluted rationale that could lead one to regulate outdoor trash cans as a pesticide because litter is an environmental pest.

This is an unfortunate example of regulators' ulterior motives leading them to torture the intention of a statute in a way that is inappropriate and was never intended. The EPA said that an intensive and comprehensive review of the ice-minus bacterium was necessary because it was the first recombinant DNA–modified organism to be "released to the environment." This was a specious rationale. It ignored the wide consensus that the use of recombinant DNA techniques, per se, does not confer risk. Also, it disregarded the fact that this ice-minus bacterium differed from its wild-type cohorts only by having a gene *deleted*. Because genes are constantly deleted and mutated naturally, the recombinant DNA–mediated genetic construction was functionally no different from what was already found commonly in nature.

Finally, as to the presence of recombinant organisms "in the environment," a study funded by the EPA itself had already confirmed that literally hundreds of millions of recombinant bacteria are released incidentally (and harmlessly) from laboratory "containment" at every standard research laboratory each day.[20] Thus, by the time of the ice-minus field trials, a vast, varied, and unregulated "release experiment" involving thousands of laboratories and millions of discrete new genotypes of recombinant microorganisms had been in progress for a decade, with no untoward effects observed.

There was virtual unanimity among scientists, including scientists within the EPA, about the safety of the test of the ice-minus organism. But just because the organism had been modified with recombinant DNA techniques, the field trial was subjected to an extraordinary, lengthy, and burdensome review. By contrast, research with spontaneous ice-minus mutants had required *no governmental review of any kind*. Even when approval for field testing of the gene-spliced ice-minus bacteria was finally granted, the agency continued its heavy-handed and inappropriate actions by conducting elaborate and unnecessary monitoring of the actual field trials in the guise of performing research on risk.[21]

The first application of the ice-minus bacteria in the field was a media circus and a journalist's dream. Julianne Lindemann, the scientist who sprayed the bacterial solution onto the plants, was attired in a super-high-containment "moon suit" more appropriate for protection against biological warfare. This scene was immortalized on the front page of the *New York Times*, imprinting in readers' minds how seriously regulators took the potential risks of the ice-minus bacteria. The meta-message was unmistakable: *biotech = danger*. But what readers and TV viewers could not see was that news photographers themselves were able to snap shots from just a few feet away in the comfort of their shirtsleeves and sandals, and with no more protective gear than wide-angle lenses. The print and electronic journalists stood around munching breakfast muffins.

Two of the major stated purposes of the EPA's extensive monitoring of the ice-minus trial were to "determine distributions of the [gene-spliced bacteria] on and off the plot during the meteorological conditions encountered during the spray and post-spray periods" and to "provide recommendations for evaluating fate and transport of recombinant organisms for future field releases."[22]

The EPA simply chose to ignore the fact that the data relevant to the first point were already available from field trial data on wild-type and spontaneous mutants of *P. syringae*. But even in the ideal case, the data would only be meaningful for *P. syringae* in the particular environments where the tests were conducted. For example, the data would have no application to soil bacteria or other microorganisms transmitted by animal or insect vectors, so the agency's second stated goal could not, in any case, be accomplished by such an experiment. In the end, the EPA's vast expenditure on monitoring obtained no data of scientific value.

Dr. Steven Lindow, the University of California at Berkeley microbiologist who proposed the experiment, had previously performed field trials with spontaneous mutants of *P. syringae* that were phenotypically identical to the recombinant ice-minus organism—trials that had required no government review, no notification, and no special safety precautions of any kind. Moreover, the data from these field trials were actually submitted as part of the proposal to test the recombinant ice-minus strain. Regulators have been similarly unconcerned about wild-type strains of *P. syringae*, which are now widely used to enhance the production of artificial snow at ski resorts. Without any scientific rationale for it, the use of recombinant DNA techniques was, and continues to be, the EPA's preferred regulatory trigger. This is irreconcilable with both the scientific consensus and the federal government's policy that regulation should be "based on the risk posed by the introduction and *should not turn on the fact that an organism has been modified by a particular process or technique.*"[23]

In spite of the demonstration that the ice-minus bacteria were safe and effective at preventing frost damage, the combination of onerous government regulation and the huge expense of doing the experiments discouraged additional research. The product was never commercialized. As a result, the supply and price of citrus, grapes, peaches, berries, coffee, and other crops remain a hostage to the vagaries of killing frosts.

"Biorational" Pesticides Fall Victim to EPA

The ice-minus fiasco is not an isolated example. At around the same time, the Monsanto Company proposed a small-scale field trial that was scientifically interesting and of potential commercial importance—the control of a corn-eating insect by a harmless soil bacterium, *Pseudomonas fluorescens*, into which scientists had spliced a gene for a protein from another, equally innocuous bacterium. In spite of the unanimous conclusion of the EPA's external scientific advisory panel and other federal agencies (one of us, Henry I. Miller, wrote the FDA's opinion) that there was virtually no likelihood of significant risk in the field trial, the EPA refused to permit it.

Two aspects of this situation are noteworthy. First, the field trial would not have been subject to any government regulation at all had the researchers used an organism with identical characteristics but crafted with less precise "conventional" genetic techniques. Second, Monsanto's response to the rejection was to dismantle its entire research program on microbial biocontrol agents—a program that could have developed biological agents as alternatives to chemical pesticides, an express goal of the EPA and long a desire of environmentalists. Instead, EPA's unscientific, undisciplined policies and decisions have had a chilling effect on the entire sector of biocontrol research and development.

Bioremediation: Another EPA Casualty

Bioremediation, the detoxification of wastes with living organisms, is another casualty of regulatory disincentives. A 1994 report in the journal *Nature* described modest success in cleaning up the beaches fouled by the 1989 *Exxon Valdez* oil spill in Prince William Sound, Alaska.[24] However, the bioremediation techniques that were employed—pouring fertilizer on the beach to stimulate the growth of any bacteria that were there—represent science and technology worthy of the nineteenth century.

Consider the observation of William Reilly, the EPA administrator at the time of the accident: "When I saw the full scale of the disaster in Prince William Sound in Alaska . . . my first thought was: Where are the exotic new technologies, the products of genetic engineering, that can help us clean this up?"[25] Good question—and the answer lay not in the stars but within Mr. Reilly's own dominions.

Innovative products of the new biotechnology for bioremediation remain on the drawing boards, because regulatory barriers and disincentives have intimidated researchers and companies. EPA officials have tried unsuccessfully for more than a decade to issue final regulations for field trials with microorganisms—including those for bioremediation. Invariably, they return to the wrong answer: proposals that discriminate against microorganisms created with recombinant DNA technology while exempting research organisms crafted with any other technique.

During the 1990s, the Clinton administration's Environmental Protection Agency encouraged and promoted expansions of these scientifically indefensible approaches, causing a further deterioration of the quality and integrity of regulatory policy.[26] As a result, recombinant DNA technology applied to bioremediation or to the development of microbial pesticides today is almost nonexistent. Indeed, because regulatory submissions for bioremediation research with recombinant DNA–manipulated microorganisms are overly burdensome and are thrust by regulatory procedures into the public domain, and because of the uncertainty of ultimate marketing approval, the U.S. bioremediation industry has largely restricted itself to research on naturally occurring and conventionally modified organisms. But because of the nature and complexity of the substances involved in most spills and toxic wastes, these organisms are usually inadequate or suboptimal for the job. The new biotechnology would provide additional, powerful tools, but bioremediation represents another sector in which scientific and commercial opportunities have been sacrificed to regulators' unwisdom.

Plant-Incorporated Protectants

Under the pesticide statute, FIFRA, the EPA has long regulated field tests (on areas greater than ten acres) and the commercial use of pesticides, as well as substances that act as plant regulators, defoliants, dessicants, and nitrogen stabilizers.[27] In 1994, the EPA proposed a rule for the regulation of gene-spliced plants that mediate "host plant resistance" to pests. Under this proposal, gene-spliced plants with new or enhanced pest-resistance traits would have been brought under the jurisdiction of FIFRA by regulating them as "plant pesticides"—but only if the traits in question were introduced with recombinant DNA techniques.[28] It was widely criticized by scientific bodies and individual scientists, sending EPA back to the proverbial drawing board.

But the EPA mindset is reminiscent of the way that one critic characterized King Charles II of France—"He never learned anything, and never forgot anything." In spite of mounting criticism from the scientific community, the EPA kept pushing the rule, with only the most cosmetic of changes. When the final regulation was published, seven years after it was first proposed, the agency had changed the term "pesticide" to "plant-incorporated protectant" (PIP), but had left the substance of the original proposal essentially intact.

PIPs are defined in a way that places them within the FIFRA definition of a pesticide—namely, substances intended to prevent, repel, or mitigate any pest. Again, though, this regulatory jurisdiction applies only if the "protectants" have been introduced or enhanced by recombinant DNA technology. The submission required for EPA's regulatory review of gene-spliced plants includes copious data on the parental plant, the genetic construction and behavior of the test plant, and so on.

It is noteworthy that EPA denies that it regulates the plants themselves, remonstrating that it is the newly introduced DNA and the PIPs that are subject to regulation. This sophistry is tantamount to saying that automobile emissions-control testing facilities regulate not cars but only their engine emissions.

Plants modified with any of the less precise, less predictable techniques of "conventional breeding" are expressly exempted from oversight under the EPA's biotech regulations. During the course of research and development on a gene-spliced plant variety that contains a PIP, however, the agency conducts repeated, redundant case-by-case reviews—before the initial trial, again when trials are scaled up to larger size or to additional sites (and even if minor changes are made in the genetic construct), and again at commercial scale.

Plant varieties have long been selected by nature and bred by humans for improved resistance or tolerance to external threats to their survival and productivity. These threats include insects, disease organisms, herbicides, and environmental stresses. All plants contain resistance traits, or they would not survive. Thus, regulators are focusing no ton the presence or absence of pesticidal properties but on their origin. In any event, there is no evidence to suggest that the origin of a pest resistance trait has any correlation with risk to the environment.

Like USDA's "regulated article," the concept of a "plant incorporated protectant" may be inventive, but it flies in the face of the prior experience with plant breeding, and it conflicts with the risk-based mandate of federal statutes. These contrived definitions ignore that genetic modification is a continuum, from relatively imprecise—but largely unregulated—traditional practices such as hybridization, intensive mutagenesis, and somaclonal variation to more precise and predictable—but intensively regulated—recombinant DNA techniques.

Likewise, these regulatory concepts fail to take into consideration the extraordinary overall safety record of genetic modification of plants, animals, and microorganisms in agriculture, whatever the techniques used. As we have noted previously, such genetic improvement of organisms has been carried out for millennia. During the past quarter-century, tens of thousands of field trials of recombinant DNA–modified plants have been performed worldwide, and more than a hundred million acres are planted with commercial recombinant DNA–modified crops annually.[29] Not once has a gene-spliced crop plant caused any demonstrable harm to human health or the natural environment, and the results of risk-assessment experiments have been uniformly reassuring.[30] Nevertheless, EPA officials, offered cover by the scare stories peddled by anti-biotechnology activists, and by occasional inconsequential transgressions of regulations, have adhered assiduously to policies marked by nonscience and nonsense.

A Science-Challenged Agency

No one should be surprised by the EPA's execrable judgements about the new biotechnology. The agency has a lengthy history of policy formulation that flouts sound science. In the 1980s, in response to a widespread media campaign waged primarily by the Natural Resources Defense Council, the EPA pressured apple growers to abandon the use of the plant growth regulator Alar™, an agricultural chemical that permits apples to ripen uniformly and consequently increases yield.

The EPA's capitulation to environmentalists' demands conflicted with the agency's own scientific findings. But faced with a public relations barrage against Alar™, EPA assistant administrator John Moore issued a statement asserting that "there is inescapable and direct correlation" between exposure to UDMH (the primary degradation product of Alar™) and "the development of life threatening tumors," and that therefore the EPA would soon propose banning Alar™.[31] Even though the EPA admitted separately that there was no data to support a finding of carcinogenicity, Moore "urged" farmers who were using Alar™ to stop.[32] Coming from a senior federal regulator, that is akin to an armed mugger "urging" the victim to relinquish his wallet.

There was more than one rotten apple in the EPA barrel. During the Alar™ episode, one of Moore's senior subordinates, lawyer Steven Schatzow, attempted to intimidate the members of an advisory panel because their opinion differed from his own:

> Apparently, the EPA officials had expected the [Scientific Advisory Panel] to rubber-stamp its decision [that Alar or UDMH was a carcinogen]. When it did not, Uniroyal [the manufacturer of Alar] officials were jubilant. But after the meeting, Steven Schatzow, then director of EPA's Office of Pesticide Programs, herded SAP members into his office. The angry Schatzow demanded, "How can you do this to us?" After a heated exchange with the scientists, he concluded, "Look, I can't tell you what to do, but you might like to think about this one again." The scientists were stunned by such flagrant interference, and all refused to back down.[33]

The EPA's lack of integrity and defiance of science has long been criticized by eminent extramural scientific groups. An expert panel commissioned by then–EPA administrator William Reilly reported in 1992 that "the science advice function—that is, the process of ensuring that policy decisions are informed by a clear understanding of the relevant science—is not well defined or coherently organized within EPA." It continued, "In many cases, appropriate science advice and information are not considered early or often enough in the decision making process." Further, while "EPA should be a source of unbiased scientific information[,] . . . EPA has not always ensured that contrasting, reputable scientific views are well-explored and well-documented." Most damning of all, the expert panel concluded that "EPA science is perceived by many people, both inside and outside the Agency, to be adjusted to fit policy. Such 'adjustments' could be made consciously or unconsciously by the scientist or the decision-maker."[34]

The panel was charitable. Generation after generation of EPA officials seem to be incapable of performing comparative risk assessment. They are relentlessly political, ideological, and self-serving. Any overlap of regulators' self-interest and the public interest appears to be purely coincidental.

Abuse of Scientific Advisors

The EPA's shortcoming are intimately related to the manner in which the agency handles its extramural advisory process. Not infrequently, on policy issues related to the new biotechnology, the EPA directs scientific advisory panels toward a predetermined conclusion. When scientists on those panels offer independent perspectives, federal officials are enraged. For example, during the administration of President George H. W. Bush, when University of California microbiologist Dennis Focht, an academic member of the EPA's Biotechnology Science Advisory Committee, observed in a letter to the committee's chairman that a policy decision to regulate on the basis of genetic technique rather than according to risk had been based on nonscientific considerations, he was subjected to a written rebuke from EPA assistant administrator Linda Fisher.[35] A lawyer, Fisher chided this distinguished scientist on his inability to "provide the Agency with [an] unbiased assessment of the scientific issues at hand" and, in effect, invited him to resign from the committee.[36] This unseemly treatment of a scientific advisor is not an isolated occurrence, and it is disturbingly similar to the Alar™ incident described above.

Incidents like these subvert the ability and willingness of scientists to contribute fully to public policy decisions. Thereby, they undermine the public interest. However, in accord with the Washington, D.C., tradition that no bad deed goes unrewarded, in the second Bush administration Linda Fisher was appointed to the number-two job at the EPA, deputy administrator. (She resigned in July 2003.)

The Focht example is a situation in which an extramural advisor, an eminent academic scientist, was genuinely committed to providing rigorous, objective, and apolitical advice to federal regulators. This is the usual case at agencies like the National Institutes of Health and the FDA, where although advisory committee members often are NIH grantees (and NIH and FDA are sister agencies, located within the Department of Health and Human Services), that is not considered to constitute a conflict of interest. Advisors to NIH and FDA are usually asked to apply narrow scientific expertise to review and rank grant applications, express opinions about research areas ripe for additional funding, or evaluate the results of clinical trials. In these cases, the federal agency involved does not itself have a large vested interest in any particular decision by its extramural committees.

However, a different and perverse situation frequently prevails at the EPA. Instead of narrow scientific questions, the biotechnology-related committees are often asked for opinions on *policy* issues—for example, what should be the scope of agency regulation. More to the point, they are often asked, in effect, to rubber-stamp a course of action that will manifestly benefit the EPA. As discussed above, the EPA consistently has chosen policy directions that serve bureaucratic ends (such as larger budgets and regulatory empires) but that disadvantage academic and most industry research.

This places extramural advisors in a position that is at the least uncomfortable and at worst frankly conflicted. It is noteworthy that at the time the EPA was proposing and its advisory committees were recommending such scientifically indefensible and regressive policies as those described above, some members of EPA's Biotechnology Science Advisory Committee were receiving substantial agency funding. It should not be a source of solace to those who favor honest, effective government to learn that the EPA's "science and technology" budget is now on the order of a billion dollars a year.

Washington Infighting

In addition to manipulating advisory committees in order to obtain concurrence with flawed policies, EPA staff members indulge in chicanery in day-to-day interactions with Congress, other agencies, governments, and international organizations. This includes intriguing with congressional staffers, leaking confidential government documents to "green" nongovernmental organizations, divulging U.S. negotiating strategies to foreign governments, and falsifying the "reporting cables" required by the State Department to summarize international conferences.[37] The EPA of the past two decades seems to fit the definition of a rogue agency.

In an effort to elevate the EPA's scientific profile, in 1989 the agency brought on board as the senior science advisor Dr. William Raub, a former NIH deputy director. Raub was known to be a smart, savvy, and collegial scientific administrator. The EPA staff proceeded to make his life miserable. From the beginning, they ignored him when they could. When they couldn't, they sent him drafts of important documents too late for a meaningful review—often just days before a court-ordered deadline for an agency action.[38] EPA Administrator Carol Browner excluded Raub from her inner circle and finally replaced him with a less-threatening, lower-level EPA staffer.[39]

The EPA's policies and practices are collectively an affront to good government and a major obstacle to the progress of the new biotechnology. Regulatory disincentives, increasingly enshrined in final regulations, will continue to deter researchers and companies from biological control strategies that could substitute safer recombinant DNA–modified microorganisms and plants for chemical pesticides. Innovations that may not provide sufficient financial return to offset the huge costs of testing and registration are especially vulnerable.[40] By limiting available technological choices, the EPA's regulatory philosophy and policies damage, rather than protect, both agricultural research and the natural environment.

(MODEST) KUDOS TO THE FDA

The FDA regulates several kinds of products under mandates of the Federal Food, Drug and Cosmetic Act (FFDCA) and the Public Health Service Act. Its oversight of human drugs and biologicals, veterinary drugs, and diagnostic tests is beyond the scope of this volume, which focuses primarily on agricultural applications of the new biotechnology.

Under the FFDCA, the FDA has responsibility to ensure the safety of all foods in interstate commerce, except meat and poultry products, which are the USDA's responsibility. The FDA has broad authority to regulate all foods that are derived from new food crops and other organisms, whether obtained through conventional breeding, hybridization, mutation breeding, or other techniques, such as recombinant DNA. In all cases, the law places the burden of ensuring the safety of foods and food ingredients on those who produce them. The FFDCA prohibits the adulteration (contamination) or misbranding (mislabeling) of food, but the agency does not inspect food prior to its sale in shops, supermarkets, or restaurants.[41] Rather, federal oversight relies on market surveillance, or postmarketing regulation. Ultimately, the onus of ensuring safety is on the producer or seller, and FDA takes action only if there is an apparent problem. With very few exceptions, this approach has worked quite well over the years.

The act does require a premarketing review for certain food-related products. Most *food additives*—a class of ingredients that includes preservatives, emulsifiers, spices and sweeteners, and natural and synthetic flavors or colors, among many others—must be approved by the FDA before they are marketed.[42] In general, a food additive must be approved by the agency if it becomes a component of or otherwise affects the characteristics of a food and is "not generally recognized as safe (GRAS) by qualified experts for its intended use."[43] When introducing a new food additive onto the market, the producer is responsible for determining whether or not the substance is GRAS. The agency only routinely reviews food additive applications for safety when the substance in question has been determined not to be GRAS by the producer. If the producer determines that a substance is GRAS, only a notification of that decision to the FDA is necessary (which is then subject to agency review).

A RISK-BASED POLICY

Where does all this leave the new biotechnology—that is, gene-spliced plants, microorganisms and other organisms, and foods derived from them? As early as 1980, the FDA agreed with the prevailing scientific consensus and affirmed that only factors actually related to risk would drive its biotechnology regulation. The agency steadfastly resisted activists' demands that biotechnology foods and drugs be more stringently regulated simply because they were perceived by some as "different." In particular, the FDA rejected demands that foods obtained from recombinant organisms actually undergo clinical trials similar to those required for drugs, and that labeling identify biotech-derived foods or ingredients. In 1992, the FDA published its official policy regarding foods derived from "new plant varieties."[44] This announcement, intended to clarify the FDA's position on the regulation of recombinant DNA technology and gene-spliced plants, explained that the "regulatory status of a food, irrespective of the method by which it is developed, is dependent upon objective characteristics of the food and the intended use."

The policy reiterated that plant breeders and food producers have "an obligation under the Act to ensure that the foods they offer to consumers are safe and in compliance with applicable legal requirements." It treated gene-spliced and other foods no differently, and it required case-by-case review by regulators only when the products raised specific safety concerns. Thus, the agency's approach was consistent with the consensus of the scientific community regarding the regulation of gene-spliced products, with the federal government's policy on "scope," discussed above, and with its own policies regarding other foods and ingredients. This approach was widely applauded as regulation that made sense, relied on scientific principles, protected consumers, and did not unnecessarily inhibit innovation.

To guide developers of new plants on how to satisfy regulatory requirements, the FDA policy defined certain potentially hazardous characteristics of new foods that, if present, would require greater scrutiny by the agency and could result in additional testing and labeling or, in extreme cases, exclusion from commerce. In other words, characteristics related to risk—not simply the use of one technique or another—would trigger heightened regulatory scrutiny. According to the FDA's 1992 policy, such characteristics include the introduction of genes that code for proteins, or that mediate the synthesis of other substances such as fatty acids and carbohydrates, if any of these substances differ substantially in structure or function from those typically found in the food supply. Heightened scrutiny by regulators would also be required if the genetic change altered a micro- or macronutrient (such as a new variety of citrus lacking or with a significantly lower amount of vitamin C), caused an allergen to be present in a milieu in which a consumer would not expect it (a peanut allergen in a potato, for example), or enhanced levels of a natural toxicant or antinutrient.[45]

The Carrot and Stick Approach

Thus, the FDA's official 1992 policy codified a genuinely risk-based approach to the oversight of new plant varieties. However, at the same time, and without the benefit of rule making or formal notification to industry, the agency created a "voluntary consultation procedure," in which the producers of gene-spliced plants were expected to consult with the agency before marketing their products.[46] Without exception they did so, because of the existence of two factors that might be thought of as, respectively, a carrot and stick.

The carrot is the fact that for marketing purposes, the biotechnology and food industries have long sought a kind of "FDA Seal of Approval" that would come from a formal review of new gene-spliced products. Although the FDA has not yet succumbed to pressure to institute a mandatory review of each new biotech food, the consultation procedure has served—for better or worse—as a proxy for such a governmental endorsement.

The stick is the considerable discretionary authority the FDA maintains over companies whose products it regulates. That discretion and the agency's reputation for vindictiveness have discouraged companies from ignoring or challenging the FDA's de facto requirement that they participate in the "voluntary" consultation process. Currently, thousands of food products in U.S. supermarkets contain gene-spliced whole foods or ingredients that have been regulated jointly under the FDA's formal 1992 policy and the consultation procedure. None has ever been shown to cause any harm at all to human health.

The effectiveness of the 1992 FDA policy was tested in a way that in scientific terms would be considered a "positive control"—a challenge by a known hazard. Allergenicity common to Brazil nut proteins had been transferred into gene-spliced soybeans by researchers hoping to add an essential amino acid that would make soybeans more nutritious, and the allergen was readily identified by routine procedures.[47] The plant breeder, Pioneer Hi-Bred International, consulted with the FDA during product development, and during the course of consultation and subsequent analysis, the allergenicity was identified. Confronted with the dual prospects of potential product liability and the costs of labeling all products derived from the new plant variety, Pioneer abandoned all plans for using the new soybeans. In a small way, this episode validates the FDA's 1992 risk-based policy. Not a single consumer was exposed to or injured by the newly allergenic soybeans (which, in any case, were intended only for animal feed).

The approach described in the FDA's policy statement is consistent with scientific consensus—namely, that the risks associated with new-biotechnology-derived products are fundamentally the same as for other products—and reflects the fact that dozens of new plant varieties modified with traditional genetic techniques, such as hybridization and mutation breeding, enter the marketplace every year without premarket regulatory review or special labeling. Many of these products are from (pre-gene-splicing) wide crosses, in which genes have been moved across natural breeding barriers.

None of these plants derived from wide crosses exists in nature. None requires or gets a premarket review by a government agency. Safety tests by plant breeders consist primarily of assessments of taste and appearance and, in the case of plants with high levels of known intrinsic toxicants (such as tomatoes and potatoes), the measurement of levels of certain alkaloids. Nonetheless, plants from mutation breeding and wide crosses have become an integral, familiar, and safe part of our diet. These include wheat, rice, oats, squash, tomatoes, potatoes, and others that are consumed daily by hundreds of millions of Americans.

Occasionally, the imprecise, trial-and-error nature of conventional plant breeding techniques leads to unforeseen and harmful outcomes. Two conventionally bred varieties each of squash and potato and one of celery were found to have dangerous levels of endogenous toxins and were barred from the marketplace. Nevertheless, standard assessment methods for new plant varieties generally have been sufficient to allow for the identification of genuinely harmful products, and it is in the best interests of plant breeders and food companies to do what they can to keep the food supply safe. Furthermore, as we have observed repeatedly throughout this volume, recombinant

DNA techniques, by virtue of their increased precision and predictability, provide an extra margin of safety to the field-testing of organisms and the foods derived from them.

In January 2001, however, with support from the food and biotechnology industries, the FDA proposed to make the voluntary consultation procedure mandatory[48]—a prototypic example of fixing something that wasn't broken. Fortunately, in 2003, the FDA dropped the proposal from the formal regulatory agenda that it submits biannually to the federal Office of Management and Budget. This positive development creates a little-appreciated schism between the official policies of the FDA on one hand (which operate under the risk-based, scientifically defensible 1992 approach) and the process-driven, unscientific policies of the USDA and EPA. Unfortunately, it would be quite easy for a future presidential administration, under pressure from activist groups or the packaged food industry, to revive the proposal for mandatory FDA review.

A Label We Don't Need

Although the FDA has wavered on the need for premarket review of gene-spliced foods, the agency continues to oppose their mandatory labeling. As part of their campaigns to stigmatize biotech foods and artificially inflate their production and distribution costs, activists have demanded labeling that would identify foods that contain ingredients made with the techniques of the new biotechnology. The ostensible rationale—to let consumers know what's in their breakfast cereal and let them choose whether or not they want it—sounds reasonable, even libertarian. But a closer look reveals that mandatory biotech labeling would not offer consumers any relevant information and would actually restrict, not promote, consumer choice.

Advocates of labeling point to public opinion surveys in which majorities of respondents agree that labeling would be a good idea.[49] However, those same surveys also show that large majorities of respondents admit to knowing little or nothing about biotechnology and gene-splicing techniques (as discussed in chapter 3).[50] When one adds to the mix the fact that few consumers have any inkling that virtually all of the meats, grains, fruits, and vegetables in their diets are derived from organisms that have been genetically improved in some way, it is difficult to credit activists' claims about public opinion.

In one typical survey, for example, 70 percent of respondents agreed that "the words "genetically engineered" should appear on the label of a food product where one or more ingredients were genetically engineered." However, 25 percent of respondents admitted that they were "not at all familiar" with genetically engineered foods, 30 percent said "not very familiar," 38 percent said "somewhat familiar," and only 5 percent said they were "extremely familiar." What are we to make of largely uninformed opinions about complex public policy issues?

In that same survey, in which 70 percent of respondents said they favored labeling of biotech foods, 40 percent agreed that foods "made from cross-bred corn" should be labeled.[51] But virtually *all* the corn grown in the United States is from crossbred, or hybrid, varieties (including every gene-spliced variety, the "parent" of which was a hybrid). Labeling in this case would, therefore, convey no useful information and would make absolutely no sense. It would be tantamount to labels on bottled water to inform consumers that the products contain hydrogen and oxygen. In any case, we wonder how many of the respondents who say they support biotechnology labeling have any knowledge of the FDA's existing policies for food labeling in general, or biotech foods in particular.

Since the first biotech-derived food products were marketed, the FDA has only required specific labeling of new foods the composition of which differs "significantly" from their conventional counterparts. Such differences would need to be risk-related factors, such as the presence of a substance that is completely new to the food supply, an allergen presented in an unusual or unexpected way, changes in the levels of major dietary nutrients, increased levels of toxins normally found in foods, or a change in the expected storage or preparation characteristics of the food.

To date, the only biotech-derived food products that would have to bear such a label are cooking oils from certain varieties of soybeans and canola, modified specifically to alter their fatty acid composition to make them healthier. But there is no requirement to disclose the use of particular techniques to make food or food ingredients, such as a "product of biotechnology" or "genetically engineered" label for foods from plants or animals that have been improved with recombinant DNA techniques. The labels on these products need only specify what "material" changes have been made. This risk-based labeling requirement applies to all foods, whether they have been developed through conventional breeding methods or the more advanced gene-splicing techniques.[52] Thus, this policy is consistent with the scientific consensus that plants developed with the new biotechnology do not pose inherently greater risk than those developed with conventional techniques, and that regulation (including requirements for labeling) should be based on the specific characteristics of the products that could make them more or less safe, not how they were created. Consequently, the FDA's biotech labeling policy has been endorsed by such scientific organizations as the American Medical Association[53] and the Institute of Food Technologists.[54]

Contrary to the claims of activists and the results of spurious polls, most consumers find the FDA's current policy satisfactory once they learn what it is. In a series of surveys commissioned by the International Food Information Council (IFIC) and conducted by a professional market research firm, respondents were read a summary of the FDA's policy on labeling and asked if they supported or opposed it. In each of nine surveys from 1997 to 2004, a majority of respondents agreed with the FDA policy.[55] Because respondents were given a summary understanding of the agency's current policy *before* they were asked to comment on it, the results of the IFIC surveys are far more credible than surveys of otherwise uninformed members of the public. Given the limited level of background knowledge upon which the results of other research on public attitudes is based, there is no persuasive evidence that the public genuinely supports mandatory labeling.

The FDA's policy is also consistent with the Federal Food, Drug and Cosmetic Act, which requires that food labels be truthful and not misleading. Federal law prohibits label statements that are likely to be misunderstood by consumers, even if they are, strictly speaking, accurate. For example, although a "cholesterol-free" label on a certain variety or batch of fresh broccoli is accurate, it could run afoul of the FDA's rules because it could be interpreted as implying that broccoli usually does contain cholesterol, when in fact it does not.[56]

In an analogous way, instead of educating or serving a legitimate consumers' "right to know" certain information, mandatory labels on biotech foods would imply a warning about some important but unspecified difference. One legitimate concern about mandatory labeling of all gene-spliced foods is that the presence of a label would be misconstrued by some consumers as suggesting that biotech-derived foods differ in an important way (such as safety or nutrition) when they do not.[57] The FDA's current approach toward labeling, which has been dubbed "*need* to know"—as opposed to the European Union's view that consumers have a "*right* to know"—has been upheld both directly and indirectly by two different federal court decisions.

Is There a Consumers' "Right to Know"?

In the early 1990s, a group of Wisconsin consumers sued the FDA, arguing that the agency's decision not to require the labeling of dairy products from cows treated with gene-spliced, or recombinant, bovine growth hormone (bGH, also known as bovine somatotropin, or bST) allowed those products to be labeled in a false and misleading manner. In the case, *Stauber v. Shalala*, the plaintiffs failed to demonstrate any material difference between milk from treated and untreated cows. The federal District Court for the Western District of Wisconsin ruled that because the dairy products in question did not differ in a significant way, "it would be misbranding to label the product[s] as different, even if consumers misperceived the product[s] as different."[58] Thus, the logic of the law trumps the illogic of public opinion.

In the second case, which is sort of a mirror image of the first, several food industry associations and firms challenged a Vermont statute that required labeling to identify milk from cows treated with the gene-spliced bovine growth hormone. In *International Dairy Foods Association et al. v. Amestoy*,[59] the U.S. Second Circuit Court of Appeals ruled that a labeling mandate grounded in consumer perception, rather than in a product's measurable characteristics, raises serious constitutional concerns. The court held that food labeling cannot be mandated simply because some people would like to have the information, and rules both the labeling statute and companion regulations unconstitutional because they forced producers to make involuntary statements contrary to their views when there was no material reason to do so. "The right not to speak inheres in political and commercial speech alike . . . and extends to statements of fact as well as statements of opinion." Because the state of Vermont could not demonstrate that its interest represented anything more than satisfying consumer curiosity, it could not compel milk producers to include that information on product labels. In the words of the court:

> We are aware of no case in which consumer interest alone was sufficient to justify requiring a product's manufacturers to publish the functional equivalent of a warning about a production method that has no discernable impact on a final product. . . . Absent some indication that this information bears on a reasonable concern for human health or safety or some other sufficiently substantial governmental concern, the manufacturers cannot be compelled to disclose it.[60]

In other words, there exists no consumer "right to know" obscure information about food. "Were consumer interest alone sufficient," said the court, "there is no end to the information that states could require manufacturers to disclose about their production methods." Illustrating the court's concern, some California activists have demanded labels to identify machine-harvested—as opposed to handpicked—tomatoes. Where will it end? In order to be constitutional, labeling mandates must be narrowly tailored to provide information that serves a genuine and identifiable governmental or consumer need.

Another aspect of the labeling controversy is the unfavorable asymmetry encountered by those who might wish to develop or sell gene-spliced foods, as well as the impact that mandatory labeling can have on consumer choices. As General Mills' Senior Vice President Austin Sullivan observed, "With no manufacturing or consumer benefit to offer and only downside risk of adverse consumer behavior, mandatory labeling would lead manufacturers to ask their suppliers for non-bioengineered ingredients only."[61] Although we would argue that lower production costs and the many important environmental benefits of gene-spliced crops do benefit consumers, the fact that these attributes are not immediately obvious to most consumers validates Sullivan's point.

The European experience reinforces that view. The United Kingdom's mandatory-labeling law, touted by a senior regulator at its inception several years ago as "a question of choice," has had the opposite effect. It sparked a stampede by food producers, retailers, and restaurant chains to rid their products of all biotech ingredients so they wouldn't have to introduce new "warning" labels and risk the debacle of Greenpeace and other NGOs picketing, vandalizing, and making inflammatory, false accusations.

Economic Terrorism

University of California at Riverside Professor Alan McHughen calls this distortion of market forces "economic terrorism," in that the "the terrified food industry is responding to threats of shakedown by the NGOs," not to consumers' concerns or preferences.[62] He notes that gene-spliced tomato paste brightly labeled to the effect that "GM techniques" had been used in its production was successfully marketed in the United Kingdom during the 1990s. These affirmatively labeled (and less expensive) cans of processed paste from the Zeneca company's gene-spliced tomato variety sold well in British grocery stores—until retailers were hounded by anti-technology activists to remove biotech foods from store shelves.[63] And labeled cooking oils from gene-spliced oilseeds continue to sell well even in such European countries as France, where anti-biotechnology sentiments are at their greatest.[64]

This supports McHughen's contention that "surveys show consistently that consumers generally are unconcerned, and that [only] a relatively small proportion of consumers would refuse to buy" gene-spliced foods.[65] In the few cases where labeled gene-spliced foods are available in European stores, most shoppers do not in fact seem to be turned off by them.[66]

In the face of this consumer indifference, activists have adopted a two-pronged strategy—trying to coerce food processors into rejecting the new biotech and inducing government agencies to over-regulate. Mandatory labeling to identify biotech foods and ingredients is an important element of these efforts, because once foods containing gene-spliced ingredients are identifiable, activists can demonize them and terrorize their producers, distributors, and retailers.

This strategy has worked, even in the absence of compulsory labeling. Two of the largest U.S. producers of baby food, Heinz and Gerber, responding to intimidation by activists, announced in 1999 that they would use only non-gene-spliced materials for their products—even if these were nutritionally inferior to or less safe than those made from gene-spliced plants.[67] In other words, they decided to boycott grain from plants modified to reduce the need to spray with chemical insecticides, and soybeans modified in ways that make high-quality soy protein cheaper to obtain.

The companies' rejection of a superior technology solely because of the demands of a few activists has important implications. Consider, for example,

"Bt corn," which was crafted by splicing into commercial corn varieties a gene from the bacterium *Bacillus thuringiensis*, that codes for a protein that is toxic to corn borer pests. As it fends off the insect pests, the gene-spliced corn also reduces the levels of Fusarium, a toxic fungus often carried into the plants by the insects. Lowering the amounts of Fusarium, in turn, reduces the levels of fumonisin, a potent fungal toxin that can lead to fatal diseases in horses and swine that ingest infected corn, and can cause esophageal cancer and other maladies in humans. Thus, using the gene-spliced corn for food processing lowers the levels of fumonisin—and also the concentration of insect parts—found in the final product.

But merely because anti-biotechnology extremists have demanded it, companies like Heinz and Gerber have chosen to forgo such genetically improved sources of foods that could yield healthier and safer products. Worse still, Gerber has announced that it will shift to organic corn, which is especially prone to insect, fungal, and bacterial infestations and—because raising corn without insecticide and other chemicals is labor-intensive and lowers per-acre yields—will be far more costly. The organic corn will also likely have greater amounts of fumonisin, insect parts, and bacterial contamination.

Is that what purchasers of baby food expect? Is that kind of decision making consistent with the rhetoric of Al Piergallini, president and chief executive officer of Novartis Corporation's U.S. consumer health operations, of which Gerber is a part: "I have got to listen to my customers. So, if there is an issue, or even an inkling of an issue, I am going to make amends."[68]

This is an industry that understands and uses advertising aggressively— an industry that could outspend activists a thousand to one, in order to explain and defend a policy of using the best ingredients and state-of-the-art technologies to guarantee a top quality product. Therefore, we don't call Gerber's decision to reject a superior, safer technology "making amends"; we call it cowardly capitulation. We call it selling out, in one fell swoop, the interests of the company, its commitment to making a superior product, and its customers. If this trend continues, farmers and food producers eventually will find that although biotech foods and ingredients may be superior, there's no market for them.

More Effects of Compulsory Labeling

Compulsory labeling of biotech foods would enable activists to apply even greater pressure on retailers and end users (like baby-food producers) to reject gene-spliced ingredients in their products. But there are other, more compelling reasons why it is a pernicious idea. First, it implies risks for which there is no evidence. Second, it flies in the face of worldwide scientific consensus about the appropriate basis of regulation—namely, that oversight should focus on palpable risks, not the use of certain techniques. Third, the requirement constitutes, in effect, a punitive tax on a superior technology.

Fourth, such gratuitous and difficult to meet requirements can create legal liability for everyone in the production and distribution pathway, in the event of inconsequential noncompliance (as discussed in the next chapter). Finally, because mandatory labeling implies the need to segregate conventional and gene-spliced foods, it will raise the costs of all foods.

Although it might seem that labeling would not be very costly, the costs would actually be quite high—far more than simply a one-time expense to analyze the product and prepare new labels, as was the case for the now-ubiquitous nutrition labels on food that provide information on calories, amounts of protein, fat, carbohydrates, and so forth. In order to ensure the accuracy of the labeling and guarantee compliance, elaborate systems of segregating biotech-derived foods from conventional foods in all stages of production (including seed development, planting, harvesting, distribution, processing, and packaging) would be necessary. Much of the cost involved in labeling biotech-derived foods arises from the fact that most biotech and nonbiotech products are indistinguishable from one another, unless and until one applies state-of-the-art analytical techniques. This is true even for most freshly harvested foods, because the new traits are seldom obvious from visual inspection. Segregation becomes even more difficult for processed food products like cooking oils, sugars and other sweeteners, and cheeses and fermented beverages, because the processing tends to break down the proteins and DNA strands that are the only evidence that they originated from gene-spliced DNA. For example, the oils from conventional soybeans, organic soybeans, and gene-spliced soybeans often are totally indistinguishable from one another.

Consequently, to ensure accuracy in labeling, an elaborate system of separation and record keeping would have to be imposed so that every single ingredient or additive in every food product could be traced through every step of the food chain—from breeder to farmer, to shipper, to processor, and to retailer—as was recently mandated in the EU (see chapter 8). Such segregation and "traceability" require extensive DNA and protein testing at each step of the food production process, the creation of a superfluous duplicate network of grain elevators, processing mills, and storage facilities, as well as exhaustive record keeping. New methods of third-party verification (government or private sector) could also be required.

The considerable cost for each of these services will have to be borne by both food producers who use gene-spliced ingredients and those who do not; producers of *nonbiotech* foods would not be immune, and would likely have to bear costs equal to producers willing to accept gene-spliced ingredients, because every ingredient would need to be tested for "purity" at each step of the production process. Under various labeling proposals the failure to label accurately a product that contains gene-spliced ingredients would result in criminal penalties (to say nothing of civil liability, discussed in the next chapter), so producers who do not use biotech-derived ingredients would have to ensure that none is accidentally introduced into their own supply chains.

In a study commissioned by the University of Guelph in Ontario, Canada, KPMG Consulting estimated that a proposed Canadian labeling mandate, which was far less strict than the current European labeling and traceability rule, would raise the cost of producing, handling, shipping, and processing gene-spliced commodity grains between 35 and 41 percent (the estimated cost increase to farmers alone would be approximately 14 percent). Because the cost of such grains accounts for about one-fourth of the total costs associated with making the average processed-food product, the study further calculated that a labeling mandate would be expected to raise the retail price of processed foods by at least 9 to 10 percent.[69] That estimate is based on the limited number of gene-spliced crops now commercially available. If additional gene-spliced species (such as wheat, rice, and other major staples) were to be marketed, those cost estimates could soar.

Similarly high cost estimates were found in another KPMG study commissioned by the Australia/New Zealand Food Authority,[70] and in an econometric literature survey conducted by researchers in the European Union's Directorate General for Agriculture.[71] A 1994 analysis by the California Department of Consumer Affairs (CDCA), a state watchdog agency, predicted that although "the American food processing industry is large, it is unlikely to be either willing or able to absorb most of the additional costs associated with labeling biotech foods."[72] The analysis concluded that "there is cause for concern that consumers will be unwilling to pay even the increased price for biotech foods necessary to cover biotechnology research and development, much less the additional price increases necessary to cover the costs associated with labeling biotech food."

It is worth reiterating that all of these ill effects derive from the gratuitous overregulation of a superior technology, and that conformance to these requirements and the expense of complying with them confers no gain in either public health or environmental safety. Moreover, because overregulation (including labeling requirements) leads to less competition in the marketplace—which keeps prices high—the CDCA assessment implies another outcome of unwarranted but compulsory labeling. Overregulated, and therefore overpriced, biotech products will tend to become limited to upscale, higher-income markets. Wealthier consumers will be able to pay more for the improved products, while the less affluent will simply do without them. That prospect should serve as food for thought, given that low-income consumers could otherwise benefit most from the nutritionally improved gene-spliced foods that are nearing commercialization.

To serve the consumer best, mandates concerning labeling should focus on genuine risks and require information about a food's origin or use only when it is relevant to safety and promotes informed choice. Mandatory labeling of all biotech foods would achieve none of this. If enough people really want to avoid gene-spliced foods, niche markets will arise, as they have for kosher, halal, and organic products. Assuming that consumers are willing to pay a premium for foods certified to be "gene-splicing free," as they would in any case under a mandatory labeling system, no government mandate for labeling is needed.

THE RIPPLE EFFECTS OF BAD PUBLIC POLICY

Throughout most of the world, gene-spliced crop plants, such as herbicide-tolerant soybean and canola, and insect-resistant corn and cotton, are subject to lengthy, hugely expensive mandatory testing and premarket evaluation, while plants with similar properties but developed with older, less precise genetic techniques are exempt from such requirements. This sort of anomaly is irreconcilable.

Regulators' inconsistent, illogical approach to the introduction of new plant varieties violates both a basic principle of regulation—that the degree of oversight should be commensurate with risk—and the legal dictum that similar situations should be treated in similar ways. Likewise, it defies common sense, in that regulators have adopted an approach in which there is *inverse* proportionality between risk and the degree of oversight. Some regulators remonstrate that their regulatory reviews do indeed focus on such risk-related characteristics as weediness, pathogenicity, toxicity, and potential for outcrossing. But like building a handsome edifice on a shaky foundation, one cannot ignore the effects of the flawed scope of what is encompassed by the oversight regime—namely, the noncategory of gene-spliced organisms. Without proportionality of oversight and risk, a regulatory regime is discredited, and resources are misallocated. One might as well decide to require a review only of applications that arrive on certain days of the week. Requiring review of gene-spliced plants while excluding all others is so flawed and inappropriate that it compromises the integrity of the regulatory regimes.

Regulatory Inconsistency in Practice

What do this regulatory inconsistency and illogic mean in practice? If a student doing a school biology project takes a packet of "conventional" tomato or pea seeds to be irradiated at the local hospital X-ray department and plants them in his backyard in order to investigate interesting mutants, he need not seek approval from any local, national, or international authority. However, if the seeds have been modified by the addition—or even deletion—of one or a few genes via gene-splicing techniques, this would-be Mendel faces a mountain of bureaucratic paperwork and expense (to say nothing of the very real possibility of vandalism by anti-technology activists, because the site of the experiment must be publicized). The same applies, of course, to professional agricultural scientists in industry or academia.

Although the handful of large agribusiness companies involved in agricultural biotechnology may actually have benefited in the short term from such extensive and expensive regulatory regimes—buying up small competitors unable to tolerate hugely inflated regulatory costs—academic researchers, the ultimate engine for innovation, have been among the most severely affected victims of excessive, ill-conceived regulation. Operating on small budgets, their ability to perform field trials of recombinant plants and microorganisms has been markedly restricted.

In the United States, USDA's requirements for paperwork and field trial design make field trials with gene-spliced organisms ten to twenty times more expensive than the same experiments with virtually identical organisms that have been modified with conventional genetic techniques.[73] By EPA's own radically conservative estimates, the regulatory costs of its Plant-Incorporated Protectants regulation will raise the average expense per "permit submission" for testing a new plant from $200,000 to $500,000—a 150 per cent increase—*only because the field trials employ a more completely characterized, precisely constructed, and predictable plant variety!*[74] And that is only one of several components of the costs of federal biotechnology regulation.

Don Gordon, president of the Agricultural Council of California, has predicted that the EPA's regulatory approach will have profound impacts: "Research and development of 'plant pesticides' will continue; but only a few very large companies will have the resources necessary to cope with this new and costly bureaucratic process."[75]

A specific example will illustrate the real-world problems engendered by the flawed regulatory policies being applied to the new biotechnology. Agriculture in northern California, one of the region's major industries, is under threat from a disease spread by an insect called the glassy-winged sharpshooter. These leaf-hoppers carry Pierce's disease, a lethal bacterial infection of grapevines, citrus, and other plants, for which there is no cure. The insect vectors have migrated north from Mexico and are now causing millions of dollars in damage annually to California's vineyards, but the worst is surely yet to come. The infestation currently threatens the San Joaquin Valley's eight hundred thousand acres of table, raisin, and wine grapes, and involvement of the premier winemaking regions of Napa and Sonoma cannot be far off.

The meager weapons available to attack the sharpshooter currently include the inspection of plants shipped from areas infested by glassy-winged sharpshooters and the spraying of chemical pesticides. In the long run, however, detection and insect control are doomed to fail. As Dale Brown, president of the Napa Valley Grape Growers Association, acknowledges, "Genetic resistance is where we want to go."[76]

There are several ways to introduce or enhance the resistance to Pierce's disease in new variants, or varieties, of grapevines. One logical approach is to transfer genes that confer resistance into California's grapes from distantly related, noncommercial grapes that possess natural immunity; but conventional grape breeding is a notoriously slow, difficult, and unpredictable process, which may not work well or at all in some cases. Unfortunately, attempts to use the more sophisticated and efficient gene-splicing techniques to introduce resistance and to induce new vines to bear fruit years earlier than usual have become hugely expensive and impractical because they are subject to the EPA's PIP rule. In addition, grape growers and winemakers face the problems of anti-biotechnology activism and possible rejection of exports. In the end, the exploitation of California's liberal referendum process by individual counties to ban the planting of gene-spliced plants, as Mendocino County did in March 2004, may prove to be the coup de grâce.

Flawed policies such as those of the USDA and EPA (and those contemplated recently by the FDA) impose huge costs and divert resources from other legitimate public and private sector endeavors. Such miscarriages of federal authority breed well-deserved cynicism about the government's motives. New, gratuitous responsibilities—and the larger budgets and bureaucratic apparatuses that accompany them—benefit primarily one special interest: the regulators themselves. In order to appreciate fully the vast scope of unnecessary federal activities in this area and their direct and indirect costs, it is instructive to go to the agencies' websites—www.usda.gov, www.epa.gov, and www.fda.gov—and perform a search for "biotechnology." The returns are copious, reflecting the creation of new bureaucracies and all manner of gratuitous busywork; biotechnology regulation has itself become a major "industry"—the product of which we can well do without.

Misguided public policy—not limited to biotechnology, by any means—is causing an invisible economic bloodbath. The costs of developing and enforcing federal regulations have increased fifty-five-fold since 1960,[77] and this trend shows no signs of abating. The untold billions of dollars diverted to (that is to say, squandered on) the direct and indirect costs of unnecessary biotechnology regulation—most of it ultimately transferred to consumers as higher prices on agricultural and food products—are unavailable for the creation of wealth and health.

The Real Reasons for Unnecessary Regulations

Those of us who study public policy are often asked *why* government regulatory policy and its implementation are so often unnecessarily expansive, expensive, ponderous, poorly conceived, badly implemented, and politicized. Nobel Prize–winning economist Milton Friedman has spent decades studying and writing about this phenomenon. He notes two fundamental—and related—reasons:

1. The influence of special interests, who often induce the government to provide substantial benefits to a few while imposing small costs on many; and
2. The self-interest of government officials themselves.

Friedman cites as an example of the first point the licensing of taxicabs in New York City. The number of cabs is limited by government fiat, and this has pushed the price of the medallion required to operate a taxi to more than three hundred thousand dollars. The removal of this arbitrary limitation would have wide benefits: consumers would have a wider range of alternatives, the number of cabs and demand for drivers would increase, and drivers' salaries would rise.

So why does the limitation of cabs persist? Because the people who now own the medallions and those who finance their purchase would lose if the limitation were ended, and they apply intense economic and political pressure to prevent reform. Conversely, there is no group whose interest in change is large enough to lobby for reform.[78]

Friedman's second point is that you can usually rely on individuals and institutions (including regulatory agencies) to act in their own self-interest. In the case of regulators, their behavior is influenced both by their yearning for more responsibilities, larger budgets, and grander bureaucratic empires, and by the desire to avoid errors of commission, even at the cost of committing errors of omission (discussed in chapter 4).

Max Planck said more than half a century ago that an important scientific innovation rarely makes its way by gradually winning over and converting its opponents. Rather, its opponents gradually die out and the succeeding generation is familiarized with the idea from the beginning.[79] In a sense, then, time is on the side of biotechnology in the longer term. We suspect that in a decade or two many products made with the new biotechnology will be as much a part of our routines as cell phones and computers are to children today. But that isn't good enough. Overregulation and the relentless propaganda of anti-biotechnology critics are stifling research, development, and commercialization of agricultural and food products.

For many reasons, including those pertaining to economic equity and justice—the poor suffer most from unnecessarily high consumer prices—it is tragic when biotech products' acceptance and potential growth are even minimally limited or delayed. For the inhabitants of less developed countries who are at or below the subsistence level, justice delayed is justice denied. The greater the unnecessary burden and expense for research and development using the new biotechnology, the more likely that the marketed products will be high-value-added ones, available predominantly to wealthier countries and populations, and at higher prices than necessary. With regulatory costs at astronomical levels and agricultural and food biotechnology companies struggling to survive, what incentives are there to work on subsistence crops like millet, sorghum, and sweet potatoes?

The battle for the adoption of sound public policy toward biotechnology is not an intellectual exercise akin to a debate at the Oxford Union. Nor is this an issue that has "two sides," a phrase that one often hears from television producers, journalists, and conference organizers who misunderstand what it means to offer a "balanced" presentation. Rather, it is a real-life struggle for the freedom to carry on legitimate research and development without undue interference—and ultimately, for the wide availability of products that will enhance, prolong, and enrich lives. It is a struggle for life, liberty, and the pursuit of happiness, to borrow a phrase.

Regulation exerts wide influence beyond even the profound direct effects that we have described. The more something is regulated, the greater the presumption that it poses some sort of risk—to public health or to the natural environment, for example—a presumption that has important implications for liability issues in case of allegations that something or someone has been damaged by a product of the new biotechnology. Moreover, regulation creates the expectation of compliance by producers, retailers, and others in the manufacturing and distribution pathway, another factor related to potential legal liability. These issues of legal liability, which return us yet again to the "product versus process" debate, are addressed in the next chapter.

CHAPTER 6

· · · · · · · · · · · · · ·

Legal Liability Issues

with Drew Kershen

ALTHOUGH FORMAL AGENCY regulations are perhaps the most prominent and obvious "regulatory influences" that affect plant breeders, farmers, and food processors, they are not the only ones. Innovators are also "regulated" by less formal restrictions on the testing and commercialization of new products that arise from the common law and from legal liability for harms their products may cause. For producers, the fear of legal liability can be just as potent a restraint as formal agency rules—and, as we shall see, in some cases, an even greater restraint.

Especially in industrialized countries like those in North America and Europe, where well-established legal systems provide injured parties ready access to redress for damages, tort liability laws promote safety by providing strong incentives for companies to ensure that their products are neither defective nor otherwise unsafe.[1] Although legal liability in tort law often has an impact on the behavior of innovators that is just as important and compelling as formal regulations, there are important differences.

Formal government regulation applied to the new biotechnology focuses (at least ostensibly) on whether a particular gene-spliced plant, microorganism, or animal (or a product derived from them) is safe to humans and the environment, and whether producers must be required to meet a minimum threshold of safety.

More specifically, regulation determines whether and under what conditions products of the new biotechnology may be tested, marketed, and used. But regardless of what regulatory permissions and approvals are obtained, these products—as well as their counterparts made with conventional technology—may at times still cause damage to property, persons, markets, the environment, or social structures. Legal liability in tort claims provides a basis for punishing those responsible if damage occurs during product testing or from a commercialized product, whether it is gene-spliced or not. In many regards, it is therefore more potent—and also more fair—than formal agency regulation.

DOES BIOTECHNOLOGY REQUIRE ITS OWN LAWS OF LEGAL LIABILITY?

Many of the concerns voiced by the critics of biotechnology—such as the coexistence of gene-spliced and conventional or organic agriculture, possible health effects from "biopharmed" crops (which are engineered to produce pharmaceuticals or industrial compounds), and hypothetical environmental damage—are already being addressed by courts in tort actions. Like many aspects of regulation discussed in this volume, a vigorous debate is being waged about whether a special, dedicated regime is needed for gene-splicing, in this case for legal liability.

Echoing their biases about regulation, critics of the new biotechnology argue that a novel liability system is necessary for gene-spliced organisms and their products. Thus, once again, the critical policy question becomes whether the new biotechnology is so fundamentally different from other analogous technologies used for genetic enhancement that it requires a special legal liability regime, or whether the legal liability regimes commonly used for other agricultural activities can be applied.

NEW ZEALAND, U.S., AND EU POSITIONS

Although few governments have formally investigated the adequacy of existing civil liability standards for resolving disputes about gene-spliced organisms, a commission established by New Zealand's parliament considered this question in depth. Its deliberations are instructive.

Part of the charge of the Royal Commission on Genetic Modification was to gather information on "the liability issues involved, or likely to be involved now or in the future, in relation to the use, in New Zealand, of genetic modification, genetically modified organisms, and products."[2] Some of the submissions to the commission argued that the kind and magnitude of risks of gene-splicing applied to agriculture were so different that this technology should be considered inherently dangerous.[3] Not surprisingly, these submissions called for a legal liability regime specific to the new biotechnology and possessing the following attributes, among others: strict liability (that is, liability even when there has not been negligence or wrongful intent, as discussed below) for any and all damages caused; extended periods of exposure to legal liability for damages (e.g., thirty years or even in perpetuity); and a requirement that as a condition for approval, applicants provide proof of financial responsibility through insurance, a bond, or payments into a public compensation fund.[4]

Other submissions to the commission argued that on the contrary, the new biotechnology was not fundamentally different from other technologies for genetic modification. Generally, they contended that the existing tort and regulatory laws of New Zealand were sufficient in scope and flexibility to address any damages that might occur through the use of the new biotechnology, and that a special, dedicated legal regime for gene-splicing and its products would serve only to create a disincentive to research and development and impose additional, unnecessary costs upon an emerging and beneficial technology.[5] (Of course, this may very well have been the goal of those demanding a special liability scheme).

The Royal Commission considered the submissions and recommended "that for the time being there be no change in the liability system":[6]

> The Commission considers it is unnecessary to recommend legislation providing special remedies for third parties, where they may have been affected by the release of a [gene-spliced] organism. As technology advanced with ever-increasing pace throughout the 20th century, the common law (that is, law based on court decisions, as distinct from statute law) showed it was well able to mould new remedies for novel situations. Parliamentary intervention has rarely been needed in this area. From a legal liability perspective we have not been persuaded there is anything radically different in genetic modification as to require new or special remedies.[7]

As of January 2003, the U.S. government's position on legal liability was similar to that of the New Zealand Royal Commission. At least in theory, the U.S. government's view is that the new biotechnology applied to agriculture is not fundamentally different from other technologies used for similar purposes, a doctrine clearly enunciated in the 1986 Coordinated Framework for Regulation of Biotechnology.[8] Hence, the United States leaves the issue of legal liability for products of the new biotechnology to the laws generally applicable to agricultural products—primarily the common law of torts, discussed below.

In contrast to New Zealand and the United States, the European Union has proposed classifying gene-splicing as an inherently dangerous technology and, along with other listed activities, making it subject to a special legal liability regime.[9] The proposed EU regime provides for "strict liability" for a wide range of environmental damage that is over and above civil liability for damages to persons, property, or economic interests, and for which there exists no statute of limitations. The EU proposals also suggest (but have not made compulsory) that member states encourage those subject to the special legal liability to have insurance or other forms of financial security.

Nevertheless, in Europe, New Zealand, the United States and elsewhere, the producers and users of the new biotechnology are subject to the usual rules of civil legal liability that apply to all persons and products. Specifically, if a producer or user of gene-spliced plants, microorganisms, or animals causes damage to the property, person, or markets (economic interests) of another person, the offending party may be liable for those damages.[10] Consequently, the behavior of these actors will often be influenced by concerns about *ex post* legal liability that could arise from their products or actions.

Below, we discuss the various types of damage claims by category—property, person, and markets—and focus on unique issues that may arise when these ordinary claims are applied to the new biotechnology.

DAMAGE TO PROPERTY

Claims of property damage from products of the new biotechnology will most likely be related to the flow of pollen from a gene-spliced crop to conventional plants that damages seed production or harvested products intended to be sold as "non-biotech" in order to capture some price premium—including, but not limited to, organic crops.

Because gene-spliced products cannot be used in organic agriculture, producers of certified organic foods may claim, for example, that "contaminating" pollen from gene-spliced crops planted nearby has damaged their organic crop production, causing it no longer to meet the definition of "organic." Likewise, conventional seed producers may claim that the movement of gene-spliced pollen has damaged the purity and integrity of their seeds, making them no longer certifiable as meeting specified standards of purity (see discussion of seed certification in chapter 1 and below).

As discussed below, there are four primary types of tort claims—trespass, strict liability, negligence, and private nuisance—each with somewhat different applications and usage.

Trespass

Producers of seeds or organic crops, for example, who believe they have suffered damages from contamination with pollen from gene-spliced plants may bring a common law cause of action against a neighboring farmer growing gene-spliced crops that is based in "trespass," the physical invasion of the possessory interests of the property (land, in this case) of the person claiming damages.[11]

The physical spread of gene-spliced pollen to neighboring fields may itself be enough to establish the physical invasion element of trespass. However, pollen flow between varieties of the same plant and between related plant species is common both in nature and farming. Hence, if pollen flow by itself were sufficient to give rise to legal liability for trespass upon a neighbor's crops, all farmers would be exposed to legal liability for trespass for almost every crop they grow. To differentiate between pollen flow that constitutes trespass and pollen flow that is accepted as a biological fact of life inherent in farming, the law requires that the physical invasion cause demonstrable damage. Pollen flow from gene-spliced to non-gene-spliced crops may, under certain conditions, meet this threshold of demonstrable damage, but individual cases will vary.

It is noteworthy that if trespass were to become a widely adopted source of legal liability in this context, organic and conventional farmers too would be subject to legal liability for pollen flow *from their crops to gene-spliced crops*, if the pollen flow from the organic or conventional plants were to cause damages to the gene-spliced variety. For example, if the ability of a gene-spliced crop to produce a high-value pharmaceutical or enhanced nutrient content were compromised by pollen flow, the grower might use the trespass claim.

The relevant rules and standards regarding claims for damage to "organic" foods are somewhat counterintuitive. In the United States, federal law sets standards for "organic" foods through the National Organic Program (NOP) of the U.S. Department of Agriculture.[12] These standards specifically exclude from the production of organic foods "methods used to genetically modify organisms,"[13] in spite of the fact that, as discussed in chapters 1 and 2, virtually all of the fruits, vegetables and grains on our farms and in our diet are from plants that have been genetically modified, or improved, by one technique or another. In this context, USDA uses the term "genetically modified" to encompass only organisms altered with recombinant DNA techniques.

Even more problematic are the comments accompanying the official rule on organic standards that pertain to pollen flow, which place USDA squarely on the wrong (that is, unscientific) side of the "product versus process" discussion in chapter 1—though, ironically, in a way that works to the benefit of growers of both gene-spliced and organic crops:

> When we are considering [pollen] drift issues, it is particularly important to remember that organic standards are process based. Certifying agents attest to the ability of organic operations to follow a set of production standards and practices that meet the requirements of the [National Organic Production] Act and the regulations. This regulation prohibits the use of excluded methods in organic operations. The presence of a detectable residue of a product of excluded methods alone does not necessarily constitute a violation of this regulation. As long as an organic operation has not used excluded methods and takes responsible steps to avoid contact with the products of excluded methods as detailed in their approved organic system plan, the unintentional presence of the products of excluded methods should not affect the status of an organic product or operation.[14]

Thus, USDA seems to reward effort and intent, whether or not the "integrity" (for lack of a better word) of the product is compromised. As long as the organic producer follows the process requirements specified in his own approved organic system plan, the unintentional presence of gene-spliced crops in the organic food supply does not constitute a violation of USDA organic production standards. This process-oriented regulatory policy has important implications for allegations of damages related to trespass caused by gene-spliced pollen drift. Because neither pollen flow nor the presence of genetic material or other substances derived from gene-spliced crops, per se, constitutes a violation of the standards for organic crops, organic farmers may face significant difficulties in proving that pollen flow from gene-spliced crops caused any damage. Organic certification in some export markets, however, may require that there is no detectable gene-spliced material, and that *could* be taken into consideration by courts as well.

Seed producers, on the other hand, operate under both process and product standards, in which both the characteristics of the final product and how it was produced matter. In the United States, the Association of Official Seed Certifying Agencies (AOSCA), which works through forty-two affiliated entities throughout the country, sets "the minimum standards for genetic purity and identity and recommended minimum standards for seed quality for the classes of certified seed."[15]

The seed standards of the Nebraska Crop Improvement Association (NCIA), a state affiliate of AOSCA, are typical of those used in the United States. In order to gain seed certification in Nebraska, seed producers must comply with requirements related to land use (such as isolation distances between fields of different varieties of the same crop and the use of buffer rows) and agronomic practices (such as removal of slow growing or otherwise undesirable plants, weed control, and detasseling). Additionally, the seed crop must conform to the tolerance levels for genetic purity.[16] Such methods are used routinely and have been proven equally effective for gene-spliced and non-gene-spliced plant varieties.

Split Approvals

Liability may also arise when there is cross-contamination in a situation in which a crop variety is intended for one use (such as for animal feed or for an industrial purpose) but not for another (such as human consumption). The potential for liability in such cases, however, applies to both gene-spliced and non-gene-spliced crops.

As we discussed in chapter 3, rapeseed is a plant in the *Brassicae* family that is grown in many countries to produce an industrial lubricant that is toxic when consumed by humans. Canola is a *Brassicae* variety of the same species but is grown widely to produce cooking oil. Canola was developed by plant breeders from rapeseed with conventional breeding methods used to suppress the genes that direct the synthesis of the anti-nutrient glucosinolate and the toxic erucic acid. To avoid cross-contamination, the two varieties are routinely segregated by growers, in the field and throughout processing, because consumption of those substances from rapeseed could be harmful to human health.

Recent studies of pollen flow in two varieties of canola, one gene-spliced and one non-gene-spliced, found that the usual isolation distances—such as those in the seed certification standards for canola—are sufficient to produce certified seed at the 99.75 percent level of genetic purity.[17] Also, because canola is among the most highly outcrossing species, these standards would be adequate for most other crops as well (although there are published standards for common crops). As is the case with organic production, the mere presence of detectable levels of gene-spliced material does not disqualify seed batches from being certified, but because seed certification sets limits on the permissible contamination of the end product, seed breeders might have a stronger claim of trespass if those limits are exceeded.

Agricultural processors and food companies should already be aware of the broader applicability of trespass. Therefore, it should come as no surprise to them that—usually for reasons related to commerce rather than safety—some agricultural crops must be segregated from others with specialized traits not readily visible to the naked eye. Thus, as new crops with a range of traits applicable to nutritional, medicinal, industrial, and environmental uses become commercialized—crafted with techniques new and old—it is not unreasonable to expect that growers will continue to take the precautions necessary to prevent the inappropriate mixing of varieties. (See also the discussion of "biopharmed" crops and zero tolerance in chapter 5.)

Strict Liability

A person who believes that his land or crops have been damaged by a neighbor's gene-spliced crops may, in certain cases, also bring a tort claim in "strict liability." This claim applies if the activity of growing gene-spliced crops could be judged to be abnormally dangerous, regardless of whether the defendant has been negligent and in spite of the exercise of even the utmost care.[18] Claims of strict liability turn on whether or not individual gene-spliced crops, or all such crops, are considered abnormally dangerous. To answer that crucial question, the following factors would be taken into consideration:

(a) Existence of a high degree of risk of some harm to the person, land, or chattels of others
(b) Likelihood that the harm that results from it will be great
(c) Inability to eliminate the risk by the exercise of reasonable care
(d) Extent to which the activity is not a matter of common usage
(e) Inappropriateness of the activity to the place where it is carried on

(f) Extent to which its value to the community is outweighed by its dangerous attributes[19]

In the United States, where the official, overarching government policy holds that the new biotechnology is not different in kind from other technologies for genetic improvement, those who allege a strict liability claim may have difficulty establishing the existence and likelihood of factors (a) and (b).[20] Moreover, inasmuch as American farmers have, for the past few years, planted significant acreage of gene-spliced crops, those alleging strict liability may also have difficulty in establishing factors (d) and (e).[21]

In addition, organic farmers or others hoping to produce non-gene-spliced products may face an additional hurdle to establishing strict liability against gene-spliced crops, because section 524A of the Restatement of Torts states, "There is no strict liability for harm caused by an abnormally dangerous activity if the harm would not have resulted but for the abnormally sensitive character of the *plaintiff's* activity."[22]

Although the presence of "contamination" from gene-spliced crops, per se, does not cause organic farmers to lose their organic certification under USDA-NOP standards, some private nongovernmental organic certifiers or other process-oriented organizations may impose stricter standards that deny the private certification if any amount of gene-spliced crops is detectable.[23] Adherence to these stricter standards may be interpreted as a choice by growers to produce crops that have "an abnormally sensitive character."[24]

When considering damage claims under strict liability, it is also important to differentiate between gene-spliced commodity crops (such as canola, corn, cotton, and soybean) and gene-spliced crops that produce a nonfood product—a pharmaceutical or a substance used industrially, for example. If damage occurs, biotechnology companies and farmers are likely to be at greater risk that a court will rule that a pharmaceutical gene-spliced crop is abnormally dangerous. However, the likelihood of such an outcome would depend upon the characteristics of the particular crop and on whether a regulatory agency overseeing the activity has established a tolerance for the presence of the crop or the pharmaceutical in food and animal feed (As we discussed in chapters 3 and 5).

Finally, as part of the process of deciding whether something is "abnormally dangerous," courts are allowed to perform "social-utility balancing," which means that even for gene-spliced pharmaceutical crops, a court could decide against strict liability and in favor of a negligence liability standard if the crop in question were determined to have special value.

Negligence

Although strict liability applies regardless of any efforts the defendant might have made to prevent damage, parties who believe their crops or property have been harmed because neighbors growing gene-spliced plants failed to take adequate precautions may have a claim for "negligence." Such a claim could be filed against a neighbor who is growing a particular plant variety, or possibly even against the biotechnology company that created it.

Negligence, defined as "conduct which falls below the standard established by law for the protection of others against unreasonable risk of harm," is a fault-based claim arising from the fact that the negligent person failed to take adequate precautions.[25] Plaintiffs have the burden to prove four traditional elements of a negligence claim: first, that the defendant had a duty of care to the plaintiff; second, that the defendant's unreasonable conduct breached that duty; third, that the defendant's actions caused the damages claimed; and finally, that a harm or injury that can be valued in a monetary amount actually occurred.[26]

If courts decide that the presence alone of material from gene-spliced crops (such as from pollen or volunteer plants) on another person's land does not constitute grounds for a trespass or a strict liability claim, negligence liability for growing gene-spliced crops would not differ from negligence for growing non-gene-spliced crops. In either case, farmers would owe their neighbors reasonable care to avoid causing injury or harm to nearby land or crops.

Although farmers would have no new or additional negligence liability solely because they decided to grow gene-spliced crops per se, biotechnology companies and farmers growing certain gene-spliced crops may have the obligation to take additional reasonable precautions if, for example, the agronomic evidence showed that a particular gene-spliced crop manifested weediness, pollen flow, or volunteer plants to a greater degree than similar, nonbiotech crops.

Companies and farmers would likely have the duty to adopt additional reasonable precautions if, for reasons of safety, a gene-spliced or conventional crop (such as one producing a pharmaceutical or industrial chemical, as discussed in the previous section) needed to be segregated from commodity crops destined for food or animal feed. With this burden in mind, biotechnology companies and farmers are devising and implementing various techniques to prevent pollen flow and volunteer plants. One technique is to introduce into the crop biological barriers against pollen flow and the survival of volunteer plants. These include male sterility to produce infertile pollen, seed sterility to prevent volunteer crops, and control of flowering time to prevent cross-pollination.[27]

Ironically, although one reason for the implementation of such techniques is to avoid legal liability, it is possible that their availability could in the future expose seed breeders and biotechnology companies to claims of "design defect." How could that be? A product has a design defect when "foreseeable risks of harm posed by the product could have been reduced or avoided by the adoption of a reasonable alternative design . . . and the omission of the alternative design renders the product not reasonably safe."[28] Consequently, if at some point in the future these biological barriers become feasible to incorporate into gene-spliced plants but a biotechnology company failed to do so, the company could be held liable for a products liability claim for design defect if the plants were to cause damage to property or persons.

Certain agronomic practices, such as employing sufficient isolation distances between fields, barrier crops, border rows, and refugia, can also reduce pollen flow and the frequency of volunteer plants. In addition, biotechnology companies may have the duty to educate farmers about these best-management practices and to police their farmer customers through contractual and monitoring arrangements, and farmers may then have an obligation to abide by these agronomic practices. If biotechnology companies and farmers fail to adopt best-management practices and consequently cause damage, they may face legal liability through negligence claims.

Private Nuisance

The tort claims of trespass, strict liability, and negligence focus on the *conduct* or the *activity* that causes harm to the property of another. By contrast, the claim of "private nuisance" focuses not on conduct but on the interest to be protected—that is, the private use and enjoyment of land free from nontrespassory invasion by others. By focusing on the use and enjoyment of land, nuisance may overlap with the other common law claims that are concerned with conduct, but nuisance is a distinct and independent basis for legal liability.

Fundamental to the nuisance claim is the idea that persons must not interfere with their neighbors' use and enjoyment of their own land and property; however, the legal claim of nuisance recognizes that neighbors must be accommodating to one another in order to allow a peaceable coexistence. As one can imagine, determining what actions are required for a peaceable coexistence requires a careful balancing of each party's interests. To make such judgments, courts have defined the elements of nuisance to include an invasion that meets two conditions: First, the action must be either intentional and *unreasonable*, or unintentional and otherwise actionable (such as a legal claim for trespass, strict liability, or negligence); and second, it must cause significant harm.

For example, individuals who bring a legal claim for nuisance must provide proof that nearby fields of gene-spliced crops have unreasonably interfered with the use and enjoyment of their own land. In view of the widespread planting of gene-spliced crops with regulatory permission in the United States (more than one hundred million acres annually), persons bringing nuisance claims are unlikely to be able to establish that gene-spliced crops per se are unreasonable. The legal claim of nuisance is oriented to the specific facts and circumstances between neighbors and to what constitutes "unreasonableness" in a specific situation. Therefore, it will probably be difficult to bring private nuisance actions against biotechnology companies.

Private nuisance may be a more viable legal claim against a neighbor growing gene-spliced crops than against a biotechnology company, but in either case the courts are unlikely to endorse a claim that insists on zero tolerance of pollen flow or volunteer plants. As courts engage in balancing of the gravity of harm against the social utility of each neighbor's use and enjoyment of his own land, they expect neighbors to exhibit a reasonable level of tolerance toward one another.

Individuals who bring a private nuisance claim must also establish that the invasion caused significant harm, which has two components—its gravity and its "normality" in a particular geographic region. More specifically, significant harm requires that there be "harm of importance, involving more than slight inconvenience or petty annoyance."[29] Normality addresses whether "normal persons in [the region would] be substantially annoyed or disturbed by the situation."[30] Persons claiming private nuisance will need to establish that a significant harm has occurred and that the harm is more than merely philosophical opposition to gene-spliced crops.

DAMAGE TO THE PERSON

A claim of personal damage, as opposed to damage to one's property, might assert that gene-spliced crops or food products caused toxicity or an allergic response, or other ill effects to health. The very nature of gene-spliced crops and foods derived from them and their intensive regulation (discussed in chapter 5) should prevent significant exposure to products with toxic or other harmful effects, but because allergenic reactions are difficult to predict and to verify, the most likely personal damage claim would be an allegation that the gene-spliced crop or food caused an allergic reaction.[31] The basis for such a claim could be strict liability, products liability, nuisance, or negligence, with the same elements and burdens of proof as discussed above for property damage claims.

Compared to non-gene-spliced crops and foods, the presently approved gene-spliced products pose no new legal liability risks with regard to personal damage claims related to food safety. (Also, it should be noted that once the EPA has approved a gene-spliced plant, federal law preempts damage claims based on failure to warn, improper labeling, and related torts.) Indeed, in an interesting twist, the *failure* to use gene-spliced crops as food ingredients when these crops reduce food safety risks means that food companies could be exposed to legal liability for design defect (as we discuss below).[32]

In the one instance in the United States in which injury from consuming food derived from a gene-spliced crop was alleged (StarLink™ Bt-corn, which contains a bacterial protein, Cry9C, that is toxic to certain insects), the corn variety had been approved only for animal, but not human, consumption. The EPA granted this "split" approval due to then–unresolved concerns about the safety of the novel StarLink™ protein—it takes slightly longer than most proteins to be digested, a characteristic it has in common with many known allergens.

The activist organization Friends of the Earth paid a laboratory to test a large selection of packaged food products made with corn (including corn chips, tortillas, and taco shells) and found the unintended presence of the Cry9C protein in some of them. After newspaper and television news reports announced that the unapproved, and possibly allergenic, protein was found in food products taken from grocery store shelves, twenty-eight people reported that they experienced allergic-like reactions after eating corn-containing food products. Nevertheless, intensive investigation of adverse effects reports (AERs) by the Centers for Disease Control was not able to confirm a single allergic reaction:

> Although the study participants may have experienced allergic reactions, based upon the results of this study alone, we cannot confirm that a reported illness was a food-associated allergic reaction. Although our results do not provide any evidence that the allergic reactions experienced by the people who file AERs were associated with hypersensitivity to Cry9C protein, we cannot completely rule out this possibility, in part because food allergies may occur without detectible serum IgE to the allergens.[33]

This was a very tepid and cautious conclusion (typical of scientists), given that none of the blood sera tested showed a reaction consistent with an allergic response to the Cry9C protein. But in light of the CDC's equivocation and the absence of regulatory approval for StarLink™ in human food, a class-action lawsuit alleging that consumers ate food unfit for human consumption was successfully concluded with a settlement against Aventis, the producer of the StarLink™ corn variety.[34] Thus, gene-spliced crops not approved for human consumption present the risk of legal liability *even if no consumer has suffered any toxic, allergic, or other health-related harm.*

Although this may appear to be an anomalous outcome, in that the fault lies not with the product itself or the legal system but in flawed regulatory policy, such problems are the inevitable result of regulations that treat gene-spliced products as though they pose some inherent, unique risks, when it is clear that they do not.

The real culprits are the regulatory policy that required EPA's review of the variety in the first place and the agency's insupportable decision thereafter to approve it only for animal feed. Note that, as discussed in chapter 5, affirmative regulatory approvals are not required for conventional crops or foods but only for those derived from gene-spliced organisms—a situation that creates the opportunity for precisely the kind of mischief represented by the StarLink™ debacle.

The greatest jeopardy to biotechnology companies and growers for damages to the person may lie in the cultivation of gene-spliced plants that produce pharmaceuticals or industrial chemicals.[35] In most instances, in order to avoid adverse effects and to prevent claims of toxic, allergic, and unfit food harms, regulators, farmers, and drug companies will seek to prevent the substance(s) newly synthesized by the plants from being transferred into food and feed crops, or the gene-spliced crop from being accidentally commingled with food or feed. The USDA has proposed new guidelines for the segregation of gene-spliced pharmaceutical and industrial crops from food and feed crops (as discussed in chapter 5),[36] but for the purpose of preventing civil liability, these regulatory measures would ordinarily be viewed as minimum standards. Compliance with the government's formal regulatory requirements may not alone be a sufficient defense against claims of negligence or strict liability if particular products still cause genuine harms. In order to minimize the risk of legal liability, from the field to the pharmaceutical processing facilities biotechnology companies will need to develop contractual provisions with their growers for segregation measures, control of volunteer plants, and identity preservation of the pharmaceutical crop. Such measures also will help to ensure the integrity of the value-added gene-spliced crop, so that the end product can be manufactured in a consistent and controlled way.

If tort claims are asserted because the new trait from an approved gene-spliced pharmaceutical or industrial crop is transferred inadvertently into a food product, courts will have the power to choose between strict liability and negligence standards for legal liability. In order to decide whether strict liability applies, courts would balance the social benefit (i.e., the creation of useful pharmaceutical products) against the likelihood of possible harm (the risks of toxicity or allergenicity) in the food supply. If the social benefit were judged to outweigh the risk, that might persuade the courts to decide against strict liability.

They may be influenced in this decision by the thoroughness and effectiveness of the contractual stewardship programs and by any tolerances adopted by the regulatory authorities. If the courts decide against the applicability of strict liability, they would look to negligence as the source of legal recovery. In that case courts would then need to determine whether the company and the grower had acted reasonably in their crop production, harvesting, control of volunteers, and handling. If they had, no liability would exist.

DAMAGE TO ECONOMIC INTERESTS

Economic injury is not identical to property damage, although the two can overlap. While "property damage" refers to an event that actually harms one's real property or makes it less valuable (usually, though not always, through a direct physical impact), "economic damage" refers more narrowly to an event that harms one's ability to sell products or services, or otherwise to generate income. Naturally, not all damage to economic interests is actionable—one such case would be the sale by a competitor of a superior product at a lower price that makes one's own product unprofitable or unmarketable. But current and future cases, such as *Sample v. Monsanto*, discussed below, will test just how broadly or narrowly applicable the "economic loss" doctrine is when it comes to gene-spliced crops. This legal tenet has its origins in products liability law, at the interface between tort law and contract law, but it has evolved such that the "economic loss" doctrine precludes recovery in tort even in the absence of a contractual dimension to the legal dispute.

In lawsuits that claim damage by gene-spliced crops to economic interests, the defendant usually will be the agricultural biotechnology companies or other developers of gene-spliced organisms, because it is they who place new biotech products on the market and thereby may impact the market access and prices of non-biotech crops. Individual farmers who grow gene-spliced crops are at negligible risk of economic-interests lawsuits.

To date, farmers of conventional crops have filed several lawsuits, claiming that the introduction of gene-spliced crops increased their production and equipment costs and depressed the price for their products. They claimed that their particular crops have suffered property damage through cross-pollination and through the presence of the gene-spliced crops in the agricultural sector generally, which has affected market access and prices for their nonbiotech crops.

In order to understand the potential for claims of damages to economic interests (i.e., markets) in the United States, it is necessary to distinguish among: (1) crops approved for limited uses in the United States, (2) crops approved for all uses in the United States, and (3) crops approved in the United States but unapproved in major export markets.

Gene-Spliced Crops Approved for Limited Use in the United States

The "approved for limited use" category includes certain varieties undergoing permitted field trials, biopharmaceutical crops, and the anomalous circumstances of the corn variety known as StarLink™, which contains the bacterial Cry9C gene. StarLink™ is the only gene-spliced crop variety ever to have been granted a limited use commercial approval—that is, for use only in animal feed but not for human consumption.

When the Cry9C gene was found to be present in foods (though without evidence of actual harm), there were three options open to the EPA: grant an exemption from the existing zero tolerance for the Cry9C gene in foods, set a higher tolerance level, or deny a tolerance and consider the foods adulterated. When the EPA decided against either an exemption or setting a nonzero tolerance, the FDA (which enforces pesticide tolerances established by the EPA) was required to recall the hundreds of completely harmless food products that were suspected of containing trace amounts of the Cry9C gene or protein.[37] Several parties, including farmers, grain handlers, and food processors, were then stuck with various amounts of corn or processed food made from corn they were unable to sell for human consumption.

With zero tolerance as the regulatory standard, it is no surprise that a trial judge in the Northern District of Illinois allowed a multidistrict, class-action case to proceed to trial on the tort legal liability claims of negligence, negligence per se (that is, statutory violations), strict liability, private nuisance, and public nuisance.[38] At trial, the plaintiffs (farmers alleging damages to economic interests) and the defendant (Aventis Corporation) would have presented evidence establishing and rebutting, respectively, the elements of these tort claims that must be proven to create legal liability. There was no trial, however, because the parties reached a settlement in February 2003 in which Aventis would compensate farmers growing non-StarLink™ corn for property damage and economic loss based on pollen flow or mixing of StarLink™ corn with non-StarLink™ corn.

In order to avoid a repetition of the StarLink™ debacle, the EPA announced in March 2001 that it would no longer grant limited use, or split, registrations for gene-spliced crops.[39] However, as gene-spliced crops that produce pharmaceutical or industrial products enter field trials and commercial production, the USDA and FDA will face an issue analogous to split approval—namely, whether and under what circumstances to grant consent for the cultivation of plants for pharmaceutical production, while prohibiting their use for food or feed. (It should be noted that plants cultivated for pharmaceutical production—gene-spliced or not—would not formally fall under the FDA's pre-market jurisdiction until the sponsor sought permission to begin clinical trials.) While undergoing USDA-permitted field trials, gene-spliced crop plants that include a pesticidal trait not yet approved by the EPA would pose a similar problem, unless future policy makes an allowance for trace amounts of the "Plant Incorporated Protectant" in the food supply.

If the FDA insists on a zero tolerance standard for the detection of nonfood traits or substances in the food supply, the biotechnology companies will have three options. The first is to grow the nonfood crop only in contained and confined structures such as greenhouses. The second is to grow it in fields under conditions of sufficient "biological containment" or physical isolation (but subject to the tort claims identical to those pursued in the *StarLink™ Corn Products Liability Litigation*). The third is to abandon the gene-spliced crop as a production method for nonfood products.

Gene-Spliced Crops Approved for All Food and Feed Uses

Another multidistrict, class action lawsuit—this one in the Eastern District of Missouri—presented the questions of tort liability for an agricultural biotechnology company with fully approved gene-spliced crops.[40] The plaintiff farmers in the *Sample v. Monsanto Company* case alleged that the presence of gene-spliced material in the corn and soybean commodity streams (either from gene transfer into their non-gene-spliced crops as the result of cross-pollination, or as a result of commingling with their crops during harvesting, transport, nor storage) increased the plaintiffs' costs of production and depressed the prices for corn and soybeans. The plaintiffs claimed only negligence and public nuisance as tort causes of action; they did not allege private nuisance or strict liability. However, the failure of the *Sample* plaintiffs to allege these two torts does not preclude plaintiffs in other cases from using them as alternative or additional claims for liability in similar cases.

The farmers in the *Sample* case alleged the same elements of negligence as in the StarLink™ case, but in claiming damages to economic interests, they faced an additional defense by the agricultural biotechnology companies and farmers growing transgenic crops: the "economic loss" doctrine. As noted above, the economic loss doctrine holds that for plaintiffs to prevail in a negligence claim there must be actual "physical harm," not merely disappointed commercial expectations.

In addition to the negligence claim, the farmers in the *Sample* case also sued under the doctrine of "public nuisance," which should be distinguished from private nuisance, defined above. Public nuisance is an unreasonable interference with a right common to the general public.[41] Because of its focus on public rights, the tort of public nuisance is not limited to plaintiffs who must prove damages to their property. Although public nuisance is usually enforced by public officials, plaintiffs who can prove a harm different in kind from that suffered by the general public may use public nuisance to recover damages for themselves while simultaneously protecting public rights for themselves and others.

In September 2003, the court dismissed both the negligence and public nuisance claims in the *Sample* case because the economic loss doctrine applied and the plaintiffs were unable to show that their own crops had been "contaminated" with gene-spliced material. The farmer plaintiffs only experienced disappointed commercial expectations when European commodity buyers began purchasing corn and soybeans from other countries; no actual damage to their crops was demonstrated.

In the *StarLink™ Corn Products Liability Litigation*, on the other hand, the court ruled that the economic loss doctrine did not apply and the plaintiffs might be able to recover damages if they could prove that the unapproved crop cross-pollinated or was commingled with the farmer-plaintiffs' nonbiotech crop, thereby damaging the property (nonbiotech corn) of the farmers who did not grow the StarLink™ variety. The "physical harm" would have been the presence of StarLink™ in the plaintiffs' corn that prevented it from being sold for food. Part of the court's discussion of this issue may have particular significance for fully approved transgenic crops that can be sold for all uses. The *StarLink* court wrote:

> What these [bridge or road closure cases, to which the court referred for guidance] share in common with traditional economic loss doctrine jurisprudence is the lack of property damage. Moreover, because the only harms alleged were profits lost due to customer's inability to access the premises, these damages fit neatly within the rubric of "disappointed commercial expectations."
>
> Still, as the access cases aptly demonstrate, the economic loss doctrine has grown beyond its original freedom-of-contract based policy justifications. Farmers' expectations of what they will receive for their crops are just that, expectations. Absent a physical injury, plaintiffs cannot recover for drops in market prices. Nor can they recover for any additional costs, such as testing procedures, imposed by the marketplace. But if there was some physical harm to plaintiffs' corn crop, the lack of a transaction with defendants affects what will be considered "other property."[42]

Judging by the opinions in *Sample v. Monsanto* and the *StarLink™ Corn Products Liability Litigation*, we can foresee that in future cases, courts will need to decide whether cross-pollination or commingling of a fully approved gene-spliced crop causes a "physical harm" to non-gene-spliced crops. If those courts decide in the affirmative, they will likely allow cases to proceed to trial for proof of the harm under the negligence tort claim. If, however, the courts decide that no physical harm occurred, they will likely hold that the economic loss doctrine bars tort claims.

In order to determine whether growing a fully approved gene-spliced crop is a significant, unreasonable interference with a right common to the general public, and therefore subject to claims under public nuisance, the courts will likely consider two pivotal questions. First, what is the effect of compliance with the regulations applicable to gene-spliced crops, assuming that such compliance can be demonstrated by the agricultural biotechnology companies? Second, whatever the general utility of gene-spliced crops may be, has there been an identified harm that would be unreasonable if left uncompensated?

This latter question raises another policy issue called the "socialization of harm"—that is, even if an identifiable harm exists, under what circumstances should society as a whole bear its cost?[43] The New Zealand Ministry for the Environment has observed correctly that

> it would clearly be counter-productive to design liability rules that provided full compensation in all eventualities, if the practical consequence was that the costs and risks of engaging in the activity were prohibitive. Liability rules must fit

with the basic goal of preserving opportunities. . . . Any move to a more onerous liability regime may have negative impacts. Depending on the strength and
design of the regime, it may create a disincentive for investment in [gene-
splicing-based] innovation.[44]

Gene-Spliced Crops Approved in the United States but Not Approved in Major Export Markets

The approval of a particular gene-spliced crop variety in the United States
but not in a major export market amounts to a de facto zero tolerance for
that particular gene-spliced crop in the foreign market, unless there has been
established some other level of acceptable comingling. An example would
be the unintentional and "unavoidable" mixture from cross-pollination or
other mechanisms (often referred to as "adventitious presence") that is permitted under some countries' regulations.

Thus, the companies and the farmers who wish to grow U.S.-approved
gene-spliced crops in the United States can either forgo the benefits of that
particular variety or attempt to satisfy the zero-tolerance standard for crops
exported to the market where it has not yet been approved. If they opt for
the latter, the companies and their farmer-clients would need to create an
identity preservation system that segregates gene-spliced crops from conventional crops (or segregates approved from unapproved varieties) to achieve
the required tolerance. This would require the development of stewardship
practices and standards for growing, harvesting, storing, and marketing non-
gene-spliced varieties.[45]

Although these stewardship and identity preservation programs are challenging to create, U.S. farmers are already showing that it is possible to segregate and preserve the identity of non-gene-spliced grains for export
markets, providing there is a technically-achievable tolerance level for the
adventitious presence of gene-spliced material.[46] It is futile, however, to attempt to attain zero tolerance under real-world conditions of cultivation,
harvesting, processing, and distribution. According to the European
Commission's Scientific Committee on Plants, "The Committee is of the
opinion that a zero level of unauthorized [gene-spliced] seed is unobtain-
able in practice. A zero level would have severe consequences for [the EU
law governing releases into the environment of gene-spliced crops, for] field
releases, for biosafety research and for evaluation of new [gene-spliced] plant
varieties."[47]

Even worse, now that the Cartagena Protocol on Biosafety has come into
effect as a binding international treaty for countries that have ratified it, its
article 18 may be interpreted to require a "less than zero" tolerance for
unapproved gene-spliced crops. Less than zero tolerance occurs when an
importing nation is legally authorized by the protocol to refuse agricultural
commodities if those commodities *may contain* an unapproved variety.[48]

If this absurd option were to become an established principle of international law, stewardship and identity-preservation programs would become irrelevant, because the only way to avoid a "may contain" refusal is to prohibit completely the field testing and commercialization of any gene-spliced varieties in geographical regions from which farmers wish to export their crops—that is, to keep entire exporting regions gene-splicing-free.

This is reminiscent of the situation in some less developed countries, such as Zambia and Zimbabwe, that wish to export food or animal feed to European Union member nations. Because of the EU's regulatory policies and intimidation, these African countries have resisted not only commercialization of gene-spliced crops but also the importation of harvested grains from gene-spliced corn and soybean plants (as we discussed in chapter 1).

Although the purpose of field tests often is to gather data for the approval process, the mere fact of their having been conducted may trigger the "may contain" restriction. Thus, field testing of even a preliminary sort would not be permissible if there were a legal obligation to protect the ability to export to nations that had established a "less than zero" tolerance. Finally, it is unclear what implications "may contain" regulatory restrictions have for the inevitable false positives that would be found in the analytical tests performed to detect putative contamination of stored or transported agricultural products.

If lawsuits were brought by farmers of non-gene-spliced plants or by commodity organizations in order to prevent the field testing or commercialization of gene-spliced crop varieties not approved in a major export market, the plaintiffs would likely rely prominently on the doctrine of public nuisance, alleging that the introduction of a gene-spliced crop that lacks export market approval would cause such widespread economic losses that it constitutes an unreasonable interference with the public peace, comfort, or convenience. The plaintiffs would allege that the access to the export market with its zero tolerance standard can best—or possibly only—be protected through an injunctive remedy that the public nuisance liability claim allows.

These cases would pose a genuine dilemma to the court. A decision to protect access to the export market would affirm the ability of the foreign export markets' hostility (quite possibly stemming from protectionist motives) to control what research and development may be undertaken in the United States. It would also raise the question of the ability of a court to use the grounds of public nuisance, in effect, to overrule regulatory agencies' actions under a mandate created by the Congress. Moreover, if the case pertained to the ability to pursue field trials and commercial production of pharmaceutical gene-spliced crops, the court's ruling would imply that access to export markets takes precedence over the development of new medicines and corporate and individual freedom to undertake legitimate research.

By contrast, a decision to protect the field testing and commercialization of gene-spliced crop varieties that have been duly approved in the United

States could subject American farmers to rejection of their crops in export markets that apply zero tolerance or less-than-zero tolerance toward unapproved gene-spliced crop varieties.

This situation illustrates the complex interplay among various elements of public policy, including regulatory, trade, and liability issues. We believe it makes clear the importance of scientific principles as the basis for policy making in all of these realms.

CIVIL LIABILITY: THE BIG PICTURE

A court adjudicating a public nuisance injunction lawsuit, in effect, brings public policy full circle. Although the forum is a judicial one, the fundamental policy issue is the same one discussed at great length throughout this volume. Is the new biotechnology so fundamentally different from other agricultural technologies that it requires special treatment—in this case, an expanded and sui generis legal liability regime?

As legislatures and judges engage this question and deliberate about the applicability of precedents, they must keep in mind that there exists a seamless continuum between conventional biotechnology and the new biotechnology. This so essential because the legal liability issues that pertain to the new biotechnology could just as well arise with conventional techniques of genetic improvement, or even with undomesticated plant species that have undergone no human-mediated genetic improvement at all.[49]

Consider, for example, the devastation caused by the southern corn leaf blight epidemic of 1970, which was due to plant breeders' inadvertent introduction of sensitivity to a fungal plant pathogen into commercial corn varieties developed with conventional hybridization techniques.[50] The National Research Council's 1989 report observes, "The southern corn leaf blight epidemic was a highly publicized event: an epidemic ensued, and economic loss resulted. The year 1970 was certainly a bad year for corn production," with 15 percent of the American harvest destroyed. The report goes on to emphasize the importance to agriculture of the new biotechnology: "Because an occasional unexpected crop loss may occur, it is important to have an arsenal of genetic modifications, techniques and genetic resources available that can be used promptly to limit unacceptable losses. New molecular methods for gene introduction will be beneficial in this regard."

Jurists must also consider that many agricultural crop varieties currently in commercial use are mutants that were created through chemical or radiation mutagenesis.[51] If activists' persecution of gene-spliced crops were to expand to these mutant varieties, pollen flow from such varieties might also elicit demands for zero tolerance. If gene-spliced crops establish the precedent for significant legal liability for government-approved agricultural crops, the currently small risk of potential legal liability could be raised for mutated varieties that, like new non-gene-spliced varieties generally, undergo little or no formal regulatory scrutiny. However, assuming that mutant crops do not give rise to an expanded, specialized legal liability, the principle of treating like cases alike should mean that gene-spliced crops likewise should not be subjected to such liability.

In the end, we must confront the fundamental question, "Are current tort law remedies sufficient for handling cases that are likely to arise as a greater variety of gene-spliced crops becomes more widely cultivated for more diversified purposes?" As we have shown, the answer appears to be yes.

LIABILITY OF *REJECTING* THE NEW BIOTECH

To this point, our discussion has focused on the civil liability of farmers who grow gene-spliced crops, and on agricultural biotechnology companies that produce and market them. Agricultural processors and food companies too may face civil liability, but from a different, and perhaps unexpected, direction—for their *refusal* to purchase or to use gene-spliced varieties. To see how, consider that the response by some in the food industry to anti-biotechnology protesters and to controversies like StarLink™ corn has been to try to avoid gene-spliced crops altogether in their food or feed products. This strategy also carries risks of civil liability that must be carefully considered.

Design Defect Liability: The Gerber Example

As we discussed in chapter 5, in 1999 the Gerber foods company succumbed to activists' pressure, announcing that its baby food products would no longer contain any gene-spliced ingredients. Indeed, Gerber went further and promised to shift to the use of organic crops that are grown without synthetic pesticides or fertilizers.

However, in its attempt to head off a potential public relations problem, Gerber may have unintentionally increased the health risk for its baby consumers—and, thereby, its legal liability. Studies by USDA entomologist Patrick Dowd and Iowa State University plant pathologist Gary Munkvold show that gene-spliced Bt-corn crops have a significantly reduced incidence of infestation by the mold *Fusarium* and therefore lower concentrations of the mold's cancer-causing mycotoxin, fumonisin.[52]

For the sake of argument, let us assume a mother discovers that her Gerber-fed baby has developed liver or esophageal cancer. On the child's behalf, a plaintiff's lawyer can allege strict products liability based on mycotoxin contamination in the baby food as the causal agent of the cancer. Such a claim would allege that under products liability law, the contamination is a *manufacturing defect* caused by the baby food's departing from its intended product specifications, "even though all possible care was exercised in the preparation and marketing of the product."[53]

The plaintiff's lawyer can also allege a *design defect* in the baby food, because Gerber knew of the existence of a less risky design—namely, the use of gene-spliced varieties that are less prone to *Fusarium* and fumonisin contamination—but deliberately chose not to use it. Instead, Gerber chose to use non-gene-spliced, organic food ingredients, knowing that the foreseeable risks of harm posed by them could have been reduced or avoided by adopting a reasonable alternative design—that is, by using Bt-corn, which is known to have a lower risk of mycotoxin contamination.[54]

If Gerber attempted to answer this design defect claim by contending that the company was only responding to consumer demand, the company would encounter a facet of the law that subjects a design defect to a risk-utility balancing in which consumer expectations are only one of several factors used to determine whether or not the product design (i.e., the use of only non-gene-spliced ingredients) is reasonably safe.

The Restatement of Torts holds that "The mere fact that a risk presented by a product design is open and obvious, or generally known, and that the product thus satisfies expectations, does not prevent a finding that the design is defective." However, the fact that "a product design meets consumer expectations may substantially influence or even be ultimately determinative on risk-utility balancing in judging whether the omission of a proposed alternative design renders the product not reasonably safe." Nevertheless, conformance with consumer expectations may not serve as an independent basis for denying a liability claim.[55]

Gerber could also attempt to respond to this design defect claim by arguing that if its baby food, which contains no gene-spliced ingredients, were judged not to be reasonably safe, consumers would be denied a market choice. However, this argument would enable the plaintiff's lawyer to add an additional claim to the lawsuit: that Gerber is liable because it failed to provide adequate instructions or warnings.[56] For example, Gerber could have labeled its nonbiotech baby food with a statement such as: "This product does not contain gene-spliced ingredients. Consequently, this product has a very slight additional risk of mycotoxin contamination. Mycotoxins can cause serious diseases such as liver and esophageal cancer."

The Hypoallergenic Foods Example: Peanuts and Soybeans

The example above, which postulates damage from higher levels of toxin in non-gene-spliced corn, is probably a less likely scenario than liability for an allergic reaction. Allergies to peanuts and soybeans, for example, are quite common. Between 6 and 8 percent of children and between 1 and 2 percent of adults are allergic to soybeans. Although only about 1 percent of the population is allergic to peanuts, some individuals are so highly sensitive that exposure causes anaphylactic shock. Dozens die every year.

Fortunately, biotechnology researchers are well along in the development of peanuts, soybeans, and other crops in which the genes coding for allergenic proteins have been silenced or removed.[57] According to University of California–Berkeley biochemist Bob Buchanan, scientists are rapidly accumulating knowledge about how to reduce the allergenicity of major allergens, work that has been accelerated significantly by a dog model that he and his colleagues have shown to be effective for a variety of foods (peanut, tree nuts, cereals, and milk). He estimates that candidates for commercial hypoallergenic varieties of wheat could be developed within the decade, and nuts somewhat later.[58] Once these products are commercially available, agricultural processors and food companies that refuse to use these safer food sources will open themselves to products-liability design-defect lawsuits.

Property Damages and Personal Injury: Contribution and Indemnity Exposure

Potatoes are a booming crop, primarily due to the vast consumption of french fries at fast-food restaurants like McDonald's, Burger King, and Wendy's. However, growing potatoes is not easy, because they are preyed upon by a wide range of voracious and difficult-to-control pests, such as the Colorado potato beetle, aphid-spread viruses, potato blight, and others.

To combat these pests and diseases, potato growers use an assortment of fungicides (to control blight), insecticides (to kill aphids and the Colorado potato beetle), and fumigants (to control soil nematodes). Although some of these chemicals are quite hazardous to farm workers, forgoing them could jeopardize the sustainability and profitability of the entire potato industry. Standard application of chemical inputs enhances yields more than 50 percent over organic potato production, which eschews most synthetic inputs.[59]

Consider a specific example. Many growers use methamidophos, a toxic organophosphate nerve poison, for aphid control. While methamidophos is an EPA-approved pesticide, the agency is currently reevaluating organophosphate use and could ultimately prohibit or greatly restrict the use of this entire class of pesticides.[60] As an alternative to these chemicals, the Monsanto Company developed a potato that contains an endogenous Bt gene to control the Colorado potato beetle and another gene to control the potato leaf roll virus spread by the aphids: Monsanto's NewLeaf® potato is resistant to these two scourges of potato plants, which allowed growers who adopted it to reduce their use of chemical controls and increase yields.

Farmers who planted NewLeaf® became convinced that it was the most environmentally sound and economically efficient way to grow potatoes, but after five years of excellent results it was withdrawn from the market. Under pressure from anti-biotechnology organizations, McDonald's, Burger King, and other restaurant chains had informed their potato suppliers that they would no longer accept gene-spliced potato varieties for their french fries. As a result, potato processors such as J. R. Simplot inserted a non-biotech potato clause into their farmer-processor contracts and informed farmers that they would no longer buy gene-spliced potatoes.[61] In spite of its substantial environmental, occupational, and economic benefits, NewLeaf® became an unacceptable variety. Talk about market distortions!

Now, let us assume that a farmer who is required by contractual arrangement to plant non-gene-spliced potatoes sprays his potato crop with methamidophos (the organophosphate nerve poison) and that the pesticide drifts into a nearby stream and over nearby farm laborers. Thousands of fish die in the stream, and the laborers immediately report to hospital emergency rooms complaining of neurological symptoms.

This hypothetical scenario is, in fact, not at all far-fetched. Fish kills attributed to pesticide runoff from potato fields are commonplace. In the potato-growing region of Prince Edward Island, Canada, for example, a dozen occurred in one thirteen-month period alone, between July 1999 and August 2000.[62] According to the UN's Food and Agriculture Organization, "normal" use of the pesticides parathion and methamidophos is responsible for some 7,500 pesticide poisoning cases in China each year.[63]

To continue our hypothetical scenario, the state environmental agency brings an administrative action for civil damages to recover the cost of the fish kill, and a plaintiff's lawyer files a class-action suit on behalf of the farm laborers to recover personal injury damages.

Several possible circumstances could enable the farmer's defense lawyer to shift culpability for the alleged damages to the contracting processor and the fast-food restaurants that are the ultimate purchasers of the potatoes. These circumstances would include the farmer's having planted Bt potatoes for the previous several years; his contractual obligation to the potato processor and its fast-food retail buyers to provide only non-gene-spliced varieties; and his preference for planting gene-spliced, Bt potatoes, were it not for the contractual proscription. If these conditions could be proven, the lawyer defending the farmer could name the contracting processor and the fast-food restaurants as cross-defendants, claiming either contribution in tort law or indemnification in contract law for any damages legally imposed upon the farmer client. The farmer's defense lawyer could argue that those companies bear the ultimate responsibility for the damages because they compelled the farmer to engage in higher-risk production practices than he would otherwise have chosen. These companies chose to impose cultivation of a non-gene-spliced variety upon the farmer although they knew that in order to avoid severe losses in yield, he would need to use organophosphate pesticides. The defense lawyer could argue that the farmer should have a legal remedy to pass any damages arising from contractually imposed production practices back to the processor and the fast-food chains.

Companies that insist upon farmers using production techniques that involve foreseeable harms to the environment and humans should be legally accountable for that decision. If agricultural processors and food companies manage to avoid legal liability for their insistence on non-gene-spliced crops, they will be "guilty" at least of externalizing their environmental costs onto the farmers, the environment, and society at large.

THE CHALLENGE TO THE LEGAL SYSTEM

Life is filled with risk, and the production, distribution, and sale of food are not exceptions. But as discussed in chapter 4, there is also risk in rejecting new technologies and products, and in establishing public policy—through legislatures, regulatory agencies, and the courts—that inhibits innovation. When public policy discriminates against the use of a product or technology with benefit/risk characteristics that are overwhelmingly positive—which is the case with the new biotechnology today—all of society loses. Dozens of scientific bodies have examined the risks inherent in the modification of organisms with gene-splicing techniques, and none has produced evidence that they pose any new or unique risks. On the contrary, there is overwhelming evidence that because of the greater precision and power of these molecular techniques, gene-spliced organisms and products made from them are actually safer and more predictable.

In the same vein, there is no scientific basis for courts to impose legal liability for events associated with the cultivation and marketing of gene-spliced crops that is different or greater than that for non-gene-spliced crops. Existing legal remedies are sufficient to address the issues that are likely to arise from the use of, or failure to use, gene-spliced crop varieties. The creation of a special liability system solely for the products of agricultural biotechnology would therefore unjustly punish the innovation of new products and techniques that are in many ways superior. Moreover, it would endorse and perpetuate the damaging mythology that there is something uniquely dangerous about the new biotechnology, impede agricultural research and development, and distort markets in agricultural products. In this way, the courts would be acting contrary to the public interest.

Battles over the future of some biotechnology applications already are being waged in a number of courtrooms, and in the future the liability concerns discussed in this chapter will affect directly and indirectly the regulation of gene-spliced crops. The advantage of applying such a tort liability approach to many of these vexing questions is that while the common law sets a basic level of behavioral expectations among producers and users of gene-spliced products, tort law can evolve along with the progression of the technology.

Society need not depend solely on prescriptive regulatory mechanisms to prevent harm from occurring; effective liability law also promotes safety. But, as legal scholars Peter Huber and Robert Litan warn, "Liability law will not promote anything systematically if it is imposed capriciously, if it imposes costs on superior options, or if it imposes damages that swing wildly."[64] The courts must scrupulously avoid these pitfalls.

We are particularly intrigued by the potential for the legal system actually to *encourage* the use and diffusion of the new biotechnology where it is likely to be the safer option and, by imposing legal liability upon those who cause damage directly or indirectly by their rejection of the technology, to discourage antisocial corporate decision making. If the courts seize these opportunities, in the short term they will be throwing a legal cat among the stakeholder pigeons, but in the longer term they will reduce market distortions and exert a positive effect.

The overall challenge for the courts—as for legislators and regulators—will be to apply the law in a way that rejects ignorance, bias, superstition, and uninformed opinion in favor of science and common sense. The scientific consensus about the new biotechnology is clear and widely held. We shall see whether the legal precedents will be as clear as the scientific ones.

This discussion of legal liability illustrates the interconnectedness of what might seem to be distinct and unrelated public policy issues—the subtle interplay, for example, among tort liability, domestic regulation, international trade, and foreign countries' internal regulation of consumer products and restriction of imports. For that reason, the next chapter addresses "The Vagaries of Foreign and International Regulation."

This chapter was written by the authors and Drew L. Kershen, Earl Sneed Centennial Professor of Law at the University of Oklahoma College Law. Kershen is also a member of the Oklahoma Water Law Advisory Commission and is a past member of the Board of Directors and past president of the American Agricultural Law Association.

CHAPTER 7

The Vagaries of Foreign and International Regulation

Aᴌᴛʜᴏᴜɢʜ ᴛʜᴇ U.S. government's biotechnology policies are unscientific and inconsistent, their shortcomings pale in comparison with those of many other countries and international organizations. Although they are grossly overregulated, products do move through the American regulatory pipeline, and a handful of gene-spliced commodity crops have been commercialized and become hugely popular with U.S. farmers. Likewise, there has been a trickle of approvals and great popularity for the products in Canada, China, Argentina, and a few other countries. However, attempts by mostly U.S.-based technology firms to move gene-spliced crops more broadly into global markets have encountered intense resistance from foreign regulatory officials, anti-biotechnology activists, and public opinion.

THE OBSTACLES TO EXPORTING GENE-SPLICED CROPS

In the year 2003, the total area planted to gene-spliced crops worldwide was 167 million acres (67.7 million hectares). Although this may seem impressive, it represents less than 1.5 percent of total global cropland. Fully 99 percent of this acreage was confined to just six countries: the United States (63 percent), Argentina (21 percent), Canada (6 percent), Brazil (4 percent), China (4 percent), and South Africa (1 percent). Small numbers of farmers in twelve other countries (Australia, Bulgaria, Colombia, India, Indonesia, Honduras, Germany, Mexico, the Philippines, Romania, Spain, and Uruguay) also were legally growing some gene-spliced crops.[1]

Plantings in many of those latter countries, however, were restricted to pre-approval field trials, with no marketed varieties. In sum, most countries do not allow farmers to plant gene-spliced crops, and where they are available, they often are limited to just a handful of varieties.[2]

Governmental Resistance

Most governments that have sought to block the planting of gene-spliced crops have done so ostensibly because of biosafety concerns, claiming that the use of recombinant DNA techniques inherently gives rise to special risks that require heightened regulatory scrutiny.[3] In spite of the overwhelming support that gene-spliced crops and foods enjoy within the scientific community and among farmers, regulatory requirements are largely unscientific, excessive, and burdensome, particularly in the European and Asian countries that are some of the world's biggest importers of agricultural products. Thus, because of the growing interconnectedness around the world of environmental and public health (including food safety) policies, and the interdependence of global markets, the prospects for the continued adoption of gene-spliced crops even in the United States are uncertain.

Because the most widely planted gene-spliced food and animal feed crops—corn and soybeans—are heavily traded and exported commodities, the rules that govern trade between nations have become pivotal to the expansion of the new biotechnology. The United States exports approximately 35 percent of its soybean crop (86 percent of which is from gene-spliced plants) and 20 percent of its corn (46 percent from gene-spliced plants),[4] and gene-spliced and conventional varieties are routinely intermingled in most bulk commodity shipments. Therefore, importing nations' refusal to approve the corn and soybean varieties that have been approved and grown in the United States and the total rejection of gene-spliced crops by some countries pose a serious challenge to commodity exporters.

Several existing trade treaties could in time help to resolve these problems, but if international trade rules are interpreted or altered to permit import restraints or labeling requirements that discriminate against gene-spliced crops, exporting countries will face potent disincentives to planting them, including higher research, development, and production expenses, and issues of special legal liability.

Consumer Resistance

If consumer resistance causes private importers in international markets not to purchase gene-spliced commodities or, even worse, to avoid importing from nations that are known to plant gene-spliced crops, there is little, other than the creation of educational programs, that can or should be done by governments to change these behaviors. The aggregated purchasing decisions of a multitude of individual customers *should* drive the outcomes of freely operating markets. In that sense, the customer is always right—even when acting on assumptions about products (including gene-spliced crops) that are wrong. An example is the widespread success of organic produce, which is more costly than nonorganic food, even though it has never been shown to be more healthful or safe.

By contrast, when government policies rather than voluntary consumer choices restrict the availability and sales of gene-spliced products in world markets—effectively removing consumer choice—there is reason for concern. Governments should not mistake the opinions of political majorities for the choices of individual consumers. Unless products can be shown to have dangerous and unmanageable effects, governments should not substitute their own judgments for those of individuals. Although in a democracy the actions of the government should generally reflect the wishes of the majority, they should not unduly infringe on the right of minorities to make free and unencumbered choices in the marketplace. The restriction of consumers' access to products because the technology used to make them is opposed by a vocal minority of citizens, or even a majority, is not the same thing as believing that the customer is always right. These distinctions have often been lost on governments and anti-technology activists who try to justify restrictive policies that keep products off the market.

Among the most critical international regulatory issues faced today by the developers of gene-spliced crops is when and to what extent national governments will be permitted to block imports of gene-spliced commodities at their borders or to require stigmatizing labels on food products derived from them. Some major importing regions, such as the European Union, have implemented restrictive policies that go beyond even the exceptional risk aversion embodied by the precautionary principle, by claiming that food products made with gene-splicing conflict with the "social values" of their consumers.

The arbitrariness and utter imbecility of such claims are reminiscent of Jonathan Swift's brilliant parody in *Gulliver's Travels*: "The primitive way of breaking eggs before we eat them, was upon the larger end: but his present Majesty's grandfather, while he was a boy, going to eat an egg, and breaking it according to the ancient practice, happened to cut one of his fingers. Whereupon the Emperor his Father published an edict, commanding all his subjects, upon great penalties, to break the smaller end of the eggs."

The international institutions that govern such matters ultimately will need to resolve this growing divergence between the policy preferences of the dominant players and to decide which will end up with egg on its face. Currently, the struggle is being joined in a number of venues, including bilateral U.S.-EU negotiations, World Trade Organization panels and committees, the UN's Codex Alimentarius Commission, and within the continuing negotiations on a multilateral, UN-based environmental agreement known as the Cartagena Protocol on Biosafety. Ultimately, the resolution of this larger looming U.S.-EU bilateral trade conflict will largely determine whether agricultural biotechnology remains a boutique industry with a narrow range of products found mainly in wealthy industrialized nations, or evolves into one that reaches beyond high-profit crops to create new varieties of subsistence crops for the masses in less developed countries.

Tragically, political power may win in the end, because in today's global commodity markets importing countries usually have the advantage.[5] Inasmuch as the EU is a dominant importing region, and because the U.S. resolve to defend science-based regulation and free trade is uncertain, the smart money perhaps should be on the EU's anti-scientific, anti-technology, anti-American outlook to win the day.

TRADE ISSUES AFFECT THE DIFFUSION OF THE NEW BIOTECHNOLOGY

Trade policy issues should not dominate the global debate over the testing and use of gene-spliced organisms. Unless actual health or environmental risks can be identified, the decision whether or not to develop, test, and use agricultural applications of the new biotechnology should be made by plant breeders, agronomists, biotechnology researchers, and farmers working together to predict which crop varieties are most appropriate for local conditions and which foods are most likely to be desired by food processors and consumers. But because governments in most countries overregulate the testing and use of gene-spliced crops, practitioners at every link of the long food supply chain, from seed producers to farmers, to shippers, to processors, to retailers, feel the sting of regulation, not just on their own activities but at every other link of that food chain as well. In many locales, the biggest single obstacle to producing gene-spliced crops and foods is regulatory policy established in *other* countries, supposedly to protect the environment and to ensure the safety of food.

The case-by-case screening of gene-spliced crops for biosafety risks is now standard regulatory policy in all industrialized countries, and increasingly is becoming the norm in most developing countries as well.[6] As is done routinely in agricultural research and development, breeders and farmers should consider possible risks to the environment when any new plant variety is introduced into a farming system—whether or not it was developed with recombinant DNA techniques. But gene-spliced plants are subjected without any justification to extraordinary scrutiny, which in the vast majority of cases is unwarranted—especially in view of the virtual absence of government oversight of varieties crafted with less precise and predictable technology.

Discriminatory Review Systems

At least in theory, U.S. regulatory policy has held since 1986 that the oversight of gene-spliced organisms should be essentially the same as for conventional crops,[7] but in practice, agencies have created separate, discriminatory review systems for gene-spliced plants and microorganisms. Other nations also quickly abandoned science in favor of political expedience, bureaucratic self-interest, and short-term commercial advantage. The early consensus of an experts' group at the Organization for Economic Cooperation and Development[8] that recombinant DNA techniques create no new or unique risks began to lose *political* support, especially in Europe, even before the widespread commercial releases of gene-spliced crops that began in 1995.

In 1990, the EC's environment directorate rushed to publish its first process-based directives, specifically to preempt consensus reports from the scientifically stronger, apolitical Group of National Experts on Biotechnology of the OECD. Various reports from the OECD and other organizations have reiterated that neither new regulatory paradigms nor new regulations are necessary for biotechnology products. Nevertheless, in order to define what should be the "scope" of case-by-case review, EU directives co-opted the once-generic term "genetic modification" (and its abbreviation "GM") to describe only the products of gene-splicing, singling them out for discriminatory regulation. The rules, which were sweeping and more strict than even those in the United States, established a regulatory process that has been not only unscientific but complex and difficult to navigate, and the rules have been administered capriciously and inconsistently.

By 1999, fourteen gene-spliced crop plants—including varieties of corn, canola, soybean, chicory, and several nonfood species—had been approved for commercial or precommercial cultivation in the EU, but only two (one each of corn and soybean) had been approved for use in food. Fortunately for such products as oil from corn and soy, neither DNA nor proteins remain in the consumer product, so under the original EU rules in force until April 2004, those gene-spliced food products could be commercialized if the producer demonstrated that they were "substantially equivalent" to the non-gene-spliced counterparts in nutritional value, metabolism, intended use, and other characteristics. Sixteen corn, canola, and cottonseed varieties were approved for use as cooking oils.[9]

None of this has mattered much in practice, however, because of the strong negative opinion of gene-spliced foods held by a sizable minority of the European public, constant protests by anti-biotechnology organizations, and the consequent belief among food processors and retailers that gene-spliced foods would elicit brand boycotts and other negative attention from activists. As a result, few food processors use gene-spliced ingredients and few grocery stores will stock biotech foods.[10]

Manipulating Public Opinion

The public resistance to biotech foods is the result of clever manipulation. Groups opposed to the new technology repeatedly and relentlessly raise the specter of hypothetical negative effects of gene-spliced organisms, without acknowledging that identical risks are routine—and often *greater*—with other methods of genetic improvement and that such risks are minimal and manageable. The public concerns stimulated by such emotion-laden claims lead to demands by those same activist groups for much tighter biosafety screening processes. Thus, activists roll out a vicious circle of anti-biotechnology propaganda—exaggerating and misrepresenting the risks of biotechnology to elicit public opposition, then using that opposition as a justification for more regulation.

The media have been willing collaborators. Environmental activists in the European Union, and in the United Kingdom in particular, have been aided and abetted by a sympathetic press willing to report activists' scaremongering uncritically as a way to sell more newspapers and magazines.[11] In the late 1990s, England's *Express* ran such headlines as "Mutant Crops Could Kill You," and "Is Baby Food Safe?" The *Daily Mail* chimed in with "Mutant Crops' Threat to Wildlife," and the *Guardian* contributed "Gene Crops Could Spell Extinction for Birds." Exposed to both refulgent yellow journalism and incessant propaganda from activists, the public in most EU nations has become far more skeptical of recombinant DNA technology than in the United States.[12]

That European public skepticism is not likely to abate any time soon. Unwarranted regulatory attention focused on gene-spliced organisms ensures that there will continue to be spurious accusations, pseudo-crises, and governmental overreactions, such as those following upon the allegations that pollen from gene-spliced corn could kill Monarch butterflies, that StarLink™ corn "contamination" of food was somehow a threat to public health, that genes from recombinant corn had "invaded" and "contaminated" native varieties in Mexico, and that "biopharmed" corn is a threat to the food supply. The media will be right there, continuing to mine a rich vein of sensationalism and titillation.

In the late 1990s, European government overregulation of gene-spliced crops turned from bad to worse. Beginning in the fall of 1998 Austria, Denmark, France, Greece, Italy, and Luxembourg openly pledged that they would block the EU's approval of all new gene-spliced varieties until an even stronger set of biotechnology regulations could be created by the European Parliament and implemented by individual member states. The new rules were created and went into effect in the spring of 2004. EU politicians boast that they are "the toughest [biotechnology] legislation in the world," and tout them as just the trick to restore public confidence in the technology.[13]

This is wishful thinking: Because the new requirements are so much more strict, complex, and costly, they are likely to make it even more difficult to grow and sell biotech crops. Any positive impact on public opinion—itself a dubious expectation—will be swamped by the negative impact of drowning biotech researchers and farmers in a sea of red tape, vast expense, and public opprobrium. And in the first votes on gene-spliced products following implementation of the new rules, several governments continued to vote against approving new varieties. A provision in the new regulations that permits the European Commission to break a political deadlock when there are neither enough votes to grant or deny approval allowed the EC to approve one variety. Even then, the variety—Syngenta's Bt-11 sweet corn—was approved only for import (harvested and canned), not for cultivation within the EU.[14]

EXPORTING RESISTANCE TO NON-EUROPEAN COUNTRIES

Europe's regulatory excesses toward the new biotechnology initially were seen as a regional problem, but the wealthier countries of East Asia have begun to take a similar precautionary approach to biotechnology regulation. Japan, a longtime leader in biotechnology research, has tightened restrictions on biotech food imports, and South Korea has followed its neighbor's lead.[15] Even China, a world leader in research and development of gene-spliced food and fiber crops, has approved no new biotech food crop varieties since 2000.[16]

The European Union is also aggressively trying to insinuate its regulatory approach into international treaties that will bind countries around the world. The EU was the primary advocate of the Cartagena Protocol on Biosafety, for example, which regulates the planting of gene-spliced plants and international trade in grains, vegetables, and fruits harvested from them. It was in the context of this intensifying political debate in the industrialized world that officials in many less developed nations were forced for the first time to confront the problematic world of biotechnology regulation.

In most industrialized nations, well-established biosafety policies governing the movement and introduction of new plants were in operation long before the advent of the new biotechnology. In many less developed nations, however, the formal evaluation of new crop or ornamental plants for biosafety had not been well-established prior to the appearance of gene-spliced varieties. Such evaluation had traditionally been viewed as a costly and technically demanding task that was far less important than boosting farm yields and addressing public health problems.[17] But the EU and United Nations reckon that what less developed countries really need is bureaucracies to "enable scientists to test for transgenic crops." That is "like offering swimming lessons to people in the Sahara," according to Calestous Juma, a former executive secretary of the UN's Convention on Biological Diversity, now director of the Science, Technology, and Innovation Program at Harvard University, which focuses on the role of research and development in less developed countries.[18]

Obstacles to Biotechnology in Less Developed Countries

In practice, the challenge for governments is to enact biosafety policies that can detect possible biohazards associated with new plants—whatever the techniques used to develop them—while not blocking the use of new crop varieties on speculative grounds alone or exceeding the technical or administrative capacity of regulators. But governments in less developed countries have not met the challenge. Instead, they have chosen the same scientifically indefensible regulatory approach that industrialized nations have chosen for themselves—holding all gene-spliced varieties to standards that could not possibly be met by the products of conventional breeding and exempting virtually all non-gene-spliced plants, regardless of risk.

Part of the reason is that UN agencies have dangled funding in front of these poorer countries for "capacity building"—that is, establishment of regulatory apparatuses—if the countries sign on to agreements to regulate gene-splicing excessively, such as the Cartagena Protocol on Biosafety and the evolving Codex standards.

The United Nations Environment Program has announced a $38 million initiative to help developing countries set up infrastructure for the testing and commercialization of products made with recombinant DNA technology.[19] The three-year project will center on "building capacity for assessing risks, establishing adequate information systems and developing expert human resources in the field of biosafety."

But the proposal is problematic. Many of the countries for which the project is intended lack virtually any regulation of *acknowledged* high-risk activities, such as public transport and dangerous occupations, and their expenditures on public health are woefully inadequate. It is not unusual in poor tropical countries, for example, to observe preteens performing welding or using dangerous machinery, with no protective gear and wearing only shorts or a loincloth. Malaria, schistosomiasis, and bacterial and viral diseases that have been all but eradicated from industrialized countries remain epidemic in many underdeveloped nations. Surely the UN's $38 million dollars would be spent much more productively if it was allocated to address any of these more important problems.

The UNEP's cynical offers of bribes to get countries to ratify the Cartagena Protocol offer Faustian bargains to less developed nations. They would receive small grants up front, but in the long term, unscientific, excessive regulation of this promising new technology—and the resulting uncertainty among innovators about their ability to conduct research and market products—would ensure that the biotechnology revolution all but passes them by. Such strategies—on which the UN bureaucrats publicly congratulate themselves—are a moral outrage.

As a direct consequence of such efforts, some less developed nations have now adopted official biosafety regulations for gene-spliced organisms, but very few have granted any approvals for commercial releases. By the end of 2003, for example, the only nation in all of Africa to have granted commercial planting approvals for gene-spliced crops was South Africa—which grows varieties of corn, soybean, and cotton. In all of Asia, only China, India, and the Philippines have so far given any commercial planting approvals—the first two for Bt-cotton and the last for Bt-corn, respectively.[20]

This represents a surprisingly high degree of risk aversion, given that most developing countries—where insecticide spraying, the mismanagement of irrigation, encroachment into forests, and the destruction of wildlife habitat are all common features of agriculture—have never been greatly concerned about the biosafety risks of new crop introductions. With good reason—the greatest biosafety and environmental hazards in rural areas of the developing world have in the past come not from crop plants but from intentional destruction of wildlife habitat for agricultural expansion or other development, and from pathogenic microorganisms and various non-domesticated non-coevolved ("exotic") plant and animal species introduced intentionally or accidentally into new ecosystems.

Real Dangers in Poor and Developing Countries

Crop plants (gene-spliced or otherwise) are seldom invasive, because crops bred for human use are generally poorly competitive outside of their protected and high-maintenance farming environments.[21] By contrast, non-coevolved, or exotic, species can do devastating damage if introduced into farming environments in circumstances in which the natural competitors or predators that usually control them are absent. According to some estimates, the introduction of such exotic species (which have nothing at all to do with the new biotechnology) in the developing world currently generate losses to agriculture in the tens of billions of dollars annually.[22]

Examples include losses from virus-carrying whiteflies in South and Central America, and from the exotic cattail weeds now strangling rice in the wetlands of northern Nigeria. In China, the introduction of cord-grass (*Spartina anglica*) from Europe in 1963–1964 caused huge losses of biodiversity in fish ponds and shrimp ponds in southern coastal areas, and more than two hundred indigenous species were made extinct. Consequently, it would be understandable if governments' primary concern were the introduction of entirely new plant species into their ecosystems. Instead, they perseverate about gene-spliced organisms, the vast majority of which belong to species that have a long history of safe use in a wide range of ecosystems on all the habitable continents. They persist in subjecting gene-spliced plants to extraordinary regulatory scrutiny while subjecting true exotics to only cursory (if any) oversight.

It might also be understandable for poor countries to resist gene-spliced crops on environmental grounds if the specific biotechnology applications at issue had never been tried anywhere in the world. These countries are perhaps understandably sensitive to being the victims of "dumping" of untested or dubious products. But most of the crops being considered in less developed nations, such as herbicide-tolerant soybeans in Paraguay, Bt-corn in Kenya, and Bt-cotton in Indonesia, were first approved and cultivated widely and without incident for years in the United States, Argentina, Canada, Australia, China, and South Africa.

Rather than generating new biohazards, the best evidence shows that herbicide-tolerant and insect-resistant gene-spliced crops have reduced rural environmental damage by allowing farmers to engage in less harmful soil-tillage practices, spray herbicides that are less toxic and less persistent (and to do so less often), and decrease the spraying of chemical insecticides that commonly poison nontarget species and field workers.[23]

Finally, one could understand a scenario in which governments in the developing world were eager to obtain the latest agricultural technologies but were frustrated by the reluctance of their own highly traditional, conservative farming communities to use those new tools. In many nations, however, the opposite is happening. Rather than trying to promote access to gene-spliced crops, many government officials have worked to keep those technologies unavailable, especially through regulatory and trade policy decisions.

Developing nations' representatives in the negotiations that led to the Cartagena Protocol on Biosafety collaborated to create a mechanism that would impede the transfer of this technology into their own countries. (It is noteworthy that at these kinds of negotiations most countries—including both less developed and industrialized—are often represented by officials from environment ministries rather than those concerned with science, agriculture, or public health.) Meanwhile, many farmers in those countries have been eager to plant gene-spliced crops but are prevented from doing so by their own governments.

For years, Brazilian and Paraguayan soybean growers were so enamored of gene-spliced varieties that they routinely but illegally planted seeds smuggled in from Argentina, risking harassment and arrest.[24] In September 2003, the Brazilian government granted a provisional, one-year approval for gene-spliced soybeans primarily because so many farmers were already growing them.[25] Ironically, the Indian government very nearly opted *against* approving the commercialization of Bt-cotton after it was discovered in 2001 that farmers were planting seed obtained illegally from field trials of the gene-spliced variety under consideration.[26] We find it revealing that when biotech varieties *have* been made available to farmers in less developed nations, they have been adopted quickly and eagerly.

Economic Obstacles

Other factors that contribute to the inability of poor developing countries to benefit from gene-spliced crops include mistrust of and unwillingness to cooperate with large, multinational corporations and a lack of substantial funding for charitable or public-sector biotechnology research.

Public-sector funding for agricultural research has declined substantially since the days of the Green Revolution, and ewhat funds are available are largely spent on more conventional technologies. The Consultative Group on International Agricultural Research (CGIAR), a network of World Bank–sponsored research institutes established in the 1970s to help poor farmers in the tropics breed better crops, devotes only about 10 percent of its $340 million budget to any kind of biotechnology;[27] much of that goes not to research that involves gene-splicing but to the least controversial crop biotechnology techniques, such as tissue culture and marker-assisted plant breeding.

Some of the most effective international assistance for agricultural biotechnology has come from the New York–based Rockefeller Foundation, which between 1985 and 2000 spent about $100 million on plant research and training for more than four hundred developing-country scientists who work on both gene-spliced and conventional rice varieties in various overseas locations.[28] However, most international support is more targeted to training local scientists or building regulatory capacity than for funding research on the improvement of crops with gene-splicing techniques.

It is lamentable that organizations like the Rockefeller Foundation, which possesses financial clout and the ability to exercise moral suasion, have not been a force for science-based public policy. For example, had Rockefeller and the CGIAR adopted a policy of not funding research in countries that adopt unscientific regulations, the regulatory landscape might be altogether more pleasant to behold.

In order to obtain new plant varieties, farmers in the developing world have relied mainly on commercial firms selling locally adapted cultivars of the varieties first introduced in industrialized countries. In some cases, such as Bt-corn in South Africa and Bt-cotton in China and India, this has worked well. However, research on plants such as rice, millet, cassava, sweet potato, and others that are staple crops in less developed nations but far less significant in industrialized countries must often be funded by aid institutions or national governments. It is ironic, then, that countries such as Brazil, China, India, Mexico, the Philippines, and Thailand have adopted highly risk-averse, overregulatory biosafety policies while at the same time spending large sums of government money to develop gene-spliced crops. Government both giveth and taketh away.

In Brazil, India, and Kenya, government-funded scientists complain bitterly about the slowdown in the development of gene-spliced crops caused by stifling environmental regulations.[29] Relatively large public-sector expenditures—at least, by the standards of poor countries—are difficult to justify in light of the coexistence of paralyzing biosafety rules, especially when research funds are devoured by regulatory requirements. Just as in the United States, a field trial with a gene-spliced plant may be many times more expensive than the same experiment performed with a plant that has virtually identical characteristics but that was modified with less precise genetic techniques. This is a tragic waste of scarce research funds, which are squandered on paperwork and unnecessary experimental procedures. In return, there is no enhancement of environmental safety or public health, merely a marked diminution in the amount of research bang for the buck (or peso or rupee).

THE SPREAD OF ANTI-BIOTECHNOLOGY POLICIES

The initially positive outlook of many less-developed countries toward the new biotechnology became less favorable only after gene-spliced crops became controversial among consumer and environmental advocacy groups in the industrialized world. For example, the Indian Review Committee on Genetic Manipulation was designed originally to promote biotechnology[30] but has become a highly risk-averse regulatory body. Brazil's National Technical Commission on Biosafety (CTNBio) initially granted approval for gene-spliced soybeans as long ago as 1998, but that decision was challenged in court by Greenpeace and a consumer-activist organization. The courts ruled that CTNBio did not have authority to make approvals, and the review process was reconstituted to make it more precautionary. It wasn't until September 2003 that Brazilian president Luiz Inàcio Lula da Silva granted a one-year approval for farmers to grow that variety. In Brazil, India, and elsewhere, the regulatory approval process has been obstructed by lawsuits, media campaigns, and direct political actions by anti-biotechnology activist organizations, many of which receive funding and leadership direction from Europe and North America and are direct extensions of overseas radical organizations such as Greenpeace.

India finally relented and approved Bt-cotton in 2002, but seven months later the government's interministerial Genetic Engineering Approval Committee (GEAC) deferred a final decision on gene-spliced mustard (used commonly in Asian nations to produce cooking oil) in the face of an often vicious and mendacious media campaign mounted by environmental activists.[31] It also refused to grant an expanded approval to additional Bt-cotton varieties in the spring of 2003, granting only limited additional approvals in the spring of 2004.[32] This trend toward unscientific, anti-social regulatory policies and decisions is due to a combination of restrictive policies in industrialized nations, UN-based regulatory agreements, and lobbying by activists.

The anti-biotechnology nongovernmental organizations (NGOs), unsuccessful in their attempts to block completely biosafety approvals of gene-spliced crops in rich countries, are not deterred. They have shifted their efforts to obstructing new approvals and preventing the penetration of gene-spliced crops into poorer nations. For the most part, their objections to agricultural biotechnology are usually part of an ideology that fears and resists modern technology and is antagonistic toward the globalization pursued by U.S.-based multinational corporations and neoliberal global institutions such as the World Bank and World Trade Organization. This wider ideological agenda is a core feature of the anti-biotechnology appeals made by NGOs to urban constituencies in less developed countries.

It is convenient for the activists' agenda that so many of the gene-spliced crops being offered to poorer nations have been produced by U.S.-based multinational giants, including Monsanto and DuPont. If the first generation of biotech crops had come out of government laboratories in the developing world or even out of the publicly funded Consultative Group on International Agricultural Research, anti-biotechnology activists might have had more trouble generating apprehension about them. No matter how good its products may be, the "Mon-Satan" Company makes a good target.

Neocolonial Influence Gives Rise to Overregulation

Biosafety policies in poorer countries are also often driven by the direct influence of NGOs and governments from industrialized—primarily European—countries, which have done no favors for the inhabitants of the developing world. As Wellesley College political scientist Robert Paarlberg has observed, "Instead of helping Africa's hungry to grow more food, European donors are helping them grow more regulations."[33] In a kind of politically correct neocolonialism, Europeans (aided by their overfed, overcompensated chums at the UN) have provided much of the funding and legal expertise for the creation of biosafety policies, which, not coincidentally, end up resembling their own.

These policies set unrealistic, inappropriate standards for testing and data evaluation that poor countries often do not have the capacity to meet, even when the product applications are otherwise complete and unassailable. Donors work hard to help poor nations craft strict biosafety standards, but they invest much less in building the technical and administrative capacity needed to implement them. Knowing that they lack much of the technical capacity necessary to implement their highly complex biosafety regulations and that they will be challenged at every turn by NGOs and the media if they release any gene-spliced crops for commercial use, biosafety regulators in low-resource countries have every incentive to move slowly.[34] Intoning the regulator's all too common lament, Achyut Gokhale, former chairman of India's GEAC, told a *Newsweek International* reporter, "We took a lot of flak over GM cotton. . . . It was my job to ensure we weren't accused of over-hastiness."[35] Thus, we have regulators making decisions not on the merits of products but on the basis of their guesses about public perceptions of the likelihood that regulators are making hasty decisions.

Another reason that many countries, both industrialized and less developed, have slowed their biosafety approval processes is the fear that they will lose export sales if they introduce gene-spliced crops into their agricultural systems. The possibility that major commodity-importing countries such as Japan, South Korea, and the nations of the EU will eventually reject shipments that contain certain gene-spliced products has been enough to cause a number of export-oriented developing countries to slow or halt their commercial approvals entirely. These kinds of concerns, which are especially acute in poor countries, where it would be too costly to segregate farm products into separate gene-spliced and non-gene-spliced commodity streams, have caused horrific situations in places like Uganda.

That country is suffering from several years of devastation by a fungus of its banana crop, the primary food staple. A few years ago, the government was encouraging the testing of gene-spliced fungus-resistant banana plants developed by Belgian scientist Rony Swennen, but it backed off in the face of the EU biotech moratorium.[36] This is doubly tragic, not only because farmers are being devastated and people are starving but because in Uganda the banana should be the least worrisome gene-spliced plant imaginable. It doesn't produce pollen, so the introduced genes cannot be transferred, and the plants won't produce volunteers. The genetic alterations are in the leaves and stem, so the fruit is not affected. Also, inasmuch as Ugandans eat almost all of the bananas they grow, any impact on export markets would be small.

Still, the negative attitudes held by Europeans have been spread by NGOs throughout Africa. It is all too common to hear Ugandans ask, "If Europeans are concerned, shouldn't we be too?"[37] Let us not forget, though, that all of this controversy and turmoil is over whether a demonstrably safe, superior product should and can merely be *tested* so that ultimately it might become available to farmers and consumers who desperately need it. Especially in this case, the risk-risk and risk-benefit calculations are unequivocal.

Remaining "Biotech-Free"

Similar to the situation in Uganda, the decision by the Zambian and Zimbabwean governments to refuse gene-spliced corn as food aid in the face of famine reflects the belief that the surest way to compete for the business of wary buyers in Europe or Japan is to remain entirely "biotech-free."

Other countries, including Argentina, Australia, China, Thailand, and Brazil, have curtailed their approvals for the same reason. Because Brazil's only known gene-spliced crop is soybean, Brazilian corn could (more or less) credibly be sold as "non-gene-spliced." In January 2002 the country's farmers captured a premium of six to seven dollars a ton over U.S. corn in overseas sales.[38] In most markets, however, there is no price premium for other non-gene-spliced crops, such as canola, because nearly all canola is processed in such a way that oil from gene-spliced and conventional varieties are indistinguishable from one another.[39] That may change, however, under the new labeling and traceability rules instituted by the European Union in April 2004 (which we discuss in the next chapter).

The strategy of remaining "officially" biotech-free is not foolproof, though. Some European food importers have declined to purchase beef from Namibia because the cattle is partly raised on gene-spliced corn grown in South Africa.[40] By 2000, more than three years before the legal planting of gene-spliced soybeans in Brazil, sophisticated foreign customers were reluctant to pay premiums for supposedly non-gene-spliced Brazilian soybeans, because illicit planting of seeds smuggled in from Argentina had become commonplace. By one estimate, Brazil had become the world's fifth-largest grower of gene-spliced crops that year.[41]

Brazil was unusual in having such quantities of bootlegged seeds, however, so it may still be possible for other nations to capture the business of European and Japanese commodity buyers by prohibiting the cultivation of gene-spliced crops. That is the gamble being taken by several Australian state governments which, for marketing reasons, forbade the planting of gene-spliced canola early in 2004, shortly after it was approved by the Australian federal government's Office of Gene Technology Regulator.[42]

The ability to command a premium price for what is arguably an inferior product is not unlike the marketing of unpasteurized milk—known to harbor pathogenic bacteria, including *Mycobacterium bovis*, *Listeria*, and *Salmonella*—which persisted at low levels in the United States until recently because certain consumers demanded it. Nevertheless, when it comes to gene-spliced crop plants, many governments are hoping to capitalize on the irrational policies in major export markets.

Research, Development, and Trade in China

The evolution of policy in China is another reflection of the interplay between biotech research and development and international trade. For years, China pushed ahead aggressively with the development and planting of gene-spliced crops while paying little more than token attention to biosafety. The Chinese State Council began to invest heavily in gene-spliced crop research during the 1980s, and the authorities were eager to get the results of this research into the field. China planted gene-spliced tobacco over wide areas in the early 1990s before its Ministry of Science and Technology had even promulgated an official policy for field testing gene-spliced organisms. The government went on to grant field trial permits for dozens of cultivars from a range of different plant species.[43] There was no danger, of course, that in China commercial releases would be blocked by activist NGOs promoting obstructionist lawsuits or anti-gene-splicing media campaigns; opposition NGO groups are not permitted to operate in mainland China, and there is neither a free press nor an independent judiciary.

In spite of the absence in China of NGOs or outspoken negative public opinion, China's aggressive move on gene-spliced crops has stalled. By 1999, China had approved thirty agricultural biotech products for field trials, including twenty-four for commercialization.[44] But since 2000, because of concerns that new approvals could compromise the acceptability of Chinese agricultural exports, China's Committee on the Safety of Agricultural Biological Genetic Engineering has been reluctant to approve any additional gene-spliced food crops for commercial cultivation. By September of 2000, there was a backlog of nearly two hundred products for various kinds of field trials that had not yet been approved.[45] In April 2001 Chinese officials announced that new commercial releases, especially for food crops, would be frozen at least temporarily, specifically citing international consumer resistance to gene-spliced foods as one reason for the halt.

China's policy change coincided with the decision in late 2000 by importers in Japan and South Korea to look for completely non-gene-spliced shipments of corn, after it became known that some U.S. corn shipments contained traces of StarLink™, a gene-spliced variety that had been approved in the United States for animal feed use but not for human consumption. Japan, in particular, reduced purchases from the United States and increased purchases from Brazil, where regulators had not yet approved the planting of any gene-spliced corn. China, an occasional exporter of corn, began to imagine there might be some commercial advantage in remaining, like Brazil, a biotech-free source of corn and other crops. As recently as summer 2004, China had not yet approved any gene-spliced corn varieties, even though successful field trials had been under way since 1998.

China is also an occasional exporter of rice to Japan, so the possible commercial advantage of remaining biotech-free in domestic rice production arose as well. Thus, although China boasts one of the largest and most advanced research programs on gene-spliced rice, the prospects seem remote for near-term market approvals. The anti-biotechnology views of many in Europe also had to be of concern to China, given the increasing diversity and global reach of its agricultural exports. Even before the StarLink™ episode, at least one shipment of Chinese soy sauce known to have been produced in Shanghai from U.S.-grown gene-spliced soybeans was turned back by skittish EU importers.[46] The commercial advantage to China of remaining a biotech-free source of soybeans was underscored late in 2001, when as an alternative to "contaminated" U.S. and Argentine beans Korea purchased three hundred thousand tons of Chinese soybeans for food use.

Fear of Lost Export Sales

It is not only China that has begun adjusting its gene-spliced crop approval practices to take commercial realities into account. Argentine officials, who at first aggressively approved gene-spliced soybeans and corn, more recently have refrained from approving any gene-spliced corn varieties not yet approved by regulators in the EU. Argentina learned a lesson from the situation in the United States, where biotech firms commercialized new varieties of gene-spliced corn after the EU began its unofficial moratorium on approvals in 1998. Since then, American corn has faced a variety of export difficulties. Bulk shipments that contain any non-EU-approved gene-spliced varieties have been turned away from the EU market, at a loss to U.S. exporters of more than $200 million in sales annually.[47]

Taking heed of this experience with corn, U.S. commodity producers and exporters decided not to seek commercial approval for any varieties of gene-spliced soybeans that had not yet been approved by the EU. As of mid-2004, only Monsanto's Roundup Ready® soybean variety was fully commercialized around the world—even though other gene-spliced soybeans were available for marketing—because Roundup Ready® was the only soybean variety fully approved in the European Union. U.S. and Canadian regulators are reluctant to approve gene-spliced wheat, partly for fear of discouraging purchases by Europe or Japan. The chairman of the Canadian Wheat Board has estimated that the first exporting country to begin planting gene-spliced wheat could immediately lose one-third of its export customer base.[48] And in the spring of 2004, Monsanto announced that it was indefinitely delaying plans to introduce its Roundup Ready® wheat variety due to these concerns.

U.S. food producers are taking other measures to prevent their grains (which are of superior quality!) from becoming unexportable. In remarks at the U.S. Chamber of Commerce in December 2002, Department of Agriculture special counsel David Hegwood identified a particularly "troubling development" in agricultural trade—American food producers moving production facilities abroad and using non-U.S. food ingredients to avoid the labeling required by the EU, Japan, Korea, Australia, and New Zealand. "The food companies have been very clear: They do not want to put GMO [genetically modified organism] labels on their branded food products," he said. "They, too, are afraid of the European attitudes toward biotechnology. If it is happening to U.S. exports and U.S. companies, it will happen to every other country that utilizes biotechnology. If they can do this to biotechnology, they can do it to any other issue that captures the attention of the European public."[49] Hegwood might have added, "or that can be *alleged* to capture the attention of the European public, or to conflict with its 'social values.'"

Fear of lost export sales has thus become the single most important constraint on additional plantings of gene-spliced crops around the world. In export-oriented nations such as the United States, where farmers have planted gene-spliced crops aggressively since the mid-1990s, the full-scale retreat from gene-spliced crops by other exporting nations has been viewed with justifiable alarm. U.S. farmers and exporters had expected that gene-spliced commodities would flood export markets worldwide, eliminating any realistic opportunity for anti-biotech importers to find and purchase a large-volume, biotech-free source of commodity grains. This is now the case with soybeans, where over 90 percent of global exports come from the U.S., Brazil, and Argentina, each of which plants substantial acreage with gene-spliced varieties.[50] However, this degree of diffusion never materialized with any other crop species, and the future prospects for the technology now depend heavily upon whether importing countries will be able to get away with unscientific government-sanctioned protectionist policies, blocking imports of gene-spliced organisms, and requiring stigmatizing labels on foods derived from them.

Several aspects of this situation are troubling. First, the most risk-averse, anti-technology players are being permitted to set the rules of the game. Second, there is strong and obvious protectionism behind the rejection of the products of a superior technology. Third, leaving aside narrow commercial advantages that may accrue to certain players who adopt anti-technology policies, the market distortions that are part of this game are damaging to overall international trade and to the interests of consumers throughout the world.

We cannot overemphasize that regulators' risk aversion toward and rejection of gene-spliced crops in no way confers any sort of protection of the natural environment or public health. The reality is quite the opposite. We discuss the ongoing U.S.-EU dispute in more detail in the next chapter.

CHAPTER 8

European Resistance
to Biotechnology

Tʜᴇ ᴄʜᴀsᴍ ʙᴇᴛᴡᴇᴇɴ U.S. and European attitudes and policies regarding the new biotechnology is a relatively recent development, dating only to the late 1990s. During the early days of recombinant DNA research and development, U.S. and EU policies toward gene-spliced crops were not significantly different. Prior to 1998, the European Union approved several new gene-spliced crops, based on scientific testing for food safety and biosafety risks, just as U.S. regulators did. Although these procedures were far more restrictive and burdensome than necessary, a trickle of gene-spliced crop varieties was emerging.

THE IMPACT OF MAD COW DISEASE

This approach became politically untenable in the EU after the 1996 crisis over bovine spongiform encephalopathy (BSE), or "mad cow disease," which was transmissible (as variant Creutzfeldt-Jakob disease) to humans who consumed infected meat. BSE is in no way related to recombinant DNA techniques. Indeed, rather than arising from a novel technology or agricultural practice, the inadvisable feeding customs that gave rise to BSE were centuries old. Nevertheless, BSE undercut the confidence of consumers in all official EU regulatory systems and pronouncements because early on, food safety regulators had repeatedly assured consumers it was safe to eat meat from BSE-diseased animals—a position that in retrospect appears foolish and incompetent.

Consumer confidence in foods made with gene-splicing techniques was not severely undercut, however, until the technology was attacked by a variety of anti-corporate and anti-globalization nongovernmental organization (NGO) activist groups such as Greenpeace and Friends of the Earth. Those groups were able to capitalize on the mistakes related to BSE to erode public confidence in the safety assurances offered for gene-spliced foods.

Even now, however, the intensity of negative consumer attitudes is often exaggerated. A comprehensive survey known as the Eurobarometer measured attitudes in all fifteen EU member nations in the fall of 2002 and found that some 70 percent of Western Europeans supported gene-spliced crop *plants*, though only 50 percent support gene-spliced *foods*—with respondents in Greece, France, Luxembourg, and Austria falling well below average and respondents in Spain, the Netherlands, Portugal, and Finland the farthest above average.[1] Still, the minority that remains strongly opposed to the new biotechnology is very vocal and dominates media coverage and political debates.

These activist-driven attitudes have led food processors and retailers to avoid gene-spliced products, and they have induced individual European governments, and then EU authorities in Brussels, to place a moratorium on the approval of any new gene-spliced crops for commercial production and consumption.

Dread of Consumer Backlash

The mandatory labeling of certain gene-spliced foods is among the most important factors in European resistance to the technology. Contrary to popular opinion, however, the biggest problem with mandatory labeling of gene-spliced foods has been one of neither consumer rejection per se nor added cost (which is not insignificant). Rather, it has been food producers' and retailers' dread of an NGO-led backlash that could cause even a small percentage of consumers to reject their products.

In spite of the seemingly widespread concern about so-called "genetically modified" (GM) foods throughout Western Europe, some affirmatively labeled gene-spliced products can still be found on supermarket shelves. Where both gene-spliced and non-gene-spliced products are sold, there does not appear to be any price premium for non-gene-spliced foods. Less than 5 percent of European consumers appear to be so strongly and actively opposed to gene-spliced foods that they will reject them under virtually any circumstances. Indeed, most consumers must actually have the "GM" label pointed out to them before they have any qualms about purchasing labeled gene-spliced foods.[2]

Thus, except for a very small minority, it appears that the fear of, or ambivalence toward, gene-spliced food that is revealed by consumer surveys may be real, but it is not so deeply held that it actually impacts purchasing decisions. As recently as 1999, labeled cans of processed paste from the Zeneca company's gene-spliced tomato variety sold well in British grocery stores.[3] Other labeled gene-spliced food products, mainly from the small- and mid-sized brands among which price competition is most fierce, can today be found on store shelves throughout the EU, even in such stalwart anti-biotech countries such as France and Germany.

Why would producers and retailers reject gene-spliced foods, if consumers haven't? Competition in the food industry is intense, and profit margins tend to be very small, so the defection of even a few percent of consumers could mean the difference between profitability and millions of dollars of lost revenues. With Greenpeace, Friends of the Earth, and other campaign organizations so eager to protest and retaliate against supermarket chains and food-processing companies that use gene-spliced ingredients, few firms are willing to put their carefully-guarded brand reputations at risk. The bigger the companies, the less willing they seem to use the new biotechnology in a way that subjects their products to the labeling requirements.[4]

The Moratorium

Facing intense protests from activist organizations and fearing that support of scientifically sound, if unpopular, public policy could adversely affect their reelection chances, many European politicians had come out against gene-spliced foods by the late 1990s. In 1998, political opposition to biotechnology was so strong that the governments of Austria, Denmark, France, Greece, Italy, and Luxembourg began to block the EU's approval of all new gene-spliced crop varieties. That informal moratorium remained intact until May 2004, following the introduction of new, more stringent regulations for approval and more comprehensive labeling rules.

During that time, there were a dozen new gene-spliced crop varieties stuck in the approval pipeline even though every one of them has been successfully screened by the EU's Scientific Committee on Plants.[5] The moratorium kept many bulk shipments of U.S. commodities out of Europe at a commercial cost to U.S. exporters of some $200–$300 million a year. Although one gene-spliced food product was eventually approved—because a change in the rules allows the European Commission to break the deadlock when there are neither enough countries voting to grant or deny authorization—the governments of Denmark, Greece, France, Luxembourg, Austria, and Portugal were still trying to block EU-wide approvals. Furthermore, the new regulations impose draconian hurdles to pre- and post-market-approval for gene-spliced food and animal feeds. Among the most onerous of these new rules is the requirement for labeling and "tracing" gene-spliced food products.[6]

Even prior to the new rules taking effect, gene-spliced foods had to be labeled, but the requirement extended only to products in which residues of the novel gene or gene product could be detected. In practice, this meant that many processed foods, such as oils from gene-spliced corn and canola, or cheeses made with the gene-spliced coagulant chymosin, were exempted, because no detectable evidence of gene-splicing survives the processing.

Under the new labeling and traceability rules, however, any food or animal feed produced from a gene-spliced organism must be labeled, re-

184 ·   The Frankenfood Myth

gardless of whether or not there is any detectable difference from conventionally produced foods. In order to facilitate this thorny labeling rule, seed producers, farmers, shippers, processors, retailers, and others will be required to keep detailed records of the source of the raw materials used in their products and to whom the products were sold, so they can be "traced" all the way through the food chain. What makes this especially onerous is that every single gene-spliced variety must be traced individually. This is a debilitating requirement; segregating gene-spliced products in every shipment going from the United States or elsewhere to Europe will grossly disrupt the commodity process for shipping grains and add dramatically to the cost of producing foods.

Consider one example. If a particular processed food such as ketchup was made from a single variety of gene-spliced tomatoes, vegetable oil derived from three different gene-spliced canola varieties, and corn sweetener from a dozen different gene-spliced corn varieties, the processor, packager, and retailer would all be required to track all sixteen gene-spliced ingredients, and then do the same for every single food product they receive and/or sell! Furthermore, growers and sellers of non-biotech foods would also have to bear the cost of testing at every step for the presence of adventitious gene-spliced material, lest they unwittingly pass along trace amounts of those ingredients and suffer legal sanctions.

Such draconian requirements and procedures for traceability might be justified if there were bona fide safety issues—such as contamination with new "biopharmed" crop varieties that produce potent orally active medicines—but that is emphatically *not* the case for the food crops at issue. Moreover, the scope of what is subsumed under the new labeling and traceability rules appears to have been gerrymandered for political and economic ends. Recall the arcane and obscure distinction made between items produced *from* and produced *with* a gene-spliced organism, discussed in chapter 4. Foods that contain one or more ingredients produced *from* a gene-spliced organism as an additive—say, oil produced *from* gene-spliced corn, or tofu produced *from* gene-spliced soybeans—are considered, for regulatory purposes, to be genetically modified and must be labeled. However, foods that are produced *with* the aid of a gene-spliced organism—such as cheeses produced *with* gene-spliced chymosin or beers and wines fermented *with* gene-spliced yeasts—are not considered to be genetically modified.[7]

Not coincidentally, European companies are far more competitive in the "produced *with*" group of products, which includes French and Italian wines and cheeses, and German, British, and Dutch beers. This further sophistry within a system that is already fundamentally arbitrary, capricious, and wrongheaded is reminiscent of Humpty Dumpty's view in *Through the Looking Glass* that a word means whatever he wishes it to mean.

Promoting Irrational Fears

Astonishingy, the European Commission actually acknowledges that its new, hugely costly and debilitating labeling and traceability directive does not stem from genuine concerns about the safety of any gene-spliced products currently on the market. On the contrary, the official position of the EC, as recounted by Commissioner for Health and Consumer Affairs David Byrne, is that currently marketed, gene-spliced crop varieties pose no greater food safety or environmental threat than the corresponding conventional varieties.[8] He even characterizes the European consumers who continue to fear gene-spliced foods as "irrational." But, just as heightened regulation has been promoted by some U.S. food and biotechnology companies as a way of reassuring consumers that gene-spliced products are safe, the European Commission maintains that its proposed new labeling policies will reduce irrational consumer fears and actually promote consumer confidence in gene-spliced foods.

The facts argue otherwise. Pandering to near-superstitious hysteria only serves to enhance anti-biotechnology (and more general anti-technology) mythology. As the former president of the consumer-advocacy group Consumer Alert testified to a federal investigative panel a decade ago, "For obvious reasons, the consumer views the technologies that are *most* regulated to be the *least* safe ones. Heavy involvement by government, no matter how well intended, inevitably sends the wrong signals. Rather than ensuring confidence, it raises suspicion and doubt."[9]

Surely, a better approach would be to choose progressive, rational public policy that defies the myths and favors the public interest, and then to educate the public vigorously as to the wisdom of that policy. However, having ignored the Rule of Holes—when you're in a hole, stop digging—the EU may be past the point of being able to select this option. The Brussels-based European Association for Bioindustries, a trade group, reports that since 1998, 61 percent of the private-sector institutions surveyed by the EC's Joint Research Center have canceled research projects that involve recombinant DNA technology.[10] There has been a virtual meltdown of field trials of gene-spliced organisms in Europe; from a rather unimpressive peak level of 264 field trials in 1997, there were only thirty-five in 2002, and all of *two* during the first quarter of 2003.[11] Thus, the EU's only viable strategy may be to poison the well—to make sure that the new biotechnology fails everywhere and that no competitor remains standing.

The EU touts its new labeling and traceability requirements as a way to convince individual national governments that consumers will have the information they need to make choices and predicts that it will become politically acceptable to resume product approvals. But, as we discussed in chapters 2 and 4, that seems implausible. The votes by Denmark, Greece, France, Luxembourg, Austria, and Portugal in April 2004 against approving the importation of Syngenta's Bt-11 corn appear to validate that skepticism. Because the rules seem unlikely to improve consumer acceptance, and because they pose a significant barrier to many imported food products but not many domestic ones, observers could be forgiven for suspecting less than pure motives from European officials.

Fortunately, while the moratorium hurt U.S. exports, several factors mitigated its impact. First, gene-spliced varieties that already had been approved by the EU prior to the moratorium could still be exported from the United States. The only gene-spliced soybean variety grown commercially in the United States was approved in the EU before 1998, so soybean shipments had only modest difficulty going through. In any case, most soy is used for animal feed or is highly processed into cooking oils or lecithin emulsifier, products that escaped the labeling requirements in place from 1997 to April 2004.

Second, the most heavily affected agricultural product was corn, because U.S. farmers plant several varieties that have not been approved in the European Union. However, very little U.S. corn had gone to the European market even before the moratorium, because of high import barriers resulting both directly and indirectly from the EU's Common Agricultural Policy. So, although the ability of U.S. farmers to export corn has been heavily affected, the loss amounts only to an estimated $200 million to $300 million per year. That is not an insignificant sum, but because American farmers still export many billion dollars' worth of grain and feed to various parts of the world every year, it is comparatively modest.[12] Thus, although significant, the economic damage has not been crippling.

The situation could change dramatically, however, under the EU's new labeling and traceability rules. Finalizing those new regulations has led to an end of the moratorium, but at what cost? No longer will processed oils or animal feeds escape the stigma of a mandatory "gene-spliced" or "GMO" label, even though no difference at all can be detected between heavily processed products, and the onerous traceability requirement will make growing, shipping, and using gene-spliced crop varieties prohibitively expensive in most cases.

Thus, if the activist-led consumer backlash against recombinant DNA technology persists in Europe, it may become politically unpopular for the U.S. government, as it has for others, to approve new varieties of gene-spliced plants. Political scientist Robert Paarlberg notes that the traceability rule could be the one regulation that finally drives gene-spliced products out of the European market, because the complete segregation required will mean having "two of everything—two sets of grain elevators in every county, two categories of railroad cars and river barges, separated drying and processing facilities, and segregated export elevators."[13] We would add only the caveat that not all gene-spliced products would be driven from the European market, because the labeling and traceability rules do not apply to many products of recombinant DNA technology commonly made or used by European producers.

An unfortunate corollary of this will be that occasional examples of inconsequential cross-contamination will create new "pseudo-crises" to be trumpeted and exploited by the anti-biotech lobby. All this over the disparagement of a superior technology and the enforced segregation of items that are virtually indistinguishable from one another! As we discuss below, a U.S. attempt to interrupt this domino effect by mounting a World Trade Organization (WTO) challenge to the EU rules is clearly warranted. Unfortunately, this strategy may not be effective, especially if the Codex Alimentarius Commission (the UN organization that sets food standards) legitimizes the unscientific, precautionary European approach to regulation.

THE LOOMING U.S.-EU TRADE CONFLICT

The use of sovereign power by European nations to restrict or hamper cross-border trade in gene-spliced plants, seeds, and food raises a sensitive international issue. Ordinarily, governments are free under international law to set policies that bind residents within their jurisdictions, whether or not those policies are reasonable or scientifically defensible. And, although the EU's restrictions on gene-spliced crops and foods violate the terms of several WTO agreements to which the EU is a party, they do seem to be authorized under the Cartagena Protocol on Biosafety. Thus, there remains uncertainty about how these disputes will ultimately be resolved, or even to which of several venues parties should turn for resolution.

The applicable World Trade Organization rules are contained in several agreements that have their basis in the 1986–1993 Uruguay Round of negotiations on the General Agreement on Tariffs and Trade (GATT). Uruguay Round negotiators made a concerted effort to reduce tariffs on world agricultural trade and to eliminate many spurious nontariff barriers to imported food products that had been erected by governments in the name of environmental protection or public health. Article XX of the GATT permits WTO members to restrict imports when necessary to protect "public health and safety" or to ensure environmental sustainability.[14] But in order to prevent article XX from becoming a refuge for protectionist rules, two other instruments—the Agreement on the Application of Sanitary and Phytosanitary Measures (SPS) and the Uruguay Round Agreement on Agriculture—were negotiated during the Uruguay Round. A third, the Agreement on Technical Barriers to Trade (TBT), had been negotiated during the earlier Tokyo Round of GATT negotiations and serves a similar purpose.

The cumulative effect of these agreements has been to require laws that restrict trade to be based upon scientifically demonstrable health or environmental risks posed by the end products themselves. Restrictions cannot be based upon mere speculation about potential health hazards, or on a country's amorphous "social values." Nor can they be based upon the production or process methods. Finally, WTO rules stipulate that "like" products—that is, those with similar uses and similar risk characteristics— must be regulated in a like manner. The European Union's biotechnology regulations clearly violate all of these provisions.

These trade agreements were finalized before the first gene-spliced crops were commercialized, whereas the Cartagena Protocol on Biosafety (Biosafety Protocol) was negotiated (perhaps "contrived" would be more accurate) more recently for the specific purpose of governing the transboundary movement of gene-spliced organisms, which the protocol dubs "living modified organisms," or "LMOs". The protocol's text, finalized in January 2000, allows states far more leeway to block imports and to require stigmatizing labels—at least for "living" gene-spliced organisms (defined as those that can replicate their DNA), including live plants, seeds, and unprocessed grains. Under international law, the fact that the Biosafety Protocol was negotiated more recently than the various WTO treaties suggests that it could supercede any prior agreements where the obligations or rights of parties differ, if parties to the dispute have ratified both agreements.

It is important to note that the United States is not a formal party to either the Biosafety Protocol or its parent agreement, the Convention on Biological Diversity. Therefore, it is questionable whether the protocol's requirements would take precedence over WTO obligations vis-à-vis U.S. exports. If both the exporting and potential importing nations are WTO members (as are the U.S. and the European Union) but only one of them is a party to the Biosafety Protocol, WTO obligations should take precedence.

Two Crucial Agreements

Advocates of a more restrictive, precautionary approach toward gene-splicing, including the European Union, want to be able to block imports and impose labeling requirements for as long as it takes to "prove" that gene-spliced organisms are safe for human health and the environment. (One guesses that their time frame is approximately when hell freezes over.) The practical objection to this approach is that as discussed in chapter 4, this standard of proof asks too much from experimental science. Controlled scientific experimentation can demonstrate the *presence* of specifically hypothesized risks, if they exist, but no amount of experimentation can prove the *absence* of all risk.

Consequently, open-ended restrictions based on the precautionary principle would seem to be invalid under the GATT and other WTO agreements. Nevertheless, there is a growing preference among certain WTO members for permitting open-ended precautionary restrictions for gene-spliced crops and other importable goods. As discussed throughout this volume, however, theory, risk-assessment experiments, and empirical experience have already demonstrated not only the safety but the agronomic superiority of many new gene-spliced plant varieties. Consequently, the United States decided to challenge the EU's blatantly noncompliant moratorium on gene-spliced crops.

In May 2003, the governments of the United States, Argentina, and Canada filed a formal complaint with the World Trade Organization, challenging the EU moratorium on approvals of new gene-spliced crops. Nine other countries, including Australia, Chile, Colombia, El Salvador, Honduras, Mexico, New Zealand, Peru, and Uruguay joined the complaint as informal third parties.[15] Because this complaint challenges only the moratorium but not the EU's other unscientific anti-biotechnology rules, it may prove to be only the first of many battles within the WTO to determine the outcome of this long-running dispute. Nevertheless, the unequivocal provisions of the Agreements on Sanitary and Phytosanitary Measures and Technical Barriers to Trade suggest that the case is likely to be decided in favor of the United States and its allies.

The Agreement on Sanitary and Phytosanitary Measures (SPS)

Under the terms of the Sanitary and Phytosanitary (SPS) agreement, nations are free to establish domestic levels of health or environmental protection that are as stringent or lax as they wish—but whatever *import* restrictions they enact must be consistent with internal policies so they do not discriminate against imported goods. They must also be based upon a scientific demonstration of a genuine risk and be no more restrictive than necessary to achieve the desired level of protection; nor may they be maintained "without sufficient scientific evidence."[16]

The SPS agreement acknowledges that science may not be able to identify all relevant risks easily or quickly, so it does allow states to employ temporary import restrictions in cases where experience with the product is limited and genuine scientific uncertainty exists about its risks. Article 5.7 states, "In cases where relevant scientific evidence is insufficient, a Member may provisionally adopt sanitary or phytosanitary measures on the basis of available pertinent information." However, this article also obliges members to base provisional restrictions only on available evidence and to "seek to obtain the additional information necessary for a more objective assessment or risk and review the SPS measure accordingly within a reasonable period of time."[17]

Thus, open-ended "precautionary" restrictions cannot be justified if scientific experiments have been conducted and no evidence of a risk has been found. Especially for varieties of gene-spliced crops that have been commercialized and widely used elsewhere, it is difficult to make the case that the "relevant scientific evidence is insufficient." Literally hundreds of thousands of individual laboratory assessments and field trials have been conducted, and thousands of peer-reviewed research papers can be found in the academic literature. None of this vast body of scientific evidence indicates the presence of any unique or unmanageable environmental or health risks.

The limits on invoking the precautionary principle in trade disputes have already been tested in a case filed by the U.S. and Canadian governments against the European Union. In that case (described in chapter 4), which revolved around European restrictions on American and Canadian beef from cattle given certain growth hormones, the WTO found that while the general "look before you leap" sense of the precautionary principle could be found in the SPS, it does not negate the provisions of the agreement that require regulatory actions to be based upon the findings of a full, scientific risk assessment. A large amount of scientific data had been generated over many years, and even the evidence presented by the EU in the case showed no reason to believe that the hormone residues in question had any negative health effects. Consequently, the WTO ruled in favor of the United States and Canada, and against the EU's use of the precautionary principle. The "reasonable period of time" the SPS allows for the EU to find evidence supporting its restrictions had long passed, and in any case, numerous scientific studies showed no evidence of harm.[18]

Similarly, large amounts of peer-reviewed research conducted by university-based and public-sector scientists—much of it even funded or conducted by the European Commission or EU member governments—has revealed no evidence of unique or novel health or environmental risks from gene-spliced crops or foods.[19] Thus, one would expect the WTO to conclude that the EU's biotechnology policies lack scientific foundation. In the case of the current, narrowly targeted WTO challenge to the EU moratorium, the United States and its co-complainants are almost certain to prevail, because by failing even to consider new product applications for nearly six years, the European Union was violating its *own* rules. Once the moratorium is lifted, exporting nations may have a slightly less easy time challenging the EU's labeling and traceability rules, but even those are not likely to withstand WTO scrutiny.

Winning at the WTO could be a hollow victory, however, as many observers expect that the EU would ignore such a decision. The WTO has no real enforcement power, but relies upon member nations to accept its decisions voluntarily. All the WTO can do is authorize aggrieved parties to establish countervailing import tariffs on goods from the offending nation in an amount equal to the estimated sales revenues lost by the exporters—a right sovereign nations would have even if they were not WTO members. After losing the beef hormone case, the European Union accepted the countervailing tariffs rather than change its policy. If this current or future WTO challenges prove successful, we predict a similar outcome.

European politicians claimed the WTO complaint against the EU moratorium was ill timed and "eccentric," because the moratorium was expected to be lifted once the new approval process and labeling and traceability rules were finalized.[20] But this claim overlooks the fact that, even now, many EU member nations are still reluctant to authorize new gene-spliced varieties. As recently as April 27, 2004, *after* the new regulations went into effect, farm ministers from Austria, Denmark, France, Greece, Luxembourg, and Portugal voted against approval of a gene-spliced sweet corn variety for use only as an imported food, not for planting in the EU; and the ministers from Belgium, Germany, and Spain abstained from the vote.[21] Only a feature of the new regulations that allows the European Commission to break a deadlocked vote made it possible for Syngenta's Bt-11 sweetcorn to be approved.

Even if approvals become more common, though, it will be difficult for growers, shippers, and processors to comply with the discriminatory new labeling and traceability rules. Major food companies in Europe, and exporters in industrialized countries like the United States, Canada, and Australia might, in some cases, be able to comply. Ensuring traceability for individual shipments of gene-spliced soybeans, for example, might be feasible as long as U.S. farmers do not begin to grow multiple biotech varieties. Tracing other crops or multi-ingredient food products, on the other hand, could prove too costly to justify. For poor developing countries, however, the added cost and complexity of the labeling and traceability rules could be completely beyond their ability to comply, shutting them out of the biotechnology revolution.

The mandatory labeling requirement—which supposedly serves consumers' interest by enabling them to differentiate between foods developed with different processing techniques—but which has actually decreased consumers' choices in the marketplace—also could be ruled invalid by the WTO under the terms of the SPS Agreement and the Agreement on Technical Barriers to Trade.

Technical Barriers to Trade (TBT)

The TBT agreement, which governs trade restrictions erected for reasons other than environmental or consumer safety, states that regulatory measures that have the effect of disrupting trade must be necessary to realize a legitimate objective and must not be more restrictive of trade than necessary.[22]

No evidence has ever been produced to suggest that the use of recombinant DNA techniques, per se, compromises product safety or poses any health or environmental risk. Because the EU's labeling requirements focus on the *process* used to develop gene-spliced foods rather than on the risk-related characteristics of these products, such rules would appear to be a clear-cut case of the kind of discrimination prohibited by the TBT and SPS. Consumers' desire for more information per se has never been viewed as a legitimate objective under either agreement. But, just as European governments doggedly defend their indefensible import restrictions, the EU seems ready to defend its labeling requirements as well.

No outcome of this dispute that prolongs trade restrictions—including the imposition of countervailing duties—is desirable, as European consumers would still be denied the choice of gene-spliced products, and tariffs on European exports would force American consumers to pay higher prices. However, a World Trade Organization ruling in favor of the United States and its co-complainants would send an unmistakable message to the world that arbitrary, scientifically indefensible policies and intimidating tactics are unacceptable. Perhaps fearing this outcome, EU delegates to the WTO's current Doha Round of WTO negotiations are hedging their bets by trying specifically to carve out exemptions from TBT and SPS rules when they conflict with radical environmental and consumer "protection" policies. It is unclear how successful such a tactic will be.

The Cartagena Biosafety Protocol

Drafted under the auspices of the United Nations–sponsored Convention on Biological Diversity (CBD), the Cartagena Protocol on Biosafety is nominally intended to protect biological diversity from threats posed by gene-spliced organisms. It erects a global framework for the creation of national biosafety rules that govern the international movement of gene-spliced organisms (called "living modified organisms" or LMOs, in the agreement). The CBD and Biosafety Protocol, which are both projects of the UN's Environment Programme (UNEP), were negotiated primarily by representatives of national environment ministries rather than by officials from trade, science, or agricultural ministries. This provenance has given the protocol a distinct anti-trade, anti-agriculture, and anti-innovation bias.

The terms of the Biosafety Protocol were originally drafted to resemble the Basel Convention on transboundary movement of hazardous wastes.[23] Not surprisingly, the kinds of regulatory systems that the protocol envisions for gene-spliced organisms are more appropriate for toxic chemicals, dangerous pesticides, or nuclear waste than for the relatively safe agricultural products it actually governs. The protocol's negotiators seem to be unaware that there are important differences between paraquat and plutonium on one hand, and papayas and potatoes on the other.

Under the protocol's Advance Informed Agreement (AIA) process, member governments that participate in the protocol are encouraged to require exporters to supply various information about biosafety test results before the first-time importation of any gene-spliced, or living-modified, organism intended for "environmental release" (e.g., gene-spliced seeds or gene-spliced plant materials intended to be grown outside a greenhouse or laboratory). The importing government may then require a complete and possibly redundant premarket biosafety assessment for that variety under domestic conditions.

Although the AIA provision does not apply to shipments of gene-spliced organisms that are intended for food or animal feed, or for other processing, potential exporters nonetheless are obliged to provide timely information to the international community about such LMOs through a newly created international Biosafety Clearing-House. Furthermore, if there are any gene-spliced organisms in the bulk shipments of harvested grains or other foodstuffs, they must be labeled as "May Contain Living Modified Organisms" and "Not Intended for Intentional Introduction into the Environment." Ongoing negotiations are now further defining identification and labeling requirements for such shipments—although, we hasten to mention once again, gene-spliced organisms are often indistinguishable from their conventional counterparts, differing primarily by having been crafted by more precise techniques and exhibiting more predictable behavior.

Finally, the Biosafety Protocol explicitly endorses a "precautionary approach" to risk management that would permit restrictions or outright bans, *even when assessments of individual gene-spliced products find no unreasonable risks.* The text of the agreement reiterates frequently the mantra of the precautionary principle, "lack of scientific certainty due to insufficient relevant scientific information and knowledge" should not prevent governments from taking precautionary import actions against gene-spliced organisms.[24] Of course, when it comes to the politics of precaution, the determination of how much scientific information is necessary to establish certainty is pointedly left to the discretion of individual governments.

The discrepancy between this precautionary approach and the science-based approach required under the SPS agreement was conspicuous to all at the time the Biosafety Protocol was being negotiated. Delegates sought to placate agricultural exporters—such as the United States, Canada, and Argentina—by including a caveat in the agreement's preamble that the Biosafety Protocol "does not imply a change in the rights and obligations of a Party under any existing international agreement," such as the SPS or TBT agreements. However, the preamble also asserts that the Biosafety Protocol should not be considered "subordinate" to those other agreements. This leaves the exact nature of the interrelationships about as clear as mud.

It is uncertain how this matter will be resolved. But because the SPS agreement specifically encourages World Trade Organization members to harmonize their health and environmental measures by adopting international standards whenever possible, it is conceivable that restrictions erected under the auspices of the Biosafety Protocol could be deemed permissible by the WTO. Negotiations to spell out more clearly the relationship between WTO rules and multilateral environmental agreements such as the Biosafety Protocol are scheduled to take place during the current Doha Round of WTO/GATT negotiations, but there is little indication yet as to what process will be adopted to settle these disputes. What *is* known, however, is that the SPS specifically endorses the food safety and environmental standards set by the UN's Codex Alimentarius Commission discussed below, and that therefore, EU negotiators are working within that body to legitimize and justify their illegitimate, unscientific, and unjustifiable policies.

The Codex Alimentarius Commission

Established in 1962, the Codex Alimentarius Commission is an intergovernmental body responsible for managing a joint Food and Agriculture Organization/World Health Organization food standards program. To date, the Codex has developed more than two hundred food standards for commodities and more than forty codes of hygiene and technological practice. The Codex has a nearly universal global membership of 163 participating states.[25]

Prior to 1995, however, Codex was neither a powerful nor a prominent force for global governance, because its standards are not legally binding on members. All that changed, however, when the SPS agreement entered into force at the end of the Uruguay Round of GATT negotiations. As noted above, the SPS encourages WTO members to harmonize their health and environmental measures by adopting international standards whenever possible. It specifically cites the standards set by the International Office for Epizootics, the International Plant Protection Convention, and the Codex Alimentarius Commission as valid, though it acknowledges that other internationally agreed upon standards may also qualify.

Thus, the responsibility devolved upon Codex to maintain the international standards relevant to food safety that will be recognized by the WTO. Individual members may enact standards that are *more* strict if there is sufficient scientific justification, but while Codex standards are still voluntary, the validity of national regulations are often judged by their correspondence with Codex. Any sanitary or phytosanitary restriction that complies with a Codex standard is automatically deemed to be valid under WTO rules. This point may be critical to whether the new biotechnology will be widely applied to agriculture and to the production of food, or whether its promise will be limited by overregulation.

Since assuming this important new responsibility, the character of the Codex as an institution has changed dramatically. Winning trade disputes in the WTO can now require that a regulatory clash first be won in the Codex. Accordingly, the activities of the Codex have become heavily politicized along traditional trade-interest lines. Whereas Codex meetings before 1995 were attended primarily by low-level technocrats with backgrounds in food science or food safety, now these meetings are also attended by politically motivated senior delegates from ministries of trade and industry, finance, and foreign affairs, as well as by activist NGO representatives.[26] In this more politicized atmosphere, the traditional Codex method of working by consensus has become strained. Many Codex meetings now are often, and unmistakably, major political battlegrounds.

In 2000, Codex established an ad hoc working group on foods derived from biotechnology, charging it with drafting internationally acceptable standards for assessing gene-spliced foods. At that time, the permanent Codex Food Labeling Committee was also asked to develop international guidelines for countries that wish to establish mandatory labeling of gene-spliced food and food ingredients. These Codex working groups generally are split along ideological lines that reflect the broader biotechnology dispute. On one side are the positions of the U.S. delegation and its allies in other major agricultural exporting nations such as Australia, Canada, Argentina, and a number of less developed countries. On the other are the positions advocated by the European Union—including the ten Eastern European nations that only recently joined the EU—and the industrialized nations of the Pacific Rim.

Among other things, the EU wants governments to be able to look beyond human health and environmental protection limitations of the SPS agreement and take into account "other legitimate factors," such as social values, when conducting risk analysis.[27] But consider New Zealand's experience about where this can lead:

[In August 2002] it was confirmed that [New Zealand's] moratorium on commercial releases of genetically modified organisms would not be extended. . . . Now, however, it emerges that the [national regulatory] authority is already looking at giving more weight to Maori spiritual values when it considers genetic research proposals. Scientists have good cause to be alarmed. This misguided notion has the potential to stifle their work as effectively as any prohibition on research. The authority goes so far as to suggest that Maori spiritual concerns about genetic research—even in the absence of physical or biological risk—could be reason enough to reject research applications.[28]

Accepting vague, all-embracing "other legitimate factors" as a basis on which to make regulatory policy would give the Europeans all the cover they need to restrict gene-spliced organisms with no scientific justification whatever. The EU could simply claim, as it has done for many years, that Europeans have a deep cultural appreciation for outdated, anachronistic farming practices and abhor "tampering with nature," and that accordingly the new biotechnology must be restricted.

The European Union further claims that it should be able to base mandatory labeling requirements on the use of certain processing and production methods, including the use of gene-splicing techniques. The EU is now negotiating in as many Codex working groups as possible to expand the scope of and advance the authority of the precautionary principle in risk regulation. It is also pushing for direct incorporation of the precautionary principle into hoped-for revisions of the SPS and TBT agreements, and into other World Trade Organization instruments.[29]

In principle, the United States opposes this anti-scientific approach to biotechnology regulation. Unfortunately, the U.S. position in Codex has been hampered by the flaws in its own domestic regulations for gene-spliced crops and foods, which needlessly and unscientifically single out the products of gene-splicing technology for extraordinary regulatory treatment (chapter 5). It should also be noted that the U.S. delegation to Codex's ad hoc working group on biotech food has defended its position only weakly.

We attribute the American delegation's failure to several factors, including mismanagement by the senior bureaucrats who lead the delegation, and the desire of these government officials to protect the ability of the EPA, USDA, and FDA to practice precautionary regulation domestically. As a result, several proposed standards that endorse precautionary regulation of gene-spliced foods, and that will compromise the ability of the United States to obtain favorable decisions from complaints filed with the WTO, are proceeding through the laborious Codex consensus process with little resistance from the U.S. delegation.

If Codex standards legitimize the precautionary principle and other scientifically unjustified restrictions on gene-spliced organisms, agricultural biotechnology's public policy morass will worsen and its day-to-day problems will multiply. Moreover, one should not lose sight of the virtual impossibility of getting an essentially unaccountable UN group like the Codex (or the group implementing the Cartagena protocol) to repair the damage of overregulation in the future. As sure as the inevitability of death and taxes is the tenacity of government officials at hanging on to responsibilities and bureaucratic empires.

Given the multiple jurisdictional overlaps and conflicts among existing global institutions, agreements, and regulations, what are the prospects for developing a sound, internationally harmonized system to govern trade policy toward gene-spliced organisms? The creation of such a system, if it is possible at all, may now have to await a test of strength between the two principal protagonists, the United States and the European Union. Once the WTO case involving the EU moratorium is decided, two other controversial EU policies toward gene-spliced organisms—the EU directive on labeling and traceability of gene-spliced foods, and the broader European application of the precautionary principle to health and environmental regulation—could soon provide the *casus belli* for such a showdown. How deplorable that the international governance of a critical, safe, and superior new technology should be determined through a test of political strength. Yet, all too often, this is the mode of resolution of what should be settled by the guidance of sound science and the wisdom of the marketplace.

IS THE END OF AGBIOTECH THE END OF THE WORLD?

Let us think the unthinkable. Let us suppose that the United States were to capitulate and agree to apply the precautionary principle to the oversight of gene-splicing, effectively ending the ability of the new biotechnology to contribute to modern agriculture and food production. Would an end to the planting of gene-spliced crops in major exporting countries such as the United States be such a terrible outcome?

For U.S. farmers that outcome would certainly turn back the clock, but only to about 1995. Such a loss might seem bearable, even insignificant. The demise of gene-splicing as a viable alternative for crafting genetic improvement in plants and microorganisms would, of course, be bad for the biotechnology industry and its shareholders—and for entrepreneurs who hope to back the *next* promising new technology to be assailed by activists—but otherwise, few in the United States would even notice.

If North American farmers gave up planting gene-spliced crops they could still prosper, and consumers in industrialized countries could still be well and inexpensively fed. The environmental benefits of gene-spliced crop varieties are significant, but not so great that forgoing them would spell ecological disaster. Farm production costs would rise slightly, the spraying of toxic and persistent herbicides and insecticides would increase, and there would be more runoff of chemicals and topsoil into waterways. In addition, plant breeders and farmers would lose the potential benefits of future crops designed to resist drought and specific pests and diseases—such as grapes resistant to the glassy-winged sharpshooter and Pierce's disease, and trees resistant to fungal infestations.

In other words, the impacts would be the sort seen with Type II errors, discussed in chapter 4, where the delay or abandonment of socially valuable activities or products is largely invisible. Moreover, those losses might even be seen by American agriculturists as less costly than paying for the redundant distribution and marketing infrastructures that labeling and traceability would require, to say nothing of the risk of various kinds of legal liability that result from poorly crafted regulation and inconsistencies among rules in various countries.

Turning back the clock to 1995, however, could spell catastrophe for poor farmers in tropical countries. Almost two hundred million inhabitants of sub-Saharan Africa, most of them children, are undernourished. They lack "food security"—continuous access to sufficient food to lead active, healthy lives—

reflecting harvests that on average provide yields only barely above subsistence levels. Thus, in bad years, people starve.[30]

This problem will be exacerbated as food production per capita in most African countries continues to stagnate, the result of rapid population growth and low crop yields. The latter problem, which is caused by depletion of soil nutrients in excess of replenishment, and crop losses from pests, diseases, and abiotic stresses, could be addressed in part by gene-spliced crop varieties.

A subsistence farmer in Kenya trying to produce corn to feed his family will benefit from a Bt variety to control the stem borer infestations that can destroy as much as half his crop. A woman in rural Niger trying to produce cowpeas will benefit from a gene-spliced variety to help fight against pod borers and weevils. A farmer in Uganda trying to fend off fungal damage to his bananas will benefit from fungus-resistant varieties (replacing the largely ineffective home brew of cow manure, cow urine, hot peppers, tobacco leaves, banana peels, and local herbs, all boiled and fermented together). A poor farmer with a few hectares of land in Indonesia trying to grow cotton will benefit from a gene-spliced cotton variety that resists bollworms. Rice farmers throughout Asia will reap the benefits of gene-spliced varieties that resist a multitude of insect pests and plant pathogens, and beta-carotene enriched "golden rice" may be only a few years away from saving countless children from the scourge of vitamin A deficiency.

In the future, if drought resistant and nitrogen-fixing, gene-spliced varieties were to become available, the benefit to poor farmers of this technology could be incalculable. During the next few decades, biotechnology's greatest contributions may be to water conservation. Irrigation for agriculture accounts for roughly 70 percent of the world's water consumption, and about one-third of the planet's population lives under conditions of relative water scarcity.[31] Plant biologists have already developed several major crop plants that can grow with less water or lower quality water (for example, recycled water or water containing relatively large amounts of natural salts), and they are rapidly accumulating knowledge about the genetics and physiology of drought resistance.[32] Especially during drought conditions, even a few percent reduction in the use of water for irrigation could result in huge benefits, both economic and humanitarian.

None of these possibilities, or others currently being developed in laboratories around the world, is in itself a panacea—a cure for malnutrition, starvation, or disease. But the cumulative impact of hundreds or thousands of possible applications could be monumental, arguably as great as that of the Green Revolution.

If the new biotechnology is killed in the cradle by precautionary UN-brokered agreements and by the pandering of politicians to uninformed, propagandized consumers, poor farmers and consumers in the tropics will be the big losers. If today's rich nations decide to stop or turn back the clock, they will still be rich. But if we stop the clock for developing countries, they will still be poor and hungry. And many of their inhabitants will be dead.

How can we prevent this dismal possibility from coming to pass. How can overly restrictive, unscientific policies be reformed? We offer a few suggestions in the next and final chapter.

CHAPTER 9

Climbing Out of the Quagmire

P. J. O'ROURKE, A political satirist and author, has observed that giving money and power to government is like giving whiskey and car keys to teenage boys. But this observation begs the central question: *Why* is government the problem?

There are several reasons. The most prominent is that bureaucratic self-interest often conflicts with and takes precedence over the public interest. As discussed in chapters 4 and 5, government regulators face potent incentives to expand their activities and to overregulate products under their purview. If regulators move products through the pipeline rapidly, they become vulnerable to criticism over mishaps, while overregulation and procrastination insulate them from negative media attention, public criticism, and political probes.

Similarly, the professional status of regulators in Washington and around the world is directly proportional to the perceived importance of their jobs, the volume and value of articles that they oversee, and the size of their budgets and bureaucratic empires. Given these powerful influences, it is no wonder that progressively more products, processes, and activities come under the sway of regulators.

But federal regulators of the new biotechnology have had a lot of help in crafting heavy-handed, misguided public policy. They have received aid and encouragement from well-funded activist groups that fear technological progress and loathe the profit motive. Paradoxically, part of the business community has also collaborated on the inexorable progression toward greater government control over their own livelihoods. To gain short-term advantage, some large corporations sacrifice their own long-term interests, as well as those of consumers and business in general. Excessive regulation may protect firms from the dynamism of market processes and the need to keep technologically current, and it serves as a market-entry barrier to potential competitors. Some corporate officials rationalize that competitors will be just as much disadvantaged, and that in the end they can all pass the increased costs along to consumers. Another motive for industry's support of excessive regulatory requirements is to avoid ruffling the feathers of the regulators, who wield so much discretionary control over their business and products.

Biotech's public policy miasma is becoming progressively more damaging, immutable, and taken for granted. What impetus there is for change is waning, and we are in danger of the worst becoming the norm. In this final chapter, we consider the relationships among federal agencies and the agricultural biotechnology and food industries, and we examine the system of bureaucratic incentives and disincentives, and of rewards and punishments, that influences policy making within the regulatory agencies.

Finally, we discuss possible solutions, some emanating from first principles, others from empirical experience. Some are sweeping and would introduce systematic changes, others are specific and mechanistic, but all are intended to focus regulatory policy on genuine risks, and ultimately on maximizing net benefit to society.

BUREAUCRATIC VERSUS SOCIETAL RISK

Nobel economist Milton Friedman correctly concluded that the blame for many of the distortions of the marketplace described throughout this volume—excessive, discriminatory regulation of a superior technology; the misrepresentations of activists that sow confusion among consumers; and the potential for courts to impose "prior restraint" on research and development—lies with the system itself, not primarily with the actors within it. Government regulators, like the rest of society, generally act in their own self-interest, even when those actions are inimical to the best interests of others.

This is not the way that public servants' "contract" with society is supposed to work. In return for lifetime tenure and civil service protections, career government employees are supposed to make decisions that are in the public interest and that are largely insulated from outside influences. At least, this is how, more than a century ago, political theorist Max Weber described the concept of a professional bureaucracy protected from special interests. That has become the idealized, textbook vision for bureaucracies, but even Weber realized that, in practice, bureaucracies buffeted by political winds could not achieve this ideal.[1]

The Zero-Risk Mindset

The striving by regulators to avoid at all costs the marketing of a hazardous product and the fallout from such an action gives rise to a kind of tunnel vision focused on protecting the public from unsafe products. But shouldn't regulators be equally eager to move safe and innovative new products into the marketplace? Shouldn't they consider the costs of delay or abandonment of innovative new products? Shouldn't they wish to encourage the development of improved ways to control pests, clean up toxic wastes, conserve water, and treat diseases? Shouldn't they be trying to minimize *net* risk and maximize *net* benefit?

Of course they should—and to be sure, examples of progressive, public-spirited, effective civil servants can be found in every agency. But in practice, the institutional incentives are stacked against those government officials who do try to weigh the risks of introducing a new product against the risks of not introducing it. As we described in chapters 4 and 5, the desire never to generate controversy or attract attention—to remain at what one FDA commissioner called "periscope depth"—can be a powerful motivating force in civil servants' decision making. They learn quickly to "game" their decisions and actions to avoid the kinds of mistakes that get them into the most trouble. There is also the constant reinforcement from colleagues, supervisors, and society that the prevailing risk-averse culture of their workplace *does* promote the public good, so even highly dedicated public servants face tremendous pressure to "go along to get along."

Consider the problem of the asymmetry between Type I and Type II errors we discussed in chapter 4. No matter how well vetted a product is or how beneficial it may be after it is put on the market, even a few high-profile mishaps with it can result in severe repercussions for the regulatory agency that approved it. This kind of mistake is made highly visible by the media—especially if the story is high on the "if it bleeds, it leads" scale, and the cable news networks make it the Story of the Week, flogging it twenty-four hours a day. That kind of attention puts regulators squarely in the cross-hairs of the public and Congress.

Because Americans have been so conditioned to believe that every mishap must be someone's fault, both the developers of a harmful product and the regulators who allowed it to be marketed are excoriated and punished. A regulatory official's career might be damaged irreparably by the good-faith approval of a product that is later found to have dangerous side effects—even if the outcome was completely unforeseeable and if the product continues to offer a net benefit. Therefore, on controversial or high-profile products, regulators frequently make decisions about approvals and labeling in a highly defensive manner, motivated at least in part by the desire to preempt accusations of acting hurriedly.

The public seldom connects this kind of regulatory procrastination with negative events such as the unmet need for an innovative new technology for cleaning up oil spills, or farmers' loss of crops to insects and frost. The rare counterexamples occur when single-issue advocacy groups closely scrutinize regulators' review of certain products and aggressively publicize Type

II errors—such as the AIDS activist groups that monitor and pressure the Food and Drug Administration to approve new therapies.

But where are we to find vocal, militant advocates for crop plants that grow more robustly in poor tropical soils, or for insect- and virus-resistant varieties of potato that require little or no synthetic chemical pesticide? Such advocates are few, whereas detractors and activists who rally against these products regularly, loudly, and viciously are numerous. Media determined to report "both sides" of the story uncritically promulgate the activists' groundless claims, and thereby confer undeserved credibility on those who are opposed to technology.

Erring on the Side of Caution

It should not be surprising, then, that regulatory agencies have great success at explaining away Type II errors as conscientious "erring on the side of caution." Although these errors can have dire consequences, too often the media and the public accept this euphemism uncritically. For example, during the 1980s, the Monsanto Company proposed a scientifically interesting and potentially important small-scale field trial of the bacterium *Pseudomonas fluorescens* that had been modified to control a voracious insect predator of corn (which we described in chapter 5). In spite of the unanimous conclusion of the EPA's panel of extramural scientific experts and other federal agencies that there was virtually no likelihood of significant risk in the field trial (and leaving aside the enormous potential benefit to farmers and consumers), the EPA refused to permit it, explaining that public opinion simply was "not ready" for the experiment. The field trial would have been subject to *no government regulation at all* had the researchers used an organism with identical characteristics but crafted with less precise, less predictable "conventional" genetic techniques.

Thus, instead of making a decision based on scientific considerations and the public interest, and then educating the public as to its merits, regulators based their decision on their own dubious perceptions of public attitudes. This kind of bureaucratic reasoning leaves innovators—to say nothing of farmers and the public—in a regulatory limbo, which makes planning for the future difficult, if not impossible.

Knowing that similar future proposals to test these so-called "biorational pesticides" would likely fall prey to additional Type II regulatory errors, Monsanto decided to dismantle its entire research program on gene-spliced microorganisms for pest control—and has never resumed it. Since then, few other companies have dared to brave the regulatory waters by pursuing these products.

The result of these egregious government policies and actions was catastrophic: an entire sector of biotechnology destroyed by regulatory disincentives. This outcome is especially ironic given that synthetic chemical pesticides, the only viable competing products, have fallen into public and governmental disfavor, opening a vast new potential market for microbial pest control.

Thus, we see the power of public policy: When it favors certain strategies, innovators and consumers respond positively; but when it makes other choices too difficult, expensive, or unpredictable, they disappear.

Egregious and costly Type II errors can take the form of broad agency policies as well as decisions about individual products. A good example is the "plant-incorporated protectant" policy discussed in chapter 5 that enables the EPA to regulate gene-spliced plants that have enhanced resistance to pests, diseases, or environmental stresses as though they were pesticides—an approach that makes no sense, affords no added protection to human health or the environment, squanders public and private-sector resources, and discourages research. Many Type II errors are not so obvious, however. Instead, like the EPA and the example above of the *Pseudomonas fluorescens* field trial, they reflect more the pervasive "culture" of risk aversion in which every decision, every choice is overly conservative.

While delay and uncertainty are the bane of those who are awaiting approval of a product for testing or marketing, procrastination and overcaution offer broader benefits to the regulatory agency. Only in government do we respond to poor performance and failed programs by rewarding them with more money and prominence. The longer product approvals take and the more functions a regulatory agency assigns to itself, the greater the number of regulators needed, the larger budgets become, and the more prestigious the sinecures.

The accretion of such empires is hardly a disincentive. In fact, it acts as a kind of "carrot" in a regulator's reward-punishment system, whereas risk aversion and fear of career-threatening mistakes (and the resulting avoidance of Type I errors at any cost) is a "stick." The cultural malaise at many regulatory agencies suggests the need for them and their congressional overseers to craft new carrots and sticks in a way that redresses these imbalances.

Some incentives already exist in performance plan goals and the like. But these are, as the English say, weak as water. The clever regulator can always take refuge in the "incompleteness" or "inconclusiveness" of the data and demand yet another study, another way of analyzing the data, or another meeting of an advisory committee. Consequently, real reform will require a sea change in the incentive-disincentive structure that prevails at the regulatory agencies.

CAN THIS BE FIXED?

Making government regulation of the new biotechnology more scientific and sensible will require a multifaceted solution that is both domestic and international. Regulatory policy must respect certain overarching principles:

primum non nocere—government policies must do no harm; sound science and common sense must be the basis for policy making; the degree of oversight must be commensurate with risk; extragovernmental mechanisms must have a central role; and market forces must be allowed to function to the extent possible. In addition, risk aversion must be modulated, and bureaucrats' self-interest made constructive rather than destructive.

Federal agencies also need to adopt reforms that are specific to the new biotechnology. Most important is replacing process-oriented regulatory triggers with risk-based ones. Just because the process of gene splicing is involved does not mean that a field trial or product should be strigently regulated; that would be like subjecting only automobiles of a certain color, or grant proposals that arrive on certain days of the week, to especially rigorous scrutiny. As discussed below, there do exist viable, scientifically defensible, risk-based approaches to the regulation of the new biotechnology, and these should be adopted and implemented as rapidly as possible.

At the same time the U.S. government begins to rationalize public policy at home, it must stand up to the other countries as well as intergovernmental and nongovernmental organizations that are responsible for precautionary style regulations abroad. As we discussed in chapter 7, such unscientific and inconsistent policies, often based on little more than one or another country's social and gastronomic customs (and often buoyed by a strong undercurrent of trade protectionism), have profoundly negative impacts. They not only penalize plant breeders and U.S. agricultural exports but also prevent many less developed nations from taking full advantage of the biotechnology revolution that could help them address some of their most pressing food security and environmental problems.

As Wellesley College political scientist Robert Paarlberg has noted, the continued "globalization of Europe's highly precautionary regulatory approach" to gene-spliced crops will cause the "the biggest losers of all [to be the] poor farmers in the developing world," and "if this new technology is killed in the cradle, these farmers could miss a chance to escape the low farm productivity that is helping to keep them in poverty."[2] Consequently, foreign governments, United Nations agencies, and other international bodies that implement, collude, or cooperate in any way with unscientific policies should be ineligible to receive funding or other assistance from the United States. Flagrantly unscientific regulation should become the "third rail" of American domestic and foreign policy.

U.S. government representatives to international bodies, such as the Codex Alimentarius Commission and the World Health Organization, must be directed to defend rational, science-based policies, and to work to dismantle politically motivated, unscientific restrictions. Every science and economic attaché in every American embassy and consulate worldwide should have biotechnology policy indelibly inscribed on his or her diplomatic agenda.

Uncompromising? Aggressive? Yes, but so is the virtual annihilation of entire areas of research and development, trampling of individual and corporate freedom, disuse of a critical technology, and disruption of free trade.

In order to succeed, efforts at regulatory rationalization and reform must extend beyond government. Industrial trade associations must better define and more faithfully represent the long-term interests of their constituencies. Ill-conceived, unscientific, gerrymandered regulatory policies may confer short-term advantages, but they are destined to be injurious in the long run. Discriminatory regulation, vastly inflated development costs, pathetically diminished product pipelines, increased legal liability, trepidation among end-users, consumer backlash, and vandalism are hardly conducive to a robust industry or society.

The Role of Public Opinion

Although public participation and favorable public opinion are important to a turnaround, they cannot be relied upon to drive reform. Public apathy and misapprehensions are too entrenched. In spite of that, during the past several years, a number of countries have surveyed public opinion as a prelude to setting regulatory policy toward the new biotechnology. For example, New Zealand set up a Royal Commission on Genetic Modification, which, at fifteen public meetings and three forums across the country, consulted widely and openly on a broad range of issues. Similarly, in 2003 the British government set up a series of public debates and focus groups, as part of the government's attempts to assess opinion in advance of a decision on whether to allow commercial planting of gene-spliced crops. A science correspondent for the London *Times* offered this view of the worth of the United Kingdom's half-million-pound-sterling initiative:

> For a couple of hours this afternoon, a few dozen Greenpeace types, assorted yogic flyers from the Natural Law Party, a handful of pensioners, and perhaps the odd scientist or farmer are going to sit down and talk about GM food. The gathering, in Harrogate, is the last in a series that makes up GM Nation?, the Government's public debate about whether Britain should grow transgenic crops. . . .
>
> The exercise has been farce from start to finish. I'm not sure I want the man in the street to set Britain's science, technology and agriculture policy. One of the six meetings—held midweek at major population centres, such as Taunton and Harrogate—spent much of its time discussing whether the SARS virus might come from GM cotton in China. It's more likely to have come from outer space. I can think of more useful ways to waste time and money.
>
> Then there's the fact that the meetings will tell us nothing we don't know already. The lack of advertising and helpful scheduling mean that everyone has

been stuffed with green campaigners and New Age zealots who think GM crops are the root of all evil. They were the only ones who were organised enough—or who cared enough—to attend.[3]

The urge not only to sample, but to make policy based on public opinion, flourishes on this side of the Atlantic as well. The U.S. National Science Foundation (NSF), whose primary mission is to support laboratory research across many disciplines, is funding a series of "citizens technology forums," at which average, previously uninformed Americans come together to solve a thorny question of technology policy. According to the NSF's abstract of the project, being carried out by researchers at North Carolina State University under a 2002 grant, participants "receive information about that issue from a range of content-area experts, experts on social implications of science and technology, and representatives of special interest groups"; this is supposed to enable them to reach consensus "and ultimately generate recommendations."[4]

The project, first funded in 2002 to support two panels and expanded in 2003 under a continuing grant, calls for eight more panels of fifteen citizens (who are "representative of the local population") each. Their deliberations will be overseen by a research team "composed of faculty in rhetoric of science, group decision-making, and political science" that will test both "an innovative measure of democratic deliberation" and "also political science theory, by investigating relationships between gender, ethnicity, lower socioeconomic status and increases in efficacy and trust in regulators."

At a time when federal budgets are under pressure and laboratory research funding is tight, the NSF has seen fit to spend almost half a million taxpayer dollars on this politically correct but dubious project.

Getting policy recommendations on an obscure and complex technical question from groups of citizen nonexperts (who are recruited by newspaper ads) is rather like going from your cardiologist's office to a café, explaining to the waitress the therapeutic options for your chest pain, and asking her whether you should have the angioplasty or just take medication. (It might help, of course, if there were specialists in the rhetoric of science and in group decision making having lunch at a nearby table.)

The first of these NSF-funded groups tackled regulatory policy toward agricultural biotechnology and recommended that the government tighten regulations for growing gene-spliced crops, including a new requirement that the foods from these crops be labeled to identify them for consumers. As discussed throughout this volume, both of these proposals are unwarranted, inappropriate, hugely expensive, and contrary to the recommendations of experts, including those within the government and in the scientific community. The outcome of this citizens' panel illustrates that such undertakings have limitations both in theory and practice; nonexperts are too much subject to their own prejudices and to the specific choice of materials and advocates to which they are exposed.

Although involvement of the public is critical to their *understanding* of government policy and must often play a role in setting broad policy goals, it is less useful for the *formulation* of specific policies. This is particularly true when complex issues of science and technology are involved. Science is not democratic. The citizenry do not get to vote on whether a whale is a mammal or a fish, or on the temperature at which water boils; and legislatures cannot repeal the laws of nature. Public participation is most important when answering questions to which there is no scientifically "right" answer—such as at what age persons can vote, or at which they should no longer drive, or whether we should carry out more manned exploration of the moon. Similarly, the public can guide governments in choosing the overarching acceptable level of tolerance or aversion to risk, but the public must defer to experts in assigning specific products or classes of products to risk categories.

Thus, one should regard warily the attempts in various countries to sample public opinion as a prelude to setting policy on biotechnology: In addition to the examples above, in recent years the Netherlands, Japan, Norway, South Korea, Switzerland, France, Argentina, and Denmark have undertaken similar exercises on biotechnology-related issues. Even if such opinion-sampling were better organized, widely attended, and more representative, its purpose should not be to translate the *vox populi* into policy on subjects highly dependent upon an understanding of the subtleties of science and technology. The nature of statistics—the phenomenon of statistical "clusters," for example—and concepts such as "the dose makes the poison" are not intuitively obvious. Permitting laypersons to make policy when they do not grasp the nuances of quantitative issues or the distinctions between *association* and *causation* is absurd.

The regulation of risk is complex, to be sure, but if democracy must eventually take public opinion into account, good government must also discount heuristic errors and prejudices. The eighteenth-century Irish statesman and writer Edmund Burke emphasized the government's pivotal role in making such judgments. He observed that in republics, in which we elect leaders to represent our interests, "Your Representative owes you not only his industry but his judgment; and he betrays, instead of serving you, if he sacrifices it to your opinion." Although it may be useful, and also politic, for governments to consult broadly on high-profile public-policy issues, after the consultations and deliberations have been completed, government leaders are supposed to *lead*.

Risk-Based Approaches to Regulation

Countless experiments and many years of real-world applications have shown that neither the use of recombinant DNA techniques nor the transfer of genes, per se, confers incremental risk. The risk posed by an organism is a function of its characteristics and its use—regardless of whether, or how, it has been modified.

Nevertheless, as we have described throughout this volume, the regulatory paradigms adopted in the United States and abroad for the testing and commercialization of gene-spliced organisms deny these basic verities and conflict with the scientific consensus about the safety of gene-splicing and the basic principles of risk analysis. Reform and rationalization must, therefore, begin with the recognition that certain cardinal principles should apply to any regulatory regime: triggers to regulation—that is, the criteria for determining which products and experiments warrant certain levels of scrutiny and evaluation—must be scientifically defensible; and the burden of oversight and compliance must be commensurate with the level of scientifically determined (or estimated) risk.

Some have contended that this may be obvious in theory but difficult to achieve in practice—that because we cannot know a priori which experiments and products pose significant risk, a risk-based oversight paradigm will always be little more than an idealized fiction. These assertions are insupportable. Based on educated assumptions and scientifically derived estimates about the magnitude and distribution of risk, the United States and other nations have devised stratified regulatory regimes for many kinds of products and activities. For example, we regulate potent, addicting drugs more intrusively than over-the-counter remedies, because we have enough theoretical and empirical information to know that opiates, for example, are addictive and prone to abuse while antacids are not. We regulate airplanes more stringently than cars or bicycles, because we know that an accident involving a commercial airliner can be catastrophic and that there is less margin for error.

The most apposite analogy to agricultural biotechnology is in the longstanding regulations of the Plant Pest Act and in other rules regarding quarantine of certain infectious organisms. Based on experts' assessments of risk, we require permits for field trials with certain organisms known to be plant pests, whereas we exempt other, quite similar ones that are nonpathogenic (chapter 5). The validity of these estimates about the relative risks of different drugs, modes of transport, and organisms determines the integrity of the regulatory scheme. Without them, we might as well flip a coin to decide how stringently something should be regulated.

With such proportionality of regulation in mind, the federal government's 1986 Coordinated Framework for the Regulation of Biotechnology attempted to focus oversight and regulatory triggers on the risk-related *characteristics of products* and on their intended use, rather than on the *process* used for genetic modification.[5]

This risk-based approach to biotech regulation for federal agencies was reaffirmed in the 1992 "scope announcement," which clarified how the regulation of recombinant DNA–modified organisms should be approached. It calls explicitly for "a risk-based, scientifically sound approach to the oversight of planned introductions of biotechnology products into the environment that focuses on the characteristics of the . . . product and the environment into which it is being introduced, not the process by which the product is created." It stipulates, "Exercise of oversight in the scope of discretion afforded by statute should be based on the risk posed by the introduction and should not turn on the fact that an organism has been modified by a particular process or technique."[6]

A rare example of adherence to these risk-based approaches to regulation of the new biotechnology was the FDA's 1992 policy statement about products from "new plant varieties," which did not distinguish between plants crafted by gene-splicing and those made with less precise, conventional methods of genetic modification. It defined certain potentially hazardous *characteristics* of new foods that, if present, required greater scrutiny by the agency and that could result in additional testing and labeling, or even exclusion from commerce. Thus, the agency's approach conformed to the fundamental principle that the degree of scrutiny should be commensurate with risk.

However, in spite of the intent of the Coordinated Framework and the "scope announcement," and the FDA's years of success at actually translating these policy pronouncements into effective regulation, the U.S. Department of Agriculture and Environmental Protection Agency have clung to oversight regimes that are not risk based but are focused on the use of gene-splicing techniques. These policies capture virtually all gene-spliced organisms regardless of risk, and they have created a regulatory morass that has spilled over to other areas, including questions of legal liability.

Regulators have been nothing if not creative in crafting unscientific approaches to regulation. Some regimes circumscribe for case-by-case review organisms with phenotypes that "do not exist in nature," according to the rationale that such organisms are "unfamiliar" and by extension potentially high risk. Yet, as long as gene-splicing techniques are not used, these rules exclude the products of sophisticated scientific breeding methods, including those from wide crosses (organisms that are certainly not found in nature).

Demonstrating the wrongheadedness and circularity of this approach, organisms are considered "familiar" if they are "natural" or have been created by older, more "familiar" genetic manipulation techniques; and no matter how pathogenic, invasive, or otherwise problematic or hazardous these "familiar" or "natural" organisms may be, they are intentionally exempted from the regulatory net. These sorts of anomalies are irreconcilable.

As discussed at length in chapters 4 and 5, this precautionary approach to regulation fails to protect public health or the environment effectively because the degree of regulatory scrutiny is *inversely* related to risk. Moreover, it neglects comparative risk analysis, thereby overemphasizing the possible risks of new processes and products, while underestimating the risks of older ones. Consequently, it diverts attention and resources from potentially greater harms that may result from forgoing beneficial new technologies.

In order to reduce the overall risks of agricultural practices and to enhance food safety, the regulation of new plant varieties should focus on and be triggered by the risk-related characteristics of new products, not on the techniques used in creating them. Examples of such scientifically defensible and risk-based alternatives to the bogus precautionary principle—and to our existing regulatory policies—do exist. They include the USDA's quarantine regulations for non-gene-spliced plants and the FDA's policy on food from novel plants.

A RATIONAL APPROACH TO RISK ASSESSMENT

The public policy miasma that exists today is severe, intractable, and worsening. Ironically, it is also wholly unnecessary. From the advent of the first gene-spliced microorganisms and plants a quarter-century ago, the path to rational policy was not obscure. As discussed at great length in the first three chapters of this volume, the new biotechnology is merely the culmination of less precise and predictable techniques for genetic improvement that have been used for centuries. Conventional risk analysis, supplemented with assessments specific to the new biotechnology in those very rare instances where they were needed, could easily have been adapted to craft regulation that was risk-based and scientifically defensible.

A Vertical Approach: Oversight on a Higher Plane

How do we acquire knowledge about the risks of new products, processes, and other activities? One way is to perform well-designed risk-assessment experiments. As early as two decades ago, the U.S. National Science Foundation concluded that risk-assessment paradigms and regulatory methods in use before the advent of the new biotechnology provide both a useful foundation and "a systematic means of organizing a variety of relevant knowledge" for the assessment and management of recombinant DNA–modified products.[7] Thus, when risk is not readily demonstrable, risk analysis dictates the use of established scientific principles to identify any significant gaps in understanding, which then may be addressed by the conduct of appropriate experiments.

If there were significant concerns about recombinant DNA modification conferring weediness or toxigenicity on plants, for example, such experiments might attempt experimentally to quantify the ability to transform a benign, nontoxic, noninvasive plant into one that possesses one or more undesirable traits. Or these experiments might investigate the ability of a plant with a certain newly acquired trait to transfer it by means of outcrossing. An example of the latter would be herbicide resistance under the positive selection pressure of the herbicide in the test environment. However, such experiments generally have a very low probability of a positive result unless they are carefully designed both to maximize the occurrence of a "positive" event and to detect rare events. This approach is cumbersome, provides data of only limited usefulness, and for gene-spliced plants in particular, was arguably unnecessary. In spite of these limitations, during the past two decades many such risk-assessment experiments have been performed with gene-spliced organisms, and the results have been uniformly reassuring.

As an alternative to experimental data, one can accept the consensus view that there is no conceptual distinction between organisms modified with "conventional," pre-recombinant-DNA techniques, and those modified with molecular techniques. This "vertical" approach to understanding risk relies heavily on prior knowledge about the behavior of genetic variants produced in nature and by human intervention.[8] Thus, in order to assess the risks of a new gene-spliced tomato, a tomato breeder or a government regulator would rely more heavily on background information about tomatoes modified with traditional techniques than on information about gene-spliced mice or bacteria. Similarly, a breeder experimenting with a new gene-spliced, herbicide-tolerant canola variety would rely on years of experience with conventionally modified herbicide-tolerant crop varieties, and with various conventionally modified canola varieties.

With this vertical approach in mind, and reinforced by a copious amount of experimental data, the Paris-based Organization for Economic Cooperation and Development (OECD) developed and applied the concept of "substantial equivalence" to food from novel organisms. Addressing gene-splicing generally, the OECD's Group of National Experts on Safety in Biotechnology echoed the well-established scientific consensus: "While recombinant DNA techniques may result in the production of organisms expressing a combination of traits that are not observed in nature, genetic changes from recombinant DNA techniques will often have inherently greater predictability compared to traditional techniques, because of the greater precision that the recombinant DNA technique affords." Also, "it is expected that any risks associated with applications of recombinant DNA organisms may be assessed in generally the same way as those associated with non–recombinant DNA organisms."[9]

The OECD's experts group subsequently took up food safety specifically, concluding in a 1993 report:

> Modern biotechnology broadens the scope of the genetic changes that can be made in food organisms, and broadens the scope of possible sources of foods. This does not inherently lead to foods that are less safe than those developed by conventional techniques. Therefore, evaluation of foods and food

components obtained from organisms developed by the application of the newer techniques does not necessitate a fundamental change in established principles, nor does it require a different standard of safety.[10]

The OECD experts' group described the concept of *substantial equivalence* as a kind of regulatory shorthand for defining those new foods that do not raise safety issues that require special, intensive, case-by-case scrutiny. The OECD continued to explore and reevaluate the concept, another expert group concluding in 1998, "While establishment of substantial equivalence is not a safety evaluation *per se*, when substantial equivalence is established between a new food and the conventional comparator—such as an antecedent organism—it establishes the safety of the new food relative to an existing food and no further safety consideration is needed."[11] In other words, it sets up a simple kind of transitivity: If *a* is equivalent to *b*, and *b* is known to be safe, then *a* can be assumed to be safe.

It bears repeating that substantial equivalence is intended to be a conceptual tool for food producers and government regulators, not a scientific formulation or algorithm, and it neither specifies nor limits the kind or amount of testing needed for new foods. Important scientific questions relevant to the behavior and performance of organisms in field trials and to food safety should be addressed systematically and in ways that are consistent with recognized scientific principles and procedures. Experience, precedents, scientific principles, and common sense can suggest approaches that will avoid unnecessary and costly experiments performed in the name of "risk assessment," as well as wasteful and superfluous oversight.

For example, after a field trial of an obviously innocuous recombinant DNA–modified strain of the soil bacterium, Rhizobium (*Bradyrhizobium japonicum*), Louisiana regulators "felt that continued monitoring of the field [was] needed," and a Louisiana State University professor proposed that this constituted "an opportunity to obtain valuable scientific information from the careful long-term study of the impact of this release on the environment."[12] This is nincompoopery of the first order. Employing such reasoning, there is never a logical place to end the accumulation of negative data. There is always the possibility that we just haven't yet gotten to examining the *nth* hypothetical risk; to the *nth* year of exposure, in which the risk will finally be demonstrated; or to the point at which risks from applications that haven't yet been contemplated become detectable. In other words, we are confronted by the impossibility of proving a negative amidst unchecked, unreasonable speculation about unspecified and hypothetical risks.

The vertical approach to risk emphasizes the fundamental similarities among products with similar characteristics and reflects the ways that regulators have grouped products or processes in the past.[13] It recognizes that for many decades governmental agencies in the United States, Europe, Japan, and other countries have overseen the safety of a vast array of products, including foods, pharmaceuticals, pesticides, and other consumer goods that now can be produced using newer, more refined techniques. It focuses greater regulatory attention on product classes of intrinsically high risk (e.g., prescription drugs, artificial hearts, nuclear reactors, and pathogenic organisms) and on circumstances that may be correlated with risk (such as workplace hazards).

The evil twin of the *vertical* approach to regulation and risk assessment, the *horizontal* approach, is predicated on the notion that there is something systematically similar and functionally important about the set of organisms the only common characteristic of which is the use of the techniques of the new biotechnology.[14]

The *horizontal* approach focuses on the artifactual "category" of products made or manipulated with these techniques—not unlike deciding that "doors" are a regulatory category that is amenable to one-size-fits-all standards and review, whether they are affixed to doll houses, bank vaults, or submarines. A horizontal approach to public policy seldom makes sense, but least so as a basis for crafting governmental regulation. Nonetheless, the horizontal approach, further confounded by the application of the bogus precautionary principle, is the basis for biotechnology regulation in the United States and elsewhere. At best, the horizontal approach to recombinant DNA technology has been a distraction and a wasteful nuisance. At worst, it has contributed to specious generalizations and flawed assumptions in policy making, and drastically limited the diffusion of and the potential benefits that can be realized from the new biotechnology.

Paradigm Found: Reliance on Traditional Experience

A paradigm for regulating products of the new biotechnology may be summarized in a syllogism:

1. Industry, government, and the public possess considerable, pre-recombinant DNA experience with every aspect of the testing and commercialization of organisms genetically improved by traditional techniques: plants for food and fiber, and microorganisms for agricultural, pharmaceutical, and industrial applications.
2. Existing regulatory mechanisms have generally protected human health and the environment without stifling innovation.
3. There is no evidence that unique hazards exist either in the use of recombinant DNA techniques or in the movement of genes between unrelated organisms.
4. *Therefore*, for recombinant DNA-manipulated organisms, there is no need for additional regulatory regimes to be superimposed on pre-existing regulation. (In fact, if there *were* an argument to be made for a disparity of regulatory treatment, logically one would impose *lesser* scrutiny on organisms crafted with the most precise and predictable techniques.)

The syllogism assumes, of course, that aside from the new biotechnology and its products, there exists adequate governmental control over the testing and use of living organisms and their products generally. This assumption is certainly open to question, particularly where known dangerous pathogens, chemicals, and similar products are largely unregulated or where regulations are widely ignored. Nevertheless, throughout our pre-recombinant DNA history of scientific research, in the United States and elsewhere, scientists have had a high degree of unencumbered freedom of experimentation—with pathogens as well as nonpathogens, under both contained and uncontained conditions. The resulting harmful incidents have been few, and the benefits, both intellectual and commercial, have far exceeded any detrimental effects.

More important, the fact that the regulation of products in one or another legitimate risk category may warrant reevaluation is no rationale for creating an unconscionably high regulatory bar for the pseudo-category of gene-spliced organisms. Although simply raising the regulatory hurdles for gene-spliced products may be easier to accomplish politically than a broader, scientific reevaluation of regulation, it results in an anomalous, irreconcilable situation in which most products of genuine concern are missed, while the vast majority of what is captured for case-by-case review poses negligible risk.

The syllogism can be illustrated graphically. In Figure 1A, the large triangle represents the entire universe of experimental introductions of organisms into the field. The horizontal lines divide the universe into classes according to the safety category of the experimental organism (with examples listed on the right side of the figure). These categories can take into account the effect of a genetic change, whether it is a consequence of spontaneous mutation or the use of conventional or new techniques of genetic manipulation. Such genetic changes can shift the organism from one safety category to another.

For example, if one were to grow cultures of *Neisseria gonorrhea* (which causes gonorrhea) or *Legionella pneumophila* (which causes Legionnaire's disease) in the presence of increasing concentrations of antibiotics to select for antibiotic-resistant mutants, the classification might change from, say, Class III to Class IV. Similarly, a variety of corn, usually Class I, might be considered to be Class III or higher if—say, for the purposes of biopharming—it contained the bacterial gene that directs the synthesis of botulinum toxin (the active ingredient in the drug, Botox®, widely used to remove facial wrinkles). Conversely, the deletion of the entire botulin toxin gene from *Clostridium botulinum* (the organism that causes botulinum, and that normally contains the toxin gene) could move the organism from class III to class II or even class I.

The oblique lines divide the universe according to the use of various techniques, with techniques becoming newer, moving from left to right. It should be evident from Figure 1A that the use of one technique or another, per se, does not itself confer safety or risk (except insofar as a genetic change wrought with recombinant DNA techniques is likely to be more precise,

PLANNED INTRODUCTIONS INTO THE ENVIRONMENT

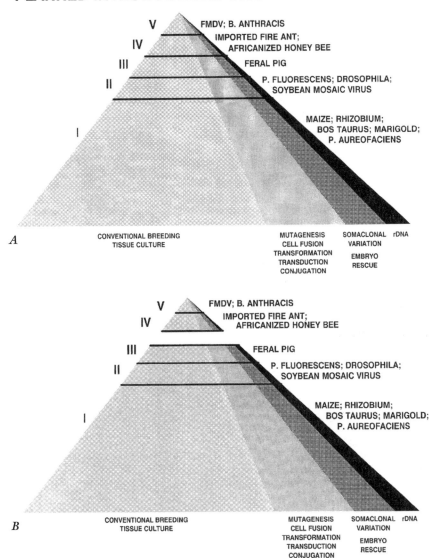

Figure 1 In both *A* and *B*, the overall figure represents the entire universe of field trials of plants, animals, and microorganisms. The horizontal lines divide the universe into classes according to the safety category of the experimental organism, taking into account the intrinsic characteristics of the parental organism and any newly introduced genetic mutation or genetic change. Examples of organisms within the categories are listed on the right. The oblique lines divide the universe according to the use of various techniques (with techniques becoming more recent as one moves from left to right). In *B*, categories IV and V are lifted off to illustrate what could be considered to constitute a "high-risk" set of organisms.

better characterized, and more predictable than, for example, a wide-cross hybridization). Whether or not an organism is "wild type" (that is, unmodified) or possesses traits newly introduced or enhanced in some way, its risk is primarily a function of its observed characteristics, or *phenotype*, which in turn is determined by its *genotype*, the genomic information that is encoded in its DNA. Some organisms are destined by their genetic constitution to exist symbiotically and innocuously on the roots of legumes (like the bacterium *Rhizobium*), while others infect and kill mammals at a low inoculum (such as Lassa fever virus).

The use of recombinant DNA techniques markedly expands the range of genes and traits that can be transferred between organisms, but greater versatility and flexibility does not imply greater risk. For an oversight scheme to be truly "risk based," the use of these molecular techniques, or the fact of genetic modification more generally, should not dictate the degree of oversight required. Rather, the trigger for oversight or for enhanced scrutiny should be a function of the characteristics of an organism, including any new traits introduced by conventional or molecular genetic modifications. Therefore, there is no coherent scientific rationale for defining the scope of a regulatory net as, say, the "recombinant DNA" slice in figure 1, although, as we have discussed throughout this volume, that approach has often been adopted.

Figure 1B differs from that in 1A by having risk categories IV and V lifted off to illustrate that this higher-risk set of organisms, rather than the recombinant DNA slice , might be an appropriate "scope" for mandatory case-by-case reviews—particularly if one were designing a regulatory scheme *de novo*. This suggestion is intended merely to be illustrative. Depending upon various considerations such as the amount of scrutiny judged to be appropriate and the degree of regulatory burden on researchers and the government deemed acceptable, the scope of what falls into the regulatory net—and what that implies with respect to data submissions and other requirements—could be appropriately stratified, or graduated. For example, category IV and V organisms might be required to undergo case-by-case, "every-case" reviews by governmental agencies prior to field trials. Category III organisms might need only a formal notification to regulators, but not an affirmative approval, while category I and II organisms might be exempt. However, some might argue that category III organisms should be lumped with either the higher or lower-risk categories and therefore be subject to greater or lesser regulatory requirements.

This kind of conceptual approach moves us away from discredited technique- or process-based oversight to a more rational consideration of the factors relevant to risk. It also affords maximum flexibility, in that by adjusting the regulatory requirements for the various risk categories the approach can be adapted to more risk-averse or less risk-averse regulatory regimes. A risk-based regulatory algorithm that uses this approach is described below.

Field Trials: The Stanford Model for Regulation

Several years ago, the Stanford University Project on Regulation of Agricultural Introductions developed a widely applicable regulatory model for the field-testing of any organism, whatever the method or methods employed in its construction. The approach is vertical and is patterned after quarantine systems such as the USDA's Plant Pest Act regulations described in chapter 5. That approach is essentially binary; a plant that a researcher might wish to introduce into the field is either on the proscribed list of plants pests—and therefore requires a permit—or it is exempt. The more quantitative and nuanced "Stanford Model," which stratifies organisms into several risk categories, more closely resembles the approach that was taken in the National Institutes of Health/Centers for Disease Control (NIH/CDC) handbook *Biosafety in Microbiological and Biomedical Laboratories,* which specifies the procedures and physical containment that are appropriate for research with microorganisms,[15] including the most dangerous pathogens known. These microorganisms were stratified into risk categories by panels of scientists. Interestingly, unlike regulators' approach to gene-spliced organisms, the NIH/CDC approach—even for the most dangerous pathogens—is only to offer guidance to researchers but not to make adherence compulsory.

The Stanford Model—applied to plants in this first demonstration project—can be readily applied to accommodate various organisms, geographical regions, and preferences for more or less stringent regulation. In January 1997, the project assembled a group of approximately twenty agricultural scientists from five nations at a workshop held at the International Rice Research Institute (IRRI), in Los Baños, Philippines.[16] The purpose of the workshop was to develop a broad, science-based approach that would evaluate all biological introductions, not just those that involve gene-spliced organisms. The need for such a broad approach was self-evident—there was already abundant evidence that severe ecological risks can be associated with plant pests and "exotics," or non-coevolved organisms.

As part of the pilot project, the IRRI conference participants evaluated and then stratified a variety of crops based on certain risk-related characteristics, or traits, to be considered in order to estimate overall risk. Consensus was reached without serious difficulty—suggesting that it would be similarly easy to categorize other organisms as well.

The participants agreed at the outset that the following risk-based factors would be integral to a model algorithm for field testing and commercial approval of all introductions:

1. Ability to colonize
2. Ecological relationships
3. Effects on humans
4. Potential for genetic change
5. Ease or difficulty of risk management.

Each of the organisms evaluated during the conference was assessed for all five factors, which enabled the group to come to a global judgment about the organism's risk category. Most of the common crop plants addressed were found to belong in Category 1 (negligible risk), while a few were ranked in Category 2 (low but nonnegligible risk). One plant (cotton) was judged to be in Category 1 if it were field-tested outside its center of origin, and Category 2 if tested in the vicinity of its center of origin.

It cannot be overemphasized that in the evolution of this Stanford Model, the factors taken into account were indifferent to either the genetic modification techniques employed, if any, or to the source(s) of the introduced genetic material. The participants agreed that whether conventional breeding techniques or recombinant DNA methods had been used to modify an organism was irrelevant to risk. They also agreed that combining DNAs from phylogenetically distant organisms—that is, organisms from different genera, families, orders, classes, phyla, or kingdoms—was irrelevant to the risk of an organism.

In other words, the group's analysis supported the view that the risks associated with field testing a genetically altered organism are independent of the process by which it was modified and of the movement of genetic material between "unrelated" organisms. The Stanford Model suggests the utility and practicality of an approach in which the degree of regulatory scrutiny over field trials is commensurate with the risks—independent of whether the organisms introduced are "natural," non-coevolved, or have been genetically improved by conventional methods or gene-splicing techniques.

What, then, are the practical implications of an organism being assigned to a "risk category?" The level of oversight faced by an investigator who intends to perform a field trial with an organism in one or another of the categories could include: complete exemption, a simple "postcard notification" to a regulatory authority (without affirmative, prior approval required), case-by-case review of all products in the category, or even prohibition (as is the case currently for experiments with foot-and-mouth disease virus in the United States).

A key feature of the Stanford Model is that it is sufficiently flexible to accommodate differences in regulatory authorities' preferences for greater or lesser regulatory stringency. Putting it another way, different national regulatory authorities could choose their preferred degree of risk aversion, some leaning more toward exemption and notification, others toward case-by-case review. However, as long as regulatory requirements are commensurate with the relative risk of each category and do not discriminate by treating organisms of equivalent risk differently, the regulatory methodology will remain within a scientifically defensible framework.

Under such a system, some currently unregulated introductions of traditionally bred cultivars and so-called "exotic," or non-coevolved, organisms considered to be of moderate or greater risk would likely become subject to regulatory review, whereas many gene-spliced organisms that now require case-by-case review would likely be regulated less stringently. The introduction of such a risk-based system would rationalize significantly the regulation of field trials, and it would reduce the regulatory and other disincentives to the use of molecular techniques for genetic modification.

By making possible accurate, scientific determinations of the risks posed by the introduction of an organism into the field, this regulatory model fosters enhanced agricultural productivity and innovation, while it protects valuable ecosystems. It offers regulatory bodies a highly adaptable, scientific paradigm for the oversight of plants, microorganisms, and other organisms, whether they are "naturally occurring" or non-coevolved organisms, or have been genetically improved by either old or new techniques. The outlook for the new biotechnology applied to agriculture, especially environmentally friendly innovations of particular benefit to the developing world, would be far better if governments and international organizations expended effort on perfecting such a model instead of on introducing and maintaining unscientific, palpably flawed regulatory regimes.

MORE STICK, LESS CARROT

Given the current political trends in biotechnology regulation, the introduction of a vertically oriented, risk-based regulatory apparatus poses no small challenge. Regardless of the success or failure of governments at reevaluating their regulation of gene-spliced organisms, however, other kinds of reforms should not be ignored. For example, we must revise the regulatory agencies' incentive structure so that they and individual regulators systematically craft more rational policies and make better decisions on individual product applications.

Avoidance of Type I errors at any cost is built implicitly into reviewers' and managers' annual performance plans. Although an employee whose actions land his bosses in front of a congressional committee to defend the mistaken approval of a hazardous product likely will be clobbered during his annual performance review, regulators are seldom held accountable for even the most egregious Type II errors.

Performance plans and employee annual reviews are a potent influence. All regulatory agency employees involved in product evaluation or compliance should be (but are not now) punished for unnecessary delays and flawed, excessively precautionary decisions—that is, Type II errors. Performance plans must, therefore, be restructured to weigh Type I and Type II errors more equally.

Similar sanctions should be applied to those who collude to craft egregiously flawed policies (chapter 5 is replete with examples). The introduction of this means of behavioral modification would require only an extension of the kind of critical judgments about employee performance that managers are routinely supposed to perform. But actually forcing managers to make such judgments and getting them to avoid the games that bureaucrats play will be more difficult. Thus, managers themselves must also be evaluated with such a risk-risk framework in mind.

The creation of ombudsman panels to evaluate agency actions and discipline misbehavior and poor performance is the kind of stick we have in mind. Such a panel must have several characteristics. First, it must have an organizational location outside the agency, to insulate it from intimidation and cover-ups by senior officials. Various offices of inspector general might be appropriate locations—for example, the FDA's ombudsman could be located in the Department of Health and Human Services' Office of Inspector General. Second, the ombudsman panel must have access to a wide spectrum of scientific, medical, regulatory, and other expertise, either via a large membership or access to ad hoc experts as necessary. Third, the panel must have the authority to recommend disciplinary sanctions, including censure, forfeited pay and bonuses, suspension, and demotion, depending on the egregiousness and impact of the transgression. Currently, most of these options are available to managers in order to sanction employees for Type I errors. The reform we suggest is intended primarily to expand the range of offenses for which employees could be punished, providing a more balanced set of incentives.

Plant breeders, companies, industry associations, consumer groups, and other interested parties could submit cases to the panel. An incident that occurred in the 1980s would have been a good candidate case for the FDA ombudsman. In spite of a demonstration that a certain proven anti-cancer agent could shrink the malignant Kaposi's sarcoma lesions often found in AIDS patients, the FDA refused to consider approval for that use. The agency said, in effect, that such an effect was merely cosmetic and that the drug's sponsor needed to show improvement of a "meaningful" end point, such as patient survival.

Although that decision eventually was reversed, the officials who were responsible for it should have been held accountable. Other examples would include the various FDA drug-approval decisions discussed in chapter 4; the EPA's review of the "ice-minus" *Pseudomonas syringae* microorganism for frost damage prevention described in chapter 5; the EPA's failure to approve the Monsanto field trial of a gene-spliced *Pseudomonas fluorescens* mentioned above; and that agency's "split approval" of StarLink™ corn, discussed in chapter 6.

Just as regulators' behavior is influenced by the fallout from Type I errors, they will respond to the sting of losing pay and promotions. The potential for these kinds of sanctions by the ombudsman panel would redress, in part, the agencies' current bias against approving innovative products, which often erects huge economic barriers to research, development, and marketing. This innovative ombudsman mechanism, which could help to create a more appropriate balance of incentives and disincentives for regulators, could be applied widely. It is a conservative means to correct regulators' predilection for eliminating product risk regardless of the cost of lost benefits.

Equally important, we need national leaders who are committed to a strong role for science in public policy and who will demand comparative risk analysis in setting federal spending and regulatory priorities. We also need a "marketplace of ideas" in which a spectrum of plausible views of policy formulation are presented and considered. We need wise regulatory czars at the Office of Management and Budget who will control and correct errant regulators. We need knowledgeable, tough, and competent agency heads at USDA, FDA, and EPA, and other senior officials who will clean house and work with the inspectors general to deal severely with the culture of risk-aversion and obstruction. We believe that such people do exist, and we hope that changing the incentive structure of the regulatory process will allow them to emerge and flourish.

Economist Milton Friedman has said that wishing for these kinds of improvements in the federal bureaucracy is like trying to design a cat that barks, and that because government functions so poorly and self-interestedly, we should have as little of it as possible. We agree with him on both counts. We must strive, therefore, for only that degree of regulation—that is, of intrusion, control, and coercion—that is necessary and sufficient. Even with a Republican president and congress, who should be strong proponents of limited government, technological progress, and the free market, there has been little movement in that direction.

SIX STRATEGIES FOR REFORMING REGULATORY ABUSES

Habituation, the gradual adaptation to a specific stimulus or to environmental conditions, is a biological phenomenon that may also be said to apply to political influences. Irrational and burdensome public policies can become so much a part of the landscape that their victims—consumers, businesses, and institutions—no longer experience a sense of outrage or push for reform. In other words, the worst becomes the norm.

We see habituation in the passivity of academic and industrial scientists toward the regulatory abuses of the new biotechnology. Rather than working to make oversight more scientific and consistent, many researchers have capitulated and tried to "work around" regulatory strictures. As a result of this strategy, much research and development has come to naught. Projects have been unable to advance to field testing, and failed companies have been sold at bargain-basement prices or have closed their doors. There are far fewer agricultural biotechnology companies today than there were only a decade and a half ago.

Earlier in this chapter, we suggested ways that government regulation could be improved by structural and management changes, including specific recommendations. But government left to its devices won't adopt these changes. One USDA regulator boasted that only the enlightened regulation by her agency has prevented damage to American agriculture from gene-spliced organisms. This banality reminds us of the story about the fellow who blows a whistle continuously while walking down Fifth Avenue in New York City. A friend asks him what he's doing, and he responds that it's to keep away the wild lions and tigers. The friend remonstrates that there aren't any wild lions and tigers within six thousand miles, and the fellow exclaims happily, "You see, it's working!"

For two decades, ever-deteriorating government policies have weighed down the progress and promise of the new biotechnology applied to agriculture and food production. But who and what can lift such a weight? Can it be accomplished at a stroke, or must it proceed according to Max Planck's observation that an important scientific innovation rarely makes its way by gradually winning over its opponents, but rather that its opponents gradually die out and the succeeding generation is familiarized with the idea from the beginning? We fear that the latter is more likely, although it is past time that those outside government began to hold policy makers accountable and to demand change.

Perhaps reflecting the triumph of hope over experience, below we suggest six strategies for "progress"—which we would define as the evolution of public policy toward more scientific, risk-based approaches to regulation of the new biotechnology.

1. Scientists Must Actively Protest Unscientific Policies and Regulations

Individual scientists must do more of what physicist and writer Freeman Dyson, the late paleontologist Stephen Jay Gould, and the late microbiologist Bernard Davis have done in their articles and books—contribute concisely and wisely to the dialogue on public policy issues. Scientists are especially well qualified to expose unscientific arguments and should do so in every possible way and forum, including writing scientific and popular articles, agreeing to be interviewed by journalists, and serving on advisory panels at government agencies.

Scientists with mainstream views have a particular obligation to expose and debunk the misrepresentations of their few rogue colleagues, whose declarations that the sky is falling receive disproportionate attention. We are reminded of Keith Schneider, the *New York Times*' environmental reporter who, when asked why he habitually included in his articles extreme and ridiculous speculations from nonmainstream scientists, responded, "They're the only ones who will talk to me on the record!"

Although an overwhelming majority of scientists opposes process- or technique-based approaches to the regulation of gene-splicing and its products, few scientists actively protest them. Even as industry trade associations, companies, and government officials conspire to implement and maintain unscientific and excessive regulation, the expected chorus of indignation from individual agricultural biotechnology researchers and farmers fails to materialize. Dr. Elizabeth Whelan, president of the American Council on Science and Health, has offered several possible explanations. She believes that most scientists are more comfortable in their labs than on *Nightline* or the pages of the *New York Times*, fear being labeled "paid liars for industry," and are so super-specialized that they are ill equipped to comment on issues of policy.[17] She could have added that, as we described in chapter 5, scientists' treatment at the hands of regulators they have agreed to advise can be manipulative and unpleasant.

Many farmers and farm organizations have played an active role in explaining and promoting the many benefits of agricultural biotechnology, but when it comes to specific regulations, farm organizations are much like other industry associations: Depending upon their narrow self-interest, they may be inclined to sit on the sidelines, or even to embrace public policy that keeps the new biotechnology from intruding into and possibly complicating their lives. Paradoxically, they seem at times to regard the promise of a superior, powerful, safe new technology more as a problem than a solution.

Scientists too may be motivated by a desire to try to reduce the uncertainty in their work environment and to placate federal governmental grant makers. But scientists are not your average interest group. They alone possess the skills necessary to debunk activists' propaganda authoritatively, and the very nature of science—that is, a systematic search for the truth, wherever it lies—should make scientists less likely to pursue narrow, short-term interests at the expense of honesty.

Perhaps it is surprising, then, that instead of demanding rationality in public policy, most scientists have settled for "transparency" and predictability—the predictability of delay, frustration, legal liability, public backlash, and loss of markets. Others have been seduced by the myth that just a little excess regulation, even if unwarranted, will assuage public anxiety, neutralize activists' alarmist messages, and bring about the technology's golden age. Although defenders of excessive regulation have made those claims for decades, the public and activists remain unappeased, biotechnology research and development continue to be shackled, and the policy miasma has only deepened.

Exceptions to this naiveté include a few professional societies and a handful of individual scientists who have called for rational regulation in editorials and communications with government agencies. These include the blunt and excellent reports from eleven scientific societies[18] and from the Council on Agricultural Science and Technology[19] that excoriated the EPA's process-based regulatory approach (chapter 3), and an analysis of food biotechnology by the Institute of Food Technologists.[20] But the threshold for definitive action is high, the organizations tire long before the activists and regulatory agencies do, and these efforts have had only limited impact.

Encouraging scientists to test the public policy waters is not, however, without its risks. No matter how brilliant a scientist may be in his specialty, acuity on public policy issues requires a broader perspective and a different fund of knowledge. An example is the *Science* editorial by eminent yeast geneticist Gerry Fink in which he recounted how in the late 1970s, National Science Foundation administrator Herman Lewis found a way to circumvent the NIH recombinant DNA guidelines' prohibition on doing certain gene-splicing experiments in yeast, thereby permitting Fink and his coworkers to perform experiments literally years before they would otherwise have been able.[21] Their experiments accelerated research leading to the ultimate development of a vastly-improved, second-generation hepatitis B vaccine. But in his editorial, Fink neglected a critical point—that other U.S. researchers who lacked a governmental Good Samaritan were stymied for years by regressive, unnecessarily restrictive federal regulatory policies and, in the end, consumers and patients were denied beneficial options. Because Lewis was such a notable exception to the rule, the real story was about how bad science makes bad policy, and about the real-world impacts of those policies. But Fink lacked a perspective on the wider dimensions of the NIH rules.

2. Scientific Institutions Must Stimulate Public Discourse

The second strategy pertains to science in its institutional forms—professional associations, faculties, academies, and journal editorial boards. These organizations should far more aggressively explore and elucidate the controversies about public policy and elevate the level of discourse on them. They should do much more to point out the flaws in current and proposed policies, and they should be as demanding about rigor on public policy issues as they are about the conduct of research.

Scientific societies can create awareness of the importance of regulatory policy by building high-profile public policy symposia into all national and international conferences. Journals can editorialize appropriately and, to return to the example of the Fink editorial, the editors at *Science* could have steered it to the more didactic and broader theme.

However, the corrupt process of policy analysis at the National Research Council (chapter 3), and editorial failures at major journals (chapter 2)—interestingly, all in the direction of the overestimation of the risks of the new biotechnology—illustrate the shortcomings of important scientific institutions and suggest that we may be asking too much.

3. The Media Must Discount Bogus Science

Reporters and their editors wield tremendous power and can do a great deal to illuminate policy issues related to science. Too often, however, they fail to do so, in the interest of "balance" conferring a kind of moral equivalence on all points of view—even after the dialogue has progressed to a point where some have already been discredited. In the post-Darwinian policy-making world, advocates of "creation biology" deserve less credibility on issues of evolutionary biology than, for example, the works of the late Harvard paleontologist Stephen Jay Gould. Claims of the invention of perpetual-motion machines, in violation of the laws of thermodynamics, should be discounted. Likewise, endless repetition of the myth that recombinant DNA technology poses inherent risk, when decades of experimental evidence and commercial use of gene-spliced products have produced no evidence of it, cannot be justified.

All viewpoints are not created equal, but a review of the news coverage by one journalism researcher found that between 1997 and 2000, the *New York Times* and the London *Times* used fewer and fewer university-based scientists as sources and that they were more than twice as likely to quote representatives from such activist groups as Greenpeace, Environmental Defense, and the Union of Concerned Scientists, whose views range from foolishness to fraud, from mawkishness to mendacity.[22]

Journalists need to learn that where there's the smoke of activists' alarmist propaganda, there isn't necessarily the fire of genuine controversy, yet we hear endless prattling about presenting "both sides of the issue." There aren't always two sides, however. If the subject were advances in blood banking, would the media seek out activists opposed to blood transfusions? Journalists seem to delight in predictably extreme and witless quotes from anti-biotechnology activists. As in the creation biology, perpetual-motion machine, and blood transfusion examples above, the media must focus on the *legitimate* portion of the spectrum of opinion if they wish to inform the public about what is truly known and unknown, the nature of the risks of using and not using the technology or product, and the importance of public policy in their lives.

The public should be exposed to *genuine* controversy, to be sure—but not to the manufactured, gratuitous pseudo-controversies that are fomented by activists, and that are bread and butter to the media. We do not believe that the public interest is served by a discussion of whether genetically engineered pigs will fly and, in so doing, disrupt air-traffic control, or whether the coronavirus that causes SARS (severe acute respiratory syndrome) originated in a field planted with gene-spliced crops.

Aggravating matters further is the common reportorial practice of using business leaders as the sole source of supposedly pro-biotechnology opinions. We discussed earlier in this chapter and in chapter 3 the often myopic and sometimes bizarre views held by individual company executives, firms, and trade associations that reflect nothing more than self-interested spin. On the other hand, there are many astute, responsible executives and scientists in the corporate sector, but reporters and consumers of news often discount their views because of perceived conflicts of interest.

4. The Biotechnology Industry Must Advocate Scientific Regulatory Policies

Companies and trade associations should eschew short-term advantage and actively oppose unscientific, discriminatory regulations that set dangerous precedents. The U.S. biotechnology industry's support for policies like the USDA's Plant Pest Act regulations, the EPA's technique-based proposals, and the FDA's proposed case-by-case review of all new-biotechnology-derived foods guarantees that they will have a long raw to hoe. It ensures recurrences of public-relations disasters like the furors over the alleged killing of Monarch butterflies; purported transfer of genes from gene-spliced crops into native corn varieties in Mexico; and supposed "contamination" of food by StarLink™ corn, biopharmed crops, and the like.

Industry's advocacy of fundamentally flawed, unscientific regulatory policies is tantamount to a farmer eating his seed corn. In the long run, commercial interests will benefit most from the predictability and logic of science-based policies—and from a robust academic research enterprise. Productivity is squandered by public policy that forces researchers to spend their time and resources doing mountains of unnecessary paperwork instead of experiments, that is anti-competitive, that lays waste to free markets, and that creates potential civil and criminal liability for inconsequential violations.

5. All Stakeholders Should Promote Science-Based Public Policy

The biotechnology industry has spent vast sums to improve its image, but this campaign has been more concerned with public relations than public health; more cheerleader than leader. As discussed above and in chapter 3, the industry has not been a staunch advocate of enlightened public policy.

However, there are others not directly involved in research and development who are important stakeholders in the ultimate applications of science and technology—venture capitalists, philanthropists, and consumer and patient groups, for example—who can contribute to needed regulatory reform. They should increase their informational activities and advocacy, by commissioning experts and lobbyists and by joining forces with organizations such as think-tanks that have similar goals.

6. Rethink the Government's Monopoly over Regulation

The devastation wreaked on the public interest by government regulators would not have been possible were it not for the federal regulatory monopoly over the new biotechnology (and the absence of effective oversight by the Congress). However, there is nothing sacrosanct about a government monopoly over regulation, which has made such a morass of the new biotechnology applied to agriculture and food production.

As we have discussed throughout this volume, recombinant DNA technology is subjected to far more stringent oversight than the various manifestations of its less precise and predictable precursor, conventional biotechnology. Most often, the latter is subject only to the strictures of good agricultural practices; and unless conventially bred organisms exhibit a high degree of risk (for example, by being classified as plant pests or noxious weeds) they are not subject to case-by-case government reviews as they move from research, through development, to commercialization. Rather, society has devised a variety of alternative institutional arrangements that effectively regulate and monitor the testing and marketing of a wide variety of products and services.[23] Nongovernmental mechanisms exist not only for conventional agriculture (including quality control for seeds) but also for hospital certification, organ transplantation, and tens of thousands of categories of consumer products. As we described in chapter 5, even when government is involved, it is often in the form of policing of the marketplace, rather than pretesting or premarketing review.

It is past time for the biotechnology regulatory pendulum to swing away from unnecessary and discriminatory government reviews, toward other models that are more efficient and favorable to innovation.

EPILOGUE

As we have argued throughout this book, the costs of the present public policy toward the new biotechnology far outweigh its benefits. We have identified several examples where the balance is overwhelmingly negative. The failures of government, industry, and the media, the excessive regulation, pseudo-controversies, and endless repetition of The Big Lie by activists collectively constitute one of the most costly and tragic hoaxes of the last century.

None of this was necessary. We would have been far better off if, instead of implementing regulation specific to the new biotechnology, governments had regulated the products of gene-splicing in the same way as they approach similar products—new plant varieties, food, pesticides and so on—made with older, less precise and predictable, techniques. Regulators could simply have applied to the products of the new biotechnology preexisting public policy, which is (more or less) risk-based and which emphasizes surveillance and policing, rather than endless, redundant case-by-case reviews of proposals to test or market products.

Whatever the level of affluence we enjoy in our personal lives, government policy toward the new biotechnology has impoverished our public lives. Government regulators, activists, and many in industry have failed the simple test proposed by Mahatma Gandhi to determine the validity of strategies designed to meet the most basic human needs: "Recall the face of the poorest and the weakest man whom you have seen, and ask yourself if the steps you contemplate are going to be of any use to him. Will he gain anything by it? Will it restore to him control over his own life and destiny?"[24] The adoption of some of the remedies described here will help to amend, even in this small realm and in a limited way, the validity of historian Barbara Tuchman's sad observation that "mankind, it seems, makes a poorer performance of government than of almost any other human activity."[25] And it will help governments, and the rest of us, to pass Gandhi's test.

Notes

FOREWORD

1. Paul Ehrlich, *The Population Bomb* (New York: Sierra Club-Ballantine, 1968).
2. Gregg Easterbrook, "Forgotten Benefactor of Humanity," *The Atlantic* (January 1997), 75–82.

PROLOGUE

1. Fish and Wildlife Service, "Endangered and Threatened Wildlife and Plants; Review of Plant and Animal Species That Are Candidates or Proposed for Listing as Endangered or Threatened, Annual Notice of Findings on Recycled Petitions, and Annual Description of Progress on Listing Actions," *Federal Register* 66 (October 30, 2001): 54807–54832; Food and Drug Administration, "Ingrown Toenail Relief Drug Products for Over-the-Counter Human Use," *Federal Register* 67 (October 4, 2002): 62218–62221.
2. David Neumark, "Raising Incomes by Mandating Higher Wages," *NBER Reporter* (Fall 2002).
3. National Research Council, *Effectiveness and Impact of Corporate Average Fuel Economy (CAFE) Standards* (Washington, D.C.: National Academy, 2001), 26–27.
4. U.S. Department of Energy, *Final Environmental Impact Statement—Summary* (DOE/EIS-0250) (Washington, D.C.: Office of Civilian Radioactive Waste Management, February 2002), esp. S-49, S-54, S-59–S61, S-64, S-69–S-70; Douglas M. Chapin et al., "Nuclear Power Plants and Their Fuel as Terrorist Targets," *Science* 297 (September 20, 2002): 1997–1999.
5. Jorge Fernandez-Cornejo and William McBride, *Genetically Engineered Crops for Pest Management in U.S. Agriculture*, Agricultural Economics Report 786 (Washington, D.C.: Economic Research Service, U.S. Department of Agriculture, May 2000), 15–17; Janet Carpenter and Leonard Gianessi, *Case Studies in Benefits and Risks of Agricultural Biotechnology: Roundup Ready Soybeans and Bt Field Corn* (Washington, D.C.: National Center for Food and Agricultural Policy, 2001); R.

H. Phipps and J. R. Park, "Environmental Benefits of Genetically Modified Crops: Global and European Perspectives on Their Ability to Reduce Pesticide Use," *Journal of Animal and Feed Sciences* 11 (2002): 1–18.

6. Gordon Conway and Gary Toenniessen, "Feeding the World in the Twenty-First Century," *Nature* 402 (December 2, 1999): C55–C58.

7. Joel I. Cohen and Robert Paarlberg, "Explaining Restrictive Approval and Availability of GM Crops in Developing Countries," *AgBiotechNet 2002* 4 (October), ABN 097.

8. *Sunday Times* (London), September 22, 2002.

9. Julian Morris, ed., *Rethinking Risk and the Precautionary Principle* (Oxford: Butterworth-Heineman, 2000).

10. Edward F. Denison, *Accounting for United States Economic Growth, 1929–1969* (Washington, D.C.: Brookings Institution, 1974).

CHAPTER 1

1. Davan Maharaj and Anthony Mukwita, "Zambia Rejects Gene-Altered US Corn Africa: Millions Face Starvation, but the Government Cites Safety Fears for Refusing Grain," *Los Angeles Times*, August 28, 2002, A1.

2. "U.S. to Give Hungry Zambia Food Despite GM Spat," Reuters News Service (December 9, 2002).

3. Robert L. McKown and George L. Coffman, "Development of Biotechnology Curriculum for the Biomanufacturing Industry," *Pharmaceutical Engineering* 22 (May/June 2002): 1–6.

4. Lee Bruno, "Biotech Beginnings: From Brewing Beer to Unraveling the Structure of DNA—Mankind Unrelentingly Endeavors to Understand Life's Blueprint," *Red Herring* (April 2000).

5. A. L. Demain and N. A. Solomon, "Industrial Microbiology," *Scientific American* 245 (1981): 66–75.

6. Ibid.

7. World Health Organization, "Health Impact of Biotechnology: Report of a WHO Working Group," *Swiss Biotech* 2 (1985): 7–16.

8. D. L. Klingman and J. R. Coulson, "Guidelines for Introducing Foreign Organisms into the USA for Biological Control of Weeds," *Plant Disease* 66 (1982): 1205–1209.

9. P. Raven, R. F. Evert, and S. E. Eichhorn, *Biology of Plants*, 5th ed. (New York: Worth, 1992).

10. R. M. Goodman et al., "Gene Transfer in Crop Improvement," *Science* 236 (1987): 48–54.

11. Ibid.

12. A. McHughen, *Pandora's Picnic Basket: The Potential and Hazards of Genetically Modified Foods* (New York: Oxford University Press, 2000).

13. International Atomic Energy Agency, *Officially Released Mutant Varieties: The FAO/IAEA Database* (Vienna: Joint FAO-IAEA Division, International Atomic Energy Agency, December 2000).

14. Ibid.

15. S. N. Cohen, A.C.Y. Chang, H. W. Boyer, and R. B. Helling, "Construc-

tion of Biologically Functional Bacterial Plamids in Vitro," *Proceedings of the National Academy of Sciences* 70 (1973): 3240–4243.

16. California Council on Science and Technology, "Executive Summary," *Benefits and Risks of Food Biotechnology* (Riverside: California Council on Science and Technology, 2002), 5–16.

17. U.S. Department of Agriculture, *Prospective Plantings* (Washington, D.C.: U.S. Department of Agriculture, National Agricultural Statistics Service, March 31, 2004).

18. P. Berg and M. F. Singer, "The Recombinant DNA Controversy: 20 Years Later," *Proceedings of the National Academy of Sciences* 92 (1995): 9011–9013.

19. James D. Watson, *DNA: The Secret of Life* (New York: Alfred A. Knopf, 2003), 99–100 [emphasis in the original].

20. James D. Watson, "In Defense of DNA," *New Republic*, June 25, 1977, 11.

21. M. Cantley, "Government, Researchers and Activists: The Crucial Public Policy Interface," in *Biotechnology*, ed. D. Brauer (Weinheim, Ger.: VCH, 1995), 515.

22. Ibid.

23. L. Altman, "Unit Backs Human Insulin," *New York Times*, October 30, 1982, 1.

24. Office of Science and Technology Policy, "Coordinated Framework for Regulation of Biotechnology," *Federal Register* 51 (June 26, 1986): 23302–23347.

25. National Academy of Sciences, *Introduction of Recombinant DNA-Engineered Organisms into the Environment: Key Issues* (Washington, D.C.: National Academy, 1987).

26. National Research Council, *Field Testing Genetically Modified Organisms: Framework for Decisions* (Washington, D.C.: National Academy, 1989).

27. B. Keating-Edh, "Testimony before the National Biotechnology Policy Board," *1992 National Biotechnology Policy Board Report* (Bethesda, Md.: National Institutes of Health, 1992) [emphasis in original].

28. F. J. Dyson, "On the Hidden Costs of Saying 'No,'" *Bulletin of Atomic Scientists* 31 (1975): 23.

CHAPTER 2

1. California Crop Improvement Association, at http://ccia.ucdavis.edu/ [accessed February 12, 2003].

2. B. D. Davis, "Evaluation, Epidemiology and Recombinant DNA," *Science* 193 (1976): 442.

3. A. Brisson-Noel, M. Arthur, and P. Courvalin, "Evidence of Natural Gene Transfer from Gram-Positive Cocci to *Escherichia coli*," *Journal of Bacteriology* 170 (1988):1739–1745.

4. P. Mazodier, R. Petter, and C. Thompson, "Intergeneric Conjugation between *Escherichia coli* and *Streptomyces* Species," *Journal of Bacteriology* 171 (1989): 3583.

5. J. A. Heinemann and G. G. Sprague Jr., "Bacterial Conjugative Plasmids Mobilize DNA Transfer between Bacteria and Yeast," *Nature* 340 (1989): 205.

6. Mary Dell Chilton, et al., "Stable Incorporation of Plasmid DNA into Higher Plant-Cells-Molecular-Basis of Crown Gall Tumorigenesis," *Cell* 11 (1977) 263–

271; E. W. Nester, M. P. Gordon, R. M. Amasino, et al., "Crown Gall: A Molecular and Physiological Analysis," *Annual Review of Plant Physiology* 35 (1984): 387–413.

7. M. W. Bevan, R. B. Flavell and M. Chilton, "A Chimaeric Antibiotic-Resistance Gene as a Selectable Marker for Plant-Cell Transformation," *Nature* 304 (1983): 184–187; L. Herrera-Estrella, A. Depicker, M. Van Montagu and J. Schell. *Nature* 303 (1983): 209–213; R. T. Fraley, S. G. Rogers, R. B. Horsch, P. R. Sanders, et al., "Expression of Bacterial Genes in Plant Cells," *Proceedings of the National Academy of Science* 80 (1983): 4803–4807.

8. K. Takemoto, M. Yano, Y. Akiyama, and H. Mori, *GenoBase 1.1, Escherichia Coli* (March 1994).

9. *MIPS 2001*, at http://biolinx.bios.niu.edu/t80maj1/arab_plot.html [accessed February 12, 2003].

10. M. J. Chrispeels and D. E. Sadava, *Plants, Genes and Biotechnology* (Sudbury, Mass.: Jones and Bartlett, 2003), 448.

11. M. J. Crawley, S. L. Brown, R. S. Hails, D. D. Kohn, and M. Rees, "Transgenic Crops in Natural Habitats," *Nature* 409 (2001): 682–683.

12. A. Trewavas and C. J. Leaver, "Is Opposition to GM Crops Science or Politics?" *EMBO Reports* 21 (2001): 455–459.

13. D. R. Lincoln, E. S. Fisher, and D. C. Lambert, "Release and Containment of Microorganisms from Applied Genetics Activities," *Enzyme and Microbial Technology* 7 (1985): 314–321.

14. F. E. Sharples, "Regulation of Products from Biotechnology," *Science* 235 (1987): 1329.

15. Anthony M. Shelton and Mark K. Sears, "The Monarch Butterfly Controversy: Scientific Interpretations of a Phenomenon," *Plant Journal* 27 (2001): 483–488.

16. S. W. B. Ewen and Arpad Pusztai, "Effect of Diets Containing Genetically Modified Potatoes Expressing *Galanthus Nivalis* Lectin on Rat Small Intestine," *Lancet* 354 (October 16, 1999): 1353–1355.

17. Harry A. Kuiper, P.J.M. Noteborn, and A.C.M. Peijnenburg, "Adequacy of Methods for Testing the Safety of Genetically Modified Foods," *Lancet* 354 (October 16, 1999): 1315–1316.

18. Ibid.; John A. Gatehouse, Unpublished letter to the editors of *The Lancet* (October 7, 1999), available at http://silver-server.dur.ac.uk/GM_Plants_Pages/Lancet.html.

19. Royal Society, *Review of Data on Possible Toxicity of GM Potatoes*, review ref. 11/99 (London: Royal Society, June 1999), available at http://www.royalsoc.ac.uk/templates/statements/statementDetails.cfm?StatementID=2.

20. "A Hot Potato," *Lancet* 354 (October 16, 1999), available at http://www.thelancet.com/journal/vol354/iss9187/full/llan.354.9187.talking_points.2953.1.

21. C.-L. Zhen, "Transgenic Food: Need and Safety," presentation to the OECD Edinburgh Conference on the Scientific and Health Aspects of Genetically Modified Foods, February 28–March 1, 2000, available at: http://www1.oecd.org/subject/biotech/chen.pdf.

22. R. Teshima et al., "Effects of GM and Non-GM Soybeans on the Immune System of BN Rats and B10A Mice," *Journal of the Food Hygiene Society of Japan* 41 (June 2000): 3.

23. J. H. Clark and I. R. Ipharraguerre, "Livestock Performance: Feeding Biotech Crops," *Journal of Dairy Science* 84, E. Supplement (2001): E9–E18.

24. John E. Losey, Linda S. Rayor, and Maureen E. Carter, "Transgenic Pollen Harms Monarch Larvae," *Nature* 399 (May 20, 1999): 214.

25. Laura C. Hansen Jesse and John J. Obrycki, "Field Deposition of Bt Transgenic Corn Pollen: Lethal Effects on the Monarch Butterfly" *Oecologia* 125 (2000): 241–248.

26. Trewavas and Leaver.

27. Ben J. Miflin, "Crop Biotechnology: Where Now?" *Plant Physiology* 123 (May 2000): 17–27; David S. Pimentel and Peter H. Raven, "Bt corn pollen impacts on nontarget lepidoptera: assessment of effects on nature," *Proceedings of the National Academy of Sciences* 97 (July 18, 2000): 8198–8199.

28. M. K. Sears, R. L. Hellmich, D. E. Stanley-Horn, et al., "Impact of Bt corn pollen on monarch butterfly populations: A risk assessment," *Proceedings of the National Academy of Sciences* 98 (October 8, 2001): 11937–11942; D. E. Stanley-Horn, G. P. Dively, R. L. Hellmich, et al., "Assessing the impact of Cry1Ab-expressing corn pollen on monarch butterfly larvae in field studies," *Proceedings of the National Academy of Sciences* 98 (2001):11931–11936; R. L. Hellmich, B. D. Siegfried, M. K. Sears, et al., "Monarch larvae sensitivity to Bacillus thuringiensis- purified proteins and pollen," *Proceedings of the National Academy of Sciences* 98 (2001): 11925–11930; K. S. Oberhauser, M. D. Prysby, H. R. Mattila, et al., "Temporal and spatial overlap between monarch larvae and corn pollen," *Proceedings of the National Academy of Sciences* 98 (2001): 11913–11918; J. M. Pleasants, R. L. Hellmich, G. P. Dively, et al., "Corn pollen deposition on milkweeds in and near cornfields," *Proceedings of the National Academy of Sciences* 98 (2001): 11919–11924; A. R. Zangerl, D. McKenna, C. L. Wraight, et al., "Effects of exposure to event 176 Bacillus thuringiensis corn pollen on monarch and black swallowtail caterpillars under field conditions," *Proceedings of the National Academy of Sciences* 98 (2001): 11908–11912.

29. Union of Concerned Scientists website (2004), at http://www.ucsusa.org.

30. L. L. Wolfenbarger and P. R. Phifer, "The Ecological Risks and Benefits of Genetically Engineered Plants," *Science* 290 (2000): 2088–2093.

31. "Trust and How to Sustain It" (editorial), *Nature* 420 (2002): 719.

32. J. E. Carpenter and L. P. Gianessi, *Agricultural Biotechnology: Updated Benefit Estimates* (Washington, D.C.: National Center for Food and Agricultural Policy, January 2001); Carl Pray, Danmeng Ma, Jikun Huang, and Fangbin Qiao, "Impact of Bt Cotton in China," *World Development* 29 (May 2001): 813–825.

33. Carpenter and Gianessi.

34. Pray, Ma, Huang, and Qiao.

35. G. Traxler et al., "Transgenic Cotton in Mexico: Eeconomic and Environmental Impacts," Department of Agricultural Economics working paper, Auburn University, Auburn, Alabama, 2001; Y. Ismael, "Smallholder Adoption and Economic Impacts of Bt Cotton in the Makhathini Flats, Republic of South Africa," report for DFID Natural Resources Policy Research Programme, Project R7946 (London: Department for International Development, 2001).

36. J. Huang, Q. Wang, and Y. Zhang, "Agricultural Biotechnology Development Research Capacity," Center for Chinese Agricultural Policy working paper (Beijing: Center for Chinese Agricultural Policy, Chinese Academy of Sciences, 2001).

37. H. Bialy, "Biotechnology, Bioremediation, and Blue Genes," *Nature Biotech* 15 (1997): 110.

38. J. Carpenter, "GM Crops and Patterns of Pesticide Use," *Science* 292 (2001): 637.

39. D. Quist and I. H. Chapela, "Transgenic DNA Introgressed into Traditional Maize Landraces in Oaxaca, Mexico," *Nature* 414 (2001): 541–543.

40. "Fremdgene in Landsorten: Gefahr für die biologische Vielfalt? [Foreign genes in landraces: Danger for biological diversity?]" *bioSicherheit*, February 10, 2003, available at http://www.biosicherheit.de/aktuell/101.doku.html.

41. P. Christou, "No Credible Evidence Is Presented to Support Claims That Transgenic DNA Was Introgressed into Traditional Maize Landraces in Oaxaca, Mexico," *Transgenic Research* 11 (2002): iii–v; J. Hodgson, "Maize Uncertainties Create Political Fallout," *Nature Biotechnology* 20 (2002): 106–107; J. Hodgson, "Doubts Linger over Mexican Corn Analysis," *Nature Biotechnology* 20 (2002): 3–4; Allan S. Felsot, "Some Corny Ideas about Gene Flow and Biodiversity," *Agrichemical and Environmental: A Monthly Report on Environmental and Pesticide Related Issues*, 193 (May 2002): 1–13; J. .P. R. Martinez-Soriano and D. S. Leal-Klevezas, "Transgenic Maize in Mexico: No Need for Concern," *Science* 287 (2000): 1399; J. P. R. Martinez-Soriano, A. M. Bailey, J. Lara-Reyna, and D. S. Leal-Klevezas, "Transgenes in Mexican Maize," *Nature Biotechnology* 20 (2002): 19.

42. Christou; G. Conko and C. S. Prakash, "Report of Transgenes in Mexican Corn Called into Question," *ISB News Report* (March 2002): 3–5, available at http://www.isb.vt.edu/news/2002/news02.mar.html#mar0202.

43. CIMMYT (Centro Internacional de Mejoramiento de Maiz y Trigo), *Transgenic Maize in Mexico: Facts and Future Research Needs* (Mexico City: Centro Internacional de Mejoramiento de Maiz y Trigo [International Maize and Wheat Improvement Center], May 8, 2002); "CIMMYT Repeats: No GM in Maize Gene Banks," *Crop Biotech Update*, May 17, 2002.

44. Martinez-Soriano and Leal-Klevezas.

45. M. Metz and J. Fütterer, "Suspect Evidence of Transgenic Contamination," *Nature* 416 (April 11, 2002): 600–601; N. Kaplinsky, D. Braun, D. Lisch, A. Hay, S. Hake, and M. Freeling, "Biodiversity (Communications Arising): Maize Transgene Results in Mexico Are Artefacts," *Nature* 416 (April 11, 2002): 601–602.

46. D. Quist, I. H. Chapela, "Reply," *Nature* 416 (April 11, 2002): 602.

47. "Editorial Note," *Nature* 416 (2002): 600.

48. Ibid.

CHAPTER 3

1. National Academy of Sciences, *Introduction of Recombinant DNA–Engineered Organisms into the Environment: Key Issues* (Washington, D.C.: National Academy, 1987).

2. National Research Council. *Field Testing Genetically Modified Organisms: Framework for Decisions* (Washington, D.C.: National Academy, 1989).

3. Ibid., 3.

4. Ibid., 13.

5. Ibid., 14.

6. Ibid. [emphasis added].

7. *National Biotechnology Policy Board Report* (Bethesda, Md.: National Institutes of Health, Office of the Director, 1992).

8. Scientific Committee on Problems of the Environment; Scientific Committee on Problems of the Environment, International Council of Scientific Unions; and the Committee on Genetic Experimentation, *Joint Statement*, Bellagio, Italy, 1987.

9. J. Fiksel and V. T. Covello, eds., *Safety Assurance for Environmental Introductions of Genetically-Engineered Organisms* (Workshop Summary), NATO ASI Series (Berlin, Heidelberg, New York: Springer-Verlag, 1988).

10. Organization for Economic Cooperation and Development, *Safety Evaluation of Foods Derived by Modern Biotechnology: Concepts and Principles* (Paris: 1993).

11. Ibid., 13.

12. Ibid., 13.

13. Institute of Food Technologists, *IFT Expert Report on Biotechnology and Foods* (Chicago, Ill.: Institute of Food Technologists, 2000).

14. Organization for Economic Cooperation and Development (1993).

15. T. F. Hoban, "Countering the Myths of Biotechnology's Acceptance," *Grand Forks Herald* [North Dakota], September 13, 2000.

16. P. S. Naik, "Biotechnology through the Eyes of an Opponent: The Resistance of Jeremy Rifkin," *Virginia Journal of Law & Technology* 5 (2000): 1522–1687.

17. Greenpeace U.S., Federal Income Tax Filing with the U.S. Internal Revenue Service: IRS Form 990, Part III, Statement of Program Service Accomplishments, "Genetic Engineering" (1999).

18. Hoban.

19. I. Meister, "Uncontrolled Trade in Genetically Manipulated Products," press release, Greenpeace International, April 7, 1995.

20. "Flowery Thoughts" (editorial), *New York Times*, February 14, 2003.

21. Meister.

22. The Mellman Group and Public Opinion Strategies, "Public Sentiments about Genetically Modified Foods," (Washington, D.C.: Pew Initiative on Food and Biotechnology, 2003), available at *http://pewagbiotech.org/research/2003update/1.php.*

23. J. D. Miller and L. Kimmel, *1999 Study of Public Attitudes toward and Understanding of Science and Technology* (Arlington, VA: National Science Foundation, November 30, 2000).

24. W. Hallman, W. Hebden, H. Aquino, C. Cuite, and J. Lang, *Public Perceptions of Genetically Modified Foods: A National Study of American Knowledge and Opinion* (New Brunswick, N.J.: Rutgers University Food Policy Institute, 2003), available at http://www.foodpolicyinstitute.org/docs/reports/NationalStudy2003.pdf.

25. E. Haas, "Diet Risk Communication: A Consumer Advocate Perspective," in *The Emerging Global Food System*, eds. G. E. Gaull and R. A. Goldberg (New York: Wiley & Sons, 1993), 133–146.

26. Hoban.

27. D. Kennedy, "The Regulation of Science: How Much Can We Afford?" *MBL Science* (Winter 1988–1989): 5–9.

28. X. Ye, S. Al-Babili, A. Klöti, J. Zhang, P. Lucca, P. Beyer, and I. Potrykus, "Engineering the Provitamin A (β-Carotene) Biosynthetic Pathway into (Carotenoid-Free) Rice Endosperm," *Science* 287 (January 14, 2000): 303–308.

29. Vandana Shiva, "Genetically Engineered Vitamin A Rice: A Blind Approach to Blindness Prevention," *Synthesis/Regeneration* 23 (Fall 2000), available at http://www.greens.org/s-r/23/23-18.html.

30. B. Palevitz, "Bowl of Hope, Bucket of Hype," *Scientist* 15 (April 2, 2001): 15.

31. Donald G. McNeil Jr., "New Genes and Seeds: Protesters in Europe Grow More Passionate," *New York Times* (March 14, 2000), available at http://www.nytimes.com/library/national/science/health/031400hth-gm-europe.html.

32. Michael Pollan, "The Great Yellow Hype," *New York Times Magazine* (March 4, 2001): 15–16.

33. S. H. Strauss, "Genomics, Genetic Engineering and Domestication of Crops," *Science* 300 (2003): 61–62.

34. J. Cayford, "Democratization Is More Than Lower Prices," *Science* 301 (2003): 167.

35. S. H. Strauss, "Response," Science 301 (2003): 167.

36. Carl F. Feldbaum, Letter to Congressman Don Young, July 17, 1995.

37. J. Nettleton, Personal communication to Henry I. Miller (1995).

38. James A. Bair, "North American Millers' Association Comments submitted in response to the January 23, 2004, Federal Register notice of intent to prepare an environmental impact statement (EIS) and proposed scope of study published by the U.S. Department of Agriculture (USDA)'s Animal and Plant Health Inspection Service (APHIS)" (March 22, 2004), available at http://www.namamillers.org/cs_biopharm_Comments_Mar04.html [italics added].

39. J. Fox, "Puzzling Industry Response to ProdiGene Fiasco," *Nature Biotechnology* 21 (2003): 3–4.

40. L. Aldrich, and N. Blisard, "Consumer Acceptance of Biotechnology: Lessons from the rbST Experience," In *Current Issues in Economics of Food Markets* (Washington, D.C.: U.S. Department of Agriculture, 1996).

41. C. Noussair, S. Robin, and B. Ruffieux, "Do Consumers Not Care about Biotech Foods or Do They Just Not Read the Labels?" *Economics Letters* 75 (2002): 47–53.

42. Kennedy.

43. S. L. Huttner and H. I. Miller, "USDA Regulation of Field Trials of Recombinant-DNA-Modified Plants: Reforms Leave Severe Flaws," *Trends in Biotechnology* (October 1997): 387–389.

44. Keith Redenbaugh and Alan McHughen, "Regulatory Challenges Reduce Opportunities for Horticultural Biotechnology," *California Agriculture* 58 (2004): 106–115.

45. Bob Buchanan, personal communication to Henry I. Miller.

46. Bruce Yandle, "Bootleggers and Baptists: The Education of a Regulatory Economist," *Regulation* 7 (1983): 12.

47. K. R. Leube, ed. *The Essence of Friedman* (Stanford, Calif.: Hoover Institution Press, 1987).

48. Howarth Bouis, "Rich Harvest for the Poor," *Guardian* (October, 23 2003), available at http://www.guardian.co.uk/letters/story/0,3604,1068809,00.html.

49. "Bio-Food Research Increasingly Concentrated," Reuters News Service (February 20, 2003).

50. A. Bouchie, "Safety of GMOs Reaffirmed by EU," *Nature Biotechnology* 19 (2001): 1095.

51. National Research Council, *Genetically Modified Pest-Protected Plants: Science and Regulation* (Washington, D.C.: National Academy Press, 2000).

52. National Research Council, *Environmental Effects of Transgenic Plants: The Scope and Adequacy of Regulation* (Washington, D.C.: National Academy Press, 2002).

53. Office of Science and Technology Policy, "Proposed Federal Actions to Update Field Test Requirements for Biotechnology Derived Plants and to Establish Early Food Safety Assessments for New Proteins Produced by Such Plants," *Federal Register* 67 (August 2, 2002): 50577–50580.

54. Environmental Protection Agency, "Plant-Pesticides Subject to the Federal Insecticide, Fungicide, and Rodenticide Act; Proposed Rule," *Federal Register* 59 (November 23, 1994): 60496–60519.

55. Environmental Protection Agency, "Plant-Incorporated Protectants; Final Rules and Proposed Rule," *Federal Register* 66 (July 19, 2001): 37772–37817.

56. George Bruening, "Safety of Foods Derived from Spliced-DNA Foods," in *Benefits and Risks of Food Biotechnology* (Riverside, Calif.: California Council on Science and Technology, 2002).

57. "Missing the Big Picture," *Nature* 421 (2003): 675.

58. National Research Council (2000).

59. Eleven Professional Scientific Societies, *Appropriate Oversight for Plants with Inherited Traits for Resistance to Pests* (Chicago: Coordinating Society, Institute of Food Technologists, 1996).

60. Council on Agricultural Science and Technology, *The Proposed EPA Plant Pesticide Rule* (Ames, Iowa: Council on Agricultural Science and Technology, October 1998).

61. National Research Council (2000) [emphasis in original].

62. J. L. Vanderveen, "Federal Regulation and Policy on Transgenic Plants," in *Benefits and Risks of Food Biotechnology* (Sacramento: California Council on Science and Technology 2002).

63. U.S. Department of Agriculture, "Introduction of Organisms and Products Altered or Produced through Genetic Engineering Which Are Plant Pests or Which There Is Reason to Believe Are Plant Pests," 7 CFR 340.

64. National Research Council (2002).

65. Ibid., 6.

66. R. H. Hall, "Pathological Science," *Physics Today* 42 (1989): 36.

67. "Editorial Note," *Nature* 416 (2002): 600.

68. F. Gould and J. Kuzma, "The Academy Responds," *Scientist*, October 14, 2002, 12.

69. H. Miller, "Nescience, Not Science, from the Academy," *Scientist*, September 30, 2002, 12.

70. D. Stetten, Jr., "Reported Laboratory Frauds in Biomedical Sciences," *Science* 226 (December 21, 1984): 1374–1376.

CHAPTER 4

1. Davan Maharaj and Anthony Mukwita, "Zambia Rejects Gene-Altered US Corn Africa: Millions Face Starvation, but the Government Cites Safety Fears for Refusing Grain," *Los Angeles Times*, August 28, 2000, A1.

2. A. Wildavsky, *Searching for Safety* (Oxford: Transaction, 1988); Julian Morris, ed., *Rethinking Risk and the Precautionary Principle* (Oxford: Butterworth-Heineman, 2000); John D. Graham and Jonathan Baert Wiener, *Risk vs. Risk: Tradeoffs in Protecting Health and the Environment* (Cambridge, Mass.: Harvard University Press, 1995).

3. T. Page, "A Generic View of Toxic Chemicals and Similar Risks," *Ecology Law Quarterly* 7 (1978): 207–244.

4. W. Kip Viscusi and Ted Gayer, "Safety at Any Price?" *Regulation* 25 (Fall 2002): 54–63; Stephen Breyer, *Breaking the Vicious Circle: Toward Effective Risk Regulation* (Cambridge, Mass.: Harvard University Press, 1993); Graham and Wiener.

5. Breyer.

6. Mary Douglas and Aaron Wildavsky, *Risk and Culture: An Essay on the Selection of Technological and Environmental Dangers* (Berkeley: University of California Press, 1982).

7. J. B. Wiener, *Precaution in a Multi-Risk World*, Public Law and Legal Theory Working Paper Series 23 (Durham, N.C.: Duke Law School, 2001), 4.

8. Joel Tickner, "A Map toward Precautionary Decision Making," in *Protecting Public Health & the Environment: Implementing the Precautionary Principle*, ed. C. Raffensperger and J. Tickner (Washington, D.C.: Island, 1999), 163.

9. European Commission, "Questions and Answers on the Regulation of GMOs in the EU," Memo/00/277 (Brussels: Commission of the European Communities Directorate General for Health and Consumer Protection, July 24, 2001), available at http://europa.eu.int/comm/dgs/health_consumer/library/press/press171_en.pdf.

10. John Hodgson, "National Politicians Block GM Progress," *Nature Biotechnology* 18 (September 2000): 918–919.

11. "End of Moratorium: GM Corn Authorised for Import into EU," *EurActiv* (May 19, 2004) available at http://www.euractiv.com/cgi-bin/cgint.exe/1107366-633?204&OIDN=1507723&-home=home; European Commission, "Commission Authorises Import of Canned GM-Sweet Corn under New Strict Labelling Conditions—Consumers Can Choose," IP/04/663 (Brussels: European Commission, May 19, 2004), available at http://europa.eu.int/rapid/pressReleasesAction.do?reference = IP/04/663&format=HTML&aged= 0&language=EN&guiLanguage=fr.

12. Alan McHughen, *Pandora's Picnic Basket: The Potential and Hazards of Genetically Modified Foods* (New York: Oxford University Press, 2000).

13. Sabine Louët, "EU Court Overrules France's *Bt* Maize Ban," *Nature Biotechnology* 18 (May 2000): 487.

14. *GM Farm Trials*, POST Note 146 (London: Parliamentary Office of Science and Technology, September 2000); John Vidal, "GM Trials Face Delay as Crops Destroyed: Company Examines Damage to Six Test Sites," *Guardian*, June 9, 2001, 20.

15. Commission of the European Communities, "Bayer Decides against GM Crop Cultivation in the UK," CORDIS News Service (March 31, 2004).

16. Alison Abbott, "Germany Holds Up Cultivation of GM Maize," *Nature* 403 (February 24, 2000): 821; Ellen Peerenboom, "German Health Minister Calls Time Out for *Bt* Maize," *Nature Biotechnology* 18 (April 2000): 374.

17. Anna Meldolesi, "GM Products Held Hostage to Political Process," *Nature Biotechnology* 18 (November 2000): 1137; Giuseppe Benagiano, "Breaching Principles," *Nature Biotechnology* 18 (December 2000): 1227.

18. Viscusi and Gayer.

19. Glen O. Robinson and Ernest Gellhorn, *The Administrative Process* (St. Paul, Minn.: West, 1974).

20. Wiener; Wildavsky.

21. B. N. Ames, M. Profet, and L. S. Gold, "Nature's Chemicals and Synthetic Chemicals: Comparative Toxicology," *Proceedings of the National Academy of Sciences* 87 (1990): 7782–7786.

22. World Health Organization, *Global Water Supply and Sanitation Assessment 2000 Report* (Geneva: World Health Organization and United Nations Children's Fund, 2000).

23. Michael Fumento and Michelle Malkin, *Rachel's Folly: The End of Chlorine* (Washington, D.C.: Competitive Enterprise Institute, 1996).

24. Christopher Anderson, "Cholera Epidemic Traced to Risk Miscalculation," *Nature* 354 (November 28, 1991): 255.

25. Enrique Ghersi and Hector Naupari, "Dirty Water: Cholera in Peru," in *Environmental Health: Third World Problems, First World Preoccupations*, ed. Roger Bate and Elaine Mooney (Oxford: Butterworth-Heinemann, 1999), 17–46.

26. Institute of Food Technologists, *IFT Expert Report on Biotechnology and Foods* (Chicago, Ill.: Institute of Food Technologists, 2000).

27. Janet Carpenter and Leonard Gianessi, *Agricultural Biotechnology: Updated Benefit Estimates* (Washington, D.C.: National Center for Food and Agricultural Policy, January 2001).

28. Gordon Conway and Gary Toenniessen, "Feeding the World in the Twenty-first Century," *Nature* 402 (1999): C55–C58; I. Goklany, "Precaution without Perversity: A Comprehensive Application of the Precautionary Principle to Genetically Modified Crops," *Biotechnology Law Report* 20 (2001): 377–396.

29. National Research Council, *Field Testing Genetically Modified Organisms: Framework for Decisions* (Washington, D.C.: National Academy, 1989).

30. F. B. Cross, "Paradoxical Perils of the Precautionary Principle," *Washington and Lee Law Review* 53 (1996): 860.

31. Wildavksy; W. Kip Viscusi, "The Dangers of Unbounded Commitments to Regulate Risk," in *Getting Better Results from Regulation*, ed. Robert W. Hahn (New York: Oxford University Press, 1996).

32. Ibid.

33. Jason Burnett and Robert W. Hahn, *EPA's Arsenic Rule: The Benefits of the Standard Do Not Justify the Costs*, Regulatory Analysis 01-02 (Washington, D.C.: AEI-Brookings Joint Center for Regulatory Studies, 2001).

34. Stephen Clapp, "Zambia Formally Rejects Biotech Food Aid," *Food Chemical News* 44 (November 4, 2002.): 1.

35. J. Harris and S. Holm, "Extending Human Lifespan and the Precautionary Paradox," *Journal of Medicine and Philosophy* 27 (2002): 355–368; Wildavsky.

36. European Commission, *Communication from the Commission on the Precautionary Principle*, COM (2000)1 (Brussels: February 2, 2000); C. Raffensperger and J. Tickner, eds., *Protecting Public Health & the Environment: Implementing the Precautionary Principle* (Washington, D.C.: Island, 1999).

37. H. G. Grabowski and J. M. Vernon, *The Regulation of Pharmaceuticals: Balancing the Benefits and Risks* (Washington, D.C.: American Enterprise Institute, 1983.); P. W. Huber, "Exorcists vs. Gatekeepers in Risk Regulation," *Regulation* 7 (1983): 23–32.

38. Centers for Disease Control, *Influenza Vaccine (Flu Shot): Questions & Answers 2002–2003.* (Atlanta: 2002), available at http://www.cdc.gov/ncidod/diseases/flu/vacfacts.htm#7 [accessed June 10, 2003].

39. Sam Peltzman, *Regulation of Pharmaceutical Innovation: The 1962 Amendments* (Washington, D.C.: American Enterprise Institute, 1974.); Grabowski and Vernon.

40. Sam Kazman, "Deadly Overcaution," *Journal of Regulation and Social Costs* 1 (August 1990): 31–54.

41. Quoted in Grabowski and Vernon, 5 [emphasis in original].

42. C. Raffensperger and J. Tickner, eds. *Protecting Public Health & the Environment: Implementing the Precautionary Principle*, ed. C. Raffensperger and J. Tickner (Washington, D.C.: Island, 1999).

43. National Research Council, *Regulating Pesticides in Food* (Washington, D.C.: National Academy, 1987).

44. P. W. Huber and R. E. Litan, "Overview," in *The Liability Maze: The Impact of Liability Law on Safety and Innovation*, ed. P. W. Huber and R. E. Litan (Washington, D.C.: Brookings Institution, 1991), 1–27.

45. G. P. Munkvold, R. L. Hellmich, and L. G. Rice, "Comparison of Fumonisin Concentrations in Kernels of Transgenic Bt Maize Hybrids and Non-Transgenic Hybrids," *Plant Disease* 83 (1999): 130–138.

46. Wildavsky.

47. H. I. Miller, *To America's Health: A Proposal to Reform the Food and Drug Administration* (Stanford, Calif.: Hoover Institution Press, 2000).

48. Dick Taverne, "Safety Quacks," *Prospect* (April 2004), 40–44.

49. United Nations, *Rio Declaration on Environment and Development*, UN Doc. A/CONF.151/5/Rev. 1, New York, 1992.

50. See Henry I. Miller and Gregory Conko, "The Science of Biotechnology Meets the Politics of Global Regulation," *Issues in Science and Technology* 17 (Fall 2000): 47–54; Gregory Conko and Henry I. Miller, "Food Safety: The Precautionary Principle Is the Wrong Approach," *European Affairs* 2 (2001): 122–128.

51. David Byrne, "Food Safety: Continuous Transatlantic Dialogue Is Essential," *European Affairs* 1 (Spring 2000): 80–85; European Commission (2000).

52. World Trade Organization, *EC Measures Concerning Meat and Meat Products (Hormones): Report of the Appellate Body* AB-1997 (Geneva: World Trade Organization, January 16, 1998).

53. Ibid.

54. European Commission (2001).

55. Mark Mansour, "Analysis of July 25, 2001 EC Traceability, Labeling, Food and Feed Proposals" (July 27, 2001), *Keller and Heckman LLP*, available at http://www.khlaw.com/index.cfm?fuseaction=publications.showPubDetail&pubID=85.

56. Food and Agricultural Organization, *FAOSTAT Agriculture Database*, available at http://apps.fao.org/page/collections?subset=agriculture [accessed March 17, 2003].

57. Daniel Dombey and James Lamont, "Brussels Refuses to Back US over GM Food for Africa," *Financial Times*, August 23, 2002, 8.

58. Raffensperger and Tickner.

59. Charles Kessler and Ioannis Economidis, *EC-sponsored Research on Safety of Genetically Modified Organisms: A Review of Results* (Luxembourg: Office for Official Publications of the European Communities, 2001).

60. A. Bouchie, "Safety of GMOs Reaffirmed by EU," *Nature Biotechnology* 19 (December 2001): 1095.

61. Anthony J. Trewavas and Christopher J. Leaver, "Is Opposition to GM Crops Science or Politics?" *EMBO Reports* 21 (June 2001): 455–459.

62. Greenpeace, 1999 Federal Income Tax Filing with the U.S. Internal Revenue Service: IRS Form 990, Part III, Statement of Program Service Accomplishments, "Genetic Engineering."

63. Sally Lehrman, "California Targets GM-Trial Vandals with New Legislation," *Nature* 404 (April 20): 799; Christopher S. Bond, "Politics, Misinformation, and Biotechnology," *Science* 287 (February 18, 2000): 1201.

64. Tickner, 163.

65. Margaret Mellon, "Ripen-on-Command: In a Society with Ample Food, Why Bother?" *Nature Biotechnology* 14 (1996): 800.

66. Donald G. McNeil, "New Genes and Seeds: Protesters in Europe Grow More Passionate," *New York Times*, March 14, 2000, available at http://www.nytimes.com/library/national/science/health/031400hth-gm-europe.html.

67. "Protests at International Biotechnology Meeting," *Japan Times*, March 16, 2000.

68. M. Laubichler,"Frankenstein in the Land of Dichter and Denker," *Nature* 286 (1999): 1859–1860.

69. Richard Hofstadter, "The Paranoid Style in American Politics," *Harper's* (November 1964) 77–86.

70. S. L. Huttner, "Government, Researchers and Activists: The Crucial Public Policy Interface," in *Biotechnology*, ed. D. Brauer (Weinheim, Ger.: VCH, 1995), 459–494.

71. L. H. Tribe, *American Constitutional Law* (Mineola, N.Y.: Foundation, 1978).

72. R. Lofstedt, "Introductory paper—The Precautionary Principle: Risk, Regulation and Politics," Merton College, Oxford, April 5–11, 2002.

73. Tribe.

74. Nicholas Eberstadt, "Population, Resources, and the Quest to 'Stabilize Human Population': Myths and Realities," in *Global Warming and Other Eco-Myths* (Roseville, Calif.: Prima, 2002), 61–91.

75. Wildavsky.

76. Ibid.

CHAPTER 5

1. S. E. Dudley, "The Coming Shift in Regulation," *Regulation* 25 (2002): 7.

2. See H. I. Miller, "Drug Tests' Costly Side Effects," *Los Angeles Times*, November 4, 2002, B11.

3. J. L. Vanderveen, "Federal Regulation and Policy on Transgenic Plants," in *Benefits and Risks of Food Biotechnology* (Sacramento: California Council on Science and Technology 2002), 101–119.

4. Ibid.

5. Environmental Protection Agency, "Environmental Pesticide Control," 7 USC 136.

6. Food and Drug Administration, "Misbranded Food," 21 USC 343; Food and Drug Administration, "Adulterated Food," 21 USC 342.

7. Food and Drug Administration, "Premarket Notice Concerning Bio-engineered Foods," *Federal Register* 66 (January 18, 2001): 4706.

8. Office of Science and Technology Policy, "Exercise of Federal Oversight within Scope of Statutory Authority: Planned Introductions of Biotechnology Products into the Environment," *Federal Register* 57 (1992): 6753–6762.

9. Ibid. [italics added].

10. U.S. Department of Agriculture, "Federal Plant Pest Act," 7 USC 150; U.S. Department of Agriculture, "Plant Quarantine Act 7 USC 151.

11. U.S. Department of Agriculture, "Plant Protection Act," 7 USC 7701.

12. U.S. Department of Agriculture. "Animal and Plant Health Inspection Service," *Federal Register* 52 (1987): 22892–22915.

13. Ibid.

14. S. L. Huttner and H. I. Miller, "USDA Regulation of Field Trials of Recombinant-DNA-Modified Plants: Reforms Leave Severe Flaws," *Trends in Biotechnology* (October 1997): 387–389.

15. U.S. Department of Agriculture, "USDA Announces Actions Regarding Plant Protection Act Violations Involving ProdiGene, Inc.," USDA News Release No. 4098.02 (December 6, 2002), available at http://www.usda.gov/news/releases/2002/12/0498.htm.

16. C. Manly Molpus, "Food Industry Comments on Proposed FDA Regulations for Plant-Made Pharmaceuticals" (Washington, D.C.: Grocery Manufacturers of America, February 6, 2003), available at http://www.gmabrands.com/publicpolicy/docs/comment.cfm?DocID=1068.

17. U.S. Department of Agriculture, "Field Testing of Plants Engineered to Produce Pharmaceutical and Industrial Compounds," *Federal Register* 68 (March 10, 2003): 11337–11340.

18. B. Ames and L. S. Gold, "Cancer Prevention and the Environmental Chemical Distraction," in *Politicizing Science*, ed. M. Gough (Stanford, Calif. and Washington, D.C.: Hoover Institution Press and George Marshall Institute, 2003): 117–142.

19. American Association for the Advancement of Science, "Sowing the Seeds of Success: USDA Funding for Agriculture," *GrantsNet* (October 29, 2002), available at http://nextwave.sciencemag.org/cgi/content/full/2002/10/29/1.

20. D. R. Lincoln, E. S. Fisher, and D. C. Lambert, "Release and Containment of Microorganisms from Applied Genetics Activities," *Enzyme and Microbial Technology* 7 (1985): 314–321.

21. R. J. Seidler and S. Hern, *Special Report: The Release of Ice-Minus Recombinant Bacteria at California Test Sites* (Corvallis, Ore.: Environmental Protection Agency, Environmental Research Laboratory, 1988).

22. Ibid.

23. Office of Science and Technology Policy (1992) [emphasis added].

24. J. R. Bragg et al., "Effectiveness of Bioremediation for the *Exxon Valdez* Oil Spill," *Nature* 368 (1994): 413–418.

25. W. Reilly, speech at Stanford University, undated.

26. See H. I. Miller, *Policy Controversy in Biotechnology: An Insider's View* (Austin, Tex.: R. G. Landes and Academic, 1997), 60–78.

27. Environmental Protection Agency, 7 USC 136-136r.

28. Environmental Protection Agency, "Plant-Pesticides Subject to the Federal Insecticide, Fungicide, and Rodenticide Act; Proposed Rule," *Federal Register* 59 (November 23, 1994): 60496–60519.

29. C. James, *Preview: Global Status of Commercialized Transgenic Crops: 2003.* ISAAA Briefs 30 (Ithaca, N.Y., ISAAA, 2003).

30. Charles Kessler and Ioannis Economidis, *EC Sponsored Research on Safety of Genetically Modified Organisms: A Review of Results* (Luxembourg: Office for Official Publications of the European Communities), 2001.

31. M. Fumento, *Science under Siege* (New York: Morrow, 1993), 19–44; "EPA Targets Chemical Used on Apples," *Washington Post*, February 2, 1989, 4A.

32. P. Shabecoff, "Hazard Reported in Apple Chemical: E.P.A. Cites a Risk of Cancer but Will Not Bar Use Yet," *New York Times*, February 2, 1989, 23.

33. R. J. Bidinotto, "The Great Apple Acare," *Reader's Digest* 137 (1990): 55–56.

34. Environmental Protection Agency, *Safeguarding the Future: Credible Science, Credible Decisions,* report of the Expert Panel on the Role of Science at EPA, Document 600/9-91/050 (Washington, D.C.: March 1992).

35. R. Hoyle, "The Leak That Wasn't," *Bio/Technology* 10 (1992): 742.

36. L. J. Fisher, EPA Assistant Administrator, letter to Dennis Focht, August 21, 1992.

37. See H. I. Miller, *Policy Controversy in Biotechnology: An Insider's View* (Austin, Tex.: R. G. Landes and Academic, 1997), 118.

38. W. Raub, personal communication.

39. R. Stone, "EPA Gives Science Adviser More Clout," *Science* 267 (1995): 1895.

40. R. J. Cook, letter to the Environmental Protection Agency, September 17, 1992.

41. Food and Drug Administration, "Adulterated Food," 21 USC 342; Food and Drug Administration, "Misbranded Food," 21 USC 343.

42. Food and Drug Administration, "Food Standards, Food Additives, Generally Recognized As Safe (GRAS) Substances, Color Additives, Nutrient Content Claims, And Health Claims," 21 USC 348[a] and 342[a][2][c].

43. Food and Drug Administration, "Definitions," 21 USC 321[s].

44. Food and Drug Administration, "Statement of Policy: Foods Derived from New Plant Varieties," *Federal Register* 57 (May 29, 1992): 22984–23005.

45. See H. I. Miller, "Foods of the Future: The New Biotechnology and FDA Regulation," *Journal of the American Medical Association* 269 (1993): 910.

46. See H. I. Miller, "Feds' Plan Will Jeopardize Food Biotechnology," *Biotechnology Law Report* 19 (2000): 18–21.

47. J. A. Nordler, S. L. Taylor, J. A. Townsend, et al., "Identification of a Brazil Nut Allergen in Transgenic Soybeans," *New England Journal of Medicine* 334 (1996): 688–699.

48. Food and Drug Administration (2001).

49. Center for Science in the Public Interest/Bruskin Research, "National Opinion Poll on Labeling of Genetically Modified Foods," available at http://www.cspinet.org/reports/op_poll_labeling.html [accessed February 11, 2003].

50. Ibid.

51. Ibid.

52. Food and Drug Administration (1992).

53. American Medical Association, "Report 10 of the Council on Scientific Affairs (I-00): Genetically Modified Crops and Foods," (Chicago, IL: American Medical Association, 2000) available at http://www.ama-assn.org/ama/pub/article/2036-3604.html.

54. Institute of Food Technologists, *IFT Expert Report on Biotechnology and Foods* (Chicago, Ill.: Institute of Food Technologists, 2000).

55. International Food Information Council, *IFIC Survey: Support for Food Biotechnology Stable Despite News on Unrelated Food Safety Issues* (Washington, D.C.: International Food Information Council, 2004).

56. Institute of Food Technologists (2000).

57. Food and Drug Administration (1992).

58. *Stauber v. Shalala,* 895 F. Supp. 1178 (W.D. Wisc., 1995).

59. *International Dairy Foods Association et al. v. Amestoy* 1996, 92 F.3d 67 (2nd Cir. 1996).

60. Ibid.

61. Pew National Policy Forum, *Labeling Genetically Modified Foods: Communicating or Creating Confusion?* (Chicago: Pew Initiative on Biotechnology and Food, June 27, 2002).

62. A. McHughen, personal communication with the authors (2002).

63. George Gaskell, Edna Einsiedel, Susanna Priest, Toby Ten Eyck, Nick Allum, and Helge Torgersen, "Troubled Waters: The Atlantic Divide on Biotechnology Policy," in *Biotechnology 1996–2000,* ed. George Gaskell and Martin W. Bauer (London: Science Museum, 2001), 96–115.

64. C. Noussair, S. Robin, and B. Ruffieux, "Do Consumers Not Care about Biotech Foods or Do They Just Not Read the Labels?" *Economics Letters* 75 (2002): 47–53.

65. McHughen (2002).

66. Noussair, Robin, and Ruffieux.

67. See H. I. Miller, "Biotech Offers (Baby) Food for Thought," *Scientist* (October 11, 1999): 13.

68. L. Lagnado, "Genetically-Altered Baby Foods Are Being Rejected—by Adults," *Wall Street Journal,* July 30, 1999, 1.

69. Geoff Golder, Flavia Leung, and Sebastien Malherbe, *Economic Impact Study: Potential Costs of Mandatory Labeling of Food Products Derived from Biotechnology in Canada* (Ottawa: KPMG Consulting, 2000).

70. KPMG Consulting, *Preliminary Report: Compliance Costs for Labeling Biotech Foods Prepared for Australia/New Zealand Food Authority* (1999).

71. European Commission, *Economic Impacts of Genetically Modified Crops on the Agri-Food Sector: A First Review,* working document, revision 2 (Brussels: Commission of the European Communities, 2000).

72. V. J. Taylor, memorandum to the Labeling Subcommittee, California Interagency Biotechnology Task Force, April 15, 1994.

73. Huttner and Miller.

74. Environmental Protection Agency, "Economic Analysis of the Plant-Incorporated Protectant Regulations under the Federal Insecticide, Fungicide, and Rodenticide Act," (Washington, D.C.: EPA, 2000).

75. J. Seibert, "Guest Opinion: Regressive EPA Policy," *California Farmer* (June 1997), available at http://www.biotech-info.net/regressive_policy.html.

76. E. Brazil, "Hopes Raised in Fight against Sharpshooter," *San Francisco Chronicle*, May 21, 2001, A3.

77. Dudley.

78. M. Friedman, "Why Government Is the Problem," *Hoover Institution Essays in Public Policy* (1993): 8–9.

79. M. Planck, *A Scientific Autobiography* (New York: Philosophical Library, 1949), 33.

CHAPTER 6

1. P. W. Huber and R. E. Litan, eds., *The Liability Maze: The Impact of Liability Law on Safety and Innovation* (Washington, D.C.: Brookings Institution, 1991).

2. Royal Commission on Genetic Modification, "Report of the Royal Commission on Genetic Modification," (Wellington, New Zealand: 2001), available at www.gmcommission.govt.nz/RCGM.

3. Ibid., app. 2.

4. UN Environment Programme, *Report of the Meeting of Technical Experts: Handling, Transport, Packaging and Identification of Living Modified Organisms*, Article 18, March 22, 2002, UNEP/CBD/ICCP/3/7/Add.1.

5. Royal Commission on Genetic Modification.

6. Ibid., 329.

7. Ibid., 328.

8. Office of Science and Technology Policy, "Coordinated Framework for the Regulation of Biotechnology Products," *Federal Register* 51 (June 26, 1986): 23302–23350.

9. Commission of the European Communities, "Proposal for a Directive of the European Parliament and of the Council on Environmental Liability with Regard to the Prevention and Restoration of Environmental Damage," COM (2002) 17 Brussels: Commission of the European Communities, January 21, 2002).

10. Stuart Smyth et al., "Liabilities and Economics of Transgenic Crops," *Nature Biotechnology* 20 (2002): 537–541.

11. Richard Repp "Comment: Biotech Pollution: Assessing Liability for Genetically Modified Crop Production and Genetic Drift," *Idaho Law Review* 36 (2000): 585–620; Margaret Rosso Grossman, "Biotechnology, Property Rights and the Environment," *American Journal of Comparative Law* 50 (2002): 215–248.

12. U. S. Department of Agriculture, "National Organic Program," *Federal Register* 65 (Dec. 21, 2000): 80547–80648.

13. Ibid., 80639.

14. Ibid., 80556.

15. Association of Official Seed Certifying Agencies, AOSCA website, available at http://aosca.org.

16. Nebraska Crop Improvement Association, NCIA website, available at http://www.unl.edu/ncia.

17. Adrian Ewins, "Study Raises Questions about GM Buffer Zone," *Western Producer* (July 4, 2002), available at http://66.102.7.104 search?q=cache:2lyBqiT2JH8J:131.104.232.9/agnet/2002/7-2002

agnet_july_5.htm+Adrian+Ewins,+%E2%80%9CStudy+Raises+Questions+about+GM+Buffer+Zone,%E2%80%9D+Western+Producer&hl=en.

18. American Law Institute, *The Restatement of Law (Second) Torts* (Philadelphia: American Law Institute, 1977): 519–524.

19. Ibid., 36.

20. Ibid., 38.

21. "Biotech Popularity Grows in US," *Agbiotech Reporter* (August 2002), available at http://www.bioreporter.com.

22. American Law Institute (1977), 51 [emphasis added].

23. Organic Crop Improvement Association, "International Certification Standards," OCIA Standards 1.2, 9.2, and 9.3 (March 2000).

24. American Law Institute (1977).

25. Ibid.

26. A. Bryan Enders, "GMO: Genetically Modified Organism or Gigantic Monetary Obligation? The Liability Schemes for GMO Damage in the United States and the European Union," *Loyola of Los Angeles International & Comparative Law Review* 22 (2000): 453–491; Repp, 613–616; Grossman, 236–237.

27. Henry Daniell, "Molecular Strategies for Gene Containment in Transgenic Crops," *Nature Biotechnology* 20 (2002): 581–586; Katie Eastham and Jeremy Sweet, "Genetically Modified Organisms (GMOs): The Significance of Gene Flow through Pollen Transfer," European Environment Agency, Environmental Issue Report No. 28 (Copenhagen: European Environment Agency, 2002).

28. American Law Institute (1977).

29. Ibid., 105.

30. Ibid., 105–106.

31. Celeste Steen, "Comment: FIFRA's Preemption of Common Law Tort Actions Involving Genetically Engineered Pesticides," *Arizona Law Review* 38 (1996): 763.

32. D. Kershen, "The Risks of Going Non-GMO," *Oklahoma Law Review* 53 (2000): 631–651.

33. Centers for Disease Control, *Investigation of Human Health Effects Associated with Potential Exposure to Genetically Modified Corn* (Atlanta: Centers for Disease Control, June 2001).

34. A. Harris, "Danger Uncertain, but Suits Multiply—Billions Could Be at Stake in Farmers' Cases," *National Law Journal*, September 9, 2002, A12.

35. Thomas Redick, "Biopharming, Biosafety, and Billion Dollar Debacles: Preventing Liability for Biotech Crops," American Agricultural Law Association Annual Conference, Indianapolis, Indiana, October 2002.

36. U.S. Department of Agriculture, "Field Testing of Plants Engineered to Produce Pharmaceutical and Industrial Compounds," *Federal Register* 68 (March 10, 2003): 11337.

37. D. Uchtmann, "StarLink: A Case Study of Agricultural Biotechnology Regulation," *Drake Journal of Agricultural Law* 7 (2002): 159–211.

38. *In re StarLink Corn Products Liability Litigation*, 211 F Supp2d 1060 (MDL, ND Ill 2002).

39. Ibid.

40. *Sample v. Monsanto Company*, Civil No. 4:01cv00065RWS (ED Mo 2001).

41. American Law Institute (1977).

42. *In re StarLink Corn Products Liability Litigation.*

43. Ministry for the Environment (New Zealand), *Improving the Operation of the HSNO Act for New Organisms,* September 2002, available at www.mfe.govt.nz.

44. Ibid.

45. T. Redick and C. Bernstein, "Nuisance Law and the Prevention of 'Genetic Pollution': Declining a Dinner Date with Damocles," *Environmental Law Report* 30 (May 2000): 10328.

46. Dick Fawcett, "Biotechnology: Farming, Environmental Impacts, and Consumer Safety," Presentation to the Royal Society of New Zealand and the U.S. Embassy, Wellington, New Zealand (March 27, 2004).

47. EU Health and Consumer Protection Directorate-General, *Opinion of the Scientific Committee on Plants Concerning the Adventitious Presence of GM Seeds in Conventional Seeds* SCP/GMO-SEED-CONT/002-FINAL (Brussels: Health and Consumer Protection Directorate-General, March 13, 2002).

48. Secretariat of the Convention on Biological Diversity, *Cartagena Protocol on Biosafety to the Convention on Biological Diversity: Text and Annexes* (Montreal: 2000).

49. Kershen.

50. National Research Council, *Field Testing Genetically Modified Organisms: Framework for Decisions* (Washington, D.C.: National Academy Press, 1989).

51. International Atomic Energy Agency, 2000).

52. G. P. Munkvold, R. L. Hellmich, and L. G. Rice, "Comparison of Fumonisin Concentrations in Kernels of Transgenic Bt Maize Hybrids and Non-Transgenic Hybrids," *Plant Disease* 83 (1999): 130–138; P. F. Dowd and G. P. Munkvold, "Associations between Insect Damage and Fumonisin Derived from Field-Based Insect Control Strategies," Proceedings of the 40th Annual Corn Dry Milling Conference, Peoria, Illinois (June 3–4, 1999).

53. American Law Institute, *The Restatement of Law (Third) Torts: Products Liability* (Philadelphia: American Law Institute, 1998).

54. Ibid.; Munkvold, Hellmich, and Rice; Dowd and Munkvold.

55. American Law Institute (1998).

56. Ibid.

57. Ricki Helms, et. al., "Hypoallergenic Foods—Soybeans and Peanuts," *ISB News Report* (October 2002): 3–5; Bob Buchanan, personal communication to Henry I. Miller (2003).

58. Buchanan, 2003.

59. J. Wyman and S. Diercks, *Organic Potatoes: They Can Be Grown, but Can They Be Profitable?* Center for Integrated Agricultural Systems Research Brief 4 (Madison: University of Wisconsin Center for Integrated Agricultural Systems, 2000).

60. Martha Groves, "Growing Debate under a Sweeping New Food Safety Law: The Government May Soon Outlaw What Some Farmers Say Are Their Best Weapons against Insects," *Los Angeles Times,* July 12, 1998, D1.

61. Scott Kilman, "Monsanto's Biotech Spud Is Being Pulled from the Fryer at Fast-Food Chain," *Wall Street Journal,* April 28, 2000, B4.

62. Colin Nickerson, "Potatoes, Pesticides Divide Island," *Boston Globe,* August 30, 2000, A1.

63. "Pesticides: ILSI Report Lists Six Organophosphates on Basis of Shared Mechanism of Toxicity," *BNA Daily Environment Report*, October 22, 1997, A-6; "Pesticides: Food Risk Posed by Organophosphate to Infants, Young Children, EPA Says," *BNA Daily Environment Report*, February 4, 2000, A-13; "Pesticides: Some Uses on Food of Organophosphates Unacceptable, Preliminary Assessments Say," *BNA Daily Environment Report*, January 12, 1999, A-7.

64. Huber and Litan, 2.

CHAPTER 7

1. Clive James, *Preview: Global Status of Commercialized Transgenic Crops: 2003*, ISAAA Briefs 30 (Ithaca, N.Y.: International Service for the Acquisition of Agri-biotech Applications, 2003).

2. Ibid.

3. Robert Paarlberg, *The Politics of Precaution: Genetically Modified Crops in Developing Countries* (Baltimore: Johns Hopkins University Press, 2001).

4. Census Bureau, *Statistical Abstract of the United States: 2001* (Washington, D.C.: 2001); U.S. Department of Agriculture, *Prospective Plantings* (Washington, D.C.: National Agricultural Statistics Service, March 31, 2004).

5. Paarlberg.

6. Ibid.

7. Office of Science and Technology Policy, "Coordinated Framework for the Regulation of Biotechnology Products," *Federal Register* 51 (June 26, 1986): 23302–23393.

8. Organization for Economic Cooperation and Development, *Safety Considerations for Biotechnology: Scale-Up of Crop Plants* (Paris: OECD Publications, 1993).

9. European Commission, "Questions and Answers on the Regulation of GMOs in the EU," Memo/00/277 (Brussels: Commission of the European Communities Directorate General for Health and Consumer Protection, July 24, 2001), available at europa.eu.int/comm/dgs/health_consumer/library/press/press171_en.pdf.

10. Michael Mann, "Tough New EU Law Opens Way for GM Crops," *Financial Times*, February 15, 2001, 8.

11. Parliamentary Office of Science and Technology, *The "Great GM Food Debate": A Survey of Media Coverage in the First Half of 1999* (London: Parliamentary Office of Science and Technology, May 2000).

12. George Gaskell, Nick Allum, Martin Bauer, et al., "Biotechnology and the European Public," *Nature Biotechnology* 18 (September 2000): 935–938.

13. Mann.

14. *EurActiv*; European Commission, "Commission Authorises Import of Canned Gm-sweet Corn under New Strict Labelling Conditions—Consumers Can Choose."

15. Robert Paarlberg, "Shrinking International Markets for GM Crops?" speech to the U.S. Department of Agriculture Agricultural Outlook Forum, Arlington, Virginia, February 22–23, 2001.

16. Paarlberg, 121–147.

17. Ibid.

18. David Adam, "UN Attempts to Boost Biosafety in Developing World," *Nature* 415 (January 24, 2002): 353.

19. "Largest Ever World Wide Project to Promote Biosafety Launched by UNEP," UNEP news release 2002/02, January 16, 2002.

20. Agriculture & Biotechnology Strategies, Inc., *GM Database: Information on GM Approved Products,* available at www.agbios.com/dbase.php [accessed March 21, 2003].

21. National Research Council, *Field Testing Genetically Modified Organisms: Framework for Decisions* (Washington, D.C.: National Academy Press, 1989).

22. Christopher Bright, "Invasive Species: Pathogens of Globalization," *Foreign Policy* 116 (Fall 1999): 50–60.

23. Janet Carpenter and Leonard Gianessi, *Agricultural Biotechnology: Updated Benefit Estimates* (Washington, D.C.: National Center for Food and Agricultural Policy, January 2001).

24. "EU Says a US Attack over GMOs Would Be 'Eccentric,'" Reuters News Service, May 12, 2003; Peter Blackburn, "Paraguay Farmers Opt for Banned GM Soybean Seeds," Reuters News Service, January 15, 2003.

25. Reuters, "Brazil Approves Planting of GM Soybeans," Reuters News Service (September 24, 2003).

264. "India's Tryst with GM Technology," *Economic Times* (India), January 2, 2003, available at http://economictimes.indiatimes.com/cms.dll/xml/comp/articleshow?artid=33106700.

27. Ismail Serageldin, "The Challenge of Poverty in the 21st Century: The Role of Science," in *Agricultural Biotechnology and the Poor,* ed. Gabrielle J. Persley and Manuel M. Lantin (Washington, D.C.: Consultative Group on International Agricultural Research).

28. Gordon Conway, "Crop Biotechnology: Benefits, Risks, and Ownership," address to the Organization for Economic Cooperation and Development (OECD) Edinburgh Conference on the Scientific and Health Aspects of Genetically Modified Foods, Edinburgh, Scotland, March 28, 2000.

29. Paarlberg.

30. Ibid., 93–120.

31. Chandrika Mago, "Industry, NGOs Face-Off on GM Mustard, Cotton," *Economic Times* (India), November 7, 2002, available at http://www.globalpolicy.org/ngos/business/2002/1107mustard.htm

32. Ibid., "No Bt Cotton, No GM Mustard—GEAC," *Times of India,* April 29, 2003.

33. Robert Paarlberg, "African Famine, Made in Europe," *Wall Street Journal,* August 23, 2002, A12.

34. Paarlberg.

35. Fred Guterl, "The Fear of Food: One by One, Countries Are Coming Out against Crops with Engineered Genes," *Newsweek International,* January 27, 2003, 40.

36. Roger Thurow, Brandon Mitchener, and Scott Kilman, "Seeds of Doubt: As U.S., EU Clash on Biotech Crops, Africa Goes Hungry," *Wall Street Journal,* December 26, 2002, A1.

37. Ibid.

38 "Brazil Wins Premium by Producing GM-Free Corn," *Bridges Trade BioRes,* January 24, 2002, 3–4.

39. State of Victoria, *Genetic Engineering-Free Zones,* Victorian Government Con-

sultation Paper (Melbourne, Australia: Department of Natural Resources and Environment, March 2001).

40. Robert Paarlberg, "The Global GM Crop Conflict: Why Europe Will Win and Poor Farmers Will Lose," presentation to the U.S. State Department Bureau of Intelligence and Research and National Intelligence Council conference, "Food Security Issues in East and Southern Africa," January 31, 2003.

41. European Commission, *Economic Impacts of Genetically Modified Crops on the Agri-Food Sector: A First Review*, working document, revision 2 (Brussels: 2000).

42. Simon Grose, "States Extend GM Canola Moratoria," *Australasian Science* (May 2004), 21–22.

43. Paarlberg, *Politics of Precaution*, 121–147.

44. Jikun Huang, Scott Rozelle, Carl Pray, and Qinfang Wang, "Plant Biotechnology in China," *Science* 295, no. 5555 (January 25, 2002): 674–677.

45. He Sheng, "GMO Research Stirs Hot Debate," *China Daily* (Beijing), September 25, 2000, available at http://www.biotech-info.net/hot_debate.html.

46. Paarlberg, *Politics of Precaution*, 137.

47. "EU Cautions US Against Taking Biotech Fight to WTO," Associated Press News Service, February 6, 2003.

48. Robert Paarlberg, personal communication.

49. "Pressure Grows to File WTO Complaint," *AgBiotech Reporter*, January 2003, 1.

50. James; Food and Agricultural Organization, *FAOSTAT Agriculture Database*, available at http://apps.fao.org/page/collections?subset=agriculture [accessed May 5, 2004].

CHAPTER 8

1. George Gaskell, Nick Allum, and Sally Stares, *Europeans and Biotechnology in 2002: Eurobarometer 58.0—a Report to the EC Directorate General for Research from the Project "Life Sciences in European Society,"* QLG7-CT-1999-00286, 2nd ed., March 21, 2003, available at europa.eu.int/comm/public_opinion/archives/eb/ebs_177_en.pdf.

2. C. Noussair, S. Robin, and B. Ruffieux, "Do Consumers Not Care about Biotech Foods or Do They Just Not Read the Labels?" *Economics Letters* 75 (2002): 47–53.

3. George Gaskell, Nick Allum, Martin Bauer, et al., "Biotechnology and the European Public," *Nature Biotechnology* 18 (September 2000), 935–938.

4. N. Kalaizandonakes and J. Bijman, "Who Is Driving Biotechnology Acceptance?" *Nature Biotechnology* 21 (2003): 366–369.

5. European Commission, "Questions and Answers on the Regulation of GMOs in the EU," Memo/00/277 (Brussels: Commission of the European Communities Directorate General for Health and Consumer Protection, July 24, 2001), available at europa.eu.int/comm/dgs/health_consumer/library/press/press171_en.pdf.

6. European Commission, "Proposal for a Regulation of the European Parliament and of the Council on Genetically Modified Food and Feed," COM (2001) 425 (Brussels: Commission of the European Communities, July 25, 2001); and European Commission, "Proposal for a Regulation of the European Parliament and of the Council Concerning Traceability and Labelling [*sic*] of Genetically Modified

Organisms and Traceability of Food and Feed Products Produced from Genetically Modified Organisms and Amending Directive 2001/18/EC," COM (2001) 182 (Brussels: Commission of the European Communities, July 25, 2001).

7. Mark Mansour, "Analysis of July 25, 2001 EC Traceability, Labeling, Food and Feed Proposals," July 27, 2001, Keller and Heckman LLP, available at www.khlaw.com/index.cfm?fuseaction=publications.showPubDetail&pubID=85.

8. Lilzett Alvarez, "Consumers in Europe Resist Gene-Altered Foods," *New York Times*, February 11, 2003, A3.

9. Barbara Keating-Edh, "Testimony before the National Biotechnology Policy Board," *1992 National Biotechnology Policy Board Report* (Bethesda, Md.: National Institutes of Health, 1992) [emphasis in original].

10. A. Hellemans, "Consumer Fear Cancels European GM Research," *Scientist*, May 5, 2003, 52–53.

11. T. M. Fenning and J. Gershenzon, "European Agbiotech Crisis?" *Nature Biotechnology* 21 (2003): 360.

12. U.S. Department of Agriculture, "Table 27: U.S. Agricultural Exports and Imports," *Agricultural Outlook* 297 (Washington, D.C.: Economic Research Service, December 2002): 67.

13. Robert Paarlberg, "The Global GM Crop Conflict: Why Europe Will Win and Poor Farmers Will Lose," presentation to the U.S. State Department Bureau of Intelligence and Research and National Intelligence Council conference "Food Security Issues in East and Southern Africa," January 31, 2003.

14. *General Agreement on Tariffs and Trade as Amended* (Geneva: World Trade Organization, 1994).

15. U.S. Trade Representative, "U.S. and Cooperating Countries File WTO Case against EU Moratorium on Biotech Foods and Crops: EU's Illegal, Non-Science Based Moratorium Harmful to Agriculture and the Developing World," Office of the USTR press release, May 13, 2003.

16. Donna Roberts, "Preliminary Assessment of the Effects of the WTO Agreement on Sanitary and Phytosanitary Trade Regulations," *Journal of International Economic Law* 1 (1998): 377–405.

17. *Agreement on the Application of Sanitary and Phytosanitary Measures* (Geneva: World Trade Organization, 1994).

18. World Trade Organization, *EC Measures Concerning Meat and Meat Products (Hormones): Report of the Appellate Body* AB-1997-4 (Geneva: World Trade Organization, January 16, 1998).

19. Charles Kessler and Ioannis Economidis, *EC-sponsored Research on Safety of Genetically Modified Organisms: A Review of Results* (Luxembourg: Office for Official Publications of the European Communities, 2001).

20. "Brazil AgMin Says Banned GM Soy Can Sell Locally," Reuters News Service, March 11, 2003; "EU Says a US Attack over GMOs Would Be 'Eccentric,'" Reuters News Service, May 12.

21. "End of Moratorium: Gm Corn Authorised For Import into EU," *EurActiv* (May 19, 2004), available at http://www.euractiv.com/cgi-bin/cgint.exe/1107366-633?204&OIDN=1507723&-home=home; European Commission, "Commission Authorises Import of Canned Gm-sweet Corn under New Strict Labelling Conditions—Consumers Can Choose," IP/04/663 (Brussels: European Commission,

May 19, 2004), available at http://europa.eu.int/rapid/press ReleasesAction. do?reference=IP/04/663&format=HTML&aged=0& language=EN&guiLanguage =fr.

22. *Agreement on Technical Barriers to Trade* (Geneva, Switzerland: World Trade Organization, 1994).

23. Aarti Gupta, "Creating a Global Biosafety Regime," *International Journal of Biotechnology* 2 (2000): 205–230.

24. Secretariat of the Convention on Biological Diversity, *Cartagena Protocol on Biosafety to the Convention on Biological Diversity: Text and Annexes* (Montreal: Secretariat of the Convention on Biological Diversity, 2000).

25. Frode Veggeland and Svein Ole Borgen, "Changing the Codex: the Role of International Institutions," Working Paper 2002–2016 (Oslo: Norwegian Agricultural Economics Research Institute, 2002).

26. Ibid.

27. Grant E. Isaac, "Food Safety and Trade Policy: Agricultural Biotechnology Issues," prepared for Seminar on Food Safety and Trade Policy, Consumers' Association and International Trade Policy Unit, London School of Economics, July 1, 1999, revised October 1999.

28. "It's Time to End This GM Nonsense," *New Zealand Herald*, December 28, 2002.

29. Robert J. Coleman, "The US, Europe, and Precaution: A Comparative Case Study Analysis of the Management of Risk in a Complex World," address by Robert Coleman, director general for Health and Consumer Protection for the European Union Commission at the Grand Hotel-Bruges, Bruges, Belgium, January 11–12, 2002.

30. Gordon Conway and Gary Toenniessen, "Science for African Food Security," *Science* 299 (2003): 1187–1188.

31. Chris Sommerville and John Briscoe, "Genetic Engineering and Water," *Science* 292 (June 22, 2001): 2217.

32. F. C. Alvim, S. M. B. Carolino, J. C. M. Cascardo, et. al., "Enhanced Accumulation of BiP in Transgenic Plants Confers Tolerance to Water Stress," *Plant Physiology* 126 (July 2001): 1042–1054; Hong-Xia Zhang and Eduardo Blumwald, "Transgenic Salt-tolerant Tomato Plants Accumulate Salt in Foliage but Not in Fruit," *Nature Biotechnology* 19 (August 2001): 765–768; Mie Kasuga, Qiang Liu, Setsuko Miura, Kazuko Yamaguchi-Shinozaki, and Kazuo Shinozaki, "Improving Plant Drought, Salt, and Freezing Tolerance by Gene Transfer of a Single Stress-inducible Transcription Factor," *Nature Biotechnology* 17 (March 1999): 287–291.

CHAPTER 9

1. M. Weber, *The Theory of Social and Economic Organization* (New York: Free Press, 1997).

2. Robert Paarlberg, "Reinvigorating Genetically Modified Crops," *Issues in Science and Technology* (Spring 2003), 20: 86–92.

3. M. Henderson, "Who Cares What the People Think of GM Foods?" Lon-

don *Times*, June 13, 2003, at http://www.scientific-alliance.com/news_archives/biotechnology/whocareswhat.htm.

4. National Science Foundation, "A Quasi-Experimental Comparison of Face-to-Face and Internet Delivery in Citizens' Consensus Conferences," NSF Award Abstract #0080810 (May 9, 2002), available at http://www.fastlane.nsf.gov/servlet/showaward?award=0080810.

5. Office of Science and Technology Policy, "Coordinated Framework for Regulation of Biotechnology," *Federal Register* 51 (1986): 23302–23393.

6. Office of Science and Technology Policy, "Exercise of Federal Oversight within Scope of Statutory Authority: Planned Introductions of Biotechnology Products into the Environment," *Federal Register* 57 (1992): 6753–6762.

7. J. Fiksel and V. T. Covello, eds., "Safety Assurance for Environmental Introductions of Genetically Engineered Organisms (Workshop Summary)," NATO ASI Series (Berlin, Heidelberg, New York: Springer-Verlag, 1988).

8. H. I. Miller and D. Gunary, "Serious Flaws in the Horizontal Approach to Biotechnology Risk," *Science* 262 (1993): 1500–1501.

9. Organization for Economic Cooperation and Development, National Experts on Biotechnology, *Recombinant DNA Safety Considerations* (Paris: OECD, 1986), 30.

10. Organization for Economic Cooperation and Development, *Safety Evaluation of Foods Derived by Modern Biotechnology: Concepts and Principles* (Paris: 1993), 10.

11. Organization for Economic Cooperation and Development, *Report of the OECD Workshop on the Toxicological and Nutritional Testing of Novel Foods*, SG/ICGB (98) 1 (Paris: September 1998).

12. U.S. Department of Agriculture, Office of Agricultural Biotechnology, Agricultural Biotechnology Research Advisory Committee Minutes, 1991, document N. 91-01, 25-30.

13. Miller and Gunary.

14. Ibid.

15. U.S. Department of Health and Human Services, *Biosafety in Microbiological and Biomedical Laboratories*, HHS Publication (NIH) 88–8395 (Washington, D.C.: 1988).

16. J. Barton, J. Crandon, D. Kennedy, and H. I. Miller, "A Model Protocol to Assess the Risks of Agricultural Introductions," *Nature Biotechnology* 15 (1987): 845.

17. B. Whelan, "The Case of the Mute Scientists," *Washington Times*, February 27, 2003, A19.

18. Eleven Professional Scientific Societies, *Appropriate Oversight for Plants with Inherited Traits for Resistance to Pests* (Chicago: Coordinating Society, Institute of Food Technologists, 1996).

19. Council on Agricultural Science and Technology, *The Proposed EPA Plant Pesticide Rule* (Ames, Iowa.: Council on Agricultural Science and Technology, October 1998).

20. Institute of Food Technologists (2000).

21. G. Fink, "Bureaucrats Save Lives," *Science* 271 (1996): 1213.

22. Anthony M. Shelton and Mark K. Sears, "The Monarch Butterfly Controversy: Scientific Interpretations of a Phenomenon," *Plant Journal* 27 (2001): 483–488.

23. See H. I. Miller, *To America's Health: A Proposal to Reform the Food and Drug Administration* (Stanford, Calif.: Hoover Institution Press, 2000).

24. M. S. Swaminathan, "Science in Response to Basic Human Needs," *Science* 287 (2000): 425.

25. Barbara Tuchman, *The March of Folly: From Troy to Vietnam* (Boston: W. W. Knopf, 1984), 4.

Index

About the Authors

HENRY I. MILLER, M.D., is a Research Fellow at Stanford University's Hoover Institution, where, since 1994, he has focused on the relationship between science and regulation, models for regulatory reform, and federal and international oversight of new advances in biotechnology. A physician and molecular biologist, he served for 17 years at the National Institutes of Health and the U.S. Food and Drug Administration. He is the author or editor of six books, including *To America's Health* and *Public Controversy in Biotechnology*, as well as hundreds of articles in such publications as *Forbes*, the *New York Times*, *The Wall Street Journal*, *Policy Review*, and *Nature Biotechnology*.

GREGORY CONKO is Director of Food Safety Policy with the Competitive Enterprise Institute, an interest group based in Washington, D.C. He is also co-founder and Vice President of the AgBioWorld Foundation, a nonprofit organization that provides information to teachers, journalists, policymakers, and the general public about developments in plant science, biotechnology, and sustainable agriculture. His writings have appeared in scholarly journals, newspapers, and magazines, and he frequently participates in international conferences on food safety and trade.